Microsoft® Exchange 2003 Deployment and Migration

Microsoft® Exchange 2003 Deployment and Migration

Kieran McCorry

Amsterdam • Boston • Heidelberg • London • New York • Oxford
Paris • San Diego • San Francisco • Singapore • Sydney • Tokyo

Elsevier Digital Press
200 Wheeler Road, Burlington, MA 01803, USA
Linacre House, Jordan Hill, Oxford OX2 8DP, UK

Recognizing the importance of preserving what has been written, Elsevier prints its books on acid-free paper whenever possible.

Library of Congress Cataloging-in-Publication Data
Applied for.

British Library Cataloguing-in-Publication Data
A catalogue record for this book is available from the British Library.

ISBN: 1-55558-316-4

For information on all Elsevier Digital Press publications
visit our Web site at www.books.elsevier.com

04 05 06 07 08 09 10 9 8 7 6 5 4 3 2 1

Printed in the United States of America

This book is dedicated to the memory of my mother, Elizabeth.

Contents

Foreword

Electronic mail, or e-mail, has been around for many years. I first used e-mail in 1979 as an engineer at Digital Equipment Corporation. In Digital, e-mail was used between engineers on what was then one of the largest corporate networks, with several hundred hosts worldwide. Most corporations didn't use e-mail at all and there was very little traffic between those that did.

How much has changed since then! Just a few years ago, if you asked most CIOs whether voice communications or e-mail was more important, 80% would say voice. Today, it's just the opposite. E-mail is now recognized as *mission-critical* by most enterprise businesses: it's essential to their operation. And almost everyone you know is reachable via e-mail, often at multiple addresses.

At the same time, the widespread use of e-mail has brought with it exploitation and attacks in SPAM and e-mail-borne viruses. Couple that with the advent of very practical wireless mobile devices and you have those timeless partners: opportunity and challenge.

Exchange has grown and evolved with those challenges through the latest version: Exchange 2003. And once again, Kieran McCorry steps up to help you meet the challenge and the opportunity, to deploy Exchange 2003 and the infrastructure that supports it, Active Directory.

Kieran is a highly regarded and respected advisor in the industry, one with many years of experience in infrastructure and messaging. He's also earned the respect of the Exchange team in Microsoft, who've happily shared their expertise with him and, at times, learned from the customer experiences he and others from HP have shared.

Significant architectural changes were made in Exchange 2000, and Exchange 2003 carries that architecture forward. One key advance was the use of Active Directory, replacing and superseding the internal directory of Exchange 5.5. Active

Directory, the backbone directory and security infrastructure of Windows, supports myriad other services such as desktop and access management. As a result, while the initial investment is higher with a common infrastructure like Active Directory, the payoff recurs as more and more services are deployed using the in-place and managed directory. Customers often first deploy Active Directory to support Exchange, but then later find steadily improved returns on their directory investment.

Exchange 2003 is the messaging and calendaring service of the larger family of Microsoft products for communication and collaboration, including Windows SharePoint Services, Sharepoint Portal Services, and Live Communication Services.

A focus on integrated innovation led directly to a quantum-leap in the e-mail experience:, Exchange 2003, used with Outlook 2003, provides seamless mobile operation, through innovative features such as cached mode ("it just works, even with network outages") and RPC over HTTP (secure remote access without VPN!).

In addition, Exchange 2003 incorporates a multitude of improvements driven by customer feedback. Many of the improvements are more evolutionary than revolutionary, the result of broad customer-focus—resulting in a high-quality release with a rich complement of tools. The Exchange team's relentless push for quality and customer satisfaction is also evident in the recently released Service Pack 1, with customer-proven reliability and with additional support tools for migration, deployment and operations.

All these things add up to one *BIG* thing: Exchange 2003 is the best messaging system for businesses. This book addresses the key areas in deploying, from basic infrastructure design to planning for upgrade from Exchange 5.5 or 2000.

In this book, Kieran McCorry helps you through the most critical part—the planning and deployment. You can leverage his experience to make the wisest and most effective infrastructure investments. And, in so doing, build your mission critical messaging service on the best product today: Exchange 2003.

Dave Thompson
Vice President
Exchange Business Unit
Microsoft Corporation

Preface

The arrival of Exchange 2003 towards the mid-point of 2003 was by no means heralded with as much hoopla as the coming of Exchange 2000 some three years earlier. Why was that? Was it because no-one was interested in Exchange? After all, according to International Data Corporation, over 55% of all enterprise messaging seats are already upholstered with Exchange! Or was it because Exchange 2003 didn't represent as much of a new departure in messaging as did Exchange 2000?

I suspect the latter is true, but the latent facts here are important. Exchange 2003 doesn't represent so much a new departure as it does a slight change of course. We live in a messaging world today where, according to the Gartner Group, over 70% of all e-mail is unsolicited commercial e-mail (SPAM) and one message in every 50 or so is infected with a virus. Surviving in this environment was the challenge that lay before the Exchange 2003 developers: how to continue to develop a world-class messaging product that was also a platform for moving forward in a secure and robust fashion in an ever more hostile world. Not only this, but users want secure and reliable access to their e-mail no matter where on the planet they might be and that includes being on the beach or while shopping.

Of paramount importance in the asymptotic quest for the perfect messaging environment is the establishment of a solid infrastructure on which to build a reliable and secure messaging environment. For new implementations of Exchange 2003, this is a straightforward process—yet still requiring knowledge and skill—but for existing Exchange environments, especially those already running Exchange 5.5, then the migration process presents many more challenges.

For reasons that can for the most part be attributed to inertia, as Exchange 2003 was shipping, the majority of Exchange seats in situ were still running Exchange 5.5 or earlier versions of Exchange. This means that the tools and techniques that we were not overly motivated to use for migration to Exchange 2000 were still valid and required for migrations to Exchange 2003. Of course, the intervening several years between the first shipment of Exchange 2000 and that of Exchange 2003 have afforded a great deal of improvement in both these tools and the techniques that can be used for Exchange migration. The Microsoft tools themselves have matured, and third-party vendors have been unswerving in their efforts to develop (and sell) simpler, easier to use, migration products.

It is with this prevailing wind in mind that I have written this book. If you are familiar with my previous book on Exchange deployment and migration [McCorry and Livengood, Digital Press, 2001], as you flick through this book you'll find much in common with it. This book, in fact, is essentially an update and a refinement of parts of that previous book. And thus, this book is a reflection of the development of the product from Exchange 2000 to Exchange 2003.

As time passes, products evolve, and experiences are gathered, learning and advice similarly improve. And if one might misquote Jean-Paul Sartre, "*The more sand that has escaped from the hourglass of Exchange, the clearer we should see through it.*"

What is This Book about?

New deployments of Exchange 2003 and migration from legacy Exchange systems have much in common with the processes that we used with Exchange 2000 deployment and migration. In this book I have laid out many of the guidelines that have served me well while working in various Exchange environments. While the early part of this book focuses on deployment, the mainstay of the book is around migration: chiefly from Exchange 5.5, but dealing appropriately with the somewhat more straightforward task of migrating from Exchange 2000.

While much of the core material in this book can be found in my previous book, all of the material in this book has been subtly updated where appropriate. Many of the techniques and approaches for migration with Exchange 2000 are still relevant with Exchange 2003 though, and over and above this the new information in this book versus its predecessor amounts to some 43% of the opus, according to my reckoning.

With this in mind, it is my aim with this book to deliver the most up-to-date and relevant knowledge that I have come upon: some through research, some through real-world experiences, and some simply through happenstance. I am hopeful that some of the information contained herein will be useful to you.

Intended Audience

This book is aimed at a wide audience. As someone responsible for the planning or design of an Exchange 2003 messaging system, you should find sufficient information in this book to help you chart a course for either deployment or migration. As a messaging system manager or someone responsible for making a deployment or migration happen, then again, I am confident that you'll find information of value in this book.

Even if you are already in the steady state of Exchange 2003 operation, you can never be sure what the future holds. With myriad mergers, acquisitions, and divestitures occurring almost weekly in the enterprise world, a migration might never be too far away!

Acknowledgments

As always, sitting down to write the Acknowledgements section of the book is my favorite part. It's a clear signal to me that the book is now 'done and dusted' and allows me to reminisce over all the fun and frolics that I've had while penning it. Primarily, though, it affords me the opportunity to thank and extend my sincerest gratitude to all of those who have helped me in some way during its production. Doing so is fraught with danger though. One always runs the risk of omitting someone who contributed in some significant part. So, if you fall into this category, please accept my deepest apology and know that I am eternally grateful for your contribution.

My immediate colleagues in the Technology Leadership Group and the Advanced Technology Group have helped me enormously during the months that I spent writing this book. Thanks are especially due to my dearest friends Pierre Bijaoui, Kevin Laahs, Dung Hoang Khac, and Donald Livengood for all of their help, patience, and knowledge transfer to me. I left Donald to the end because I'd like to extend an especial word of thanks to him for his kind efforts in reviewing this manuscript and for agreeing to my incorporation of some of the material from our previous book into this one. I have had an absolute ball with these guys over the years, and their knowledge about all things technical and stamina for having a good time never cease to inspire and encourage me.

It goes without saying that the vast army of knowledgeable professionals working in Hewlett-Packard, particularly in HP Services, have been of tremendous assistance to me as I assembled my material for this book: some in a very explicit way, others in a more implicit fashion. Nevertheless, thanks are due to Glenn Harm, Karen Eber, Tom Richer, Jeff Dunkelberger, Wendy Ferguson, Ian Burgess, Martin Simpson, Mark Loughran, Martin Bradley, Philip Sloan, Emer McKenna, Dermot Hanna, Linda Gallagher, Marc van Hooste, Martin Rasmussen, Henrik Damslund, Daragh Morrissey, Sharon Stafford, Veli-Matti Vanamo, Steve Atkins, Allan Baird, Shree Vishwanathan, Jan De Clercq, Dave Banthorpe, Aric Bernard, Warren Cooley, Ed Crowley, Mike

Daugherty, Tim Garrett, Mike Grady, Fred Grant, Guido Grillenmeier, Paul Herbert, Joe Palermo, Alain Lissoir, Dan Martin, Brendan Moon, Joseph Neubauer, Gary Sant, Jeff Smith, Nancy Wyles, and Lars Svendsen.

I'd also particularly like to thank those individuals in Hewlett-Packard's Managed Services Design and Delivery organization for patiently sharing their always impressive knowledge and experience with me. Specifically, Stan Foster, Wook Lee, Kathy Pollert, MaryEllen Kennedy, Maureen Gould Teague, Bob Holvenstot, Chris Brownstone, and Bert Quarfordt.

I am exceptionally grateful to very many individuals in Microsoft for all of their help as I compiled this book. Much gratitude is extended to the members of the Exchange development group: Geeman Yip, Erik Ashby, Ken Ewert, Dave Lemson, KC Lemson, Steve Conn, Kevin McQuiston, James Baker, Jens Trier Rasmussen, Charlie Cheung, and most especially Paul Bowden for tolerating many annoying and no doubt intruding questions! I'd also like to thank Brett Johnson and Anthony Murphy for their assistance. And of course a special word of thanks is very much due to Dave Thompson, Vice President and Exchange Server Group Manager, for very kindly writing the Foreword to this text.

Two individuals reviewed the book in its early stages and kindly supplied back cover quotes and for this I am grateful to Dave Cook and Roy Beattie for their time and efforts.

A veritable parade of other individuals have helped me in untold ways to prepare this book, some of whom I've met over the years during my career in Digital Equipment Corporation and Compaq Computer Corporation. Thanks are due to Stephen Brown, Hans Uli Tittes, Derek Flint, William C. Minor, Oliver Kane, Michael McKenna, Jerry Cochran, Missy Koslosky, Paul Robichaux, Ken Hendel, Tom Buoniello, Ratmir Timashev, Ken Niblock, and Don Vickers. And also worthy of mention are all of the other folks at C2K, namely, Jayne McIlgorm, Tim Matchett, Suzanne Reid, Catherine Barr, and Gemma O'Doherty; all of them have contributed to the book in some fashion.

I'm fortunate enough to have had much support and unending advice from Tony Redmond during my writing escapades, to whom I am deeply indebted for all of his encouragement and support throughout the many years that I've had the pleasure of working with him.

Seemingly one of the few constants in life is the professionalism and level of expertise from the folks at Digital Press, who, as always, have been excellent. I very much appreciate the support and patience that they showed as the countdown to submission deadlines approached and for their confidence in me as a "stealth author!" I am exceptionally grateful to Pam Chester and Theron Shreve, and also to Alan Rose for the technical aspects of the book production. A host of unnamed individuals are associated with the production of the book in the background, and to all of them too, thank you.

And before closing I must extend particular thanks to Penton Media and especially Amy Eisenberg, Michele Crockett, Dave Bernard, and Lisa Pere, among a host of others. Much of the material in this book has been adapted from material I've previously published in the Exchange and Outlook Administrator Newsletter and Windows .Net Magazine. It is with their kind permission that the material has been modified and reproduced in this book.

Finally of course, a very special word of thanks to my wife Catherine, who once again has helped keep me on track, tolerated my long hours and lucubrations, and offered all the love, advice, and support for which one might wish.

Kieran McCorry,
April, 2004.[*]

[*] If you've any comments or question on the material in this book, I'd be happy to hear from you. You can contact me at Kieran.McCorry@hp.com.

1

Exchange 2003 Deployment Fundamentals

1.1 Introduction

Exchange 2003 (and Exchange 2000 before it) is radically different from Exchange 5.5. Architecturally, it's a world away from the self-contained messaging system that Exchange 5.5 was, but compared to Exchange 2000 it has much in common and differs really only by refining functionality and making improvements here and there. Those components that were built into Exchange 5.5 had been separated out from Exchange and, in most cases, integrated into the underlying operating system. For Exchange 2000 that operating system was Windows 2000. For Exchange 2003 you have the choice of two operating systems on which to run the product: Exchange 2003 can run on both Windows 2000 and Windows 2003.

Exchange 2003 positively requires at least Windows 2000 Service Pack 3 in order to operate. The Exchange 2003 executables don't run under any earlier versions of Windows, and in addition, to have an Exchange 2003 mailbox, you must have at least a Windows 2000 account. Why is there such a dependency? Well, there are a variety of reasons, but one of the most important reasons is the Active Directory (AD).

Exchange 5.5 had a reliable and distributable directory service built-in. Now there is no directory service built into Exchange: Exchange 2003 relies completely on the AD to store information about mailboxes, custom recipients, and distribution lists, although these Exchange 5.5 primitives are represented differently in Exchange 2003 and the AD. Additionally, all of the configuration information about Exchange servers that was previously held in the Configuration container of the Exchange 5.5 Directory Service, is now held in the Configuration naming context of the AD. So what does all of this reshuffling mean? First, it means that Exchange 2003 has a huge dependency on the AD. Subsequently, you must get the design of your AD totally correct if you want your Exchange 2003 deployment to be successful. By implication, this means that you must carefully plan and implement your whole Windows 2000/Windows 2003 environment to provide a solid infrastructure for Exchange 2003.

In this chapter we'll revisit some Windows 2000 design principles and outline some of the improvements to Windows 2000 that have appeared in Windows 2003.

1.2 Windows 2000/Windows 2003 Refresher

Some factors are critical for any Exchange 2003 deployment (whether it is a greenfield installation or a migration) to be successful. Getting the Windows 2000/Windows 2003 infrastructure just right is the most important point, so we need to make sure that we've got our Windows 2000/Windows 2003 model soundly in place. Windows 2000/Windows 2003 brings with it many new phrases and terminology, so as a refresher, let's quickly review some basic Windows 2000 terms that we'll see repeatedly with respect to Exchange 2003.

1.2.1 Active Directory

The AD replaces the flat-structured NT4 SAM with an X.500-like hierarchical directory structure. Exchange 2003 uses the AD extensively because it no longer has a directory service of its own. The AD is essentially a container for objects held in a hierarchical fashion. The AD provides methods for search, retrieval, and update of information that it holds. The AD is a multimaster directory, and different parts of the AD can exist on different servers within an organization. The AD provides a mechanism for replication that means that information held on one particular AD server can be replicated to another AD server. As such, replication latency can be a factor that needs to be taken into consideration, and this gives rise to the concept of "loose consistency," which is said to exist with the AD: that is, information within the AD may be inconsistent and a point in time because of replication latency. The AD is used by Exchange 2003 to hold information that is used by mail routing, to provide a Global Address List (GAL), and to store configuration information.

1.2.2 Active Directory Schema

The schema, among other things, defines the type of objects that can be stored in the AD. To store new object types, the schema must be modified to describe the structure of the new object, what attributes it may contain, where it may appear in the hierarchy, and so on. The default objects with the AD are Organizational Unit objects, user objects, group objects (both distribution groups and security groups), contact objects, computer objects, and printer objects. You may of course define your own additional object types if you wish to use them with custom-built applications or you just have some free time on your hands on a rainy Sunday afternoon.

1.2.3 Windows 2000/Windows 2003 Domain

A domain is a collection of Windows 2000/Windows 2003 computers and user accounts that share a common boundary. A Windows 2000/Windows 2003 domain is a logical grouping of network computers that share a central directory database. A Windows 2000 domain may contain Windows 2003, Windows 2000, and NT4 computers as member servers or as Domain Controllers. A directory database contains user accounts and security information for the domain. This directory database is known as the Directory and is the database portion of the AD, which is the Windows 2000 directory service. Similarly, a Windows 2003 domain may contain the same types of servers.

1.2.4 Active Directory Namespaces

In Windows 2000 the AD hosts several different namespaces, called Naming Contexts. Each domain has its own namespace called the Domain Naming Context that holds information about AD objects homed within that domain. The Domain Naming Context is maintained on a Domain Controller within a particular domain, and there is one Domain Naming Context for every domain in the AD. The Configuration Naming Context holds configuration information from your environment (including information about the configuration of Exchange). The Configuration Naming Context is automatically replicated to all Domain Controllers within the AD, as is the Schema Naming Context. Windows 2003 can have additional Naming Contexts, known as Application Naming Contexts, so that other application can share private data.

1.2.5 Windows 2000/Windows 2003 Domain Controller

When a user needs authentication within a domain, it contacts a Domain Controller (DC). You may have multiple DCs within a domain, and each DC holds a complete copy of the Domain Naming Context for the particular domain in which it resides. This means that it knows about all other member servers, DCs, users, and printers that are registered within that domain. A DC also holds a copy of the Configuration and Schema Naming Contexts for the whole forest. DCs listen on Lightweight Directory Access Protocol (LDAP) port 389 for local domain queries.

1.2.6 Windows 2000/Windows 2003 Forest

A forest is essentially an instance of the AD. A forest gets its name based on the name of the first domain that is installed. The name that you use for the first domain is very important because it potentially affects the naming structure for your whole organization. Many companies are using a placeholder first domain to allow them to build a forest and thus reserve a neutral name for it. Any DCs within the forest share the same configuration and schema naming contexts. You can use the DCPROMO utility to join or leave domains in a forest. A forest is composed of a tree of domains; a tree of domains in the same branch holds a contiguous namespace. The forest represents the security boundary for the AD.

1.2.7 Global Catalog Server

The Global Catalog (GC) server holds the same information as a DC. However, the GC server also holds a read-only replica of every Domain Naming Context in the forest. Thus, a DC only knows about the objects in its domain, whereas a GC server knows about objects in its domain and every other domain. Although the GC server knows about all objects from every domain, it only has knowledge of a subset of the attributes for each object. The objects that are available for replication to a GC server are controlled by the AD Schema Manager snap-in. By default, the first DC in a domain is a GC server. GC servers listen on port 3268 (using LDAP) for queries as well as the standard LDAP port 389. Port 3269 may also be used on a GC server to process requests for GC information over Secure Sockets Layer (SSL). A DC can be made into a GC server by selecting the option from the AD Sites and Services snap-in.

1.2.8 Operations Master

An Operations Master server is also known as the Flexible Single Master Operations (FSMO) server. There are five different operations master roles: Schema, Domain Naming, Primary Domain Controller (PDC) emulator, Routing Information Daemon (RID), and Infrastructure. Only DCs can hold these roles. From an Exchange perspective, we are only concerned with the Schema Operations Master. Although Windows 2000/Windows 2003 support multimaster replication of data, some forms of replication are single-master because conflicts would be impossible to resolve in a last-writer-wins fashion. The Schema Operations Master is unique in the forest, and it is responsible for making any modifications to the schema and distributing it to other DCs. When you first install Exchange 2000/Exchange 2003, you'll need to make modifications to the schema on the Schema Operations Master server.

1.2.9 Windows 2000/Windows 2003 Site

This is similar to the definition of a site in Exchange 5.5 terms. It may also be considered as a collection of Internet Protocol (IP) subnets, which are within an area of high-speed network connectivity such as a local area network (LAN). Sites may span domains, and accordingly, domains may span sites. There is no direct correlation between a Windows 2000/Windows 2003 domain and a Windows 2000/Windows 2003 site.

1.2.10 Active Directory Replication

Windows 2003 and Windows 2000 AD replication is a huge topic that cannot be completely covered in a short section in a book on Exchange 2003. Suffice it to say, however, that many improvements have been made to the AD replication model in Windows 2003 versus what was available in Windows 2000. Specifically, these include improvements to the AD Linked Value Replication mechanism: (1) an elimination of the 5,000 direct member limit on the number of members in a distribution group, (2) less replication overhead on the wire when changes to a distribution group membership are made (only the changes in the multivalued attribute, not the entire multivalued attribute), and (3) the elimination of a complete GC server resynchronization when a change is made to the AD Partial Attribute Set.

1.3 Exchange 2003 and Its Relationship to the Forest

Information about Exchange 2003 is rooted in the hierarchy of the AD. In fact, information about your Exchange 2003 infrastructure is rooted in the Configuration Naming Context, and because a naming context can't span forests, it should be no surprise to learn that Exchange 2003 can't span forests either. This is exactly as it was with Exchange 2000 and Windows 2000. If you have multiple forests in your Exchange 2003 deployment, say one per geographical area, then this means that you'll end up with multiple Exchange 2003 organizations—essentially different Exchange 2003 implementations, so you need to plan for a homogeneous Windows 2000/Windows 2003 infrastructure if you desire just a single Exchange organization. But remember, given that the forest is a security boundary in Windows 2000/Windows 2003, if you have strict security requirements for separation of information, then multiple forests may be best for you. One typically sees this kind of structure in financial organizations, where say investment banking must be separated from the analyst arm of the organization. Such so-called Chinese Wall implementations are becoming increasingly common.

It's also important to note that you can't host multiple Exchange organizations within a single forest. Although this may not seem too important—you probably want a single Exchange 2003 environment, after all—it is important if you consider what you do about test environments. If you want a separate Exchange 2003 implementation for testing purposes, then you'll have to root this in a separate forest. With luck, Microsoft may improve this situation in the future, because all that really needs to be done is to support several different Exchange containers in the Configuration Naming Context: of course, it's simple to suggest this but somewhat more difficult to implement it. Do note, however, that the restriction on implementing just a single Exchange organization does not mean that you cannot host multiple companies' e-mail systems within a single Exchange organization. Such "hosted" Exchange implementations are common in the service provider industry, but a full description of them is outside the scope of this book.

1.4 The Importance of Domain Controllers and Global Catalog Servers

1.4.1 User Authentication

In the world of Exchange 5.5, sites were created on the basis of good network connectivity. The parameters we looked for were reasonable available bandwidth (where reasonable varied anywhere from 32 kbps to 128 kbps) and low latency. Although the concept of sites is no longer around with Exchange 2003, we do have the concept of a Windows 2000/Windows 2003 site to deal with. Technically, of course, a Windows 2000/Windows 2003 site is a collection of IP subnets, but in practice that often means that good bandwidth and low latency connectivity is available. Today we look for higher bandwidth than that which was sought after with Exchange 5.5 sites. Nowadays we expect to see LAN speeds (at least 10 Mbps, but increasingly 100 Mbps or higher) as a baseline for Windows 2000/Windows 2003 site definitions. However, in some environments it is not uncommon to see such sites spanning network connections where bandwidth is significantly lower, often in the region 512 kbps connections.

From a pure Windows 2000/Windows 2003 design perspective, it's likely that DCs will be located close to groups of users. The reason for this is straightforward: When a user logs on to a domain, the logon process contacts the DC for that user's domain to validate the user's credentials, so clearly it makes sense to locate a DC close by for efficient logon performance. The logon process actually goes a little bit further than this, because logon requires not just access to a DC, but the DC actually requires access to a GC server. Although a DC can authenticate the credentials for the user in its domain, a user logon also requires a security token to be generated with details of every universal security group to which the user belongs. Of course, it's possible that the user may belong to a security group in a different domain, so a local DC would have no knowledge of such a "foreign" group. For this reason, the DC contacts a GC server to determine which groups the user belongs to so that access control can be correctly enforced.

So for every grouping of users, whether Exchange 2003 users or not, you should expect to see a DC and/or a GC server located logically close by.

1.4.2 Global Address List Services

As well as servicing user logon requests, GC servers offer directory lookup functionality to Exchange 2003 clients such as Outlook. GC servers hold a subset of the attributes from all objects within the forest, and specifically, for Exchange 2003, they hold name and e-mail address information. This means that Exchange clients use information from the GC server in the same way that the Exchange 5.5 Directory Service offered a GAL. Different types of clients use DCs and GC servers in different ways to get access to the GAL.

Although access to GAL information is available from GC servers over LDAP on port 3268, Messaging Application Programming Interface (MAPI) clients do not use this mechanism. By default, all MAPI client directory lookup is performed using the Name Service Provider Interface (NSPI) on a dynamically assigned port higher than 1024. (See Q270836 for information on how to lock down the NSPI interface to a specific port number.) The NSPI interface is only available on GC servers, never on DCs.

1.4.3 Understanding the DSAccess Cache

DSAccess (DSACCESS.DLL) is an Exchange 2003 server component that provides an in-memory volatile cache of user directory data of size 140 MB. This is usually enough to hold about 80,000 user objects in the cache. DSAccess is a cache that helps other Exchange components interact with the AD. Essentially this directory data relates to user mailbox information, which is useful to Exchange 2003 server components including the Store and the Message Categorizer. This particular cache is not used for client-initiated GAL lookups. Among other tasks, DSAccess is responsible for keeping a list of available, unavailable, and slow DCs and GC servers. There are two essential parts to DSAccess: the Recipient cache and the Configuration cache. The Recipient cache contains information about specific users that certain Exchange 2003 components require access to, such as the Message Categorizer that was mentioned earlier. The other cache, the Configuration cache, contains only information about valid GC servers that Exchange components (including clients) should use. Specifically, the Configuration cache contains the list of up to 200 working and preferred DCs and GC servers that Outlook mail clients and other Exchange services should use. DSAccess maintains this list: it detects changes in the environment; for example, if a DC or GC server becomes unavailable, it will detect this change and augment the list if necessary.

On startup, DSAccess uses a discovery process that completes within one minute or aborts. You can control this timeout by setting values for the following registry key:

```
HKEY_LOCAL_MACHINE\System\CurrentControlSet\
Services\MSExchangeDSAccess
Value name: TopoCreateTimeOutSecs
Value type: DWORD
Value data: 60 seconds is the default value
```

In general, the one-minute timeout should be sufficient, but if you find that it is not, your first course of action should be to determine the reason for the timeout. This may be related to network or topology problems. This discovery process is repeated every 15 minutes.

During the process, DCs are identified into three key roles of Configuration Domain Controller (used for reading/writing system configuration information) and then general-purpose worker DCs and GC servers. The Configuration Domain Controller is often called the Bootstrap Domain Controller and is used as the starting point for much of the discovery process. It is selected by DSAccess through the normal DC discovery process that Windows 2000 or Windows 2003 provides. In general, it will be a high-performance DC situated on the same LAN segment as the Exchange server, and it is typically used for up to eight hours before DSAccess requests a new server.

DSAccess only uses this discovery process if you do not have a list of hardcoded DCs that DSAccess should use (more on this topic in the following sections).

The discovery process works as follows:

1. DSAccess opens an LDAP connection to a randomly chosen DC from the local domain. This is known as the Bootstrap Domain Controller.
2. DSAccess conducts an LDAP search to identify local DCs and GC servers. DSAccess determines server suitability and assigns server roles.
3. DSAccess conducts an LDAP search to determine if one or more secondary sites are connected to the local site. If a secondary site exists, then DSAccess sorts the SiteLink objects from each site from lowest cost to highest cost. DSAccess places the lowest-cost sites in a secondary topology list.
4. DSAccess conducts an LDAP search to identify the DCs and GC servers that are located in the secondary topology sites.
5. DSAccess identifies the full topology and compiles the list of working DCs and GC servers.

In step 2, the idea of a suitability test for a DC or GC server is introduced. These suitability tests are applied to individual servers during the discovery process. DSAccess uses the following process to determine server suitability:

1. *Reachability.* Depending on the type of server object (DC or GC server), DSAccess must be able to reach the server over the network on either port 389 or 3268 within a two-second timeout.
2. *Access rights.* DSAccess reads the security descriptor of the Configuration Naming Context object on the server. If the security descriptor cannot be read, the server is not suitable.
3. *Domain preparation.* The directory server must be located in a domain in which Domainprep has been run.
4. *Synchronization.* DSAccess checks whether the server has been synchronized with the rest of the AD. This is done by checking if the *isSynchronized* value returns TRUE when the RootDSE is queried.
5. *NetLogon.* DSAccess sends a DSGetDcName Remote Procedure Call (RPC) message to the directory server to test its general suitability. If the directory server is not time synchronized, is out of disk space, or is experiencing any other replication problems, it will not show up as a directory server for RPCs. Bear in mind that if you are implementing this across a network demilitarized zone (DMZ), then steps may have been taken to disable the RPC access across internal firewalls. If this is the case, then you must be sure to disable the RPC check during this suitability testing process, which you can do by setting the following registry key:

   ```
   HKEY_LOCAL_MACHINE\System\CurrentControlSet
   \Services\MSEXchangeDSAccess
   Value name: DisableNetLogonCheck
   Value type: DWORD
   Value data: 1
   ```

6. *Domain name server (DNS) priority and weight.* Each DC and GC server has an Service Location Record (SRV), which contains both a priority and a weight. DSAccess uses the weight value to determine which server the client should prefer. Therefore, administrators can use the priority value to control which servers are used for logon activity and weigh value to control which servers are used by Exchange. A higher weight results in a higher probability that DSAccess will choose a server. DSAccess treats a weight of 0 the same as it treats a weight of 1. If DSAccess cannot read the weight, it uses a default value of 100.
7. *FSMO Primary Domain Controller (PDC) role owner.* If your topology contains Windows NT4 servers, the FSMO PDC will experience heavy loads. To avoid

performance problems, you should exclude FSMO PDCs from DSAccess by setting the MinUserDC registry key:

```
HKEY_LOCAL_MACHINE\System\CurrentControlSet
\Services\MSExchangeDSAccess\Profiles\Default
Value name: MinUserDC
Value type: DWORD
Value data: Set value between 1 and 10
```

To exclude the FSMO PDC emulator server, create the above registry key and set the value to the minimum number of DCs and GC servers that are required to support the load in your environment. For example, you might set this value to 5. Thus DSAccess will always exclude the FSMO PDC emulator server for so long as at least five DCs or GC servers are available. If the number of available servers falls below this value, then DSAccess will select the FSMO PDC emulator server.

8. *Critical data.* The server must contain a minimum set of critical data. For example, the local Exchange server object must be present in the Exchange configuration container.
9. *Residential site.* DSAccess prefers local AD servers to servers located in other sites.

In the network DMZ scenario, as well as suppressing the NetLogon RPC check across an internal firewall, you may also wish to suppress the DSAccess Ping routine that is used for each server in order to demonstrate that it is available. Again, in such network environments the Internet Control Message Protocol (ICMP) echo packets are typically blocked on a firewall. If the ICMP echoes are being blocked, DSAccess assumes that the target servers are unavailable and continually tries to rediscover the topology. You can suppress the ICMP checking by setting the following registry key:

```
HKEY_LOCAL_MACHINE\System\CurrentControlSet
\Services\MSExchangeDSAccess
Value name: LdapKeepAliveSecs
Value type: DWORD
Value data: 0
```

Note that Microsoft only supports scenarios where either this registry key is not present or it is set to a value of 0. You can find good information about this kind of network configuration with DSAccess in Microsoft TechNet article Q320529.

1.4.4 Understanding DSProxy

Outlook 2000 Service Release 2 and higher clients all use a referral mechanism to the best GC server. Directory Service Referral (or Proxy) does not use the DSAccess Recipient cache.

The DSProxy component (DSPROXY.DLL) allows MAPI clients to communicate with the AD for directory lookups. DSProxy uses the cached list of GC servers (with GCs from remote domains filtered out) that DSAccess maintains and either performs directory lookups to GC servers on behalf of MAPI clients or refers certain MAPI clients directly to GC servers to perform their own lookups. The list of servers that DSProxy maintains is updated by DSAccess as the state of servers in its cached list changes. If you wish to monitor the list of GCs that DSProxy is currently using for either proxies or referrals, you can use the Event Log. Enable at least minimum diagnostics logging on the NSPI Proxy and the RFR Interface categories of the Exchange System Attendant on the appropriate Exchange 2003 server. (Select Properties of the server under the appropriate Administrative Group of the Exchange System Manager.)

All GC server lookups either by DSProxy directly or by referred clients use the Name Service Provider Interface (NSPI) on the GC server: the LDAP protocol is not used because the overhead of conversion between LDAP and NSPI has too great an effect on performance. No caching is provided via DSProxy: all lookup requests are serviced directly by GC servers, but proxied connections and GC server referrals are round-robin load-balanced. If your Exchange 2003 server is running on a GC server, then DSProxy detects this during startup and does not offer access to the AD, as shown by the event in Figure 1-1. Clients connected directly to that Exchange 2003 server for mailbox access have their directory lookups directed to the NSPI interface on the same server.

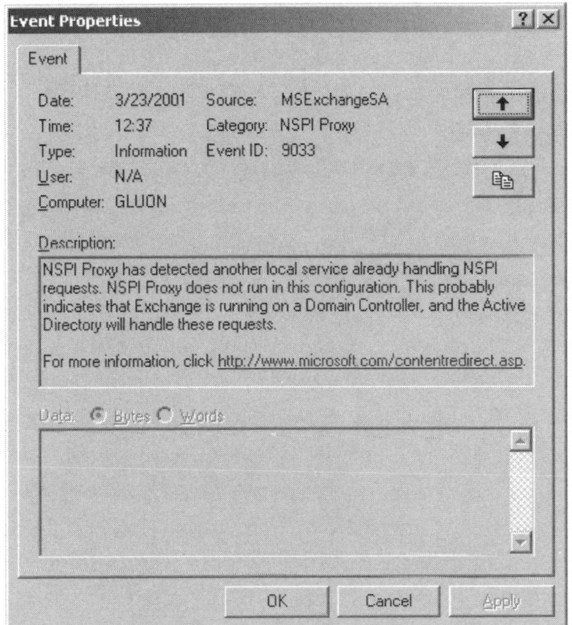

Figure 1-1
Event Log Entry Indicating NSPI Proxy Has Not Started

DSProxy starts up with one worker thread and one listener thread. The NSPI Proxy service is designed to be highly scalable. For every 512 connected clients, DSProxy creates one additional worker thread. Because additional threads consume a small number of additional resources, you can scale each Exchange 2003 server to many thousands of simultaneously connected clients. For the best performance, you should use newer versions of Outlook (Outlook XP or Outlook 2003, or really Outlook 2000 and above) that can use the referral service and communicate directly with GC servers, rather than communicating through the proxy service.

When Outlook clients send NSPI requests to the AD, the overhead is insignificant. For example, when resolving a list of names in the To: field, NSPI generates one RPC request and one RPC response packet. Because of the efficient cursor mechanisms of NSPI, scrolling through the GAL generates only a few packets on the network. Therefore, DSProxy and NSPI scalability is generally not a concern. Unlike DSAccess, DSProxy does not cache NSPI responses, so each lookup requires a request to and response from the server. Recent versions of Outlook (Outlook 2000 and higher) include a client-side cache, which reduces the number of requests.

The DSProxy process uses a load-balancing mechanism to ensure that client requests are divided equally among all available GC servers. When an Outlook client contacts the NSPI Proxy, the TCP/IP address of the requesting client is hashed against the number of available GC servers. DSProxy uses the result to either proxy or refer the client to one of the GC servers. This load-balancing method enables the client to contact the same GC server, thus ensuring consistency. The Directory Service Referral Interface (RFRI) uses a different load-balancing mechanism: when a client connects to RFRI, GC servers are returned in round-robin fashion.

1.4.5 Client Access to the Directory Service

As well as providing access to message stores, MAPI clients offer access to directory services (GC servers), which serve as a GAL. From Exchange 2003's perspective, MAPI clients come in two forms: pre–Outlook 2000 clients (i.e., Exchange 4.0 Client, Exchange 5.0 Client, Outlook 97, Outlook 98) and post–Outlook 2000 inclusive clients (i.e., Outlook 2000, Outlook XP, and Outlook 2003).

Pre–Outlook 2000 clients were designed to work with Exchange Server 5.5. Accordingly, when these clients connect to the Exchange 2003 server, which hosts a user's mailbox, they expect a directory service to be available on the same server: this was always the case with Exchange Server 5.5. Because no directory service is present on the Exchange 2003 server, DSProxy services directory lookup requests from such clients. Figure 1-2 shows how DSProxy "proxies" directory lookups to a "nearby" GC

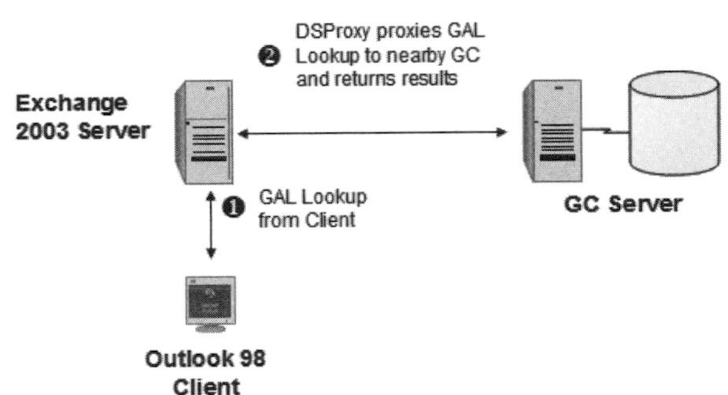

Figure 1-2
DSProxy Proxying GAL Lookups to GC Server

server and returns directory information to the client. In this case, nearby means near to the Exchange 2003 server, not necessarily near to the client.

The situation is different for Outlook 2000, Outlook XP, and Outlook 2003 clients. These "smart" clients were engineered while Exchange 2000 was being designed and before Exchange 2003, and as a result, they do not expect to only access a directory service on the Exchange 2003 mailbox server. (Service Release 2 for Outlook 98 allows it to behave as a smart client.)

Figure 1-3 illustrates the interaction between the smart clients and the Exchange 2003 and GC servers. When a smart client such as Outlook 2003 initially connects to an Exchange 2003 server, it requests a referral from DSProxy. DSProxy returns referral information, which specifies a nearby GC server to which Outlook 2003 should directly connect in the future. Again, nearby in this case means near to the Exchange 2003 server that performed the referral, not necessarily near to the client. Switching to some older clients for a while, traditional Outlook 2000 persists this GC server referral by writing the information to its MAPI profile. The client writes the fully qualified domain name of the GC server into the following easy-to-remember registry location:

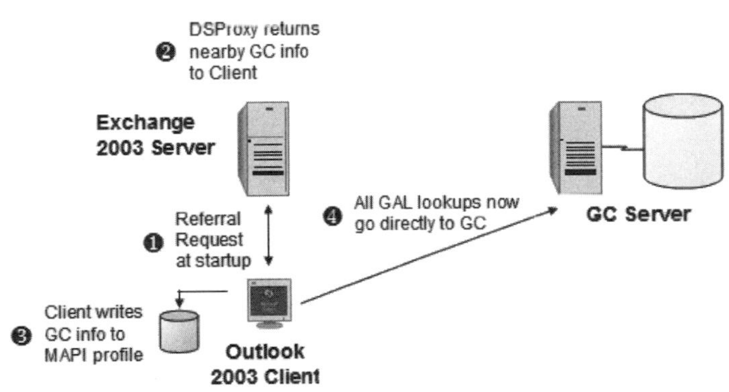

Figure 1-3
DSProxy Referring GAL Lookups to a GC Server

```
HKEY_CURRENT_USER\Software\Microsoft\Windows NT\
CurrentVersion\Windows Messaging Subsystem\Profiles\

Name\dca740c8c042101ab4b908002b2fe182
Value name: 001e6602
Value type: STRING
Value data: DN of the GC
```

All directory lookup requests from this point onward, even during the initial session, go directly to the GC server without any reference to the Exchange 2003 server. Subsequently, when Outlook 2000 next starts, it immediately attempts to access this same GC server specified in the MAPI profile. If this GC server is unavailable, it requests a new referral from DSProxy. This is not an optimal form of behavior because if for some reason the Outlook 2000 client is initially referred to a "far away" GC server, the client will continue to use this GC server until that server becomes unavailable. Only then will the MAPI profile be updated again to allow connections to the more appropriate GC server.

In general, this mechanism only allows Outlook 2000 to request a new GC server if its preferred choice is unavailable. To force Outlook 2000 to choose a new GC server, you must delete the MAPI profile registry key specified above. Additionally, Office 2000 Service Release 2C, Outlook XP, and Outlook 2003 clients implement a mechanism that allows a new GC server request every time the client starts. When these clients start, they ignore the GC server specified in the MAPI profile, request a new referral from Exchange 2003, and then write this value to the MAPI profile to be used for the duration of the session. This dynamic allocation of GC servers offers improved support for load balancing, whereas no such support is available with the persistent MAPI profile cache.

Other clients, such as Outlook Web Access or Outlook Express, will use the GC server directly over LDAP and must be configured to point to a GC server directly.

1.4.6 Using Specific Global Catalog Servers

The nature of the clients that you use will determine the placement of GC servers. In the case of proxy clients (e.g., Outlook 97 and Outlook 98), the clients will have little requirement for GC servers to be located locally. Rather, adequate numbers of GC servers must be located near the Exchange 2003 servers. This generally implies one GC server processor for every four Exchange 2003 processors, but even when fewer than four Exchange 2003 processors are deployed, you should consider using at least two GC servers (ideally dual-processor systems) for redundancy purposes. As a guiding rule of thumb, you should consider deploying one dual-processor GC server for every 5,000 users you will support. The GC servers should be located on the same network segments as the Exchange 2003 servers and preferably in the same domain and/or site. This does not mean that users of proxy clients do not need to have GC servers nearby. On the contrary, they need to have GC servers nearby so that Windows 2000/Windows 2003 logon can occur cleanly and efficiently. So for these reasons you need to have GC servers placed near to user workstations *and* near to Exchange 2003 servers as well.

The same rules of thumb generally can and should be applied when using smart clients. When Exchange 2003 provides a referral back to the client, it's referring the client to a GC server that is near to the Exchange 2003 server, not necessarily near to the client. This is not ideal because the "local" GC servers may be available to the clients via a wide area network (WAN) connection, and it is inherently inefficient because directory lookups could be better serviced by GC servers nearer to the clients. Truly local GC servers will be available in any event to service logons, so in an ideal world, the client would be referred to one of these. Although this form of GC server referral is not optimal, it's no worse than the proxy behavior or the behavior associated with Exchange Server 5.5.

It is possible for the Exchange 2003 server (and Exchange 2000 server) to define explicitly the GC server that clients will use rather than relying on DSProxy to arbitrarily assign a GC server. For proxying, you specify the fully qualified domain name of the GC server in the following registry key on the Exchange 2003 server:

```
HKEY_LOCAL_MACHINE\System\CurrentControlSet\Services\
MSExchangeSA\Parameters
Value name: NSPI Target Server
Value type: STRING
Value data: DN of the Global Catalog server
```

Similarly, for smart clients that use the referral mechanism, you can override DSProxy's GC server selection and specify the fully qualified domain name of a particular GC server to be used in the following registry key on the Exchange 2003 server:

```
HKEY_LOCAL_MACHINE\System\CurrentControlSet\Services\
MSExchangeSA\Parameters
Value name: RFR Target Server
Value type: STRING
Value data: DN of the Global Catalog server
```

If you don't wish to specify an explicit GC server for all clients that will receive referrals from this Exchange 2000 server, you can customize individual clients that are running Office SR2C, Outlook XP, or Outlook 2003. Specify the fully qualified domain name of a particular GC server to be used in the following registry key on the Outlook client:

```
HKEY_CURRENT_USER\Software\Microsoft\Exchange\
Exchange Provider
Value name: DS Server
Value type: STRING
Value data: DN of the Global Catalog server
```

But perhaps the most important client-side setting you can make to the registry is to force a smart Outlook client to use a GC server that is near to it, rather than near to the Exchange 2003 server that is executing the DSProxy sevice. To force a smart Outlook client to use the closest GC server, set the following registry key on the client computer:

```
HKEY_CURRENT_USER\Software\Microsoft\Exchange\
Exchange Provider
Value name: Closest GC
Value type: DWORD
Value data: 0x1
```

You can disable referrals altogether and force smart clients to use proxying. Set the following registry key on the Exchange 2003 server:

```
HKEY_LOCAL_MACHINE\System\CurrentControlSet\Services\
MSExchangeSA\Parameters
Value name: No RFR Service
Value type: DWORD
Value data: 0x1
```

Whatever way you look at it, there's a huge dependency on intelligent placement of DCs and especially GC servers in order to provide an efficient infrastructure for Exchange 2003 to run on top of.

1.4.7 Dealing with Global Catalog Server Failure

Neither proxy clients nor referral clients deal gracefully with the loss of a GC server. Access from the client to the mailbox is still maintained, but directory lookup functionality is not. In the case of proxy clients, although the client maintains a connection to the Exchange 2003 server, which proxies the request to a specific GC server, the client address book provider (EMSABP32.DLL) caches the GC server details locally. The caching is done so that the Exchange 2003 server always proxies the lookup request to the same GC server, thus maintaining consistency in the GAL presented to the client. However, if the GC server becomes unavailable, the client must restart (and accordingly the dynamic cache must be cleared) before a new GC server can be used for the proxy requests.

A similar scenario holds true for the smart clients. Although the GC server is available, a smart client will communicate directly with it. However, if the GC server becomes unavailable, the Outlook client must be restarted to request a new GC server. Under most circumstances DSProxy will provide the client with a new and available GC server because DSAccess will inform DSProxy that the original GC server is down. However, real-life experience has shown that DSAccess occasionally does not update DSProxy correctly, and the client may well be referred to the same GC server that is still unavailable. Because DSProxy load-balances its referrals, you can try restarting Outlook a few times to get a referral to an active GC server.

1.5 Choosing an Appropriate Domain Model

With Windows NT4 and Exchange 5.5, many restrictions could be placed on the domain model. Typically, the restrictions related to the maximum number of account objects that you could place in a domain or to management capabilities across different groups of administrators with different management interests or objectives. Using Windows NT4 and Exchange 5.5 usually resulted in an environment with one or more Master User Domains and one or more Resource Domains for Exchange 5.5 servers in all but the simplest environments (similar to that shown in Figure 1-4).

Using Windows 2000 or Windows 2003, we have an opportunity to build a more streamlined domain model either for new environments or rationalized existing environments. Ideally, a single domain model is the target for which you should aim. The ability to streamline down to a single domain model using separate Organizational Units, where once you may have used a resource domain, is a model that will be used by many organizations and that becomes achievable with Windows 2000 and Windows 2003. Most important, because of the granular access controls, this allows everything to be hosted in a single domain, yet still finely control administration. (A preferred Windows 2003 domain model is shown in Figure 1-5.)

If you find yourself in a situation where you'll be migrating a Windows NT4 domain environment to Windows 2003, it makes sense to restructure that domain environment, if it's more than just a simple domain structure. Rather than just upgrade

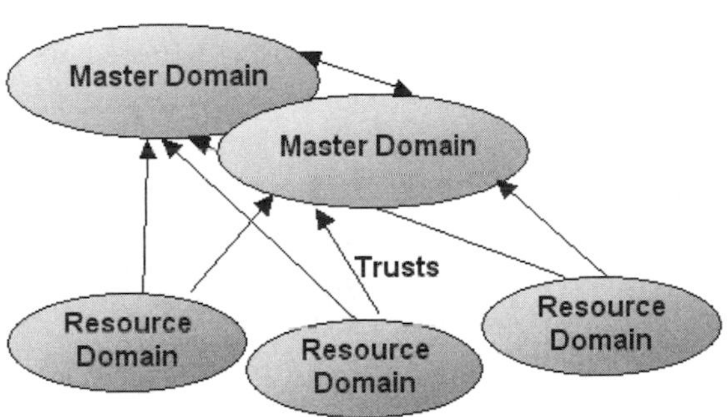

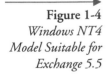

Figure 1-4 *Windows NT4 Model Suitable for Exchange 5.5*

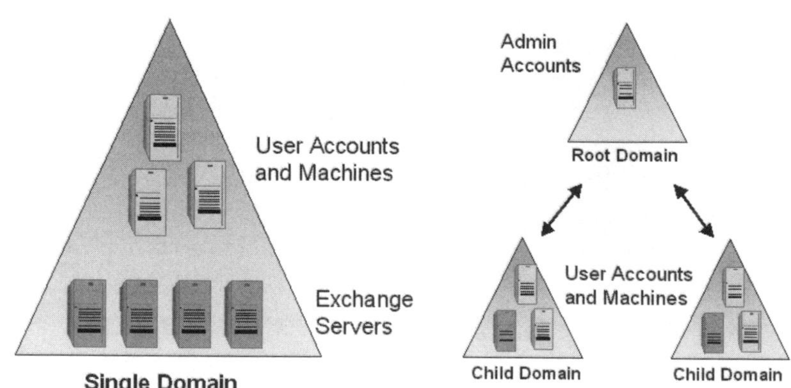

Figure 1-5
Preferred Windows 2003 Domain Models

existing systems, a more innovative approach is to build a new environment alongside the old Windows NT4 environment and then use migration tools to bring over Windows NT4 account information into the newly restructured domain. This approach is highly desirable because you get to build a new streamlined environment and impact the existing user community as little as possible during the course of the migration, other than resetting all user passwords, although some migration tools available today support limited forms of password migration. What you end up with is an optimized Windows 2003 environment ready for Exchange 2003 and possibly reducing many hundreds of Windows NT4 domains to a handful of Windows 2003 domains. Figure 1-5 illustrates two approaches for a Windows 2003 domain structure. For simple environments, it's common to see a single domain model, which includes all user and machine accounts. In more complex environments, it's common to see a tiered domain approach that typically uses just the root domain acting as a naming placeholder and holding just a handful of administrative accounts. The child domains typically hold all user and machine accounts, and it's usual to find one located to a major geographical area of business function.

Taking the former Compaq environment as an example for a Windows NT to Windows 2000 migration (which is similar to what could be done going directly to Windows 2003), we reduced the 13 Master Account Domains and more than 1,700 Resource Domains that we used in the Windows NT4 world to just four Windows 2000 domains: one placeholder domain for CPQCORP.NET and three geographical domains not-so-cryptically-named AMERICAS.CPQCORP.NET, EMEA.CPQCORP.NET, and ASIAPACIFIC.CPQCORP.NET. Of course, within this environment at the moment, work is currently underway to rationalize the Compaq Windows environment with the Hewlett-Packard Windows environment as the result of yet another acquisition.

1.6 Universal Security Groups and Windows Domain Mixed-Mode Membership

Ideally, all of your Windows 2003 (or Windows 2000) domains should be in native mode before you start to either deploy or migrate to Exchange 2003. However, there is no explicit requirement for this to be the case. And in the scenario where you have Universal Security Groups (USGs) in native-mode Windows domains, there is no requirement that the membership be drawn from other native-mode domains. This flexibility is useful, because it means that there's no restriction on the domain mode before you start to implement Exchange 2003. Having said that, as a matter of best practice you should complete the migration to native-mode Windows 2003 account domains *before* you begin to deploy Exchange 2003.

Remember that when a user logs into a domain, the GC server is consulted so that the Security Identifiers (SIDs) of any Universal Security Groups to which the user belongs are built into the user's security token. However, if the user is a member of a mixed-mode domain, then those SIDs are not placed into the token.

So clearly there is a problem, insofar as a user can be a member of a USG and, as we'll see later, you can use USGs to permission Public Folders, but those permissions will not be adhered to if the user account is homed in a mixed-mode Windows domain and the user requests access to the permissioned Public Folder. At best, this will result in the user not being granted access to the Public Folder if the USG has been used to identify those users who have access to the Public Folder. However, in the worst case, if USGs have been used to enforce explicit deny access, then users may get access to Public Folder information, which ordinarily they should not.

1.7 Token Augmentation

Obviously, it's not appropriate to allow such a lapse in the Public Folder permissions model to exist in a production environment, so a technique called *Token Augmentation* is used to plug the gap.

The problem only exists if a user's account is homed on a DC server in a mixed-mode Windows domain. (User accounts homed in native-mode Windows domains that are members of a USG are not affected.) Windows 2003 and Windows 2000 Service Pack 1 provides a function that allows an application, Exchange 2003 in this case, to discover which USGs a user is a member of and then add the SIDs of those USGs into the user's token. This results in an augmented token that is used in subsequent access checks.

In this way, Exchange 2003 (and Exchange 2000) offers the same functionality that you would expect to get with a native-mode Windows domain, although the user's domain is actually in mixed mode, with the complete token being built not at login time, but deferred until later when the user tries to access the Exchange resource. Note that the token is only augmented *on demand* (i.e., when the user requests access to the permissioned object). When the access is requested, Exchange 2003 only invokes the augmentation code if the forest in which the domains are homed is not wholly in native mode. Exchange 2003 can determine if the user is from a mixed-mode or a native-mode domain, and the token is augmented once and then cached on the server that is attempting the access.

Token augmentation becomes more complex when you have to deal with trust relationships to Windows NT4 domains and to other Windows 2000 or Windows 2003 domains in different forests:

- **Trust relationships to Windows NT4 domains** may use the Active Directory Connector to create disabled user accounts in the new Windows 2003 domain and then assign mailbox rights back to that trusted Windows NT4 account. Because we are using a trusted Windows NT4 account, the token that is generated at logon time is based on the Windows NT4 account, yet the USGs will be based on the disabled user object. In this case, Windows 2003 provides another set of function calls that allows Exchange 2003 to update the Windows NT4 token.
- **Trust relationships to domains in another forest** use a special switch, setting msExchAddGroupsToToken to TRUE, to achieve the same thing.

Token augmentation is only implemented for certain client protocols, specifically, MAPI, HTTP/DAV, and OLE-DB. However, it is not available for ExIFS, IMAP, NNTP, or POP3, so your *user experience* may vary depending on the client you're using at any particular time. This means that you may not get access to certain resources using the latter protocols.

1.8 Exchange 2003 Installation Requirements

Microsoft has used the expression "evolution, not revolution" in the past, and if ever there was a time to use it, that time is now for the relationship between Exchange 2000 and Exchange 2003. There is certainly no dramatic difference in the thinking that is required to design, plan, and implement an Exchange 2003 environment from that required for an Exchange 2000 environment.

In a nutshell, the major improvement in terms of changes between Exchange 2000 editions and Exchange 2003 editions is the addition of front-end/back-end server functionality with the Exchange 2003 Standard edition. It is still recommended that large enterprise-style configurations use Exchange 2003 Enterprise edition. This facilitates support for clustering, multiple Storage Groups, and database sizes in excess of 16 GB. Also bear in mind the importance of using Windows 2000 Advanced Server or Windows 2003 Enterprise editions so that you can use the /3 GB boot switch for large memory Exchange servers (1 GB and higher).

The most important item to note about installing Exchange 2003 is really not about Exchange 2003 at all. Exchange 2003 is supported in both Windows 2000 and Windows 2003, but it is very important to know that Exchange 2000 is ***not*** supported on a Windows 2003 server. However, do note that Exchange 2000 is supported running on a Windows 2000 member server in a Windows 2003 DC environment. Also note that only Windows 2003 DCs or Windows 2000 DCs running SP3 or higher can be used by Exchange 2003, and at least one of these must be available within the domain in which the Exchange 2003 server is installed.

Windows 2000 SP3 DCs are important to Exchange 2003 for several reasons, not the least of which is that they offer secure LDAP connectivity to many components of Exchange 2003, including the Active Directory Connector, the Site Replication Service (SRS), the Recipient Update Service (RUS), and DSAccess. Bear in mind that using secure LDAP access implies that a server certificate be installed on the DCs or GC servers that Exchange 2003 will use. And Windows 2003 is smarter here too, because it only advertises its service to act as a GC server when it has fully synchronized within the AD environment, thus issues of latency within the environment are minimized. Specifically on GC servers, there is no need to reboot (as there was with Windows 2000) when you enable the NSPI for use by MAPI clients.

For completeness, note that Exchange 5.5 can operate in most of these environments because it has no reliance on the AD, but again note that it is ***not*** supported running on a Windows 2003 server. Table 1-1 shows the operating system and Exchange version relationship. Note that an Exchange 2000 SP1 server running on a Windows 2000 server in a Windows 2003 domain requires Microsoft hotfix Q316463. The official statement for support from Microsoft is available in TechNet article Q321648.

Exchange 2003 will only install on servers that are running Windows 2000 SP3 or higher. And when installing Exchange 2003 on Windows 2000, both the .NET Framework and ASP.NET components of Windows are automatically installed. This automatic installation does not take place if you are installing on Windows 2003 though. In either case, and as before, you must install the NNTP Windows component explicitly from the Control Panel. And now, in addition, on Windows 2003 you must explicitly install the WWW Service. Not having these services installed on the Windows 2003 platform by default is part of Microsoft's initiative to make its systems

Table 1-1 *Exchange and Windows Interoperability Matrix*

Exchange/ OS version	Windows NT 4.0	Windows 2000 in Windows 2000 Domain	Windows 2000 in Windows 2003 Domain	Windows 2003
Exchange 5.5 SP3	Y	Y	Y	N
Exchange 2000 up to and incl. SP1	N	Y	Y	N
Exchange 2000 SP2	N	Y	Y	N
Exchange 2000 SP3	N	Y	Y	N
Exchange 2003	N	Y	Y	Y

more secure: no unnecessary services should be installed unless you explicitly do so as a system administrator.

The following components were featured in Exchange 2000, but have been retired in Exchange 2003:

- Instant Messaging service
- Key Management Service (KMS)
- Chat Service
- Lotus cc:Mail Connector
- MS-Mail Connector
- Directory Synchronization (DXA) Connector
- Schedule+ Free/Busy Connector

Management and administration capabilities for these components have also been retired in Exchange 2003. This means that you cannot use the Exchange 2003 version of the administration tools to manage these services.

Also not supported in Exchange 2003 are the following:

- Unified Messaging (UM) Control for OWA and Outlook
- FrontPage add-in for Exchange
- Common Messaging Calls (CMC)
- Simple MAPI (server-side)
- CDOHTML

- CDOEX (client-side only)
- ADO access via Microsoft Internet Application Publishing
- EXIFS (M:) drive (now hidden)

There are also some differences in the default configuration of Exchange 2003 versus Exchange 2000. For example, after installation, POP3, IMAP4, NNTP, and mobility services are disabled by default. There is also a 10 MB Global Message Delivery limit in place by default. And from a usability perspective, domain users cannot log on locally to an Exchange 2003 server system (similar to the fact that domain users cannot log on locally to a DC or GC server).

When using Exchange 2003 for small office locations, you should thoroughly investigate the use of Outlook 2003 cached mode for connecting users back to a central Exchange server. However, where this is not feasible, you may decide to place an Exchange 2003 server in a branch office location. Furthermore, you may wish to install Exchange 2003 on an AD server to reduce hardware and software costs. This is supported, providing the following conditions are satisfied:

- The server is not a cluster.
- You tolerate the possible performance impact of coexisting Exchange 2003 and AD.
- The server must be a GC server (not just a DC).
- You tolerate that DSAccess/DSProxy/Categorizer will not load-balance or fail-over to another DC/GC server.

You should avoid the use of the /3GB switch on coexisting Exchange 2003 and GC servers; otherwise the Exchange cache might monopolize system memory. Additionally, the number of user connections should be very low; therefore the /3GB switch should not be required.

On coexisting systems, all services run under the LocalSystem account, so there is a greater risk of exposure if a security bug is found (e.g., a bug in the AD that allows an attacker to access the AD will also allow access to Exchange, and vice versa). If Exchange Administrators will be able to log on to the local server, because they have physical console access to a DC, they can potentially elevate their permissions in the AD.

It may take approximately 10 minutes for the server to shut down. This is because the AD service (LSASS.EXE) shuts down before the Exchange services, and DSAccess will go through several timeouts before shutting down. The workaround for this issue is to manually stop the Exchange services (specifically the Store) before initiating a system shutdown or restart, which can normally be easily achieved using a script.

NT File System (NTFS) partitions are absolutely required for almost all file systems that will exist on an Exchange 2003 server, including the system volume, the volume that hosts any Exchange 2003 binaries or other application files, the volumes used for any database files or transaction logs, and any volumes where any other Exchange 2003 files will be located.

1.9 Exchange System Manager on Windows XP

The implementation of a "light" management console now becomes a distinct possibility with the Exchange System Manager (ESM) MMC snap-in now available to run on a Windows XP system. (From a management perspective you might also consider using Terminal Services.) There are several restrictions associated with this, though, and you cannot just arbitrarily install the ESM console on any old Windows XP system and expect to manage your Exchange server environment.

In the first instance, the Windows XP system must be a member computer in at least a domain within the same forest in which the Exchange server computers reside. Additionally, Windows XP Service Pack 1 must be running, and the Windows 2003 Administration Management Pack must also be present. The Windows XP Simple Mail Transfer Protocol (SMTP) service must be installed because its installation provides several dynamic link libraries (DLLs) and MMC capabilities that the snap-in requires. There is no actual SMTP communication between the administrative client and the Exchange servers under management.

As has always been the case with Exchange and Outlook, it is not a good idea to install the ESM snap-in on a Windows XP system that is already running Outlook. There is a mismatch between versions of MAPI32.EXE that are used for both functions, and this can cause both the ESM and Outlook to function incorrectly.

You should avoid using the Exchange 2000 ESM snap-in in environments where Exchange 2003 is installed. Not only will you not be able to access new Exchange 2003 features, but there is also the risk of damage to new objects that Exchange 2000 does not understand. If you must continue to use Exchange 2000 ESM, you should apply the latest Exchange 2000 SP3 roll-up to your Windows XP workstation[1]. The latest roll-up at the time of this writing includes support for the msExchMinAdminVersion attribute (also known as ESM versioning). Essentially, each Exchange object in the AD is stamped with a minimum admin version. If ESM detects that the data value is greater than the version of ESM running, it will not allow edits to that object. The following objects may become damaged if an unpatched version of Exchange 2000 ESM is used in an Exchange 2003 environment:

1. microsoft.com/downloads/details.aspx?FamilyId=E247C80E-8AFA-4C2A-96B3-F46D1808C790&displaylang=en

- A Recovery Storage Group (RSG) created by Exchange 2003
- Permissions on Outlokk Mobile Access (OMA) and ActiveSync virtual directories

These objects will only be damaged if older versions of ESM are used to manipulate (i.e., write data) directly on these objects. Additionally, some options in both Exchange 2000 and Exchange 2003 may fail to work properly if the ESM from Exchange 2000 is run against Exchange 2003 servers (e.g., the Directory Access tab on the server object returns an error if the ESM from Exchange 2000 is used against an Exchange 2003 server).

You can use Exchange 2003 ESM in environments where Exchange 2003 servers are not deployed. However, you must have performed an Exchange 2003 Forestprep to be supported. For using Exchange 2003 ESM against Exchange 2000 servers, you will automatically be able to use new features such as:

- Move mailbox
- Queue viewer
- Internet Mail Wizard
- Public Folder management enhancements (some)
- Mailbox Recovery Center

1.10 Exchange 2003 and Internet Information Services 6.0

Exchange 2003 runs better on Windows 2003 than on Windows 2000, largely because of Internet Information Service (IIS) 6.0, which brings with it several architectural improvements from which Exchange 2003 directly benefits. In general, IIS 6.0 provides improved management (simpler interface and easier to navigate to required items), better performance, improved scalability, and improved security.

The IIS 6.0 architecture is based on a more robust model employing a kernel-mode listener and the WWW (W3Svc) Service and Monitoring Agent, which is essentially a user-mode process manager. Different Web applications are effectively implemented as Worker Processes: generically, third-party application code, but just as easily a Microsoft application that uses IIS 6.0, such as Exchange 2003. This model is robust because the different Worker Processes operate independently from each other and thus can have little impact on each other from both a reliability and security perspective. This approach, using Worker Process Isolation Mode (WPIM) coupled with the WWW Service Administration and Monitoring Agent, means that if an application process fails, the Agent will detect this and take corrective action, typically restarting the process.

Furthermore, this improves the reliability of the server overall because any kernel-mode access is conducted by the kernel-mode listener, not by an arbitrary Web application. The kernel-mode listener is thus better positioned to deal with any exceptions that may result from illegal or failed operations. And the WPIM model in conjunction with the Agent mean that there are fewer occasions when the W3Svc service actually needs to be restarted.

1.11 Exchange 2003 Installation Improvements

The installation of Exchange 2000 instances (whether upgrades or new installations) required permissions such that the account running the SETUP program had Full Administrative privileges to the entire Exchange organization. With Exchange 2003 this is no longer the case. Only the first Exchange 2003 installation that you perform must be run from an account that has Full Administrative privileges, and subsequent installations of Exchange 2003 require only Full Administrative privileges at the Administrative Group (AG) level. Of course the machine account for the system on which Exchange 2003 is being installed must be added to the domain servers group, but this will typically be carried out by Windows administrative staff (if they are a separate team).

Installations of subsequent Exchange 2003 service packs will now also require only the same Full Administrative privileges at the AG level, as will the removal of a server from an AG unless that server is hosting the SRS, in which case the Full Administrative privileges for the Organization will be required. The various permissions required for installation are shown in Table 1-2.

Exchange 2000 had a requirement such that all installations of the software—no matter if it was the first server to be installed, which would be performing schema updates, or the fifth or fiftieth server—required access to the Schema FSMO role holder during installation. The particular requirement here during installation was to check for the successful presence of the schema modifications, although this is somewhat redundant given that the first installation could not proceed unless the schema modifications had first been made. Although this was by no means a major roadblock to deployment, it was an unnecessary check and could occasionally cause installations to fail if either network problems were in effect or if the Schema FSMO role holder was unavailable for whatever reason. Exchange 2003 no longer has this superfluous requirement, and the installation process only checks that the appropriate "seeding" of the organization has taken place in the Configuration Naming Context: this could not be the case unless the schema modifications had already been successfully installed.

Table 1-2 *Exchange 2003 Installation Permissions Summary*

Task	Required Permissions or Roles
Run Forestprep for first time	Member of Enterprise Administrator group and Schema Administrator group
Run Forestprep subsequently	Exchange Full Administrator at the Organization level
Run Domainprep	Member of Domain Administrator group
Install First server in Domain	Exchange Full Administrator at the Organization level
Install additional servers in domain	Exchange Full Administrator at the Administrative Group level. Machine Account added to Exchange Domain Servers group
Install server with SRS enabled	Exchange Full Administrator at the Organization level

A new option exists now with the Exchange 2003 program that now allows you to specify a particular DC to be used during the installation process: the SETUP/ChooseDC option. This is useful if you are installing a large number of Exchange 2003 servers in a short time. If each installation was to arbitrarily choose a DC to be used during the installation, then you run the risk of the installation using AD information (from the Configuration Naming Context) that is potentially out of date (i.e., suffering from replication latency). Using the SETUP/ChooseDC switch allows you to use a specific DC, thus eliminating the risk associated with replication latency.

With Exchange 2000, each time that a server was installed, the installation routine would process the access rights on the Exchange Organization object in the AD and reset them to their default value. Although this was certainly a useful precautionary measure, it is somewhat problematic if you have modified the default permissions on the Exchange Organization object. For example, you may have modified the default behavior of Exchange 2000 that allows all users to create top-level Public Folders, by removing the permissions. Subsequently reinstalling another Exchange 2000 server anywhere in the organization results in the default permissions being rewritten to the AD. This is obviously undesirable behavior.

Installing Exchange 2003 is different. The default permissions are stamped only once on the Exchange Organization object in the AD. This occurs regardless of whether this is a completely new (and the first) Exchange installation or whether you are upgrading an existing Exchange 2000 system. Subsequent installations of Exchange 2003 do not restamp any permissions.

Several groups are used for conventional operation of Exchange 2003. These are the Exchange Domain Servers and Exchange Enterprise Servers groups, created by the Domainprep utility. Their existence and correct configuration is critical to the normal operation of Exchange 2003 (and Exchange 2000). For example, a server that is a member of such a group has the permission to perform privileged lookups in the AD and access mailboxes. During the Exchange 2003 installation process, the SETUP program checks for the existence of these groups and their correct configuration. If any inconsistencies are found, then the SETUP program will terminate and the installation will fail.

Finally, with Exchange 2000, the Administrator account had the permission to open other users' mailboxes. Exchange 2003 SETUP utility locks these permissions down to prevent this possibility.

1.12 Preparing and Planning for Deployment

There are two ways in which you can begin the Exchange 2003 installation and SETUP program. You can use the conventional approach by means of the command line and executing the SETUP.EXE program (with the /Forestprep and /Domainprep in the first instance). This is no different from activities you might have carried out with earlier versions of Exchange. In a greenfield environment, you can then proceed to run the SETUP program as normal: either from the command line or simply by double-clicking the executable for Windows Explorer.

Alternatively you can be prompted for all of the various discrete tasks that need to be carried out by running through ExDeploy: a graphical user interface (GUI)-based wizard of sorts. I say wizard of sorts because it is not a true wizard in the Microsoft sense. Rather it is more of a tutorial-oriented help page that guides you through the steps required for installation, effectively just launching the executable for you. You can launch the ExDeploy wizard by double-clicking on the exdeploy.chm file, located in the \support\ExDeploy directory on the Exchange 2003 installation CD-ROM. Be sure to run this exdeploy.chm file from a local copy of the Exchange 2003 installation CD-ROM, not a remotely mounted copy. Executing it remotely results in erratic behavior, with files occasionally not being found. Similarly, be sure to have the actual installation kit locally mounted as well, because having the SETUP.EXE program located on a remote file share can cause the ExDeploy tool to fail to recognize the file.

When ExDeploy is first launched, it will present you with several options to proceed, as shown in Figure 1-6. In the case of a greenfield installation such as this, you will want to select the New Exchange 2003 Installation option.

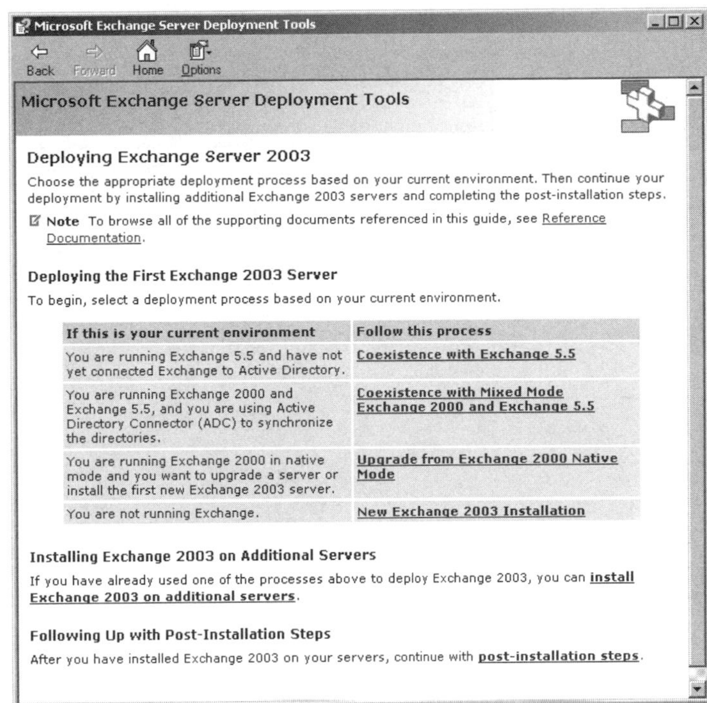

Figure 1-6
ExDeploy Initial Screen

You will then be presented with the various steps that you should carry out for installation, as illustrated in Figure 1-7. Options for Forestprep and Domainprep are presented in order, and the utility suggests that you run the DCDiag and NetDiag utilities before proceeding with the installation.

1.13 DCDiag and NetDiag Utilities

The DCDiag utility can be found in the \support\ExDeploy directory on the Exchange 2003 installation CD-ROM. DCDiag provides a basic test of network connectivity and DNS resolution to DCs in the Windows 2000 or Windows 2003 infrastructure environment.

DCDiag is typically run as a standalone tool: it is not executed as part of any other ExDeploy toolset. It is executed from the command line using the following syntax:

```
DCDIAG /s: controller name /f: file name
```

You need only specify the /s option if you are running DCDiag from a member server; otherwise executing from a DC allows DCDiag to automatically determine the domain configuration. For basic connectivity tests you do not require any administra-

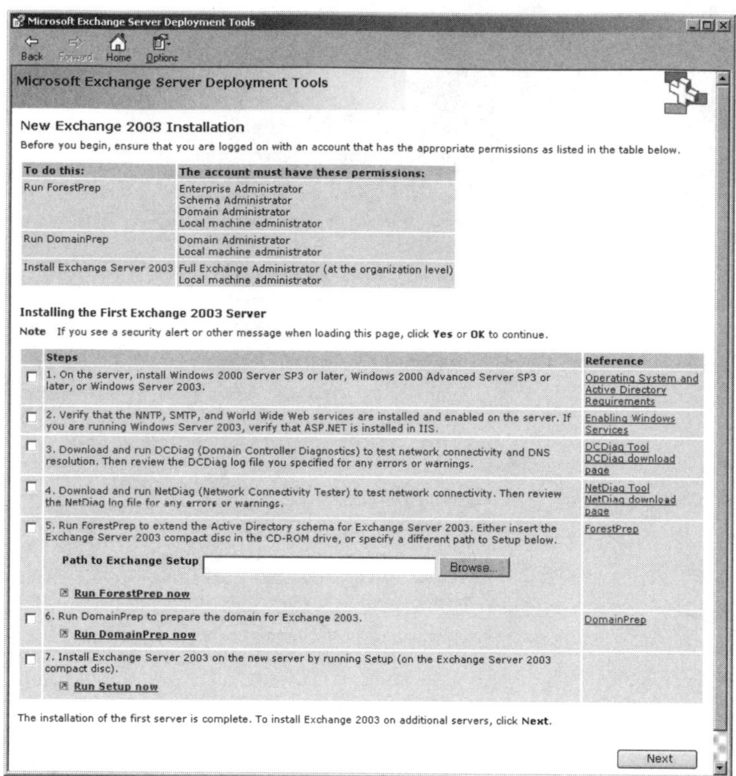

Figure 1-7 *ExDeploy Exchange 2003 Installation Screen*

tive privileges. However, if you wish to execute the complete range of tests, then Enterprise Admin privilege is required.

The NetDiag utility similarly tests basic network connectivity from the perspective of the system on which it is being executed. Essentially this test assumes that Exchange 2003 will be installed on the local system, so the point of the test is to ensure that Exchange 2003 executing on this system has access to the DC services it requires. NetDiag performs several; tests, from basic connectivity tests on the network adapter to checking that the local server can establish Kerberos and LDAP channels to a DC.

Remember that Exchange 2003 can be installed on either Windows 2000 or Windows 2003, but the means by which you invoke NetDiag is different for the two operating systems. To execute NetDiag on Windows 2000, you should run:

```
NETDIAG-W2K.EXE
```

And to run NetDiag on Windows 2003, you should execute:

```
NETDIAG-WSH.EXE
```

In an Exchange 5.5 coexistence environment, NetDiag is automatically executed as part of the DSScopeScan checks (more on this topic later). The log file for the NetDiag utility can be found in the ExDeploy Logs directory (typically on the C: drive) and is entitled exdeploy-netdiag.log. You can find supplemental information about NetDiag in the following Microsoft Knowledge base article: "HOW TO: Use the Network Diagnostics Tool (Netdiag.exe) in Windows 2000 (321708)."

1.14 Preparing Windows 2003 Domains for Exchange 2003

Because Exchange 2003 has such a huge dependency on Windows 2000 and Windows 2003, it's not surprising to learn that you need to take some explicit steps to prepare the Windows 2000/Windows 2003 environment for Exchange 2003. Two command-line options exist for the Exchange 2000 SETUP utility that allow Administrators to prepare the environment. These options are collectively known as OrgPrep but individually known as Forestprep and Domainprep. The Forestprep and Domainprep can also be executed as part of the ExDeploy toolset if you run through the packaged installation or migration scenarios.

Separating out these forest and domain preparation tasks from the Exchange 2003 installation process makes a good deal of sense in larger and more complex environments. Any sizable organization may have different teams of administrators who are responsible for pure Windows 2000/Windows 2003 administration, and preparing the forest and domain infrastructure is essentially a Windows 2000/Windows 2003 administration task that requires certain access rights. Allowing Windows 2000/Windows 2003 administrators to do this means you have the right group of people performing that task, rather than having to elevate the access rights of messaging system administrators.

1.14.1 Running Forestprep

Running the Forestprep utility for Exchange 2003 is absolutely required. This prepares the AD environment for Exchange 2003. You can perform this function in one of two ways. Conventionally you can just execute the SETUP.EXE program with the /Forestprep switch, or you can use the ExDeploy installation wizard. Whatever approach you take, Forestprep must be executed once (and only once) in the AD (whether it is Windows 2000 or Windows 2003) before you can install any Exchange 2003 servers. (If you try to run Forestprep again, the installation code will recognize that you have run it once already and will inform you of this before politely terminating its execution.)

Running Forestprep performs several important functions. First, it extends the AD Schema to add in new definitions that Exchange 2003 uses. Exchange 2003 needs to reference more attributes than just the standard ones that are in the base operating system definition. For example, Exchange 2003 needs to store extra information about your account, such as the Exchange 2003 server on which your mailbox is homed, which storage group your mailbox belongs to, and so on.

To do this, the Forestprep tool adds in some additional auxiliary classes that augment the object class definitions that are already present for user, contact, and group objects. The Forestprep utility provides the AD with 142 additional object and attribute definitions over and above those that are supplied with Exchange 2000. (Exchange 2000 provided some 1,100 or so class definitions over and above what is provided in the operating system.) These class definitions define, among other things, the hierarchy of objects and the attributes that may be associated with any given object. This means that even if this is not a new installation of Exchange, but rather an update from Exchange 2000, the new schema extensions that are part of the Exchange 2003 Forestprep utility must be executed. So the bottom line here is that you must always run Exchange 2003 Forestprep, even if you have run any other Forestprep previously! The actual schema extensions are realized as a set of LDAP Directory Interchange Format (LDIF) commands contained within 10 files named SCHEMA0.LDF through SCHEMA9.LDF found on the Exchange 2003 installation CD-ROM in the /SETUP/I386/EXCHANGE directory. You can inspect these files to satisfy your own curiosity about the actual schema extensions.

The Forestprep utility must be executed in the same domain as that which holds the Schema Operations Master server or Schema Master. (The Operations Master servers are also commonly referred to by their previous moniker of FSMO servers, or Flexible Single Master Operations servers.) Typically, the Schema Master server is the first DC installed in the Windows forest, but you may have moved the Schema Master role to some other server. If you attempt to run the Forestprep utility on a server in the wrong domain (i.e., one that is not the same domain in which the Schema Master is located), then SETUP utility will stop and a message will be displayed indicating on which server Forestprep should be executed. You do not need to execute Forestprep on the Schema Master server, but you may execute it on any other server within that same domain. The executing server will use an LDAP bind and perform the LDIF operations against the Schema Master server.

The account from which you run Forestprep must possess particular permissions. It must be a member of the following:

- The Enterprise Administrators group
- The Schema Administrators group
- The Domain Administrators group
- The Local Machine Administrators group

During the Forestprep utility, you will be asked to designate a specific Windows account that should be used to delegate other Windows accounts that can be used to install and manage subsequent Exchange 2003 server installations. You should already have created this Windows account, and after selecting it, you should use it as the account from which you will run the Exchange Administration Delegation Wizard, which you can use to assign specific Exchange administration roles to other Windows administrative accounts.

Although the AD offers multimaster replication, modifications to the schema—the very fabric of the directory—can only take place on the Schema FSMO. If you have multiple domains in your AD forest, you'll want to be sure that the schema extensions have successfully replicated to all DCs within the forest. It's important that you check for replication having been completed if you have multiple domains or DCs. If you try to install Exchange 2003 and the DC to which it connects doesn't have the appropriate schema extensions in place, then the installation will terminate with errors.

As well as simply modifying the Windows 2000 or Windows 2003 schema, the Forestprep utility performs another important task: It creates the Exchange container object within the Configuration Naming Context of the AD. The Exchange container object is that branch of the AD that holds information about the configuration of all Exchange servers within the organization. With Exchange 2000, when the Forestprep utility created the Exchange container object, the Forestprep process would prompt the user to enter the name of the Exchange organization. This organization name would then be written to the AD at the first level within the Exchange container object. This implied that when you ran Forestprep you must have decided on the name of your Exchange organization. Although this is a reasonable requirement, it was somewhat unnecessary because you really don't need to have decided on an organization name until you set about installing the first Exchange server. Exchange 2003 resolves this minor irritation by not requesting an Exchange organization name to be entered during the execution of Forestprep. Instead, Forestprep writes a placeholder globally unique identifier (GUID) to the Exchange container. The placeholder GUID is consistent across all installations and has the value:

```
{335A1087-5131-4D45-BE3E-3C6C7F76F5EC}
```

If you intend to install an Exchange 2003 server into an existing Exchange 5.5 site, then you'll also need to have at least read-only rights in the Exchange 5.5 Directory

Service. In this case, you won't be prompted to enter the Organization name, but rather, you'll be prompted to enter the name of an existing Exchange 5.5 server. Forestprep will contact the Exchange 5.5 server and interrogate the Exchange 5.5 Directory Service to get organization and site naming information that will then be configured into the AD. This configuration information is obtained by using a Configuration Connection Agreement (ConfigCA), which we'll meet later in this book. The creation of the ConfigCAs requires that the Active Directory Connector be already installed. The Exchange organization name is usually a major bone of contention for Exchange messaging administrators, especially during migrations from Exchange 5.5. There is a misconception that if you are migrating from a legacy Exchange 5.5 environment, then you are stuck with the Exchange organization name that was used in the first instance for Exchange 5.5, because when you run Forestprep it inherits the organization name from that used in Exchange 5.5. Actually, when you run Forestprep in this way, Forestprep inherits the organization name from the Exchange 5.5 Display Name associated with the Exchange 5.5 organization name. Although you cannot change the Directory Name in Exchange 5.5, it is possible to change the Display Name very easily. So if, for example, your legacy Exchange 5.5 organization was named Compaq, simply changing the Display Name to HP would mean that the Forestprep would write this value into the Exchange Organization container in the AD.

Running Forestprep is a CPU-intensive activity, particularly on the Schema Master server, which acts as the target for the LDIF operations. Most LDAP operations on a Windows server consume a lot of CPU resources. Expect to see relatively light CPU utilization on the server from which you are running the Forestprep utility, but more important, expect to see very heavy CPU utilization on the Schema Master server. By very heavy, I mean that you can expect to see the CPU utilization maxed out at 100% for the duration of the LDAP operations on a single-processor system. The process that you will see consuming the CPU resources will be LSASS.EXE—the AD process—but because LSASS.EXE LDAP threads aren't multiprocessor aware, on a two-CPU system you'll see CPU utilization max out at 50% for the duration of the LDAP operations. On a four-processor system, the utilization will be 25%, and so on. For reference and baseline purposes, performing the schema extensions on my test Schema Master server, a single-processor 500 MHz Pentium III system with 256 MB of memory, took about 19 minutes.

1.14.2 Running Domainprep

In addition to running Forestprep, you must also run Domainprep. Once again, running the Exchange 2003 version of Domainprep is an absolute requirement, regardless of whether you have actually run the Exchange 2000 version of Domainprep in all of the domains.

Domainprep performs several functions, specifically, creating the Exchange Domain Servers Global Security Group and the Exchange Enterprise Servers Local Security Group. As Exchange servers in a domain are installed, they are added into these groups, and the membership allows the Exchange server to read and to modify user and configuration information.

Domainprep also creates the Public Folder Proxy Container in each domain in which it is executed. The Public Folder Proxy object is basically an entry in the AD that holds the e-mail addresses associated with a Public Folder so that you can send mail to them. These proxies are held in the Public Folder Proxy Container.

Domainprep must be executed in every domain that will either contain an Exchange 2003 (or Exchange 2000) server and every domain that holds mail-enabled objects (i.e., Exchange mailboxes or Contacts with Exchange addresses associated with them). Additionally, Exchange 2003 (and Exchange 2000 before it) is hard-coded to expect to see the Public Folder Proxy container in the root domain of the forest, so you must ensure that Domainprep is also executed here.

Permission requirements for Domainprep are not as severe as they are for Forestprep. The account from which you execute Domainprep must be a member of the Domain Administrators group and the Local Machine Administrators group.

1.14.3 How Do You Know if Your Schema Needs Upgrading?

If you look at the end of the SCHEMA9.LDF file, you'll find an attribute called *ms-Exch-Schema-Version-Pt*. For example, with the RTM build of Exchange 2003, build 4417.5, the attribute settings in the file read:

```
dn: CN=ms-Exch-Schema-Version-Pt,emaContainerDN
changetype: modify
replace: rangeUpper
rangeUpper: 6870
```

During installation, SETUP checks the value of this attribute in the SCHEMA9.LDF file against the actual value in the AD and determines whether the schema needs to be upgraded.

Obviously, you can check the attribute settings as well, using a tool such as ADSI Edit to see the value of the AD object's attribute.

1.14.4 Best Practices You Should Observe when Preparing for Exchange 2003

Running the OrgPrep tools against your AD infrastructure is not a task that should be performed without proper planning and preparation. You are making real changes to the very definition of the AD, and as such, any changes should be properly evaluated. It makes a great deal of sense to establish a process of schema extension review (for the Exchange 2003 extensions and any other extensions you might make to tailor your AD).

Furthermore, once the schema extensions have been applied to the Schema FSMO, don't just rush off and try to install Exchange 2003 immediately. Give the AD time to replicate the changes around your organization. Visit each DC (logically of course) and verify that replication has taken place. Experience gained on other large-scale AD and Exchange 2003 deployments has always indicated the absolute importance of a functioning AD replication infrastructure.

1.15 Installing Exchange 2000

Having prepared the way for Exchange 2000 using the OrgPrep tools, all that remains is to install the software. Installation of Exchange 2000 uses a completely different User Interface (a sample of which is shown in Figure 1-8) than that used with previous versions of the product. The existing installation process was more than eight years old, and although it served well with previous versions of Exchange, it was no longer suitable for use with a more complex installation process such as Exchange 2000.

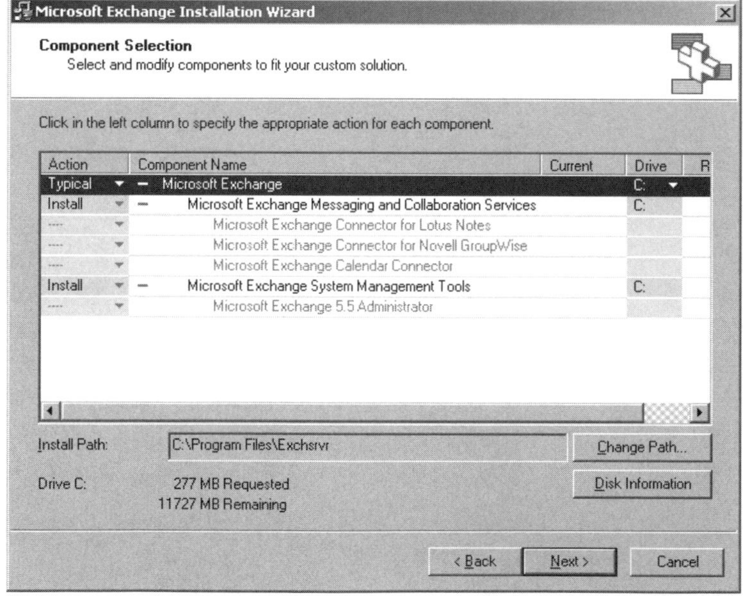

Figure 1-8
Exchange 2003 Installation User Interface

The new installation process uses a COM-based model for installing components that offers a common look and feel across all of the BackOffice applications. (It should be noted that there is no support for MSI with Exchange 2000.)

The installation process is more or less consistent with other types of installations, specifically installing Exchange 2000 on a cluster. Although a cluster installation lays down essentially the same code, some cluster-specific files get installed for cluster operation. In fact, an Exchange 2000 cluster uses its own resource DLL, which offers finer control for fail-over handling. All nodes in a cluster must receive Exchange 2000: you can't just have a few nodes in the cluster running the software.

As well as an arguably improved GUI, the installation process offers improved support for unattended installations.

1.16 Summary

Familiarity with Exchange 5.5 deployment concepts did little to help you understand the planning and activities that you would need for Exchange 2000. There was a sea change in terms of the underlying concepts in Active Directory technologies. The transition from Exchange 2000 to Exchange 2003 is markedly different though. The concepts are the same, and for the most part you have to run through the same tasks: getting Windows DCs and GC servers deployed and in the right places, installing schema extensions, and running Domainprep here, there, and everywhere. The focus for Exchange 2003 deployment is to make things simpler, and you can see how the changes in the installation process (with regard to permissions, etc.) facilitates this, even if ExDeploy doesn't really do that much singing and dancing.

2

Active Directory Connector Synchronization

2.1 Introduction

Migrating from Exchange 4.0 to Exchange 5.0, or from Exchange 5.0 to Exchange 5.5, was a relatively simplistic challenge and fairly straightforward. Then along came Exchange 2000, and we endured a steep learning curve as we all struggled to come to grips with the complexities of migration to Exchange 2000 from Exchange 5.5. You might be forgiven for thinking that migration from Exchange 5.5 to Exchange 2003 would be even more complex, but the reality is that it is no more difficult and, if anything, is slightly more straightforward because there are fewer options to confuse us. Those technologies and techniques that we learned for Exchange 2000 migration are just as relevant today for Exchange 2003, and as before the fundamentals are key so directory synchronization interoperability is critical.

The Active Directory Connector is one of the most powerful tools available to the messaging consultant. We know that Exchange 2003 doesn't have its own built-in directory service. Instead, it uses the AD. During a migration exercise from a legacy Exchange 5.5 environment to Exchange 2003, one of the most important aspects of coexistence is that of synchronizing directory information between the Exchange 5.5 Directory Service and the Windows 2003 AD. The Active Directory Connector does just that: it maps the Exchange 5.5 Directory Service object types to the AD and vice versa. The Active Directory Connector available with Exchange 2003 is not that much different from the Active Directory Connector that was available with Exchange 2000. The core functionality remains more or less the same, and only minor aspects of its operation have changed, as well as the inclusion of several bug fixes.

In this chapter we'll explore the basic operation of the Active Directory Connector, how it synchronizes data from Exchange 5.5 to AD, and vice versa. A clear and complete understanding of Active Directory Connector operation is key before you begin any Exchange 5.5 to Exchange 2003 migration project.

2.2 Active Directory Connector Core Technology Description

Many aspects of the Active Directory Connector merit broad and comprehensive discussion. In the simplest of cases, we can look at its operation in the most basic of environments. In such a case, we're concerned with how the Active Directory Connector processes information from the Exchange 5.5 Directory Service and synchronizes it with the AD. Of course, in this simple case, we're also concerned with the reciprocal process: how the Active Directory Connector synchronizes information from the AD into the Exchange 5.5 Directory Service.

As well as explaining the internals of the Active Directory Connector's operation, we also take a look at some of the less well-known functionality of the Active Directory Connector. We'll explore what's involved in using the Active Directory Connector to be selective about the objects that it will synchronize between directories and also how we can manipulate directory information "in-flight."

2.2.1 What Is the Active Directory Connector?

In any environment where interoperability between mail systems is required, there is typically a requirement to exchange directory information. The coexistence environment between Exchange 5.5 and Exchange 2003 is no exception to this rule. The Active Directory Connector can run on a Windows 2000 or a Windows 2003 server, and its installation process performs several different tasks, including installing the Active Directory Connector binaries, the management interface, and potentially some extensions to the AD schema.

The purpose of the Active Directory Connector is to synchronize information between the Exchange 5.5 Directory Service and the AD solely for the purpose of migration and not that of general directory synchronization. The Active Directory Connector provides multimaster bi-directional synchronization of data between the Exchange 5.5 Directory Service and the AD over the LDAP protocol. Active Directory Connector synchronization can take place uni-directionally if required. The Active Directory Connector operation is based on the replication model that the Exchange 5.5 Directory Service uses, but whereas the Exchange Directory Service uses object-level replication, the AD uses attribute-level replication. The Active Directory Connector sits between these two models and arbitrates the transfer of the least amount of information while synchronizing data.

Exchange 5.5 uses its own built-in directory service, whereas Exchange 2003 relies on directory services being provided by the Windows 2000 or Windows 2003 AD. As you move users from the Exchange 5.5 environment to the Exchange 2003 environment, it is imperative that you provide a consistent directory for both groups of users. The issue here is that when an Exchange 5.5 mailbox becomes an Exchange 2003 mailbox, the representation of that user in the directory moves from the Exchange 5.5 Directory Service to the AD. Because we'll have a period of time when we have a mix of both types of users, we need a mechanism to represent the new Exchange 2003 users in the old Exchange 5.5 directory, and similarly, a mechanism to represent the old Exchange 5.5 users in the new AD.

The Active Directory Connector tool is well suited to all the tasks of exchanging recipient and configuration information, and although it may not be the only tool capable of such a task,[1] it has been engineered with this role in mind.

2.2.2 How Many Flavors of Active Directory Connector Are There?

The simple answer to this question is three. You'll find an old version of the Active Directory Connector on the Windows 2000 installation CD-ROM, so obviously the Active Directory Connector has been around for a long time. Many organizations that have been experimenting with Windows 2000 or Windows 2003 for some time have also taken the time to play with the Windows 2000 Active Directory Connector and have been lifting information from the Exchange 5.5 Directory Service into the AD.

You'll find another version of the Active Directory Connector on the Exchange 2000 installation CD-ROM, and you may already have this version of the Active Directory Connector in place if you have already started a migration from Exchange 5.5 to Exchange 2000. The third version of the Active Directory Connector is the one that ships on the Exchange 2003 installation CD-ROM. This is the most up-to-date and recent version of the Active Directory Connector. You must use the Exchange 2003 Active Directory Connector if you intend to migrate users from Exchange 5.5 to Exchange 2003. In fact, if you are running an Exchange 2000 version of the Active Directory Connector and you try to install an Exchange 2003 server into your organization, the installation will detect that you have not already upgraded the Active Directory Connector to the latest version and it will terminate.

The old Windows 2000 Active Directory Connector is functional insofar as it allows you to synchronize recipient information (e.g., mailboxes, custom recipients, and distribution lists) between Exchange 5.5 and the AD, but the Exchange 2003 (and Exchange 2000) Active Directory Connector goes further. In addition to having the

1. Other tools, such as HP's LDAP Directory Synchronization Utility (LDSU) or most other directory synchronization tools, could also perform this function. Check out www.hp.com/services/message/mc_ldsu.html for more information on LDSU.

capability to synchronize recipient information, this version of the Active Directory Connector can also deal with Exchange 5.5 configuration information.

For most companies, making the move from Exchange 5.5 to Exchange 2003 will probably result in some form of coexistence between the old Exchange environment and the new one. This kind of coexistence implies mail interoperability, where Exchange 2003 servers can use RPCs to deliver messages natively to Exchange 5.5 servers. To do this, Exchange 2003 needs to have information about the Exchange 5.5 environment, and it does this by using information that's held in the Configuration Container of the Exchange 5.5 Directory Service. The Exchange 2003 Active Directory Connector creates a special type of Connection Agreement (CA), which defines an instance of synchronization called a Configuration Connection Agreement (ConfigCA). The role of the ConfigCA is to synchronize Configuration Container information with the Configuration Naming Context of the AD. The Configuration Naming Context holds all of the configuration information about the Exchange 2003 environment that Exchange 2003 servers require.

You shouldn't be too concerned with the management of ConfigCAs. Exchange 2003 automatically creates them on your behalf when you upgrade an Exchange 5.5 server to Exchange 2003 or when you install an Exchange 2003 server into an existing Exchange 5.5 site. But for this to work, you do need to make sure that you've got the correct Active Directory Connector already installed: you must use the Exchange 2003 Active Directory Connector, not the Windows 2000 Active Directory Connector or the old Exchange 2000 Active Directory Connector.

You can tell which version of the Active Directory Connector you're using by looking at the version number on the Properties Tab of ADC.EXE. On a Windows 2000 Active Directory Connector, you'll see that the version number is 6.0.3939.7, and on the Exchange 2000 Active Directory Connector the version number associated with the Active Directory Connector from the Exchange 2000 kit is something like 6.0.4368.7. On the Exchange 2003 Active Directory Connector the version number is 6.5.6944.0, as shown in Figure 2-1.

2.2.3 Active Directory Connector Operation Overview

The Active Directory Connector uses the LDAP protocol to provide multimaster, bi-directional synchronization of data between the Exchange 5.5 Directory Service and the AD. In general, you'll want to provide directory synchronization in both direc tions, but characteristics of the environment may mandate that you perform synchronization in only one direction in certain circumstances, and the Active Directory Connector can do this if required.

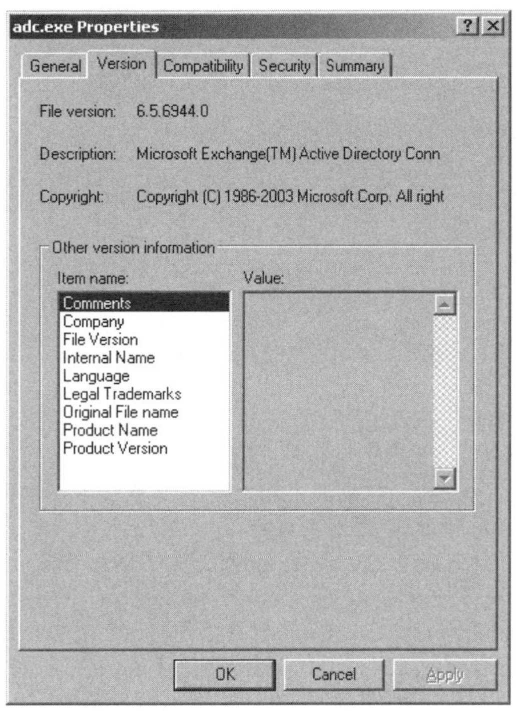

Figure 2-1 *The Active Directory Connector Properties Tab Showing Version Number*

Exchange 5.5 Directory Service object replication works using Update Sequence Numbers (USNs) that are associated with every object. When an object is changed, its USN is updated, and this change in the USN indicates that a local copy of the object requires updating. The Active Directory Connector replication engine is loosely based on this USN model, which we'll discuss in more detail later in this section.

Although the Active Directory Connector is termed a *Connector*, this isn't some special add-on to, or component of, Exchange 2003 in the traditional Exchange 5.5 sense of the term. The Active Directory Connector runs as a Windows 2000 or Windows 2003 service, named the MSADC just like any other service, and you can control it using the MMC Services snap-in. The Active Directory Connector requires either Windows 2000 SP3 or higher or Windows 2003. Alternatively, you control it from the command window using the net start msadc or the net stop msadc commands, if you like that sort of thing.

Of course, you'll need to have a Windows 2000 or Windows 2003 server available on which to run the Active Directory Connector, and you don't need to be running it on a special Windows 2000 or Windows 2003 server such as a GC server or a DC either. A simple Windows 2000 or Windows 2003 member server will be more than adequate to run the Active Directory Connector components, but you do need to make sure that this server can contact an Exchange 5.5 server and a GC server.

2.2.4 Ports and Protocols

The Active Directory Connector uses LDAP more or less exclusively for all of its operations. In the first instance, a CA (which is an instance of Active Directory Connector synchronization) accesses the Exchange 5.5 Directory Service using the LDAP protocol on port 389.

Exchange 5.5 supports the LDAP protocol as a feature of the Directory Service, and it's enabled by default. However, if you are intending to run Exchange 5.5 on a Windows 2000 DC or GC server and you need to get to the LDAP service on such a server, then you'll need to modify the LDAP protocol. (Remember that Exchange 5.5 is not supported on any form of Windows 2003 server, either member server, DC, or GC server.) DCs and GC servers also use the LDAP protocol natively, and during startup, they register their LDAP service against port 389. By the time the Exchange 5.5 Directory Service starts up, it obviously can't use port 389 as well. So, in a situation like this, you'll need to modify the protocol settings on the Exchange 5.5 server to use a different port; port 390 is the usual alternative port number to use, but any port will do. Having done so, you'll need to restart the Exchange 5.5 Directory Service for the service to be available.

The Active Directory Connector configuration takes account of this, and you can see from Figure 2-2 that you can modify the port number on which to access the Exchange directory.

You'll also notice from Figure 2-2 that it's only possible to change the port number for the connection to the Exchange 5.5 Directory Service: you can't change any settings for the AD server. The reason for this is simple: the Active Directory Connector will always connect to the AD via a GC server using port 3268. Although DCs use LDAP over port 389, the nature of Active Directory Connector operation, as described here, means that you always have to point a CA to a GC server: a DC just isn't enough. In fact, though, you can direct the Exchange 5.5 endpoint to a DC, but Windows will always redirect the connection to a GC server. Although this approach works, it imposes unnecessary overhead on the connections and slows the entire directory synchronization process.

Under normal circumstances, all network communication that the Active Directory Connector generates relies on the LDAP protocol and is limited to ports 389 (or your specified alternative) and 3268, but there is at least one exception to this rule. It's possible to use the AD Users and Computers tool to create a new Windows 2003 user object and have an Exchange 5.5 mailbox created for the object. When you do this,

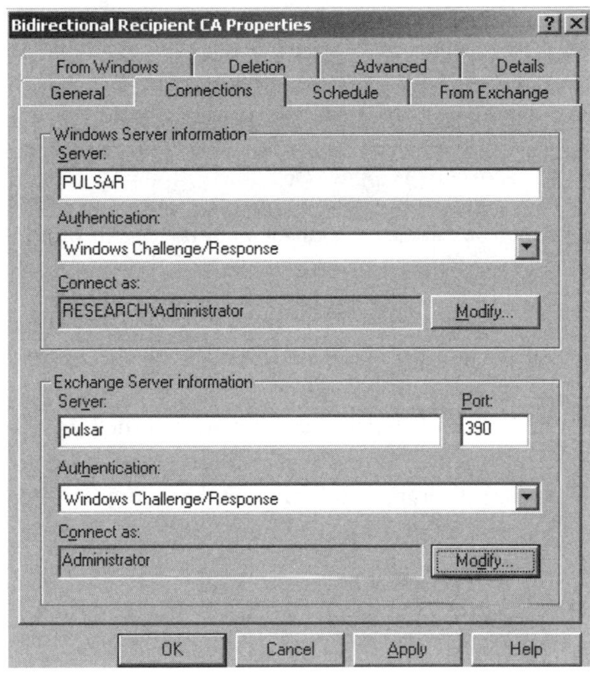

Figure 2-2 *Connection Agreement Connections Properties Tab*

although the user object is created in Windows 2003 immediately, the mailbox doesn't get created until the next time the Active Directory Connector runs the CA that deals with the particular location in the AD where the user object is homed.

As the CA executes and the Exchange 5.5 mailbox is created, proxy addresses get generated for the new mailbox. To do this, the Proxy Address Generator gets called, and unfortunately, this component of Exchange 5.5 can only be called using RPCs. In this circumstance, you'll see network activity take place against port 1026.

2.3 Connection Agreements

A CA defines an instance of synchronization between the Exchange 5.5 Directory Service and the AD. Such a CA runs on the Active Directory Connector and points to both directory services. One "end" of the CA points to a Windows 2003 GC server, while the other "end" points to an Exchange 5.5 Service Pack 3 Directory Service running the LDAP protocol.

A single CA doesn't necessarily define the complete synchronization of the two directories, but it's likely that it will define the synchronization of only a small part. In doing so, you'll probably have many CAs that collectively synchronize the whole of your two directories.

A CA, like most other Windows 2003 objects, is represented in the AD. For example, in my test environment I have a CA identified as:

```
cn=Ex 5.5 to AD, cn=Active Directory Connections, -
cn=Microsoft Exchange, cn=Services, cn=Configuration, -
cn=cantaz, cn=com
```

You can use a tool such as ADSI Edit or LDP to locate the CA objects in the AD and view or manipulate them.

But of course, directly editing the attributes in the AD is not the preferred method for configuring CAs. It's best to use the Active Directory Connector Administrator MMC snap-in for this purpose. Defining an instance of synchronization involves setting many different characteristics of the CA. These characteristics basically define the names of the servers that will take part in the synchronization, the names of the containers or organizational units that represent the source and target of synchronization, a schedule, and authorization.

On the General Properties page, as shown in Figure 2-3, you can define the direction of a CA. CAs may be unidirectional either From Exchange or From Windows (i.e., from the Exchange 5.5 Directory Service or from the Windows 2003 AD).

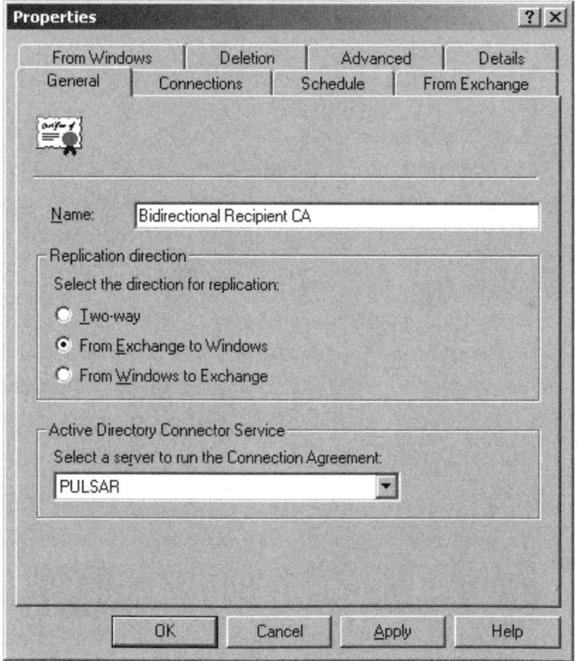

Figure 2-3 *Connection Agreement General Properties Tab*

Alternatively, CAs may be bidirectional or two-way in operation, where you specify information to be exchanged in both directions.

A single Active Directory Connector server can hold one or more CAs. There's no real architectural limit on the number of CAs that an Active Directory Connector can support, but it's related more to performance than anything else. Popular opinion suggested that around 70 CAs was a reasonable number to have on a single Active Directory Connector server with Exchange 2003, and this figure is still valid today with Exchange 2003. If anything, this number could probably go a little higher because servers have increased in performance and capability over the last few years. Your environment may never require that many CAs, but it's useful to know what the limits are. The actual load on an Active Directory Connector server isn't that great from hosting multiple CAs, but you will begin to see some load if all of the CAs are scheduled to execute at the same time. Similarly, you'll see load at either end of the CA as the LDAP operations execute in the respective directory services, although this should be relatively low. When the Active Directory Connector threads are working, the load placed on the CPU of the server running Active Directory Connector is roughly 50%. This consumption level is constant until all replication is complete. The memory consumption of the Active Directory Connector is approximately 6 MB plus approximately 2 MB per CA.

Homing a CA against a particular Active Directory Connector server is a relatively easy process. On the General Properties page, you can specify which server a particular CA should run on. So if you find that you've got too many CAs on a particular server, it's easy to change some of them to be homed elsewhere. We'll discuss when it makes sense to have multiple CAs and multiple Active Directory Connectors later in this chapter.

2.3.1 Using Real Two-Way Connection Agreements

When you configure a CA, you have the option of specifying the direction in which you want it to operate, as described previously.

In addition to specifying the direction, you need to specify which parts of the directory services you want to participate in the synchronization. Take a look at the settings shown in Figure 2-4 for a two-way CA between the systems my group uses to experiment with.

From the screenshot, you can see that I want to have any Exchange 5.5 objects that exist in containers called *DirSynced Objects*, *External People*, and *Recipients* synchronized into one single part of the AD, the *Users* OU, although strictly speaking it's a Container, not an Organizational Unit. This is a fine example of a CA because it shows the many-to-one characteristic of the Exchange 5.5 container to AD Organizational

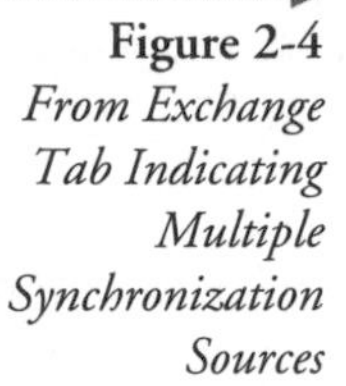

Figure 2-4 *From Exchange Tab Indicating Multiple Synchronization Sources*

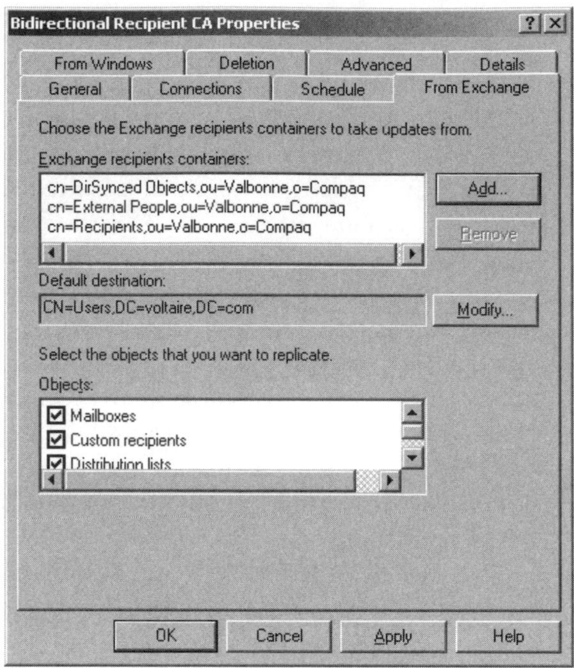

Unit mapping. If I had really wanted to reflect the same separation of objects into multiple containers in the AD, then I would have needed three CAs: one CA to map each source container to its partner Organizational Unit in the AD.

In my environment, I've got settings on the *From Windows* tab that represent the other direction for my two-way CA. You can see these settings in Figure 2-5, where my CA properties specify that objects created or changed in the *Users* Container of the AD will have their modifications synchronized back to the *Recipients* container in the Exchange 5.5 Directory Service.

Now, I want you to think about the subtlety associated with this CA. A two-way CA is only a two-way CA if you explicitly map an Exchange 5.5 source container, say FOO, to a target AD Organizational Unit, say BAR, ***and*** you explicitly provide a mapping back from the target Organizational Unit, BAR, to the source container, FOO.

In the example I've shown, the only real two-way part of this CA is between the Exchange 5.5 *Recipients* container and the AD *Users* container. Objects from the *Recipients* container will get synchronized into the AD, and if I make any changes to the object in the AD, perhaps using the *AD Users and Computers* tool, these changes will get synchronized back to the source object because an explicit synchronization path exists from the *Users* container back to the *Recipients* container.

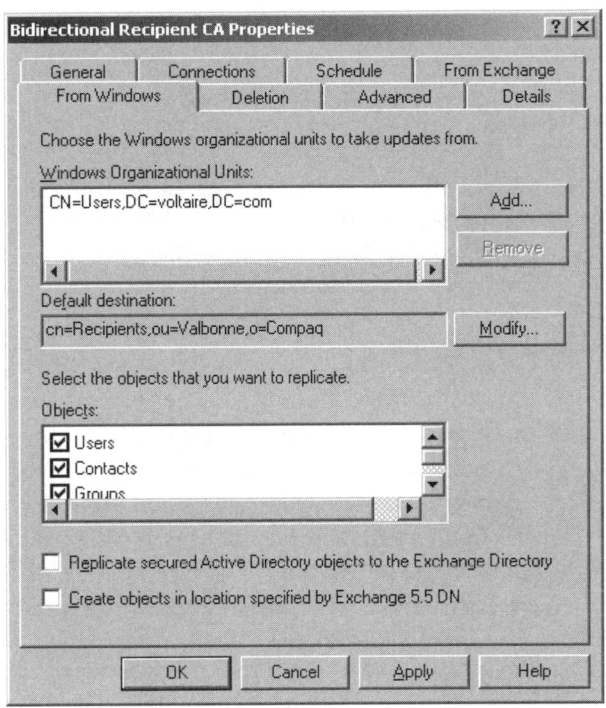

Figure 2-5 *From Windows Tab for Two-Way Connection Agreement from Active Directory Users Organizational Unit to Exchange 5.5*

Unfortunately, the same is not true for my two other Exchange 5.5 containers, *Dirsynced Objects* and *External People*. There's no explicit synchronization path back from the *Users* organizational unit to their respective Exchange 5.5 containers, so any changes I make to these objects in the AD is not synchronized back to the Exchange 5.5 Directory Service.

Each Exchange 5.5 site requires its own CA to support centralized management of both Exchange 5.5 Directory Service objects and AD objects from the AD Users and Computers MMC snap-in. You need at least one CA per site so that the CA can write changes back to objects in the Exchange 5.5 Directory Service: in Exchange 5.5, objects outside their home site are read-only.

During migration, every Exchange 2003 mixed-mode AG or site must have a two-way CA because during the process of moving mailboxes from Exchange 5.5 to Exchange 2003 servers, information is written back to Exchange 5.5 mailbox entries to reflect their move to Exchange 2003.

Note also that two one-way CAs are not equivalent to a single two-way CA, even if the endpoints of the one-way CAs have reciprocal endpoints. There are several reasons for this requirement:

- The logic of the one-way CA was not designed to support two-way replication. A one-way CA assumes that the source object is authoritative and the target object is not, whereas a two-way CA treats the objects in both directories as possible sources, thus eliminating the possibility of authoritative changes being overwritten.
- One-way CAs do not support timestamp checking, which is the process a two-way CA uses to ensure that if matching objects are modified in both directories between replication cycles, the latest change will be authoritative.
- Two-way CAs support back-replication suppression, where they check the *objectVersion* and *replicatedObjectVersion* attributes of the objects in both directories before replication. This ensures that if the Active Directory Connector was the last process to modify an object, the Active Directory Connector does not replicate that change back to the original directory. You cannot guarantee this with two one-way CAs, which can cause replication loops, where both the Exchange and Windows objects are continually modified.

2.3.2 Configuration Connection Agreements

So far when we've talked about CAs we've really been concerned with the synchronization of recipient container information between the Exchange 5.5 Directory Service and the AD. There is also the concept of the special CA, the ConfigCA that we've already met.

As well as synchronizing recipient information, cooperation between Exchange 5.5 and Exchange 2003 servers means that configuration information must be exchanged as well. Information from the Exchange 5.5 Directory Service Configuration Container is synchronized into the Configuration Naming Context of the AD using a ConfigCA. ConfigCAs are created automatically when an Exchange 5.5 server is upgraded to Exchange 2003, or when an Exchange 2003 server is installed into an Exchange 5.5 site, so there's no manual intervention required to set them up.

2.4 Active Directory Connector Schema Modifications

We've already discussed how installing Exchange 2003 extends the AD schema in section 1.14.1 and the reasons for doing so. The Exchange 2000 version of the Active Directory Connector comes with its own complement of schema extensions, but these were actually a subset of the Exchange 2000 schema extensions. The Exchange 2000 schema extensions comprised more than 1,000 modifications to the AD, whereas the Active Directory Connector schema extensions only made 188 modifications to the AD. With the Exchange 2003 version of the Active Directory Connector, the schema extensions are identical to those used during the Forestprep operation.

It's common to find organizations wishing to deploy the Active Directory Connector early in their migration plans so that the initial flood of network traffic associated with Exchange 5.5 Directory Service to AD synchronization is completed. If you intend to use the Active Directory Connector to provide directory synchronization between Exchange 5.5 and the AD for Exchange 2003 servers in the same organization (i.e., you will be performing an intraorganizational migration), then you must install the Active Directory Connector first, before you attempt to run Exchange 2003 setup with the Forestprep option. In addition to simply adding the schema extensions, running Forestprep and choosing the option to integrate with an existing Exchange 5.5 organization brings across Exchange 5.5 configuration information. To perform this configuration import, Forestprep uses a ConfigCA. Critically, the need to create the ConfigCA takes place before Forestprep can install its schema extensions, and to create the ConfigCA, some schema extensions must be in place.

So previously with Exchange 2000 you had to install two sets of schema extensions: the Active Directory Connector schema extensions and the schema extensions for Exchange 2000. Because you need the Active Directory Connector in place before Forestprep, this meant you had to install the subset of the schema modification with the Active Directory Connector and then again the complete schema extensions with the Forestprep. This resulted in two waves of GC server replication. Even if you attempted to run the SETUP.EXE program for Exchange 2000 with the /SCHEMAONLY option before installing the Active Directory Connector, two waves of GC server replication would take place because the Active Directory Connector schema extensions would again be applied when the Active Directory Connector installed. This may seem counterintuitive given that the Active Directory Connector is actually a subset of the Exchange 2000 schema extensions. It may seem logical that if you run Forestprep, all of the schema extensions, including the Active Directory Connector extensions, will be applied to the AD. However, the Exchange 2000 Active Directory Connector install always reapplied the schema extensions.

This unfortunate sequencing results in a hefty amount of unnecessary AD replication. Some of the Active Directory Connector schema extensions include new attribute definitions that are globally replicated to all GC servers in the forest in the same way that Forestprep's schema extensions include such attributes. These new objects have the *isMemberOfPartialAttributeSet* set. Just like the Forestprep extensions, adding a new attribute to the global replica set implies that all global attributes must be re-replicated, thus two waves of replication take place.

With Exchange 2003, of particular importance—and certainly most welcome—is that the Exchange 2003 Active Directory Connector schema extensions are now identical to the general Exchange 2003 schema extensions. This means that only one set of Schema Naming Context replication takes place with the AD. And in fact, in a native

Windows 2003 forest environment, no AD-wide GC server reload takes place when new objects are added to the GC server partial attribute set. Furthermore, with the Exchange 2003 Forestprep, no Exchange 5.5 organizational information is written to the AD; rather just a placeholder Exchange container is created. The actual configuration information from Exchange 5.5 is not written to the AD until you install the first Exchange 2003 server. Thus the Active Directory Connector installation is not a prerequisite for Forestprep.

With particular regard to Active Directory Connector schema extensions, do note that you do not need to install all of the Active Directory Connector: you can omit the Active Directory Connector management components and Active Directory Connector replication engine and install only the extensions: use the SETUP.EXE /SCHEMAONLY option. With the Exchange 2000 version of the Active Directory Connector, Enterprise Administrator permissions were required for the account from which the Active Directory Connector was being installed. This is no longer the case for the Exchange 2003 version of the Active Directory Connector. Only Domain Administrator privilege is now required, both to create the Active Directory Connections container within the AD and also to create the local Exchange Services and Exchange Administrators groups. This is required not just for the initial Active Directory Connector installation but also for any other subsequent installations of the Active Directory Connector within your environment. Do note that if these groups should be absent for any reason whatsoever, then any subsequent Active Directory Connector installation will recreate these groups.

2.5 Determining Which Directory Objects to Synchronize

The Active Directory Connector uses USNs to control synchronization between the Exchange 5.5 Directory Service and the AD in much the same way that Exchange 5.5 uses USNs to control both intrasite and intersite replication. Each CA uses the value of two attributes, *msExchServer1HighestUSN* and *msExchServer2HighestUSN,* to control synchronization from the AD to the Exchange 5.5 Directory Service and from the Exchange 5.5 Directory Service to the AD, respectively. We'll talk more about how these attributes are used later.

Each CA has its own signature that is defined during the configuration of the CA. As the Active Directory Connector synchronizes AD objects into the Exchange 5.5 Directory Service, it stamps the CA signature into the *Replication-Signature* attribute on the newly created Exchange 5.5 Directory Service object. Additionally, as objects are written to the Exchange 5.5 Directory Service, the *Object-Version* attribute of the Exchange 5.5 object is modified. This attribute is set to 1 if the object is being newly created or incremented by 1 if a modification is being applied. The value of the

Object-Version attribute is then written into the *Replicated-Object-Version*. Therefore, if the Active Directory Connector has just modified an object in the Exchange 5.5 Directory Service, the value of both the *Object-Version* and the *Replicated-Object-Version* attributes will be identical.

Let's look at synchronization from the Exchange 5.5 Directory Service to the AD. When a CA is activated, it obtains the value of the *msExchServer2HighestUSN* associated with that CA. The *msExchServer2HighestUSN* will have been set during the last synchronization cycle to the value of the highest USN that was encountered on an object in the source Exchange 5.5 Directory Service. If this is the first time the CA has been activated, then the value of *msExchServer2HighestUSN* will be set to 0. The Active Directory Connector then searches the Exchange 5.5 Directory Service for all objects that have a *USN-Changed* attribute with a value higher than the current value of *msExchServer2HighestUSN*. Thus all objects that have changed since the last synchronization are selected for synchronization. When the objects have been synchronized, the highest *USN-Changed* value encountered will be written to the *mxExchServer2HighestUSN* attribute, and this will define the high watermark for the next synchronization cycle.

Another check is performed in addition to looking for any changed objects. The CA excludes any changed objects that have a *Replication-Signature* value identical to the signature of the CA. This prevents the Active Directory Connector from unnecessarily resynchronizing back to the AD any objects that it synchronized in the first place. However, using this filter alone would ignore any objects that had been legitimately changed in the Exchange 5.5 Directory Service and that should be synchronized back to the AD across a two-way CA. Therefore, the object is only excluded if the *Replication-Signature* matches the CA's signature and the value of the *Object-Version* attribute is not greater than the value of the *Replicated-Object-Version* attribute.

The same process takes place in the opposite direction from the AD to the Exchange 5.5 Directory Service because AD objects use USN values to perform intrasite and intersite AD replication. It is slightly more complicated because the AD uses attribute-based replication rather than object-based replication. Therefore, in addition to using the USN values, the sum of the attribute versions of each AD object are used. However, from AD to Exchange 5.5 Directory Service synchronization, the *msExchServer1HighestUSN* attribute is used to remember the last highest USN of the object synchronized.

2.6 Active Directory Connector Block Searching

During an initial synchronization between directory services, it's possible that the Active Directory Connector may select many thousands of objects to be synchronized, although this depends on the number of objects defined in the directory services.

Take, for example, a large AD that has some 100,000 objects defined. If this is the first time synchronization is to take place, or a complete resynchronization is to take place, all of the 100,000 objects will have to be synchronized. While the synchronization process is under way, it is possible that some external factor such as a network link failure or a power failure on the remote system may occur. When the synchronization process restarts, it must perform the synchronization from the beginning again. Although this process is tolerable if the failure occurred during the early part of the synchronization process, it is less acceptable if the failure occurs towards the end.

To avoid the unnecessary resynchronization of data, the Active Directory Connector only processes objects in bands of 10,000. A search is performed of the Exchange 5.5 Directory Service, and the value of the highest *USN-Changed* is determined. The first synchronization attempt processes only objects whose *USN-Changed* attribute has the value between the current value of *msExchServer1HighestUSN* and *msExchServer1HighestUSN*+10000 (or the highest *USN-Changed* value determined). Once the changed objects in this range have been processed and committed to the Exchange 5.5 Directory Service, the *msExchServer1HighestUSN* is incremented by 10,000. If the new value of *msExchServer1HighestUSN* is less than the highest *USN-Changed* value determined, processing of the next batch of AD objects is performed. This process continues until all eligible objects have been processed, and subsequently the highest *USN-Changed* value is written to the *msExchServer1HighestUSN* attribute.

2.7 How the Active Directory Connector Uses the Active Directory

The Active Directory Connector caches significant amounts of information to improve performance. Specifically, the *msExchServer1HighestUSN* and *msExchServer2HighestUSN* is cached in memory and only written directly to the AD occasionally. When I described previously the updates that were applied to these attributes after a synchronization cycle or a search block, you should know that the updates are applied only to the memory resident versions.

In general, the *msExchServer1HighestUSN* and *msExchServer2HighestUSN* values are written to the AD every 24 hours, but for new CAs, updates to these attributes are committed to the AD every 30 minutes. A new CA is one that is executing its first synchronization cycle. Typically this can take an extended period of time and is influenced by factors such as network bandwidth and the performance of the Exchange 5.5 Directory Service and AD systems. New CAs have these attributes committed with a higher frequency because of the typically large amounts of data that is synchronized shortly after a CA is configured. If a system failure occurs on the Active Directory Connector server, the maximum of resynchronization that will take place is limited to 30 minutes.

Immediate updates to the AD are also performed under three other circumstances:

- When the Active Directory Connector Service is stopped
- At the end of the first synchronization cycle of a new CA
- When a CA is moved from one Active Directory Connector server to another

Other attributes of a CA are of interest. The *msExchServer2HighestUSNVector* attribute is not used, but the *msExchServer1HighestUSNVector* is populated. The "vector" attribute is multivalued and is only relevant to Windows 2000 servers. This attribute holds the highest committed USN for any DCs that have been contacted during a CA's lifetime. For example, if you had previously configured a CA to synchronize from a DC named JOHN and then modified the configuration so that synchronization occurred now from a DC named JOAN, you would see two values set for this attribute: one relating to the highest USN committed on JOHN and the other for the highest USN committed on JOAN. The Active Directory Connector stores this information so that no objects are missed when a CA is rehomed to another Active Directory Connector.

2.8 Mailbox-enabled and Mail-enabled Objects

It's important to understand the difference between mail-enabled and mailbox-enabled objects. Mail-enabled objects are those users that have the Mail-recipient auxiliary class associated with them. This means such objects are capable of having e-mail directed to them because they have an Exchange-style e-mail address associated with them. Mailbox-enabled objects are a special case of mail-enabled objects because they not only have the Mail-recipient class, but they also have the Mail-storage class associated with them. Mailbox-enabled objects always have an Exchange mailbox associated with their account.

2.9 Object Class Mapping from Exchange 5.5 to the Active Directory

Exchange 5.5 objects get replicated to the AD and are represented as object types, which depends on the object type they had in the Exchange 5.5 Directory Service. In all cases of replication, attributes associated with the source object are replicated to the destination object.

2.9.1 Mailbox Replication

An Exchange 5.5 mailbox that's associated with a Windows NT4 account can be mapped to a mail-enabled contact, a mailbox-enabled user, or a disabled mailbox-enabled user. You decide whether objects should be mapped to contacts or user objects, but typically the migration process is much simpler if mappings are made to either live or disabled users. However, if you've already migrated the Windows NT4 account over to the AD and the Exchange 5.5 mailbox is associated with this user account, then the mapping behavior is different. A Windows 2000 or Windows 2003 account and an Exchange 5.5 mailbox always get mapped across to a mailbox-enabled user in the AD. When an object already exists in the AD and the Active Directory Connector matches with it, attribute information from the source object is merged into the existing AD object.

When the Active Directory Connector has matched an Exchange 5.5 mailbox object with an AD user object or has created a new AD user object, the user object has several specific attributes set that correspond to characteristics of the Exchange 5.5 mailbox. Specifically they are as follows:

- The *legacyExchangeDN* attribute is set to correspond to the Distinguished Name (DN) of the Exchange 5.5 mailbox. This should be something in the form of

  `/o=<Org>/ou=<Site>/cn=Recipients/cn=<Alias>.`

- The *msExchHomeServerName* attribute is set to correspond to the Exchange 5.5 server

  `/o=<Org>/ou=<Site>/cn=Configuration/cn=Servers/cn=<Server-Name>.`

- The *replicationSignature* attribute is set to correspond to the unique signature on the CA, which replicates this object.

2.9.2 Custom Recipients and Mailbox Agents

Exchange objects such as custom recipients and mailbox agents (e.g., the Schedule+ Free/Busy Connector) are represented by objects of the same class in the AD target container. A custom recipient is created in the AD as a mail-enabled Contact object, and the e-mail address field of the Contact is set to the SMTP proxy address of the source object, even if it is a non-SMTP custom recipient.

2.9.3 Distribution Lists

Mapping Exchange 5.5 distribution lists across to corresponding primitive objects in Windows 2000 or Windows 2003 distribution groups is more complicated than it might seem. By default, the Active Directory Connector will always map an

Exchange 5.5 Distribution List across to a Universal Distribution Group (UDG) in the AD. Let's take a moment to refresh our memories on the different types of group scope you might encounter:

- **Domain Local Groups** can have membership from anywhere in the forest, but the group only has local domain scope.
- **Domain Global Groups** can only have membership drawn from the local domain, but the group has global scope.
- **Universal Groups** can have membership drawn from anywhere in the forest, and the group has global use.

UDGs have the membership and scope that Exchange 2003 requires, and they can exist in mixed-mode domains, so for the purposes of mail distribution, such groups work very well.

However, many Exchange 5.5 installations use distribution lists for more than just mail expansion. Specifically, where Public Folders are used, it's not uncommon to find users bundled into distribution lists and have public folder Access Control Lists (ACLs) put in place using a distribution list. In Windows 2000 and Windows 2003, ACLs cannot be used with any form of Distribution Group.

Although UDGs can't be used to enforce access controls in Windows 2000, USGs can be and in fact must be used if you wish to use a group of any kind to set ACLs on an Exchange 2003 Public Folder. Some characteristics of USGs are of concern to us with respect to Exchange 5.5 interoperability. USGs can only exist in native-mode Windows 2000 or Windows 2003 domains, but they can contain members that exist in mixed-mode domains.

Although the Active Directory Connector will never create USGs, it will always create UDGs, which, if they are in a native-mode domain, may get converted to USGs at a later stage by one of several methods. For this reason alone, you can see the importance of getting Windows 2000 or Windows 2003 native-mode domains in place as soon as possible.

2.9.4 Distribution Lists and Synchronization Latency

Under certain circumstances, you may find that Exchange 5.5 Distribution List objects can get synchronized before the discrete objects that make up their membership are synchronized to the AD. For example, you may find that you are using one CA to synchronize a Distribution List that's newly created, and the schedule for this has it running before another CA that is used to synchronize mailbox objects. If the Distribution List had membership objects that referenced objects that were not yet created in the AD, then the UDG could not populate its membership for those phantom objects. This is a referential integrity feature of the AD.

In this case, and if no other precautions were in place, when the CA that controls synchronization in the reverse direction would run later, there is a risk that this partial AD UDG would force the original Exchange 5.5 Distribution List to have its membership altered, thus removing perfectly good membership information.

However, the Active Directory Connector and the AD avoid this problem by using a special AD attribute called *unmergedAtts*. During the first synchronization run, if objects can't be added to the UDG because those membership objects don't yet exist, they're added to the *unmergedAtts* attribute, which is used on the subsequent back-synchronization to ensure that no membership information is lost.

This is not a problem in the reverse direction. There is no restriction on the membership of an Exchange 5.5 Distribution List that enforces the existence of a particular Exchange 5.5 Directory Service object before the DN for that object is added to the *members* attribute of an Exchange 5.5 Distribution List. Therefore, there is no need to use an *unmergedAtts* attribute with Exchange 5.5 Distribution Lists.

2.10 Object Class Mapping from the Active Directory to Exchange 5.5

In the same way that the Active Directory Connector replicates objects from Exchange 5.5 Directory Service to the AD, a similar process takes place in the opposite direction, although it is more straightforward.

Mailbox-enabled user objects in the AD are replicated as mailboxes in the Exchange 5.5 Directory Service, while mail-enabled user objects get replicated as custom recipients. Mail-enabled contacts from the AD get replicated to the Exchange 5.5 Directory Service as custom recipients. Similarly, mail-enabled groups (both Distribution and Security) get replicated as distribution lists.

If you look carefully at Figure 2-5, you'll see a checkbox at the bottom of the dialog box, which says "Create objects in location specified by Exchange 5.5 DN." In general, the Active Directory Connector will create replicated Exchange 5.5 Directory Service objects in the location specified by the Exchange 5.5 container in the CA; however, this can be overridden by the value of the *legacyExchangeDN* attribute.

When an AD object is mail-enabled (by right-clicking the object from within the AD Users and Computers tool and selecting Exchange Tasks, Establish Exchange Mail Addresses), you can associate an Exchange 5.5 site or Exchange 2003 AG with that object. Similarly, when you mailbox-enable a Windows 2003 user object, you implicitly associate it with an Exchange 2003 AG. This sets the *legacyExchangeDN* attribute. With the "Create objects in location specified by Exchange 5.5 DN" checkbox checked, the Active Directory Connector will create the replicated object in an Exchange 5.5 Directory Service container as specified by this attribute.

Exchange objects affected by the Active Directory Connector will also contain some new or changed attributes, including:

- *The ADC-Global-Names attribute*, which is blank by default for replicated objects in the Exchange 5.5 Directory Service and gets populated only when an Exchange 5.5 object is being replicated to the AD (New attribute)
- *The DSA-Signature attribute*, which is set to the Invocation-ID of the Exchange 5.5 bridgehead server specified in the CA (Modified attribute)
- *The Object-GUID attribute*, which is set to the value of the *objectGUID* attribute present on the source object in the AD (New attribute)
- *The Object-Version attribute*, which gets incremented by one after the initial replication (Modified attribute)
- *The Replication-Signature attribute*, which is set to the unique signature of the CA that made the last modification to the replicated object (New attribute)
- *The Replicated-Object-Version attribute*, which matches the *Object-Version* attribute since the Active Directory Connector made the last change to the replicated object (New attribute)

Table 2-1 defines how the Active Directory Connector maps objects from the Exchange 5.5 Directory Service to the AD, while Table 2-2 defines the mappings from the AD to the Exchange 5.5 Directory Service.

Table 2-1 *Object Mapping from Exchange 5.5 Directory Service to the Active Directory*

Exchange 5.5 Object Type	Active Directory Object Type
Mailbox and Windows NT4 Account	Mail-enabled, User Object
	Mail-enabled, disabled User Object
	Mail-enabled, Contact
Mailbox and Windows 2000 Account	Mailbox-enabled, User Object
Custom Recipient	Mail-enabled Contact
Distribution List	Universal Distribution Group
Distribution List (used for Access Control)	Universal Distribution Group initially, but converted later to Universal Security Group

Table 2-2 *Object Mapping from the Active Directory to Exchange 5.5 Directory Service*

Active Directory Object Type	Exchange 5.5 Object Type
Mailbox-enabled User Object	Mailbox
Mail-enabled User Object	Custom Recipient
Mail-enabled Contact	Custom Recipient
Mail-enabled Group (any scope, either distribution or security)	Distribution List

2.11 Synchronizing Hidden Objects

Objects in the Exchange 5.5 Directory Service that are hidden from the Address Book have their *Hide-From-Address-Book* attribute set to 1. You control whether an object is displayed in the Exchange 5.5 Global Address List by checking the *Hide from Address book* box on the *Advanced* tab of the mailbox properties when using the Exchange 5.5 Administrator program. By default the hidden objects are not displayed in recipient containers within the Administrator program unless you choose the *Hidden Objects* option from the *View* menu.

The Active Directory Connector will synchronize hidden objects into the AD, but unlike in Exchange 5.5, they are visible by default from *AD Users and Computers* when browsing through an Organizational Unit. However, a careful look at the *Hide from Exchange address book* on the *Exchange Advanced* tab will indicate that the object is hidden. (Make sure that you've selected *Advanced Features* from the *View* drop-down menu from the snap-in to see the *Exchange Advanced* tab.) Exchange 2003 users will not see AD objects (e.g., users, contacts, or groups) that have this box checked.

The *Hide from Exchange address book* checkbox on AD objects implies that the *msExchHideFromAddressLists* attribute is set to *TRUE*. Similarly, when synchronizing a hidden object from the AD to the Exchange 5.5 Directory Service, the object is hidden in the Exchange 5.5 GAL.

2.12 Dealing with Hidden Distribution List Membership

In Exchange 5.5 you can control whether membership information of a particular Distribution List is displayed to a client by checking the *Hide membership from address book* checkbox on the *Advanced* tab of the Distribution List properties when using the Exchange 5.5 Administrator program.

When the Active Directory Connector synchronizes a Distribution List from the Exchange 5.5 Directory Service, it reads the *Hide-DL-Membership* attribute and accordingly sets the *hideDLMembership* attribute on the synchronized object in the AD. This effectively applies a set of Access Control Entries (ACEs) on the group in the AD to deny access. Although the ACE prevents Exchange 2003 users from enumerating the group membership, some security principals do need to have access to the membership list: Exchange 2003, for example, needs to enumerate the membership in order to send mail to the group's members. The Active Directory Connector reads the *msExchServerGlobalGroups* attribute from the Organization container entry in the AD. This attribute contains the list of Exchange 2003 servers in the organization that must have access to the membership. Actually, the Exchange Enterprise Servers and Exchange Domain Servers groups, created by the DomainPrep utility, are granted access to membership of the group. But by default, Exchange 2003 servers are members of these groups.

In Exchange 2003, if you subsequently add a new Windows 2000 or Windows 2003 domain that includes Exchange 2003 servers, the Recipient Update Service (RUS) will detect this and it will update all groups with *hideDLMembership* set to TRUE with the security principals of the new Exchange Domain Servers group.

Synchronizing in the reverse direction, from the AD to the Exchange 5.5 Directory Service, the Active Directory Connector checks the value of the *hideDLMembership* attribute and sets the *Hide-DL-Membership* attribute on the Exchange 5.5 Distribution List. You can use the *AD Users and Computers* tool to control whether membership of an AD group is displayed or not by right-clicking on the group, selecting *Exchange Tasks* and *Hide Membership*.

2.13 Object Deletion

When you create a CA, you can define the behavior of the Active Directory Connector with respect to deleting objects from both the Exchange 5.5 Directory Service and the AD. The settings on the Deletion tab apply in both directions. Setting the CA to delete objects implies that when an object is deleted in the Exchange 5.5 Directory Service (perhaps using the Exchange 5.5 Administrator program), it is automatically deleted in the AD. The same behavior is true in the reverse direction.

If you elect not to perform directory deletions immediately, the Active Directory Connector writes non-replicated deletions to a temporary file located on the Active Directory Connector Server. Deletions that occurred in the Exchange 5.5 Directory Service are staged to a file named WIN2000.LDF, whereas deletions that occurred in the AD are staged to a file named EX55.CSV. By default, these files are located in the following location:

```
<Active Directory Connector Path>\MSADC\<Connection Agreement Name>\
```

If you wish, you can override this default location by setting the following registry key:

```
HKEY_LOCAL_MACHINE\System\CurrentControlSet\Services\MSADC\Parameters
Value name: Transaction Directory
Value type: STRING
Value data: <FullDirectory Path, e.g., C:\ADCLogs>
```

Setting this registry key creates a parent directory for the deletion logs. Each CA will create its own subdirectory under this parent directory and will write a file named MSADC.INF to the directory that contains the name and GUID of the CA associated with the directory.

You can apply these LDAP Directory Interchange Format (LDF) files to the AD and Comma Separated value (CSV) files to the Exchange 5.5 Directory Service using the LDIFDE and ADMIN /I tools respectively.

2.14 Connection Agreements and Authentication

For a CA to read or write object information from either the Exchange 5.5 Directory Service or the AD, it must make an authenticated connection to both directory services over LDAP. You can specify the credentials you will use for the connection on the *Connection Properties* tab, as shown in Figure 2-6.

You should think carefully about the accounts you use to access the directory services. The accounts specified must have the appropriate read and/or write access to the respective directory containers or Organizational Units that you specify. It's inadvisable to use an Administrator account because it suffers from the same restrictions you would have come across if you tried to use the Administrator account as the Site Services Account in the Exchange 5.5 world, such as changing the Administrator password and then slowly finding out later that services fail to start after the next reboot. In the same way, you'd expect to see Active Directory Connector synchronization fail to operate, and the cause may not be immediately obvious. So for this reason alone, it makes better sense to separate out authentication functionality and use a dedicated account. Perhaps the Exchange Site Services Account when connecting to the Exchange 5.5 Directory Service, and because there's no Site Services Account used in the Exchange 2003 environment, a dedicated account, which in the example shown in Figure 2-6 is the *ADCService* account.

The Active Directory Connector stores the credentials for the accounts used to access the AD and the Exchange 5.5 Directory Service in the Local Security Authority (LSA).[2] When you create a new CA, the Active Directory Connector MMC snap-in

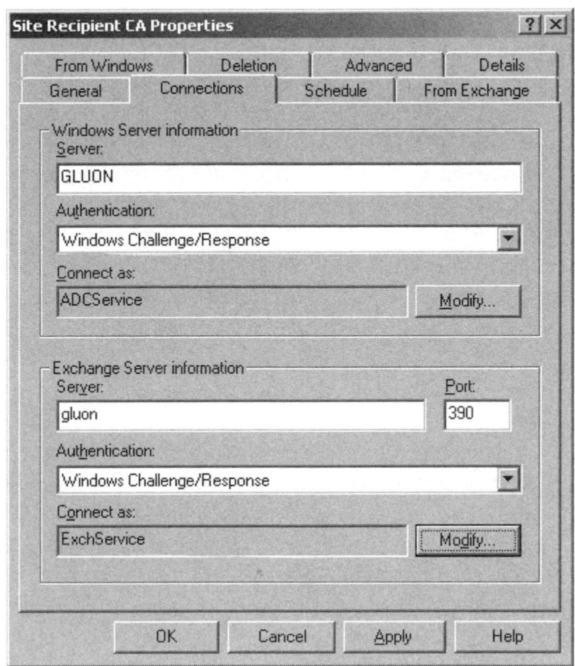

Figure 2-6 *Connection Agreement Connections and Authentications*

performs an RPC call to the Active Directory Connector service and requests storage for the credentials on the local Active Directory Connector server. The password associated with the credentials stored in the LSA can only be read by the Active Directory Connector service, not by the MMC interface. Therefore, when you modify a CA, changing either source or target containers or rehoming the CA, you must reenter the password. If you use the same set of credentials for multiple CAs, only one set of credentials is stored in the LSA to conserve space. This also saves time if you need to change the password associated with an account being used for the CA. Changing the password on one CA changes it for all other CAs that use the same credentials.

Whenever you modify the credentials using the Active Directory Connector MMC snap-in, a timestamp for that entry in the LSA is updated with the current time. Similarly, when the Active Directory Connector reads the password during a synchronization operation and the timestamp is older than seven days, it is updated again with the current time. The LSA has limited space, and the Active Directory Connector service is allocated only 64 KB on a given Active Directory Connector server. When space begins to run out, the oldest unused credentials are removed.

2. You can find more information on the LSA in the book *Mission Critical Active Directory* by Jan de Clercq and Micky Balladelli (ISBN 1555582400).

As shown in Table 2-3, any credentials that haven't been used within the last 180 days will be removed from the LSA. In the case where you create a CA, set its replication schedule to Never and then 181 days later force it to replicate, and the replication attempt will fail. You can control the minimum number of days that credentials can remain in the LSA by using the following registry key:

```
HKEY_LOCAL_MACHINE\System\CurrentControlSet\Services\
  MSActive Directory Connector\Parameters
Value name: Password Expiration
Value type: DWORD
Value data: <Minimum No. of Days to remain in LSA>
```

CAs that have replication schedules set to *Selected Times* or *Always* will never expire.

It's also important to note that you can specify the port number for the connection to the legacy Exchange 5.5 Directory Service. Connections to the AD always take place against a GC server on port 3268, but on both a GC server and a DC, port 389 is also used for general-domain scope LDAP queries. If you're running Exchange 5.5 on a Windows 2000 DC and you have enabled the LDAP protocol from within the Exchange 5.5 Directory Service, then it can't use port 389 because it has already been allocated to Windows 2000. In this case, you need to modify the port from the Exchange 5.5 Protocol settings so that a different port number is used to offer LDAP access to the Exchange 5.5 Directory. It's common to change the port number to 390, because this is not used by any other applications, but remember to then modify the port to connect on in the Connections tab.

2.15 Controlling the Synchronization Schedule

The Active Directory Connector uses a polling-based mechanism to request changes from the Exchange 5.5 Directory Service and the AD. Each request for changes and any subsequent replication activity represent a synchronization cycle. With a two-way

Table 2-3 *Expiration Limits Associated with Active Directory Connector Credentials Stored in the LSA*

Total Credentials Stored	Expiration Limit (Days)
1 to 15	180
16 to 31	120
32 to 127	90
More than 128	60

CA, the first stage in the cycle checks for changes in the Exchange 5.5 Directory Service and second in the AD. On the *Schedule* tab you can elect to have replication take place at *Always*, *Selected Times*, or *Never* (see Figure 2-7). This *Schedule* tab looks almost identical to the *Schedule* tab associated with the Exchange 5.5 Directory Replication Connector (DRC). On an Exchange 5.5 DRC, when you set the schedule to *Always*, that really translated as "try to do some replication every 15 minutes." However, on the Active Directory Connector, setting the schedule to *Always* means "try to do some synchronization every 5 minutes."

If you select *Selected Times*, you can specify times with either a 15-minute or 1-hour granularity. For each box on the schedule grid that you check, this instructs the Active Directory Connector to start polling at that moment, but does not necessarily imply that the cycle will last for exactly 15 minutes or 1 hour. When the cycle commences at the indicated time, it will continue to run until it is finished. If this is less than 15 minutes or 1 hour, the Active Directory Connector will not attempt to start another synchronization cycle until the next indicated start time on the schedule.

You can fine-tune the synchronization behavior. For example, if the Active Directory Connector is processing a very large number of modifications to objects, it is possible that a single synchronization cycle could extend for many hours. You can force interruptions to such a single cycle by setting the default number of seconds to wait between synchronization cycles by setting the following registry key:

```
HKEY_LOCAL_MACHINE\System\CurrentControlSet\Services\MSADC
  \Parameters
Value name: Synch Sleep Delay
Value type: DWORD
Value data: <number of seconds to wait between cycles>
```

This registry key causes the Active Directory Connector to pause synchronization after the defined number of seconds, wait for the same defined number of seconds, and then restart synchronization again. You can customize this behavior even further, by extending the amount of time for which the Active Directory Connector will synchronize objects without interruption. Set the following registry key:

```
HKEY_LOCAL_MACHINE\System\CurrentControlSet\Services\MSADC
  \Parameters
Value name: Max Continuous Sync
Value type: DWORD
Value data: <number of seconds that sync takes place without
   interruption >
```

The Active Directory Connector uses LDAP to get access to both the Exchange 5.5 Directory Service and the Active Directory, and as it checks to see if objects are to be synchronized it executes an LDAP search based on the container and Organizational Unit information you've specified elsewhere on the CA. LDAP operations are pretty costly, and they impose a significant amount of load on the CPU on the systems on which the searches are being executed. Executing these LDAP searches frequently will affect the performance of the Exchange 5.5 servers and AD servers that are hosting the "ends" of the CA.

If you really want synchronization to occur frequently, then you should consider having dedicated systems to host the ends of the CA. A dedicated Exchange 5.5 server in every site where CAs get terminated, hosting no mailboxes, would be a good idea. You could use existing servers: maybe your current Site Bridgeheads or Connector Servers? Similarly, you should apply the same logic to the AD servers, but you only need one such dedicated server here because AD information is read-writeable anywhere in the forest, unlike Exchange 5.5, where Directory Service containers are read-only outside their home site.

Getting the scheduling of your CAs right is pretty important. You should arrange to have CA synchronization take place after you perform any moves or updates to objects in either directory. So if you intend to migrate users from legacy Exchange 5.5 to Exchange 2003 overnight, you should be sure to run the CA immediately after those moves have taken place, so you can use the *Selected Times* option for this function. If you are moving user accounts generally at any time, then you'll probably want to set the schedule to *Always*.

You'll notice another box on the *Schedule* tab in Figure 2-7: *Replicate the entire directory the next time the agreement is run*. Ordinarily, a full replication only takes place the first time the CA is executed. Checking this box forces all directory objects to be checked for consistency, and if there are any discrepancies between the directories, objects will be replaced. If objects are found to be consistent, they will not be replicated.

You can force a full replication from Exchange 5.5 to the AD by setting the *msExchServer2HighestUSN* to 0 and a full replication from the AD to Exchange 5.5 by setting the *msExchServer1HighestUSN* to 0. Setting *msExchDoFullReplication* to *TRUE* forces a full replication in both directions.

2.16 Connection Agreement Advanced Parameters

You can define several specific settings on a CA that will result in either improved performance during synchronization or significant modifications to behavior. Advanced settings are shown in Figure 2-8, and these configuration options are described in the following sections.

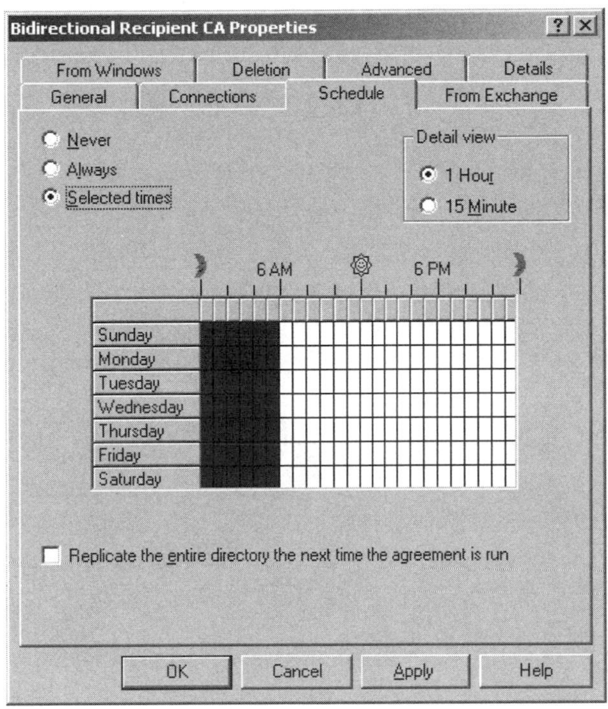

Figure 2-7 *Schedule Tab on the Active Directory Connector*

2.16.1 Paged Results

You can specify the size of a page that the Active Directory Connector expects to receive as the result of an LDAP search. Set the values for the *Windows Server entries per page* and *Exchange Server entries per page* to reflect the page size for the AD and the Exchange 5.5 Directory Service, respectively. Both of these settings are available on a two-way CA, but for one-way CAs, only the appropriate setting can be set.

Paging offers an improvement to performance by grouping together objects that are being synchronized. Larger page sizes have more entries in the page and accordingly result in fewer requests to the directory service. However, large pages require more memory.

The default page size settings for the Active Directory Connector are set to 20 entries per page. The corresponding directory service must be configured to return pages in line with these settings. In the default case, while the directory service can return pages with more than 20 entries per page, it should not be configured to return pages with fewer than 20 entries per page. Such a setting will result in replication errors.

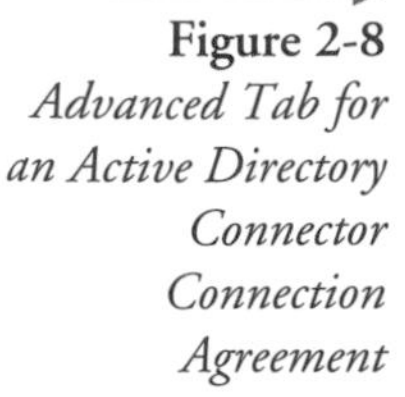

Figure 2-8
Advanced Tab for an Active Directory Connector Connection Agreement

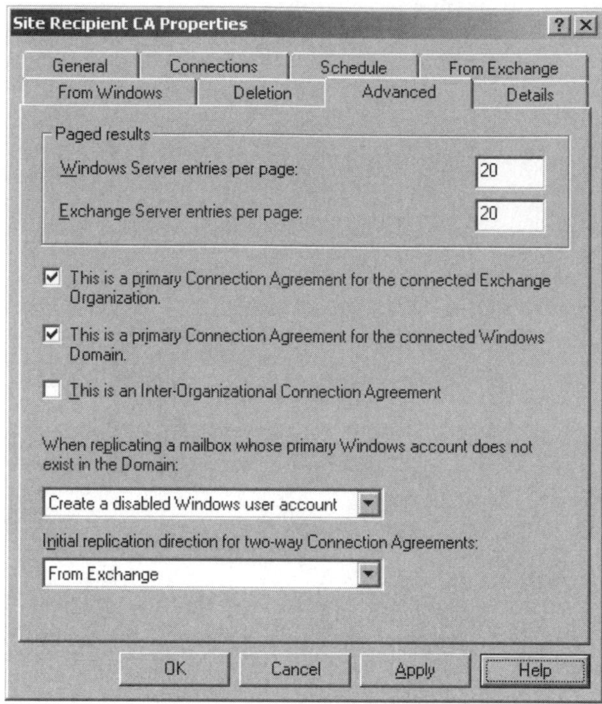

By default, the Exchange 5.5 LDAP service is configured to return 100 entries per page, although you can modify this by setting the appropriate value on the Search tab of the LDAP Protocol properties on either the Exchange 5.5 Site defaults on or a specific server, as shown in Figure 2-9.

By default, AD servers return 1,000 entries in an LDAP page. Modifying the LDAP page size on the AD can be done using the NTDSUTIL utility and the following sequence of commands:

```
ntdsutil.exe
ntdsutil: ldap policies
ldap policy: connections
server connections: connect to <domain name>
server connections: quit
ldap policy: show values
ldap policy: set maxpagesize to <value>
ldap policy: commit changes
ldap policy: quit
ntdsutil: quit>
```

This updates the *LDAPAdminLimits* attribute on the *Default Query Policy* of the AD. You can see the attribute value using ADSI Edit (shown in Figure 2-10)

Figure 2-9
Exchange 5.5 LDAP Protocol Search Settings

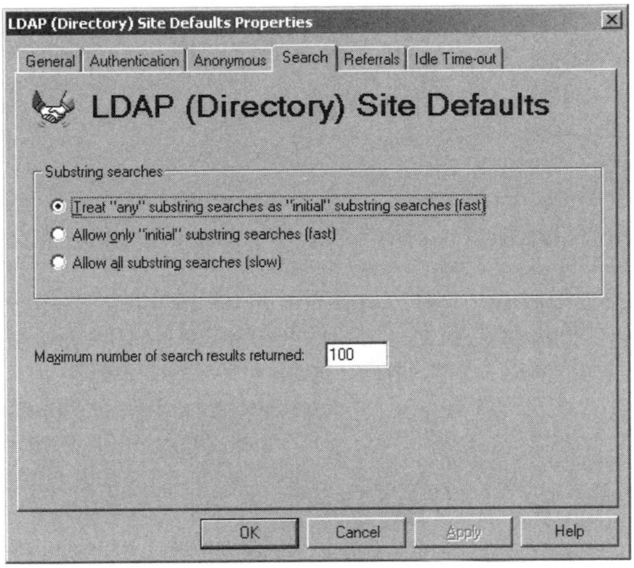

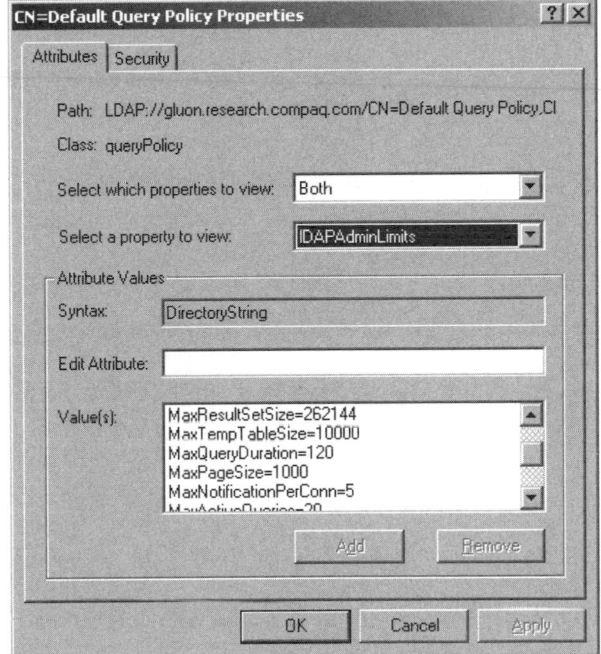

Figure 2-10
Showing LDAPAdminLimits from ADSI Edit

below the *Configuration Naming Context/Services/Windows NT/Directory Service/ Query-Policies.*

Ordinarily you shouldn't need to make any modifications to LDAP page settings: the default settings should be sufficient. However, as you can see, without modifying the source directory systems, you could change the Active Directory Connector settings to process 100 entries from the Exchange 5.5 LDAP service and 1,000 entries from the AD to glean a small performance improvement.

2.16.2 Primary and Nonprimary Connection Agreements

CAs may be either primary or nonprimary. Primary CAs can create objects in the target container or Organizational Unit, while nonprimary CAs may only modify an existing object in the target. You should have only one primary CA for any given group of recipients, although you may have nonprimary CAs for those recipients and target containers, especially if you have a large environment and you want to put *overlapping* CAs. Overlapping CAs should be avoided if at all possible, but they can be useful for those environments where an object may be moved from one location in the source directory to another and you want to retain the ability to synchronize it irrespective of its location.

Setting the Primary CA flag on more than one CA that has the same source and target should really only be done if different object classes are synchronized by each CA. Incorrectly using this setting will result in duplicate objects in the target directory. Those primary or nonprimary CAs can be either in the direction of Exchange 5.5, or the AD, or both. You can see the settings in Figure 2-8.

As a matter of best practice, it's much better to have a single point of synchronization and have your Exchange 5.5 Directory Service and AD replication schedules set to minimize latency.

2.16.3 Interorganizational Connection Agreements

You'll notice a checkbox in Figure 2-9 that reads *This is an Inter-Organizational Connection Agreement*. Setting this option essentially turns the CA into a general-purpose synchronization tool between two different Exchange 5.5 and Exchange 2003 organizations. That is, the organization names for Exchange environments are different. Using an interorganizational CA restricts the functionality of the Active Directory Connector.

When you check this box, the CA is prevented from creating mailbox-enabled users in the AD: Exchange 5.5 mailboxes get represented as mail-enabled users or mail-enabled contacts in the AD, and similarly, in the Exchange 5.5 Directory Service, custom recipients are always created for Exchange 2003 mailbox-enabled users. Custom recipients, contacts, distribution lists, and distribution and security groups are also supported over an interorganizational CA.

This functionality is designed to work hand-in-hand with the Exchange Migration Wizard, which allow mailboxes from one Exchange organization to be moved to a different Exchange organization. All combinations of Exchange organizations are supported here for interorganizational moves: Exchange 5.5, Exchange 2000, and Exchange 2003. Objects created by an interorganizational CA can be subsequently matched by the Exchange Mailbox Wizard.

2.17 Exchange 5.5 Mailboxes and Multiple Windows NT Accounts

In Exchange 5.5 it is possible to associate multiple mailboxes with a single Windows NT4 account. However, with Exchange 2003, a mailbox is a property of an AD user object, and subsequently there is a one-to-one relationship between Exchange 2003 mailboxes and AD user accounts.

Let's assume that we have an Exchange 5.5 resource mailbox with an alias name of CONFROOM. This CONFROOM mailbox is associated with the Windows NT account MARKL. However, this is not the primary mailbox associated with the MARKL account: the primary mailbox for this account actually has an Exchange alias of MARKL. As the Active Directory Connector processes mailboxes for the first time, it attempts to match against an AD user account or create a new AD object if no match can be found. If the Active Directory Connector processes the CONFROOM mailbox before it processes the MARKL mailbox, it will either match with an existing object (based on its security identifier (SID) or *SID-History*) or create a new object in the AD for the CONFROOM mailbox and associate it with the MARKL Windows NT4 account. (This is shown in Figure 2-11.) Either way this is a problem because the wrong attributes (from the CONFROOM mailbox) are associated with the AD user account: The correct attributes should come from the MARKL mailbox.

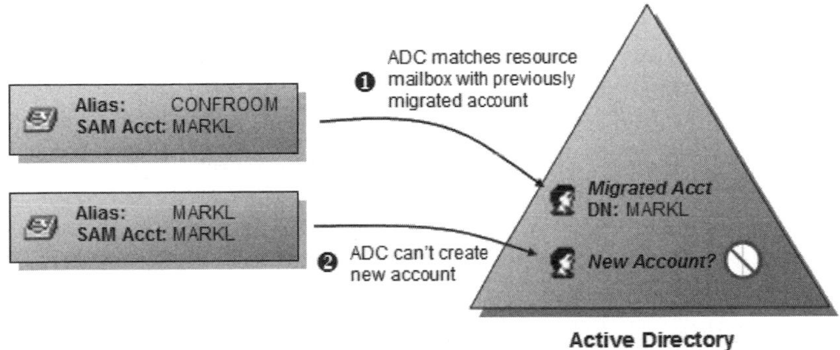

Figure 2-11 *Active Directory Connector Behavior When Two Exchange 5.5 Mailboxes Share a Windows NT4 Account*

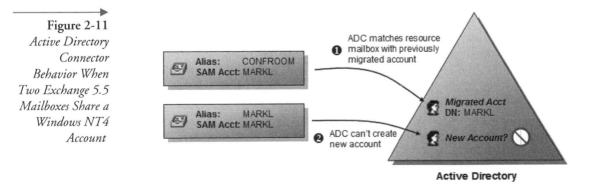

As the Active Directory Connector processes the MARKL mailbox, it will attempt to create a disabled user object. Although this seems as if it should proceed, the situation is far from correct. As the Active Directory Connector attempts to create this new AD user object, it attempts to set the *msExchMasterAccountSID* attribute to the SID of the primary Windows NT4 account associated with the mailbox. This value is identical for both Exchange 5.5 mailboxes, but AD objects must have unique values for *msExchMasterAccountSID*. Accordingly, in our example, the new AD user object cannot be created, and we end up with a wrong mailbox associated with the AD user object. (The Active Directory Connector generates Event 8281 in the Event Log to indicate that the *msExchMasterAccountSID* could not be replicated because the value exists on another AD object.)

In such cases it is desirable to mark resource mailboxes so that they are not processed by the Active Directory Connector. This can be done in one of several ways. You can use an LDAP search filter (as described in section 3.4) or use the NTDSNoMatch utility (as described in section 3.9). Ideally you should analyze your existing Exchange 5.5 mailbox and Windows NT4 account mappings and ensure that you have a separate Windows NT4 account for each and every Exchange 5.5 resource mailbox.

2.18 Mailbox Delegate Access

In the Exchange 5.5 Directory Service, the *Can send on behalf of* attribute (the LDAP *Public-Delegates* attribute) holds the Exchange 5.5 DNs of any other Exchange 5.5 users that have delegated access to a specific user's mailbox. For example, Figure 2-12 shows two Exchange 5.5 mailboxes that have delegate access to Kate Scott's mailbox.

Because this is just another attribute of an Exchange 5.5 mailbox, it should come as no surprise that the Active Directory Connector synchronizes it to a similar attribute of the AD user object. Figure 2-13 shows the AD *publicDelegates* attribute for Kate Scott's AD user object.

Thus delegate access to mailboxes is preserved in a coexisting environment using the Active Directory Connector. Note that if either of the two delegates (as shown in Figure 2-12) haven't already been synchronized into the AD, they will not appear in the *publicDelegates* attribute. Only when they, as Exchange 5.5 mailbox objects, have been synchronized into the AD in their own right can they be established as delegated user objects.

The following delegated access models are all supported with a mixed Exchange 5.5/Exchange 2003 environment with the Active Directory Connector:

- Exchange 5.5 mailbox with another Exchange 5.5 mailbox as a delegated user

Figure 2-12
Raw Properties Showing Delegated Mailbox Access

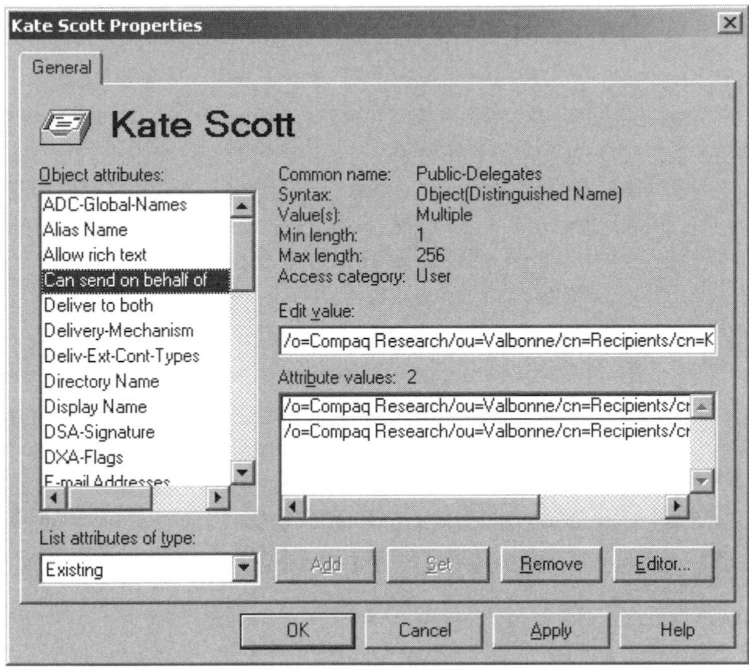

Figure 2-13
ADSI Edit View of publicDelegates of Active Directory User Object

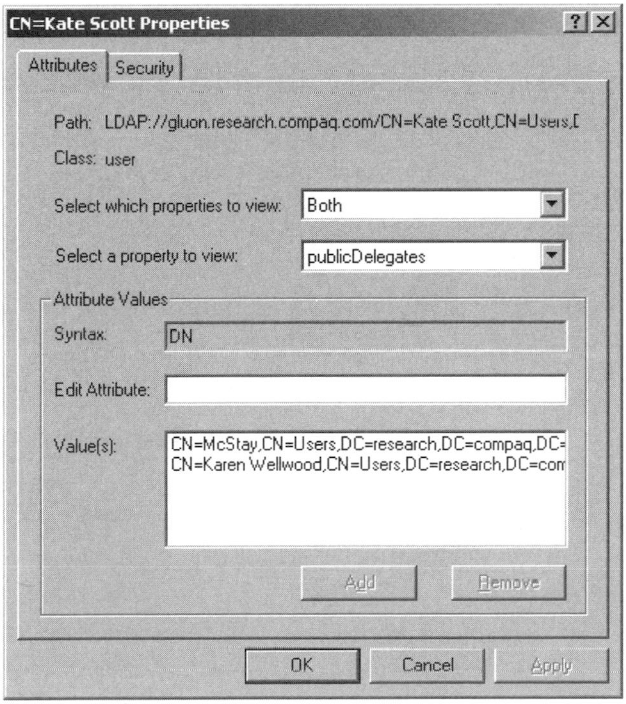

- Exchange 5.5 mailbox moved to Exchange 2000 or Exchange 2003 mailbox with another Exchange 5.5 mailbox as a delegated user
- Exchange 5.5 mailbox with another Exchange 5.5 mailbox moved to Exchange 2000 or Exchange 2003 mailbox as a delegated user
- Exchange 5.5 mailbox moved to Exchange 2000 or Exchange 2003 mailbox in a particular Storage Group on a particular Database with another Exchange 5.5 mailbox moved to the same Storage Group but a different Database as a delegated user
- Exchange 5.5 mailbox moved to Exchange 2000 or Exchange 2003 mailbox in a particular Storage Group on a particular Database with another Exchange 5.5 mailbox moved to a different Storage Group and different Database as a delegated user

2.19 Troubleshooting Active Directory Connector Synchronization Problems

After configuring the appropriate CAs, you should expect to see mail-enabled objects replicating between the Exchange 5.5 Directory Service and the AD. If objects are not synchronized, you can make several checks to determine the cause. First some basic checks:

1. Check that the Active Directory Connector process is running. Look for the service called MSADC.
2. Check that a CA exists for the source and destination containers that you need to synchronize the object from/to.
3. Check that the schedule is set on the CA so that objects are actually being synchronized. You should check that the schedule is set to *Always* or *Selected Times*. If set to *Selected Times*, wait until the activation time passes before expecting to see the object synchronized. If the schedule is set to *Never*, you should not expect synchronization to occur. You can also select the appropriate CA, right-click on it, and select *Replicate Now* from the pop-up menu.
4. Check that the Exchange 5.5 Directory Service is up and running on the source computer.
5. Check that the LDAP protocol is enabled on the source computer.
6. Check that the AD is available on the target computer.
7. On the CA, check that you've selected the appropriate object classes for synchronization. For example, if you've only selected mailboxes for replication, you should not expect to see custom recipients synchronized.

8. Check that the credentials you have associated with the CA are valid.
9. If you have created a new object in the source directory and it is not being created in the target directory, check that the CA is a primary CA.
10. If you are waiting on a newly created object to be synchronized from the source directory to the target directory, ensure that latency issues in the source environment are not to blame. For example, if you've just created a new object in one Exchange 5.5 site, but your CA points to a different Exchange 5.5 site, you'll have to wait for intersite directory replication to occur before you should expect to see the object replicated. This will take at least 15 minutes or more, depending on the schedule of your DRC. Even with intrasite replication, if you create an object on one server, it can take up to 5 minutes before the object is replicated within the site. Also, be aware of latency delays within the AD.
11. Finally, check the Application Event Log on the Active Directory Connector server for telltale errors.

If these checks reveal no insight into the problem, you can perform some other investigations as follows to explain objects not being synchronized:

1. If you have previously synchronized an object from the source directory to the target directory, and you have deleted the synchronized copy of the object in the target directory, the Active Directory Connector will not re-create the synchronized object when it is next activated. (This assumes that you are not propagating deletions with a two-way CA.)
2. If you have previously synchronized an object from the source directory to the target directory but you have subsequently moved the source or target object to a location in its respective directory where the Active Directory Connector does not have read/write access, it will not synchronize changes associated with the object.
3. If the Active Directory Connector is not creating objects with the object class that you expect (e.g., the Active Directory Connector creates an AD contact for an Exchange 5.5 mailbox), check that the CA is set to intraorganization.
4. If you have created an object in the AD and it is not being replicated to the Exchange 5.5 Directory Service, check that the object is mail-enabled. (Ensure that at least one of the following attributes is set: *mail*, *legacyExchangeDN*, *textEncodedORAddress*, *proxyAddresses*, or *msExchHomeServerName*. Objects in the Exchange 5.5 Directory Service are mail-enabled by definition.)
5. Check that any matching rules or LDAP search filters are not preventing synchronization.

2.20 The New Exchange 2003 Active Directory Connector Features

Although the Exchange 2003 Active Directory Connector functionality is basically the same as the Exchange 2000 Active Directory Connector functionality, a significant number of enhancements to the MMC snap-in can simplify configuration of CAs.

Basically, the MMC snap-in now boasts a series of buttons that will perform checks against the Exchange 5.5 Directory Service and the AD. You will see these options in the right-hand view pane of the snap-in if you click the Active Directory Connector Tools item on the navigation pane (left-hand side of the snap-in), as shown in Figure 2-14.

In order to run through the procedure you must first specify the Exchange 5.5 Directory Service connection information of at least one Exchange 5.5 server in any site: only read access is required, so any site will suffice. You can then run through the tests, the first of which simply collects various data items about the Exchange 5.5 environment. Subsequently, running the Resource Mailbox Wizard performs the NTDS Attrib checks (to identify problematic Exchange 5.5 mailboxes), and following this a CA replication check can be performed to check the integrity of Exchange 5.5 Direc-

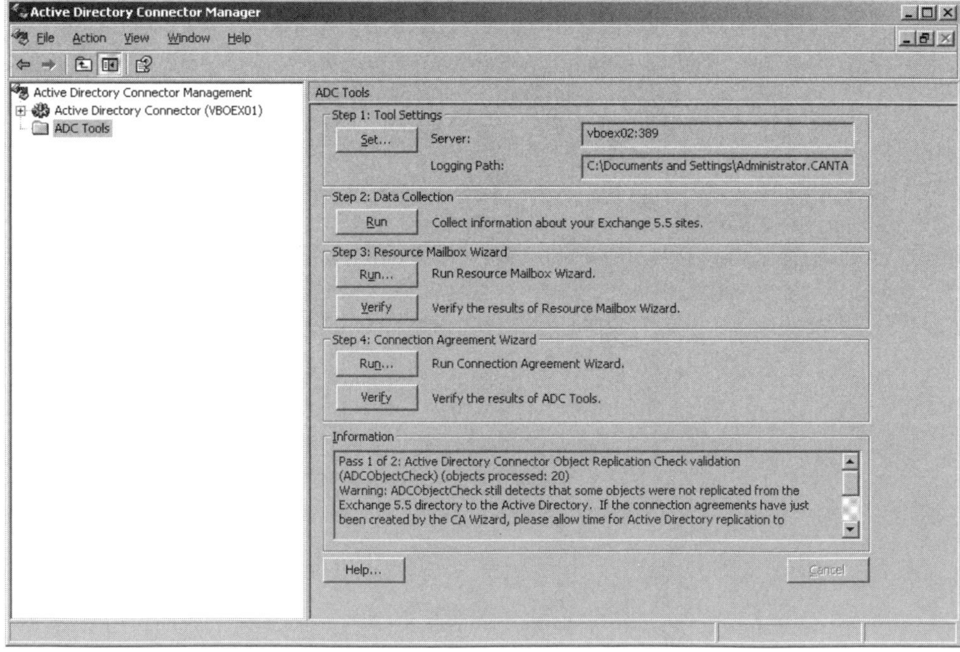

Figure 2-14 *Active Directory Connector MMC Snap-in Featuring the Active Directory Connector Tools*

tory Service to AD replication, if you have previously manually created any CAs. Information from these tests is written to the *ADCTools.log file*, to be found in the *C:\ExDeploy Logs* directory.

You must run these Active Directory Connector Tools checks at least once if you wish to install an Exchange 2003 server into an existing Exchange 5.5 environment. The installation process for Exchange 2003 explicitly checks for the results of these tests before it will allow installation to proceed. The check flag is written to the AD so that it is globally available throughout the organization: thus even if you try to run an Exchange 2003 install on any other Exchange server, the dependency on the Active Directory Connector Tools check is still valid.

Although not strictly required, you may proceed to execute the CA Wizard. This utility will analyze your Exchange 5.5 environment in conjunction with the AD environment and automatically create the CAs that it believes will be most applicable for your organization. Proceed with caution, though. The CA Wizard works in a rather rudimentary fashion, and if you have an Exchange 5.5 Directory Service container hierarchy and/or a complex AD Organizational Unit hierarchy, then likely as not the Wizard will not offer the most optimal configuration. Similarly, if you wish to use a temporary Organizational Unit in the AD and will ultimately move objects in the AD to a final location—perhaps because of a staggered Windows NT4 migration strategy—then the Wizard is not recommended. In such cases, you should continue to apply grey matter to develop the best CA architecture.

2.21 Summary

The Active Directory Connector is a powerful tool that does a great job of facilitating coexistence between Exchange 5.5 and Exchange 2003. In addition, it can be used in other innovative ways to provide interorganizational directory synchronization. But it's not a straightforward tool. Its power stems from its sophistication, and that sophistication means that you have to treat it with respect. If you want to have a successful deployment of Exchange 2003, you must get to know *exactly* how the Active Directory Connector works. Build a test lab that mirrors your production environment and test and retest until everything makes sense to you. I've outlined most of the features that I like about the Active Directory Connector in this chapter, even if I don't feel compelled to utter a Wilhelm scream!

3

Advanced Active Directory Connector Configuration

3.1 Introduction

By now you are probably familiar with the basic operation of the Active Directory Connector. In short, it's a utility that uses CAs to define an instance of synchronization between the Exchange 5.5 Directory Service and the AD. At first glance, its granularity of operation seems limited. From the Exchange 5.5 Directory Service you select the contents of one or more recipient containers to be synchronized into a single Organizational Units in the AD. Similarly, from the AD, you select the contents of one or more Organizational Units to be synchronized into a single recipient container in the Exchange 5.5 Directory Service.

In general, if the source recipient container or Organizational Units contains only mailbox entries or user objects, you must synchronize all of those mailbox entries or user objects; if the source recipient container or Organizational Units contains only custom recipients or contacts, you must synchronize all of those custom recipients or contacts; and similarly for distribution lists or groups. However, it's often desirable to be able to synchronize just a subset of the objects within a recipient container or an Organizational Units. For example, you may wish to exclude Exchange 5.5 mailboxes that are shared between multiple users and not associated with any Windows NT4 account in particular, the so-called resource mailboxes. Similarly, synchronizing from the AD to the Exchange 5.5 Directory Service, you may wish to select only those mail-enabled user objects in a particular geographic location, even though they may all reside in the same Organizational Units in the AD. This kind of granularity makes for a sophisticated migration technique from legacy Exchange 5.5 organizations to Exchange 2003.

In this chapter, we look at some less well-known configuration options that you can set on the Active Directory Connector that will give you much greater flexibility with Active Directory Connector synchronization. Specifically, we'll look at two different mechanisms by which you can control the selection of objects for Active Directory Connector synchronization: using LDAP search filters and using Active Directory Connector custom object matching.

3.2 Default Object-Matching Behavior

The default behavior of a CA is restrictive when it comes to freedom to select just those objects that you want to synchronize. Figure 3-1 shows a typical set of configuration settings that you might use to synchronize the contents of the Exchange 5.5 Directory Service Recipients container to the AD Users Organzational Unit. As the settings show, this intraorganizational CA will synchronize mailboxes, custom recipients, and distribution lists to the AD. In the AD, these synchronized objects will be represented as user objects, contacts, and distribution groups, respectively.

You can be slightly more selective with what you'll synchronize between the directories. For example, if you only wanted to synchronize mailboxes from the Recipients

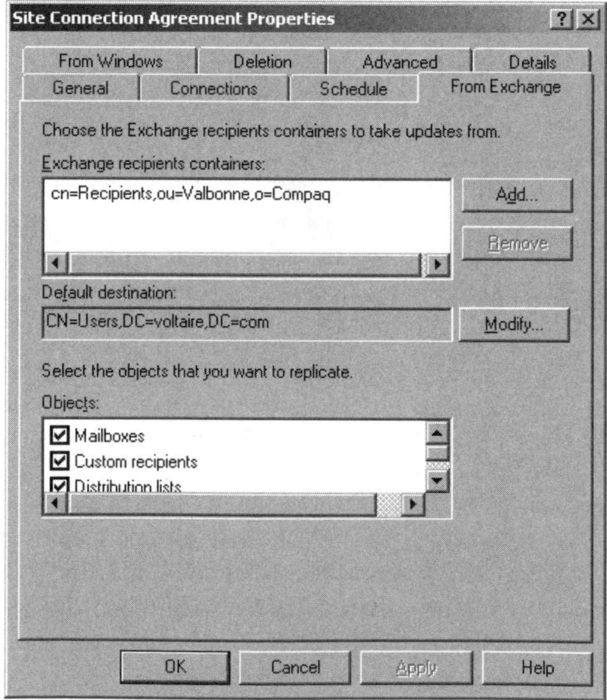

Figure 3-1 *From Exchange Properties for a Site Connection Agreement*

container, you can uncheck the boxes that indicate that custom recipients and distribution lists should be synchronized. And in the opposite direction, you can use more or less the same options on the *From Windows* tab to control whether you'll synchronize users, contacts, and groups to the Exchange 5.5 Directory Service.

3.3 How the Active Directory Connector Uses LDAP

Let's assume that you have several mailbox objects defined in the Exchange 5.5 Recipients container, as shown in Figure 3-2. As you can see, four mailbox objects are represented in the Recipients container. Three of those mailboxes have their *Office* attribute set to the value Valbonne, while the mailbox for Donald Livengood has its *Office* attribute set to the value Atlanta.

Under normal circumstances, the CA with the properties defined in Figure 3-1 would synchronize all four of these mailbox objects across to the AD, and there are no configuration options anywhere on the properties of the CA or the Active Directory Connector that allow you to specify that only a subset of these mailboxes should be synchronized. But let's assume that synchronizing a subset of the mailboxes is exactly what you want to do: have the CA synchronize only the Valbonne mailboxes, but ignore the Atlanta mailbox.

The Active Directory Connector operates by executing an LDAP query on the Exchange 5.5 Directory Service with a search base that specifies the containers that should be used as sources for the CA. This search base is effectively the containers specified in the Exchange Recipients Containers box shown in Figure 3-1. By default the LDAP query will select all mailboxes (if you checked the *Mailboxes* object), but you

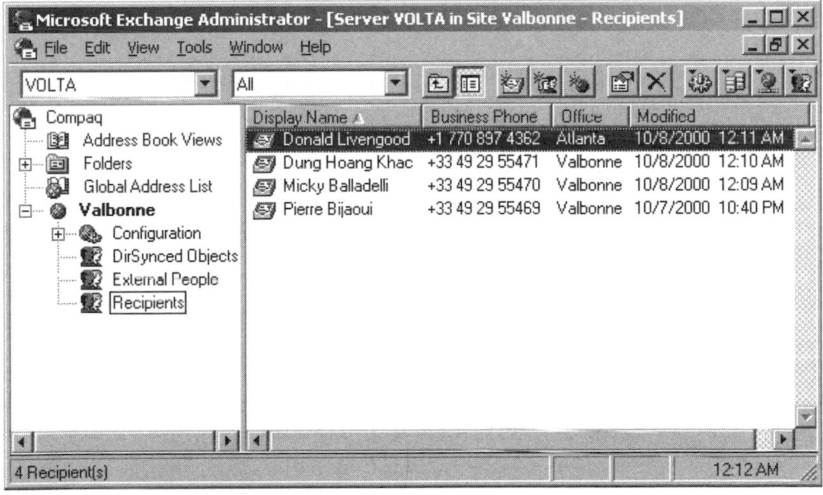

Figure 3-2 *Mailbox Entries in the Exchange 5.5 Recipients Container*

can customize the LDAP query so that it selects only some mailboxes. Specifically, the following LDAP search filter is defined by default for the CA with the settings shown in Figure 3-1:

```
(|(objectclass=organizationalPerson)(objectclass=remote-address)(object
class=groupOfNames))
```

This default search filter states that the CA should use a mailbox (*organizationalPerson*), a custom recipient (*remote-address*), or a distribution list (*groupOfNames*) as a valid object to be synchronized.

3.4 Using a Customized LDAP Search Filter

To refine the synchronization process such that only Valbonne objects are synchronized, you could modify this CA's LDAP search filter so that it reads:

```
(&(|(objectclass=organizationalPerson)(objectclass=remote-address)(obje
ctclass=groupOfNames))(physicalDeliveryOfficeName=Valbonne))
```

This search filter dictates that only mailboxes, custom recipients, or distribution lists that have their *Office* attribute (with LDAP terminology, this attribute is named *physicalDeliveryOfficeName*) set to the value Valbonne will be processed by the Active Directory Connector. You could further refine this search filter so that any custom recipient or distribution list, but only mailboxes in Valbonne, get synchronized using the following expression:

```
(|(objectclass=remote-address)(objectclass=groupOfNames)(
&(objectclass=organizationalperson)(physicalDeliveryOfficeName=Valbonne
)))
```

3.5 Understanding LDAP Search Filters

LDAP search filters use the prefix notation in the definition of an expression, unlike everyday mathematical expressions, which use infix notation. In prefix notation, the operator precedes the operands, and the precedence of operators is implicit within the expression. For example, with infix notation, you would represent the expression that adds three to four as (3 + 4). With prefix notation, you represent this as (+ 3 4).

The notation used with LDAP search filters uses | (vertical bar) to represent the logical OR operator; & (ampersand) to represent the logical AND operator; and ! (exclamation mark) to represent the logical NOT operator.

It's sometimes difficult to understand just what an LDAP search filter defines when it is represented as a long string of text. You should find it useful, either when defining your own search filters or evaluating existing search filters, to format the text into separate lines using horizontal tabs. For example, I find the following representation of this search filter:

```
(|
  (objectclass=remote-address)
  (objectclass=groupOfNames)
  (&
    (objectclass=organizationalperson)
    (physicalDeliveryOfficeName=Valbonne)
  )
)
```

easier to read and understand than this representation:

```
(|(objectclass=remote-address)(objectclass=groupOfNames)(
&(objectclass=organizationalperson)(physicalDeliveryOfficeName=Valbonne
)))
```

The syntax for LDAP search filters is fully defined in RFC 2254, and it's worth reading this RFC if you intend to build complex search filters and use them to achieve sophisticated Active Directory Connector synchronization. You can find RFC 2254 at www.ietf.og/rfc.html.

3.6 Setting an LDAP Search Filter on a Connection Agreement

I've already mentioned that there's no mechanism exposed via the Active Directory Connector management interface that allows you to set properties on either a CA or the Active Directory Connector to control the LDAP search filter that is being used for a particular CA. To customize the search filter on a given CA, you have to directly modify objects held in the AD.

Just like any user object, contact, or group that's represented in the AD, any CAs that you define for a given Active Directory Connector are similarly represented in the AD. Exchange 2003 stores its configuration information in the Configuration naming context of the AD, and appropriately, the Active Directory Connector stores configuration information for itself and its CAs in the Configuration naming context as well. Drilling down through the AD to the Microsoft Exchange branch, as shown in Figure 3-3, you'll find the entry for the CA; in our case it's called Site Connection Agreement.

Although many attributes are associated with a CA object, we're specifically interested in the *msExchServer2SearchFilter* attribute. This attribute defines the search filter that is used when the Active Directory Connector selects objects for synchronization

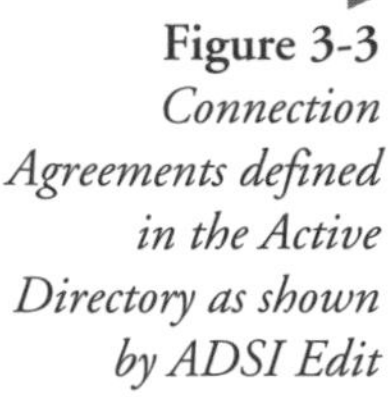

Figure 3-3 *Connection Agreements defined in the Active Directory as shown by ADSI Edit*

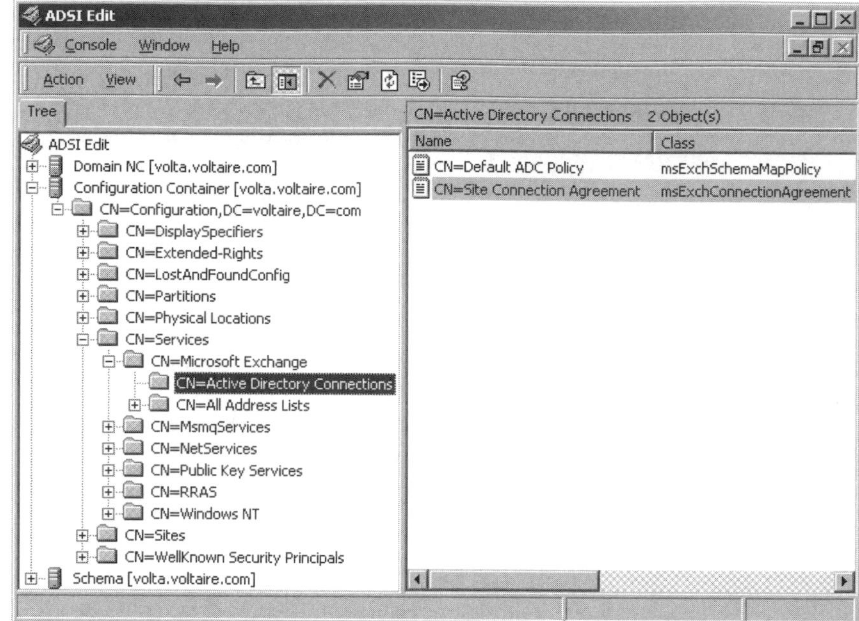

from the Exchange 5.5 Directory Service *to* the AD. (Correspondingly, the *msExchServer1SearchFilter* defines the search filter that is used when the Active Directory Connector synchronizes objects in the opposite direction; i.e., from the AD to the Exchange 5.5 Directory Service.)

The only way to set the value of this attribute is to manipulate the attribute directly in the AD using a tool such as ADSI Edit or the AD Administration Tool (LDP.EXE). Both of these tools are available on the Support Tools kit on the Windows 2000 or Windows 2003 CD-ROM.

Using ADSI Edit, as shown in Figure 3-4, you can select the attribute and then set its value by typing the search filter into the *Edit Attribute:* field and clicking the *Set* button. The next time you run the CA, the search filter will be active and objects that correspond to its scope will be able to participate in Active Directory Connector synchronization.

3.7 Default Active Directory Connector Object-Matching Behavior

The Active Directory Connector has a default set of matching rules that control the actions the Active Directory Connector takes when it processes an object in one direc-

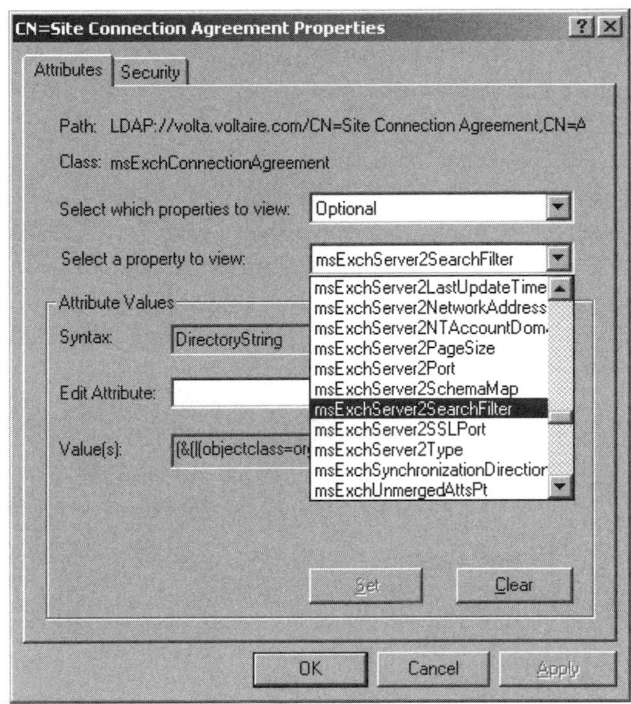

Figure 3-4 *The msExchServer2-SearchFilter Attribute Properties*

tory system and attempts to match it with an object in another. While processing objects in, for example, the AD, the Active Directory Connector attempts to match any given AD object with a corresponding object in the Exchange 5.5 Directory Service by searching on a fixed set of attributes. These matching rules work for simple synchronization cases when the environment is straightforward.

3.7.1 Matching between Exchange 5.5 Directory Service and the Active Directory

When a CA attempts to synchronize an object from the Exchange 5.5 Directory Service to the AD, it will search the AD in an attempt to find an existing object with which it can match the source object.

If the source Exchange 5.5 object has previously been synchronized to the AD, the Active Directory Connector will search for an object that has an *msExchADCGlobalNames* attribute that matches with the Distinguished Name of the source object. The Active Directory Connector populates the *msExchADCGlobalNames* attribute when an object is first synchronized, and this helps the Active Directory Connector keep track of synchronized objects. Figure 3-5, for example, shows the value of this attribute

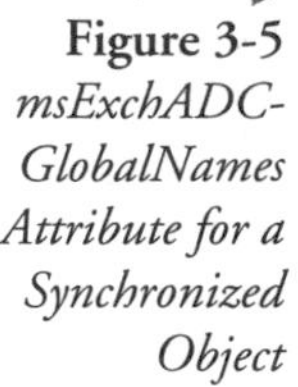

Figure 3-5 *msExchADC-GlobalNames Attribute for a Synchronized Object*

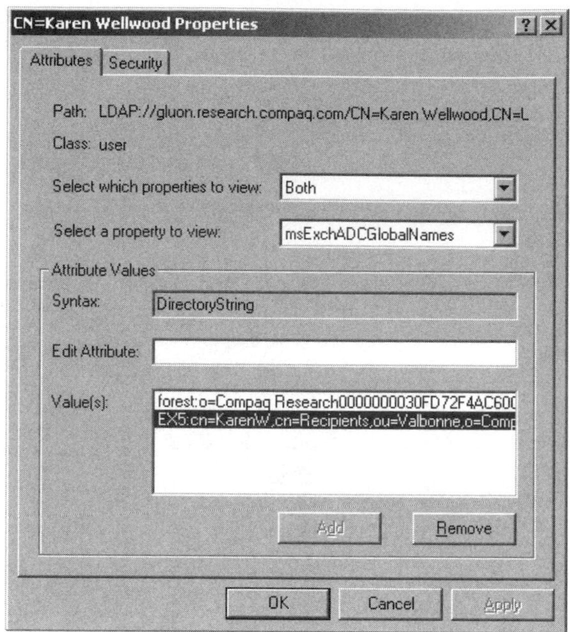

for an Exchange 5.5 mailbox with an alias of KarenW located in the *Recipients* container of the site Valbonne in the organization Compaq Research.

If this match fails, the Active Directory Connector then tries to match based on the object's GUID. The GUID of the synchronized AD object is written into the *ADC-Global-Names* attribute of the original Exchange 5.5 object when it is first synchronized. The Active Directory Connector uses the NT5 string in this attribute, which is really the GUID of the AD object, and searches the AD looking for a match. (The *ADC-Global-Names* attribute is added to the Exchange 5.5 Directory Service schema during the installation of Exchange 5.5 Service Pack 3.) Do note that the search base for a GUID-based search is not limited to the OU to which the CA is directed, but rather to the forest as a whole.

If a match is found, the Active Directory Connector assumes that the AD object corresponds to the 5.5 Directory Service object and it synchronizes attribute information from the 5.5 Directory Service object to the AD object. If no match is found, a new search is tried using the Distinguished Name of the 5.5 Directory Service object against the *legacyExchangeDN* attribute of the AD object. Again, if a match is found, the Active Directory Connector merges attribute information from the 5.5 Directory Service object with the AD object.

If no match has been found at this point, the Active Directory Connector uses the *Primary Windows NT Account* attribute (*Assoc-NT-Account*) of the Exchange 5.5 object to match against an object in the AD with a matching SID. If a matching object is found, the Active Directory Connector merges the attribute information from the Exchange 5.5 Directory Service object into the existing AD object. In such cases where no match is found, a new object is created in line with the CA settings (either an enabled or disabled user, or a contact) and accordingly, the Exchange 5.5 attribute information is merged into the new AD object.

3.7.2 Matching between the Active Directory and Exchange 5.5 Directory Service

A similar process takes place in the reverse direction when the Active Directory Connector synchronizes from the AD to the Exchange 5.5 Directory Service. The Active Directory Connector searches through the 5.5 Directory Service looking for objects in the AD with an Object-GUID attribute that matches the GUID of the current AD object. If this match fails, the Active Directory Connector matches the *legacyExchangeDN* of the AD object against the Distinguished Name of the Exchange 5.5 object. The last match attempted uses the SID of the AD object against the SID of an Exchange 5.5 object. If any of the above matches are successful, then the attribute information is merged between the two objects. If the matches fail, then the Active Directory Connector creates a new object in the Exchange 5.5 Directory Service to represent the AD object.

3.8 Using Custom Object-Matching Rules on the Active Directory Connector

Using an LDAP search filter allows you to specify which objects you will permit the Active Directory Connector to process during a synchronization run between the Exchange 5.5 Directory Service and the AD, or vice versa.

As well as using search filters, an alternative method exists for controlling the objects that you will allow the Active Directory Connector to process. While LDAP search filters are applied on a per-CA basis, you can set custom object-matching rules on the Active Directory Connector. Setting a custom matching rule means that the rule applies to all CAs that are homed on the particular Active Directory Connector in question. These custom object-matching rules override the default object-matching rules that exist as a basic component of the Active Directory Connector functionality.

3.8.1 Setting simple custom matching rules

The Active Directory Connector presents an interface to allow you to define simple customized matching rules. You access the interface by right-clicking on Active Directory Connector Management from within the Active Directory Connector Manager MMC snap-in, and then selecting *Properties*. You can set custom matching rules for synchronization *From Exchange* or *From Windows*. Any rules that you set in one direction should be balanced with a corresponding rule in the opposite direction to ensure symmetry of synchronization.

For example, Figure 3-6 shows a new custom matching rule that I created, which matches the *Primary Windows NT Account* (*Assoc-NT-Account*) of an Exchange 5.5 Directory Service object against the *sIDHistory* attribute of an AD object.

This is a useful custom matching rule to employ in an environment where you have migrated accounts from Windows NT4 domains to Windows 2000 domains using the migration tools that use the ClonePrincipal API, to preserve the "old" SID value of the Windows NT4 account in the *sIDHistory* attribute of the new Windows 2000 or Windows 2003 account. In such environments, the original Windows NT4 account may have been the *Primary Windows NT Account* associated with the Exchange 5.5 mailbox. After the Windows NT account has been migrated to Windows 2000 or Windows 2003, the Active Directory Connector would fail to match an Exchange 5.5 mailbox object against the migrated Windows 2000 or Windows 2003 object (the new Windows 2000 or Windows 2003 object will have a different SID) unless you used this form of matching rule against the *SIDHistory* attribute.

You can select a variety of attributes from an Exchange 5.5 Directory Service object to match against a similar variety of attributes from an AD object to suit your interoperability environment. For example, you could match the Exchange 5.5 mailbox *Alias* (*Mail-Nickname*) against the Windows 2000 or Windows 2003 account name (*SAM-Account-Name*), as shown in Figure 3-7, if you're confident that these attributes are unique and tie together the Exchange 5.5 mailbox with the new Windows 2000 or Windows 2003 account.

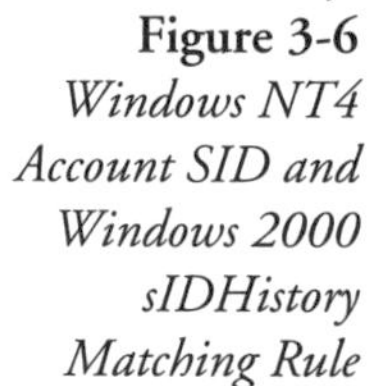

Figure 3-6
Windows NT4 Account SID and Windows 2000 sIDHistory Matching Rule

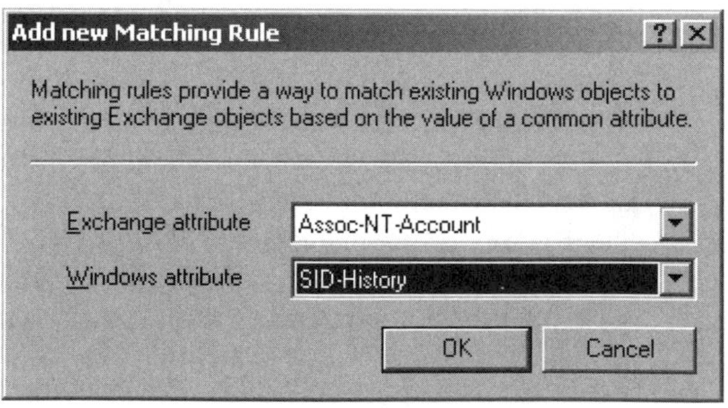

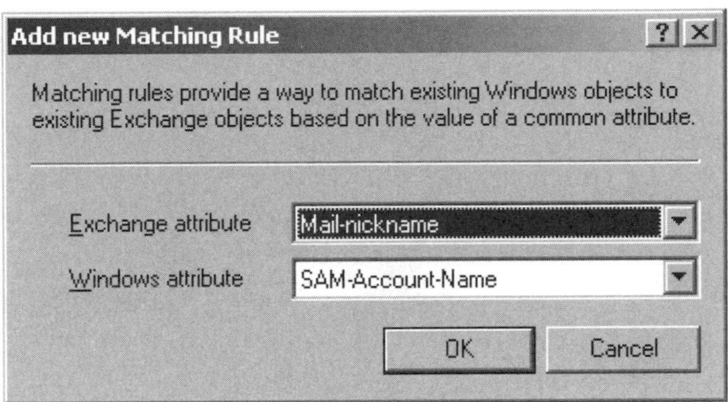

Figure 3-7 *Mailbox Alias and Windows 2000 Account Matching Rule*

Similarly, there's a variety of other attributes to match with, including mail address attributes and the complete set of 15 extension attributes from the Exchange 5.5 Directory Service, should your particular environment and migration technique rely on the use of perhaps custom attributes to store employee ID numbers or social security numbers.

3.8.2 Defining custom matching rules

When you set custom matching rules using the interface described previously, the logic associated with the rules is stored in the AD as attributes of the *Default Active Directory Connector Policy*. Figure 3-3 shows where this AD object is located in the AD hierarchy. Particularly, for the custom matching rule defined, which matches the *Primary Windows NT Account* with the *sIDHistory*, this rule is stored in the *msExchServer2ObjectMatch* attribute. Figure 3-8 shows a view of this attribute from ADSI Edit.

The *msExchServer2ObjectMatch* attribute stores custom matching rules used when the Active Directory Connector matches objects from the Exchange 5.5 Directory Service to the AD, while the *msExchServer1ObjectMatch* attribute stores matching rules used from the AD to the Exchange 5.5 Directory Service.

The value of the *msExchServer2ObjectMatch* attribute, which isn't fully displayed in Figure 3-8, specifies the matching rule. The full text of the rule is:

```
ObjectMatch###Assoc-NT-Account#sIDHistory#sid_match#
```

Similarly, if you define multiple custom matching rules using the interface, these rules are all stored in the *msExchServer2ObjectMatch* attribute. For example, if both matching rules (as shown in Figures 3-6 and 3-7) are defined, the attribute value is:

```
ObjectMatch###Assoc-NT-Account#sIDHistory#sid_match#
ObjectMatch###UID#sAMAccountName#sid_match#
```

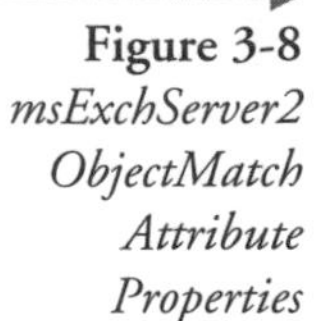

Figure 3-8
msExchServer2 ObjectMatch Attribute Properties

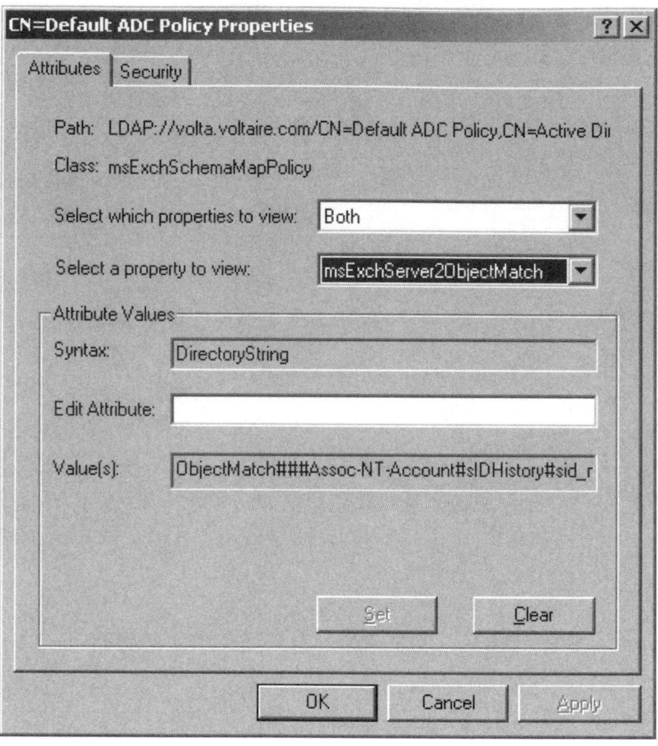

The examples I've shown all rely on creating or modifying the matching rules set on the msExchServer2ObjectMatch attribute. Just as you use ADSI Edit to view these rules, similarly you use ADSI Edit to set new values on the attribute.

3.8.3 Matching rule syntax

The syntax of the custom matching rules is defined as follows:

```
<name>#<soc>#toc<#<sa>#<ta>#<flags>
```

where

```
<name> defines an arbitrary name for the matching rule
<soc> defines the object class of the source object used in the
      attempted match
<toc> defines the object class of the target object used in the
      attempted match
<sa> defines the source attribute/value used in the attempted match
<ta> defines the target attribute/value used in the attempted match
<flags> is one of a fixed set of values that define the behavior of the
        matching rule
```

The object class values are optional. If you leave an object class blank, then all objects will be valid for processing by the particular rule. If you do wish to restrict the types of objects to which a rule can apply, then you must specify the complete hierarchy of the object class, using a dollar sign delimiter. For example, if you want the *sIDHistory* matching rule (as specified in Figure 3-6) to be applied only against user objects in the AD, you must change the rule so that it reads:

```
ObjectMatch##user$organizationalPerson$person$top#Assoc-NT-Account#sIDH
istory#sid_match#
```

3.8.4 Matching rule flags

Each matching rule has a flag associated with it that controls the processing that takes place. In the previous example, the *sid_match* flag allows matching to proceed based on SID comparison. A *guid_match* flag also exists, and its presence assumes that the objects being synchronized have previously been matched (in the AD to Exchange 5.5 Directory Service direction).

For example, the default matching rule that controls how Exchange 5.5 Directory Service objects are matched and synchronized to the AD is as follows:

```
ObjectMatch###Assoc-NT-Account#ObjectSID#
sid match EscapeBinaryBlob#
```

This matching rule attempts to match the NT4 SID of the Exchange 5.5 Directory Service object with the SID of an object in the AD. The *EscapeBinaryBlob* flag is used along with the *sid_match* or *guid_match* flags when the source attribute is in ASCII format, but the target attribute is in binary (which is the case with the SIDs referenced here). If no match is found between two objects that already exist, then the Active Directory Connector will attempt to create a new object in the AD to correspond to the 5.5 Directory Service object.

Let's say you want some way to prevent this from happening. For example, you may decide that Exchange 5.5 Directory Service objects that have an *office* attribute set to Atlanta should not be synchronized. To do this you can change the ruleset to:

```
ObjectMatch###Assoc-NT-Account#ObjectSID#
sid_match EscapeBinaryBlob#
ObjectMatch###physicalDeliveryOfficeName#"Atlanta"#veto-previous#
```

The *veto* and *veto-previous* flags indicate that the current object that is being processed should not be replicated if a match is found on the source attribute and the target attribute value. The *veto* flag (not shown here) indicates that the object won't be replicated at all and abandons all matching for that particular object. The *veto-previous* flag indicates that if the current match is true, then the previous matching rule should be ignored, but match processing should continue with the next matching rule.

This set of rules indicates that if the *office* attribute matches with the text string Atlanta, then the previous rule (that defines the matching between SIDs) is ignored. In this case, the Atlanta mailbox will not be synchronized and no corresponding user object will be created in the AD. Similarly, you could add further matching rules to, say, ignore all Exchange 5.5 Directory Service objects that have *Custom Attribute 5* set to *IgnoreADC*:

```
ObjectMatch###Assoc-NT-Account#ObjectSID#
sid_match EscapeBinaryBlob#
ObjectMatch###physicalDeliveryOfficeName#"Atlanta"#veto-previous#
ObjectMatch###Extension-Attribute-5#"IgnoreADC"#veto-previous#
```

Or, any Exchange 5.5 Directory Service objects that have any value set in Custom Attribute 6 to be ignored by the Active Directory Connector:

```
ObjectMatch###Assoc-NT-Account#ObjectSID#
sid_match EscapeBinaryBlob#
ObjectMatch###physicalDeliveryOfficeName#"Atlanta"#veto-previous#
ObjectMatch###Extension-Attribute-5#"IgnoreADC"#veto-previous#

ObjectMatch###Extension-Attribute-6#NotNULL#veto-previous#
```

The Active Directory Connector has some default matching rule behavior just like that described previously to deal with objects that have the value *NTDSNoMatch* in *Custom Attribute 10*. In such cases, the Active Directory Connector will not attempt to match Exchange 5.5 mailboxes with existing AD user objects or create new user objects in the AD.

3.9 The NTDSNoMatch Utility

The NTDSNoMatch utility can be run from a Windows 2000 or Windows 2003 system using an account that has the appropriate permissions to read the Exchange 5.5 Directory Service. Executing the following command:

```
NTDSNOMATCH <servername>:<optional LDAP port number>
```

causes the NTDSNoMatch utility to scan the complete Exchange 5.5 Directory Service using LDAP and highlight those mailboxes that it determines to be resource mailboxes. The logic for determining if a mailbox is a resource mailbox or not is straightforward and fairly simple. NTDSNoMatch compares the Exchange 5.5 alias of the mailbox with the SAM Account Name of the associated Windows NT4 account. If the values match (e.g., the alias is MARKL and the SAM Account Name is MARKL), then NTDSNoMatch assumes that this is a primary mailbox and Windows account. If the alias and SAM Account Name do not match (e.g., the alias is CONFROOM and the SAM Account Name is MARKL), then NTDSNoMatch assumes that this is a resource mailbox.

The NTDSNoMatch utility produces a series of CSV files, one for each Exchange 5.5 Site that contains the appropriate data such that when you import the CSV file in the Exchange 5.5 Directory Service for each site, resource mailboxes are updated with the value NTDSNoMatch in Custom Attribute 10. (You need one CSV file for each site because Exchange 5.5 Directory Service objects are read-only outside the site.)

For environments where the Exchange 5.5 alias for a user mailbox coincides with the SAM Account Name, NTDSNoMatch can be a useful tool for identifying resource mailboxes. However, in those environments where there is no synergy between mailbox aliases and SAM Account Names, the utility is of little use because of its primitive logic. In such circumstances, you might consider initiating an exercise to align the mailbox aliases with the SAM Account Name Values.

Whatever approach is taken, you should invest adequate resources in sanitizing your Exchange 5.5 Directory Service before you start any Active Directory Connector synchronization. Use third-party tools to analyze your environment or write your own scripts. If you have not aligned Exchange 5.5 aliases with SAM Account Names, there is the potential for name clashes as you begin Active Directory Connector synchronization. (The Exchange 5.5 Directory Service does not enforce uniqueness checking on aliases outside the boundary of a container.) Even if you have aligned alias names with SAM Account Names, large environments that use multiple domains may incur name clashes because SAM Account Names are unique only within the domain.

3.10 Summarizing Object-Matching Behavior

The Active Directory Connector is a powerful tool for controlling those objects that you will synchronize from one directory to another. In this chapter, we've looked primarily at controlling the flow of objects from the Exchange 5.5 Directory Service to the AD. But the same sophistication for controlling object flow in the direction of the AD to Exchange 5.5 Directory Services is available using a very similar set of attributes on CAs and on the Active Directory Connector policy.

Using LDAP search filters and/or custom matching rules affords those designing and overseeing migrations from Exchange 5.5 to Exchange 2003 great flexibility when it comes to sequencing object synchronization and controlling the synchronization of so-called resource mailboxes (i.e., multiple Exchange 5.5 mailboxes sharing a single Windows NT4 account).

3.11 Introduction to Attribute Mapping

The central aspect of Active Directory Connector functionality is the bi-directional synchronization of objects between the Exchange 5.5 Directory Service and the AD. When an object is being synchronized, let's say from the Exchange 5.5 Directory Service to the AD, more or less all of the attributes associated with the Exchange 5.5 object get synchronized to their attribute counterparts in the AD object.

Although you can exercise some control over which attributes you'll synchronize from one directory to another, there's little you can do with the out-of-the-box functionality of the Active Directory Connector to control the mapping of individual attributes. This part of the chapter examines some techniques for customized attribute mapping, specifically from the Exchange 5.5 Directory Service to the AD, and gives you an insight into how to refine Active Directory Connector behavior for your environment.

3.12 Default Attribute Mapping Behavior

The Active Directory Connector Manager MMC snap-in gives you little opportunity to control the mapping of attributes for an object in the Exchange 5.5 Directory Service to the AD and vice versa. The snap-in offers a predefined list of attributes that you can elect to either be included in the synchronization activity or not.

By default, most attributes of an Exchange 5.5 mailbox or custom recipient that would be useful to have replicated to the AD are synchronized automatically when a CA is established between the source container and the target Organizational Unit. Useful attributes include those such as naming and addressing information, telephone and location details that can be used in a GAL, and mailbox properties such as the *HomeMDB* (indicating on which server a user mailbox is located) that are necessary for Exchange to allow mail to be delivered.

To control which attributes you want to be synchronized, you should modify the *Default Active Directory Connector Policy*. You can do this by right-clicking on the *Active Directory Connector Management* root in the Active Directory Connector Manager MMC snap-in, then select *Properties* and either *From Exchange* or *From Windows* depending on the flow direction in which you're interested. Figure 3-9 shows the interface you'll see: If the box beside an attribute is checked, then the Active Directory Connector will synchronize the attribute.

You shouldn't need to spend too much time modifying these settings. Microsoft has already decided which attributes you'll most probably need, and typically you may only want to suppress the synchronization of an attribute—say, a Custom Attribute

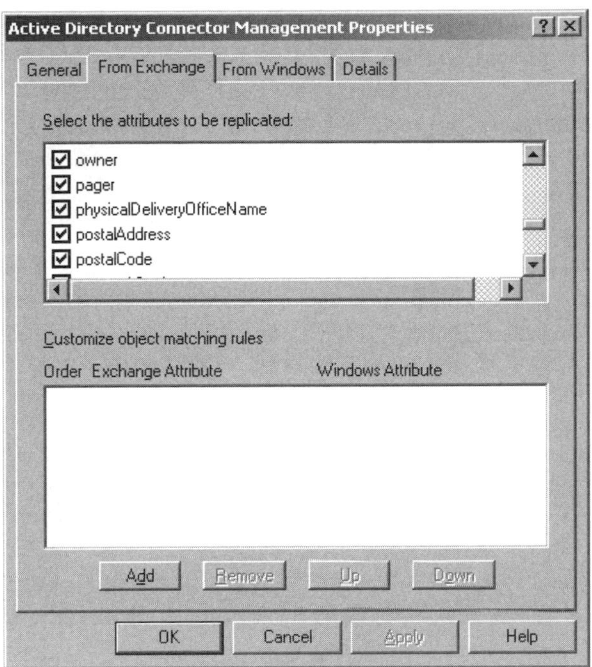

Figure 3-9 *Controlling Attribute Flow from Exchange on the Default Active Directory Connector Policy*

that holds some legacy information whose value you don't want to synchronize to the AD—because the value of the AD attribute is coming from some other directory source.

3.13 Moving Beyond the Schema Mapping GUI

As you can see from Figure 3-9, you're very limited in terms of what you can do with the mapping of Exchange 5.5 Directory Service attributes to AD attributes when you use the Active Directory Connector Manager MMC snap-in: either you map the attributes or you don't. If you wish to perform more complex attribute synchronizations, such as mapping the value of one attribute in the source directory to a different attribute in the target directory, then you need to use something other than the Active Directory Connector Manager MMC snap-in.

Unfortunately, that other method is not too sophisticated. In fact, all that the Active Directory Connector Manager snap-in does to control attribute flow is to manipulate settings on the Default Active Directory Connector Policy. However, the snap-in presents only a limited interface to the policy. If you want to perform more complex mapping operations, you need to bypass the snap-in and manipulate the policy directly by changing settings in the AD. Direct access to the policy in this way is

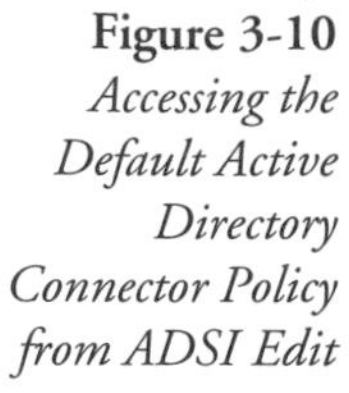

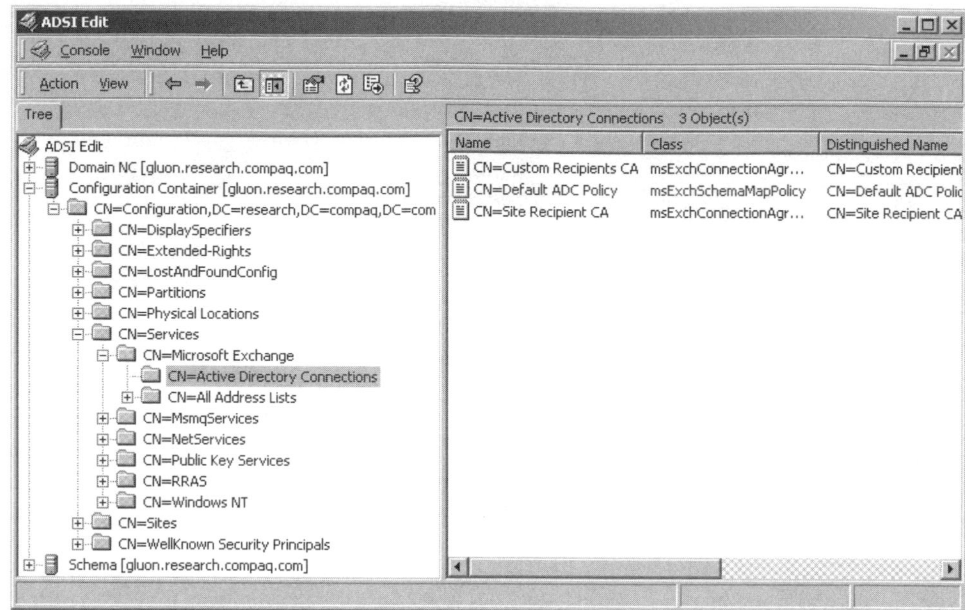

Figure 3-10 *Accessing the Default Active Directory Connector Policy from ADSI Edit*

only available by using that tool that you'll become very familiar with when using the Active Directory Connector: ADSI Edit.

You can install ADSI Edit from the *Support* directory on the Windows 2000 or Windows 2003 CD-ROM. Figure 3-10 shows the view of the policy from the ADSI Edit snap-in.

Because you define attribute mapping rules on the Default Active Directory Connector Policy, these rules are enforced for all CAs that are homed on a given Active Directory Connector. Although it appears that you can set individual mapping rules for each CA homed on an Active Directory Connector, any rules that you set in individual CAs will be overwritten by the settings on the Default Active Directory Connector Policy.

3.13.1 Modifying the mapping tables

The attribute mapping rules are defined on two attributes of the Default Active Directory Connector Policy or a CA. The *msExchServer1SchemaMap* and *msExchServer2SchemaMap* define attribute mapping rules for AD to Exchange 5.5 Directory Service and Exchange 5.5 Directory Service to AD, respectively. Figure 3-11 shows a sample of what you'll see when you look at the properties of the policy object and specifically at the *msExchServer1SchemaMap*.

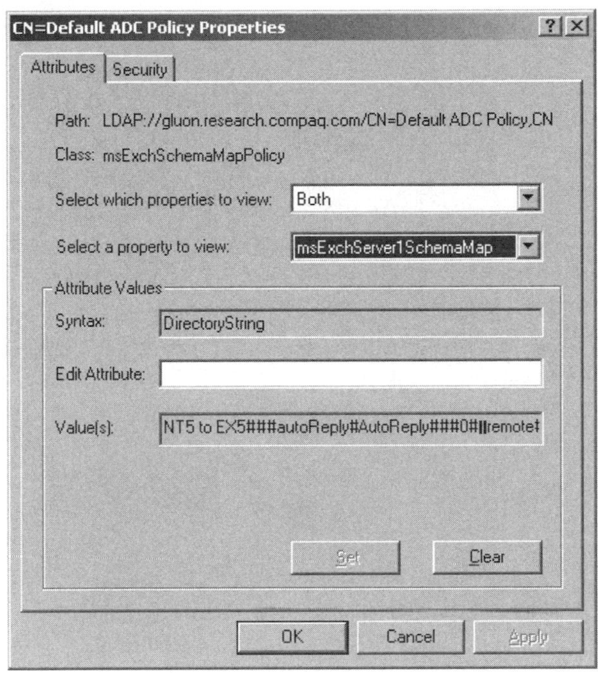

Figure 3-11 *Accessing the Value of the msExchServer1-SchemaMap Attribute*

The string shown in the *Value(s)* text box in Figure 3-11 is really just the first few characters of a rather long string that continues for some 18,029 characters, or 269 individual lines in the attribute mapping rule table. These rules are set when you install the Active Directory Connector and reflect the settings that Microsoft believes to be optimal for synchronizing attribute data to and from the 5.5 Directory Service and the AD.

To customize the mapping rules, you first need to click on the *Clear* button, at which time the mapping rule is displayed in the *Edit Attribute* text box. (You can't edit the rule when it's displayed in the *Value(s)* text box.) Once you've made changes to the rule to reflect your requirements, click on the *Set* button, and the new rule will be written to the AD and become active. Personally, I find it quite challenging to edit these rules by making changes to the text string in the *Edit Attribute* text box. To make life easier, you should copy the text string from the *Value(s)* text box, and then paste it into your favorite editor—Notepad or Wordpad is sufficient for this—where the embedded CR/LFs cause the text to be rendered in a much more readable fashion. Using an editor, it's much simpler to find the rule you wish to modify and understand other related rules. However, you can't make changes to the mapping rules using an editor and then paste the new rules back into the AD. You must make changes directly to the AD by finding the rule in the long text string and perform the editing there.

When you install the Active Directory Connector, the attribute mapping tables are populated from some predefined text files on the Exchange 2003 distribution CD-ROM. Specifically, in the ADC\I386 directory, you'll find two files: LOCAL.MAP and REMOTE.MAP. The LOCAL.MAP file contains the complete set of mapping rules that populate the *msExchServer2SchemaMap* attribute, while the REMOTE.MAP file defines the rules for the *msExchServer1SchemaMap*. If you know which modifications you need to make to the attribute mapping files, you can edit these text files (provided you copy the installation kit onto writeable media) before you install the Active Directory Connector. Doing so makes for a much easier mapping table editing experience. This technique is particularly useful and efficient if you will deploy multiple Active Directory Connectors and you need to make consistent modifications to the mapping tables.

If you want to edit these files before you install Active Directory Connector, copy the original files to a safe place, make the necessary changes to the files, and then install Active Directory Connector. The Active Directory Connector setup program does not replace these attributes if the Default Active Directory Connector Policy entry already exists. If you have already installed Active Directory Connector and you want to make changes to these files, you must delete all of the existing CAs, as well as the Default Active Directory Connector Policy entry, before you run the Active Directory Connector setup program.

On a related point, in the unlikely (but possible!) event that you need to restore the mapping tables to their default configurations, the only way to achieve this is to reinstall the Active Directory Connector. Any changes you make to the attribute mappings only affects the mapping tables in the AD, and an Active Directory Connector reinstall normalizes the Active Directory Connector tables by reading the original set of mapping rules from the LOCAL.MAP and REMOTE.MAP files for new CAs only; existing CAs and the Default Active Directory Connector Policy must be updated by hand.

3.13.2 Changing attribute mappings

Editing the schema mapping file allows you to change how the value of one attribute is mapped to another. For example, you may want to change the mapping between the *City* and the *Office* attributes as you synchronize Exchange 5.5 Directory Service objects to the AD. Take a look at the Exchange 5.5 mailbox shown in Figure 3-12.

When the Active Directory Connector synchronizes this mailbox into the AD, it will map the Exchange 5.5 *Office* attribute to the *Office* attribute of the object in the AD. However, in this case, let's say I don't want to have the value Belfield (which, incidentally, is a suburb of Dublin, Ireland) written to the AD *Office* attribute, but instead

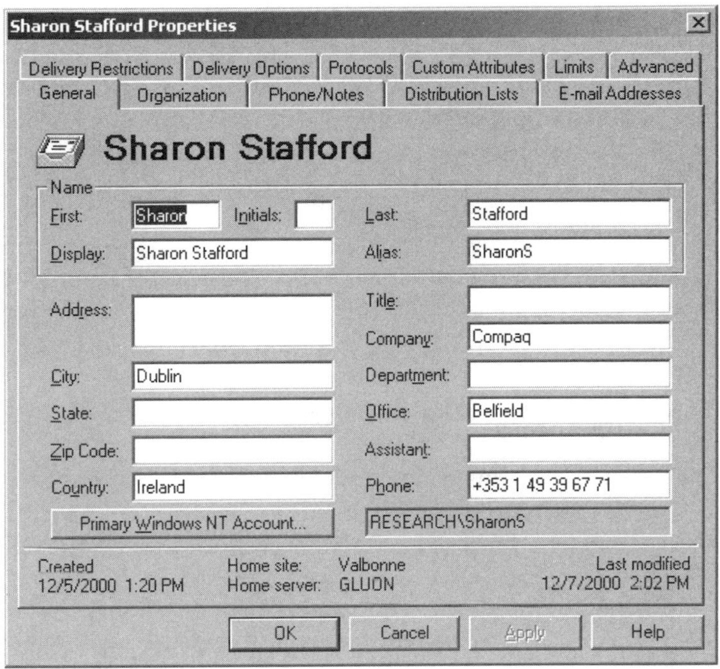

Figure 3-12
Exchange 5.5 Mailbox Properties for Sharon Stafford

I'd rather have the value of the Exchange 5.5 *City* attribute written to the AD *Office* attribute.

Looking at the mapping rules as specified in *msExchServer2SchemaMap*, you'll see that the value of the Exchange 5.5 *Office* attribute is defined to map directly to the value of the AD *Office* attribute; the appropriate rule (let's call it Rule 1) is shown as follows:

```
local###physicalDeliveryOfficeName#physicalDeliveryOfficeName###0#
```

This rule states that for all objects in the Exchange 5.5 Directory Service that will be processed by the Active Directory Connector, map the Exchange 5.5 *Office* attribute to the AD *Office* attribute. Of course, you won't be surprised to read that another mapping rule exists in the mapping table that maps the Exchange 5.5 *City* attribute value to the AD *City* attribute. The rule (let's call it Rule 2) used to effect this mapping is as follows:

```
local###l#l###0#
```

For our customized mappings, we want the AD *Office* attribute to take on the value of the Exchange 5.5 *City* attribute. This is simply done by changing Rule 1 so that it reads as follows:

```
local###1#physicalDeliveryOfficeName###0#
```

There's no need to change Rule 2, because the Active Directory Connector can map a single Exchange 5.5 attribute to multiple attributes in the AD. Thus, when the Active Directory Connector synchronizes the Exchange 5.5 mailbox shown in Figure 3-12, Sharon will be represented in the AD (see Figure 3-13) with an *Office* value of Dublin, not Belfield.

Furthermore, if you were to look at the AD *City* attribute for Sharon, you'd see that the value of that attribute held *Dublin,* so this synchronization really has done a one-to-many mapping of attribute data.

3.13.3 Dealing with conflicting mapping rules

In the schema mapping table, there is no concept of mapping rule precedence. That is, if you have two rules that map to the same target attribute, the latter rule will not override the former, nor will the former override the latter. In this example, with the

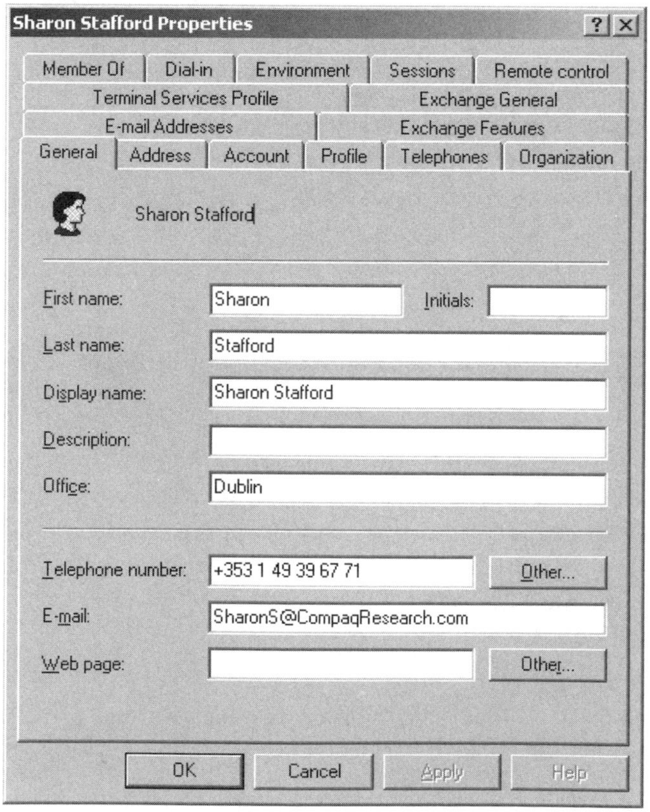

Figure 3-13
Active Directory User Object Properties

physicalDeliveryOfficeName target AD attribute, if you have two rules trying to write to this attribute, the entire synchronization operation for this object will fail. Figure 3-14 shows the event that you'll see in the Event Log if you have two mapping rules directed to the same target attribute.

In this case, the *Constraint Violation* error is returned because *physicalDeliveryOfficeName* is a single-valued attribute and the Active Directory Connector actually processes both mapping rules and attempts to assign both values to the target attribute. This results in an error, and the synchronization operation for this object is abandoned. However, for multivalued attributes, having multiple mapping rules targeting the same attribute is valid, and processing will be carried out as normal.

3.13.4 When mapping table changes take effect

When you make a change to the attribute mapping table, the changes in mapping policy take effect the very next time the Active Directory Connector initiates a synchronization activity. If the Active Directory Connector will create a new object during a synchronization run, then the new mappings will be honored, but for existing objects

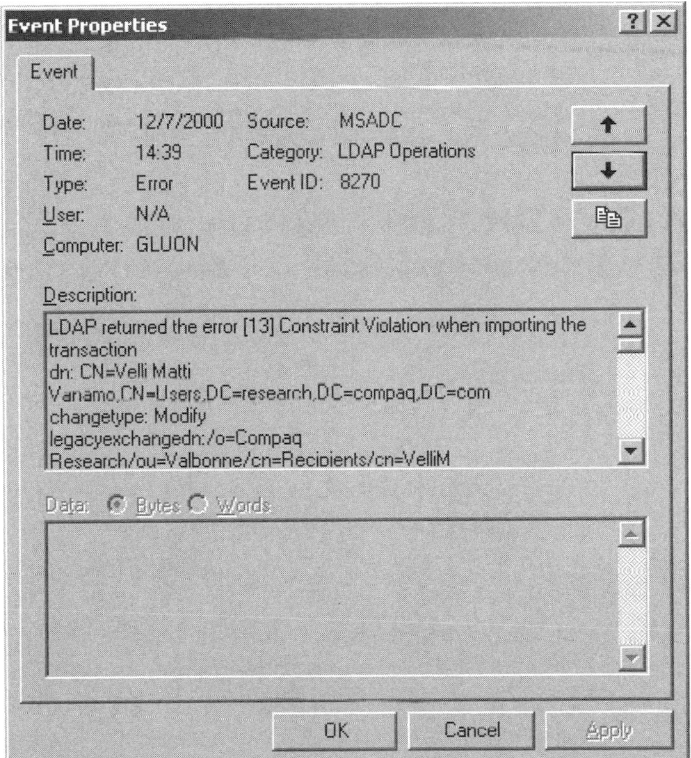

Figure 3-14
Constraint Violation Event

that have already been synchronized into the AD, the mere action of changing the attribute mapping policy is not sufficient to see the AD object updated in line with the new mapping rules. In our example, if Sharon's Exchange 5.5 mailbox had already been synchronized into the AD as a user object, you would see no changes to the AD object after you had applied the new policy and the Active Directory Connector initiated its next synchronization run.

Updates in line with the new attribute mapping rules will only be applied to already synchronized objects if some change on the source object causes the Active Directory Connector to process it again for the synchronization. Such a change would include updating a telephone number attribute or an address field, for example.

Exactly the same rules hold true for attribute mapping operations in the reverse direction (i.e., from the AD to Exchange 5.5 Directory Service), although during migration operations as a system administrator you will most likely be more interested in attribute mapping customizations from Exchange to the AD.

I've used the manipulation of the *Office* and *City* fields in this example more to illustrate the point than anything else, but you can apply these rules to all attributes associated with the directory objects. In most cases, you will want to map the attribute values as is, but other attributes may deserve some special attention. The custom attributes are the most likely candidates for nonstandard handling, because organizations have used them in different ways for different reasons. With the introduction of the AD and the way in which organizations are using it, it's likely that you may have to redefine some custom attribute mappings.

3.14 Active Directory Distinguished Name Mapping with the Exchange 2000 Active Directory Connector

Previously with the Exchange 2000 version of the Active Directory Connector, objects created in the AD by the Active Directory Connector had a Distinguished Name that is built from a combination of the AD container into which the object is being created and an Exchange 5.5 attribute of the source object.

For example, for Sharon's mailbox as shown in Figure 3-13, the Distinguished Name that is built in the AD (let's call it DN 1) is as follows:

```
CN=Sharon Stafford,CN=Users,DC=research,DC=compaq,DC=com
```

Specifically, the least significant Relative Distinguished Name (RDN) part of the Distinguished Name, in this case *CN=Sharon Stafford*, is determined directly from the Exchange 5.5 mailbox *Display Name* attribute. In the Exchange 5.5 Directory Service, the LDAP name for the *Display Name* is *cn*. Accordingly, a special rule in the *msEx-*

chServer2SchemaMap table explicitly defines the RDN for any AD objects that the Active Directory Connector will create. This rule is the last rule on the mapping table and is defined as follows:

```
local###cn#Override_RDN_Value###140#
```

The syntax of this rule is slightly different from the other rules in the mapping table. There's no real AD attribute that's shown in the rule, but the *Override_RDN_Value* string acts as a directive that tells the Active Directory Connector to modify the RDN of the Active Directory Connector–created object.

You can modify this rule to change the source attribute for the RDN. For example, you may replace the source *cn* attribute with the *sn* attribute, or possibly with the *mailNickname* attribute. Doing so forces the Active Directory Connector to build the RDN using the surname or Exchange 5.5 mailbox alias, respectively.

As well as applying to new objects that the Active Directory Connector creates in the AD, this rule also affects existing objects in the AD. For example, let's say that you had migrated a Windows NT4 user account to a Windows 2000 or Windows 2003 account using a tool such as Microsoft's Active Directory Migration Tool (ADMT) before you started using the Active Directory Connector. When ADMT creates the new user object in Windows 2000 or Windows 2003, it builds the least significant RDN part of the Distinguished Name using the Windows NT4 SAM account name—let's assume that it's Stafford. This creates an object in the AD with a Distinguished Name (let's call it DN 2) of:

```
CN=stafford,CN=Users,DC=research,DC=compaq,DC=com
```

So far, so good. When the Active Directory Connector gets to work, it matches the Exchange 5.5 mailbox object with the already existing account in the AD. (It matches the Exchange 5.5 mailbox *Assoc-NT-Account* attribute with the *sIDHistory* attribute of the AD object.) When the match is made, apart from synchronizing attributes from the Exchange 5.5 mailbox into the existing AD object, the RDN override rule forces the AD object's Distinguished Name to be updated from that shown in DN 2 to become based on the Exchange 5.5 *Display Name* attribute, and ultimately it becomes that shown in DN 1.

Although this *RDN* mapping yields pretty Distinguished Names, some administrators dislike it. Reasons for this emotion are varied, but they include (1) the confusion associated with Distinguished Names that change during the course of the migration; (2) the possibility of duplicate Exchange 5.5 Display Names, which results in the appending of '-1' to the Distinguished Name; and (3) the potential impact to applications or processes that rely on consistent Distinguished Names.

In any event, as an administrator you may wish to either disable the RDN mapping rule using the 0x10 flag (see following section) or map it to an attribute consistent with the existing RDN structure—perhaps using the Exchange 5.5 mailbox alias if it corresponds to the Windows NT4 SAM account name. (You can also disable the RDN mapping by setting the *msExchServer1Flags* attribute to the value of 2. See TechNet article Q269843 for more information.)

3.15 Distinguished Name Mapping with the Exchange 2003 Active Directory Connector

The Exchange 2003 version of the Active Directory Connector operates somewhat differently from the old Exchange 2000 version when it comes to generating the *samAccountName* and Distinguished Names for Active Directory Connector–created objects.

With the Exchange 2003 version, the generated *samAccountName* and Distinguished Name is of the following form:

```
ADC_<pseudo alphanumeric value>
```

For example, ADC_31C41A5C926H54E. Microsoft decided on this changed format primarily because some organizations were incorrectly relying on Active Directory Connector–created users' accounts as fully migrated accounts. Unfortunately, because such accounts have no *sidHistory* values associated with them, they cannot be used correctly to access legacy resources.

Personally, I think this is a mistake from Microsoft. They fix one problem (which most organizations that know what they are doing wouldn't make anyhow) but introduce another. Because the *samAccountName* for an Active Directory Connector–generated object is now pseudo-random, migration tools that previously used the *samAccountName* to match with the Exchange 5.5 mailbox alias are rendered useless. Unfortunately, Microsoft seems to have overlooked this issue, nor does it provide any mechanism to turn the old *samAccountName* generation algorithm back on. Pity!

3.16 Exchange 5.5 and LDAP Names

In the mapping rules shown, *physicalDeliveryOfficeName* in Rule 1 is the LDAP attribute name for the Exchange 5.5 *Office* attribute. Similarly, the letter *l* (ell) in Rule 2 is the LDAP attribute name for the Exchange 5.5 *City* attribute.

You can determine the LDAP name of any Exchange 5.5 attribute by running the Exchange 5.5 Administrator program in raw mode (ADMIN.EXE /R). While in the

Administrator program, drop down from the *View* menu and select *Raw Directory*. On the left-hand side of the Administrator Window, you'll see the *Schema* displayed underneath the site, and when you select it, you'll see the entire Exchange 5.5 Directory Service schema displayed in the right-hand pane. Select an object by Display Name, and the LDAP attribute name can be found by looking at the value of the *Description* attribute. Figure 3-15 shows this for the *City* attribute.

3.17 Attribute Mapping Rule Syntax

The syntax of the attribute mapping rules is defined as follows:

```
<name>#<soc>#<toc>#<sa>#<ta>#<prefix>#<syntax>#<flags>
```

where

```
<name> defines an arbitrary name for the mapping rule
<soc> defines the object class of the source object used in mapping
<toc> defines the object class of the target object used in the mapping
<sa> defines the LDAP name of the source attribute used in the mapping
<ta> defines the LDAP name of the target attribute used in the mapping
<prefix> defines a prefix to the source attribute used in the mapping
<syntax> defines the mapping syntax used in the mapping
<flags> define the behavior of the mapping rule
```

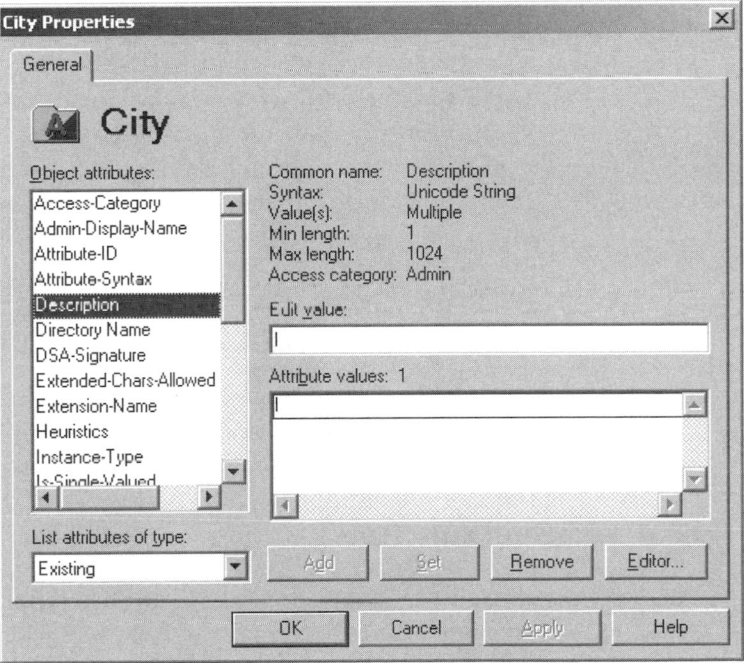

Figure 3-15 *Determining the LDAP Name of an Exchange 5.5 Directory Service Object*

In most cases, the syntax definitions are intuitive, but let's look at a few of the constructs.

3.17.1 Source and target object classes

If no source or target object classes are defined, then the mapping rule applies to all objects processed by the CA—this typically includes mailboxes, custom recipients, and distribution lists from Exchange 5.5 and mail-enabled user objects, contacts, and groups from the AD.

You can be more specific with your mapping rules by specifying the entire object class hierarchy to which you would have the mapping rule apply. For example, the following mapping rule is only applied when an Exchange 5.5 distribution list is being mapped to an AD group:

```
local#groupofnames$person$top#group$top#home-MTA#msExchExpansionServerN
ame###0#
```

3.17.2 Prefix

Using the prefix allows you to insert a fixed text string into the target attribute. The text string should not be quoted, and all characters in this field will be written directly into the target attribute.

3.17.3 Syntax

In most cases you can leave the Syntax construct blank, but if the attribute you are mapping is a Distinguished Name, then you must specify the value *DN* in this part of the mapping rule. For example, in Rule 1, the attribute we're mapping (*physicalDeliveryOfficeName*) is of syntax DirectoryString. (You can see this from the *Syntax* text box when using ADSI Edit.)

However, the following mapping rule (let's call it Rule 3):

```
local#organizationalPerson$person$top#user$organizationalperson$person$
top#Manager#Manager##DN#2#
```

defines a mapping for the *Manager* attribute, which is a Distinguished Name. Accordingly, you must set the syntax to *DN* on the rule.

3.17.4 Mapping rule flags

A mapping rule flag is a hexadecimal number that refines some specific behavior of the individual mapping. You can aggregate flags to provide composite functionality. For example, a flag of 0x140 causes the behavior associated with both the 0x100 flag and the 0x40 flag. Table 3-1 provides a summary of the flag mapping behavior.

3.18 Summary

In many environments there is no need to interfere with the natural order of all things related to Active Directory Connector attribute mapping. Attributes in the Exchange 5.5 Directory Service have natural counterparts in the AD, and mappings between the two environments are predefined when you install the Active Directory Connector.

Table 3-1 *Flag Descriptions for the Attribute Mapping Rules*

Flag	Description
0x1	Used when the source attribute is multivalued but the target attribute is single-valued and causes the first source value to be mapped into the target attribute.
0x2	Used when the source attribute has a DN syntax but the Active Directory Connector can't find the Distinguished Name in the target directory. In such cases the source value is written to the unmerged attributes list for fix-up later when the Distinguished Name can be resolved.
0x4	Used when the source attribute is single-valued, but the target attribute is multivalued and causes the source value to be written into the first target value.
0x8	Used when the source attribute is multivalued and the target attribute is single-valued and causes all values from the source attribute to be written as a single value in the target attribute as a comma-separated list.
0x10	Disables the mapping rule.
0x20	Used when the source attribute is a custom attribute used for mapping purpose and not exposed in the directory schema. Reserved for internal Active Directory Connector use.
0x40	Used when the target attribute is a custom attribute used for mapping purposes and not exposed in the directory schema. Reserved for internal Active Directory Connector use.
0x100	Mapping rule is hidden from the Active Directory Connector Manager snap-in interface.
0x200	If the Connection Agreement allows, merge the source value into the target attribute rather than overwriting.
0x400	If the source value is of type DN syntax and the link cannot be resolved, add the value into the Exchange 2003 unmerged attributes list.

Some unique circumstances may require the odd mapping modification here or there, especially if an organization has made heavy use of custom attributes.

But while the requirement to change mapping rules is likely to be minimal, what's certainly more likely is the requirement to change the way in which the Active Directory Connector creates or modifies the Distinguished Name for objects in the AD. Being able to suppress Distinguished Name modification or map it using a different source attribute is sure to be a big plus for anyone who is responsible for integrating the old Exchange 5.5 Directory Service with the new AD.

4

The Site Replication Service

4.1 Introduction

The Site Replication Service (SRS) is in general a poorly understood component of Exchange 2003, and Exchange 2000 before that. For the most part, it's perceived to be a component that allows an Exchange 2003 server to synchronize directory information with an Exchange 5.5 server. In some part, this is true. However, the SRS's role in life is merely to allow an Exchange 2003 server to participate in Exchange 5.5–style directory replication. Why might an Exchange 2003 server need to do this? The remainder of this chapter sets out to explain just that.

4.2 Positioning the Site Replication Service and the Active Directory Connector

Only the Active Directory Connector provides the mechanism to perform directory synchronization between the Exchange 5.5 Directory Service and the AD. The SRS has nothing to do with this exchange of information. The SRS presents itself as an Exchange 5.5 Directory Service to other Exchange 5.5 servers but runs on an Exchange 2003 server. The SRS is only available if you're running Exchange in mixed mode. (A mixed-mode Exchange organization includes Exchange 5.5 Service Pack 3 legacy servers. In Exchange 2000, a mixed-mode organization could also support Exchange 5.0 and Exchange 4.0 servers, but these legacy versions are not supported in terms of interoperability with Exchange 2003.)

Using the SRS to provide a shadow Exchange 5.5 Directory Service allows other Exchange 5.5 servers to continue with Exchange 5.5 directory replication to a particular server in the same way that they always did, even if that particular server has been upgraded to Exchange 2003. We'll see later why maintaining this kind of operation is beneficial to both the existing Exchange 5.5 servers and the new Exchange 2003 servers.

4.2.1 Exchange 5.5 directory replication

In Exchange 5.5, we have the concepts of intrasite replication and intersite replication between servers. Intrasite replication takes place between servers in a site using RPCs, whereas intersite replication is mail-based and takes place over a DRC between bridgehead servers in separate sites. The SRS supports both of these forms of Exchange 5.5 replication in conjunction with Exchange 2003.

4.2.2 Defining when the Site Replication Service is enabled

Although the SRS components are provided with every Exchange 2003 installation, you don't always get the SRS enabled on every Exchange 2003 server. The components are installed by default, but the SRS is only configured and enabled under certain circumstances:

- When the first Exchange 5.5 server is upgraded to Exchange 2003 (or Exchange 2000) in an Exchange 5.5 site
- When the first Exchange 2003 (or Exchange 2000) server is installed into an Exchange 5.5 site
- When an Exchange 5.5 bridgehead server is upgraded to Exchange 2003 (or Exchange 2000)

The SRS works with the Active Directory Connector to make the whole concept of Exchange 5.5 Directory Service to AD synchronization easier. Specifically, the SRS helps make the management of CAs simpler.

4.3 Components that Comprise the Site Replication Service

The SRS consists of three major components:

- An Exchange 5.5 Directory Service with its replication engine
- The *Knowledge Consistency Checker* (KCC) from Exchange 5.5
- The *Site Knowledge Consistency Checker* (SKCC), which understands the AD configuration information as well as the legacy Exchange site topology and thus has a complete view of a mixed-mode Exchange 2003 organization

This functionality is implemented by a set of files that provide directory replication functionality between the Exchange 5.5 Directory Service and an SRS database on an Exchange 2003 server. To make it all happen, you'll find these files on your Exchange 2003 server:

- SRS.EXE, which provides the main Exchange 5.5 Directory Service look-alike code and other functions
- SRSCHECK.DLL, which provides directory replication consistency checking
- SRSMAPI.DLL, which provides directory replication mail services
- SRSPERF.DLL, which provides performance counters
- SRSMSG.DLL, which provides event logging functionality
- SRSXDS.DLL, which provides the SRS XDS API (the API that is used to access the Exchange 5.5 Directory Service)
- SRS.EDB, which provides the directory service database file (the file formerly known as DIR.EDB)

These files all provide the SRS that runs with the key MSExchangeSRS, under the display name of Microsoft Exchange SRS.

4.4 The Site Replication Service in Intrasite Replication Operation

Let's look at some example environments involving the Active Directory Connector and the SRS.

Figure 4-1 shows an Exchange 5.5 site (holding only Exchange 5.5 servers) with a CA homed against one of the servers, S4. This is a perfectly valid configuration and operates well. Specifically, the CA to the AD is well defined because it has a valid source of Exchange 5.5 directory information. The Active Directory Connector gets information from the 5.5 Directory Service on server S4.

4.4.1 Importance of the Site Replication Service as Exchange 5.5 servers are upgraded

But what happens when I wish to upgrade the server S4 from Exchange 5.5 to become an Exchange 2003 server? The integrity of my CA is immediately compromised because if S4 is an Exchange 2003 server, then it won't have an Exchange 5.5 Directory Service. In such a case my CA becomes unusable. My only option is to rehome the Exchange 5.5 end of the CA onto another server, say server S5. This would reestablish the integrity of my CA, but again, I'd have to go about rehoming this CA when subse-

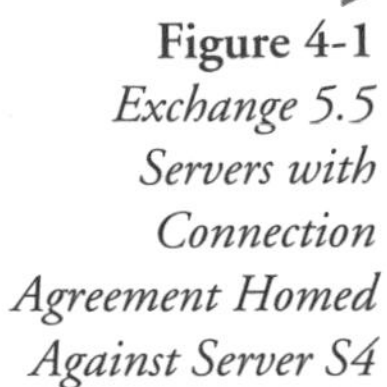

Figure 4-1
Exchange 5.5 Servers with Connection Agreement Homed Against Server S4

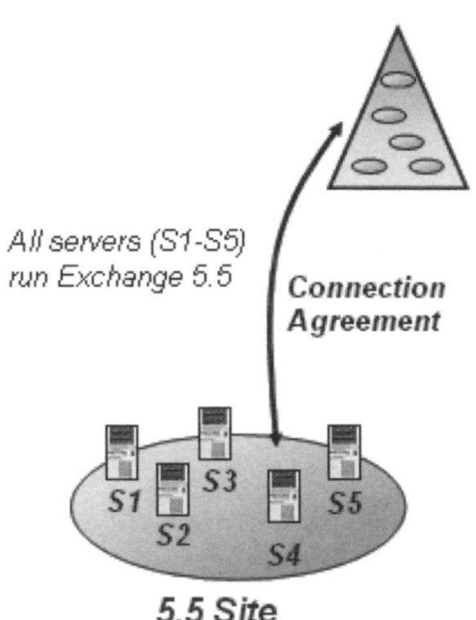

quently I upgrade server S5 to Exchange 2003. This rehoming activity could repeat itself for some time unless I made sure to initially home my CA against a server that I was confident would be the last one in the site to be migrated to Exchange 2003.

Having to devote this kind of administrative attention to your CAs and Exchange 5.5 servers isn't a matter of life or death, but it is troublesome, and really, life would be much simpler if you could just not have to worry about it. The SRS takes this worry away from you.

4.4.2 Retaining Connection Agreement integrity

From Figure 4-1, let's assume that the first Exchange 5.5 server in the site to be upgraded to Exchange 2003 is server S4. This satisfies one of the rules for having the SRS enabled: It's the first server in the site. In this circumstance, when the upgrade is performed, the SRS (which is really the Exchange 5.5 Directory Service in disguise) becomes active. Because it takes part in Exchange 5.5 directory replication just like any other Exchange 5.5 service, it has a perfectly valid view of the Exchange 5.5 directory in its SRS database. This is shown in Figure 4-2.

The live SRS on server S4 means that I haven't broken the existing CA that's homed against S4. Because the SRS is there, I have a valid source of Exchange 5.5 directory information and there's no need to manually rehome the CA. This is much simpler than having to worry about rehoming CAs time after time to different Exchange 5.5 servers. Having a single server that you can be confident will always provide a source of Exchange 5.5 directory information is a big benefit.

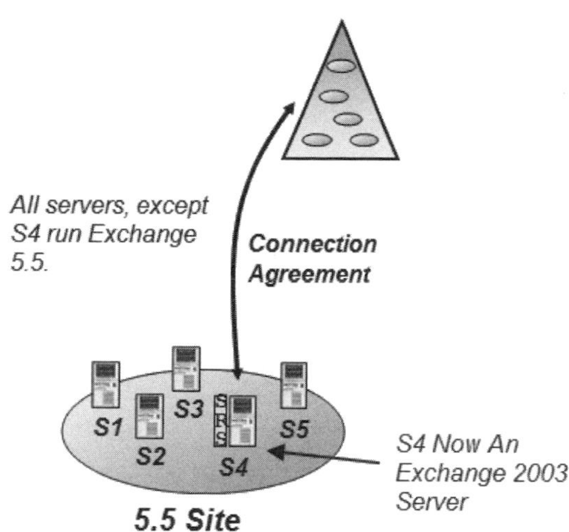

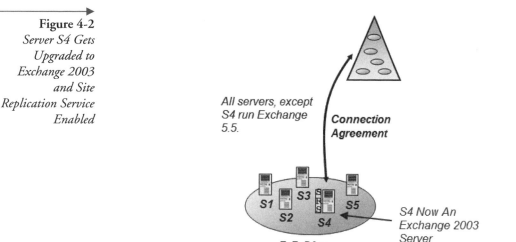

Figure 4-2
Server S4 Gets Upgraded to Exchange 2003 and Site Replication Service Enabled

4.4.3 Homing your Connection Agreements against the Site Replication Service

When you home a CA against a regular Exchange 5.5 server, you'll need to bind the Exchange 5.5 end of the CA against the LDAP protocol of the Exchange 5.5 Directory Service. By default, the Exchange 5.5 LDAP protocol listens on port 389, but you can enable LDAP on another port if you wish. Typically, you'll only do this for an Exchange 5.5 server if you're running Exchange 5.5 on a Windows 2000 or Windows 2003 DC. You'll remember that the AD on a Windows 2000 or Windows 2003 DC listens on port 389 as well, and as Windows is starting up, it will seize control of port 389 before the Exchange 5.5 Directory Service can get to it.

You'll find a similar issue with the SRS. The SRS will only ever be running on a Windows 2000 or Windows 2003 system, and it's entirely possible that this system may be a DC. A CA will always want to connect to a source of Exchange 5.5 directory information over LDAP, and to avoid confusion, the engineering team designed the SRS so that it offers its LDAP service from port 379. This being the case, if you had previously homed your CA against an Exchange 5.5 Directory Service on port 389, you'll have to modify the CA so that it now points to port 379 to get to the SRS directory service.

In reality, there is little management work you need to do. You do have to modify the CA to direct it to a different port after the upgrade to Exchange 2003, but this is a small change to an existing CA, rather than having to rehome onto an altogether different server.

4.4.4 Modifying the existing intrasite replication chain

Within an Exchange 5.5 site, an Exchange 5.5 server communicates with other Exchange 5.5 servers to keep the information in its directory service consistent with the information in the directories of all of the other Exchange 5.5 servers. This is the essence of intrasite replication. The component responsible for controlling this process is the KCC—which can be found on every Exchange 5.5 server—and it maintains a table of all Exchange 5.5 servers that are to take part in the replication chain.

As many Exchange 5.5 servers in the site are upgraded to Exchange 2003, most won't have the SRS enabled. In these cases, the upgrade code removes the entry for each respective server from the KCC table. For example, for the systems shown in Figure 4-2, presuming that they're not bridgeheads, servers S1, S2, S3, and S5 will be removed from the Exchange 5.5 intrasite replication chain. (Actually, the DSA object for these servers gets removed from the KCC table.) This ensures that they no longer take part in Exchange 5.5 intrasite replication. If the upgrade process didn't remove these DSA objects from the KCC table, you'd see numerous errors in the Event Log, indicating that Exchange 5.5 directory replication failed against the newly upgraded servers.

4.5 The Site Replication Service in Intersite Replication Operation

When an Exchange 5.5 Directory Replication bridgehead server gets upgraded to Exchange 2003, it must maintain a means by which it can communicate site information to its other Exchange 5.5 bridgehead replication partner. Using the SRS allows this to be done because it appears to the replication partner that there is still an Exchange 5.5 Directory Service with which to communicate. This is shown well in Figure 4-3, where the diagram shows the original situation with two Exchange 5.5 Directory Replication bridgehead servers (S9 and S1, respectively) communicating across a DRC.

The scenario that develops, as shown in Figure 4-4, results from an upgrade of server S1 from Exchange 5.5 to Exchange 2003.

The SRS is indispensable in this circumstance, because once again, it reduces the administrative effort associated with upgrading servers. Notice that there is no CA in the pure Exchange 5.5 site, Site B. This means that all site and topology information for Site B must come in from traditional Exchange 5.5 directory replication. In the absence of an SRS, Exchange 5.5 DRCs would need to be rehomed onto different servers as bridgehead servers were upgraded from Exchange 5.5. In our example, upgrading

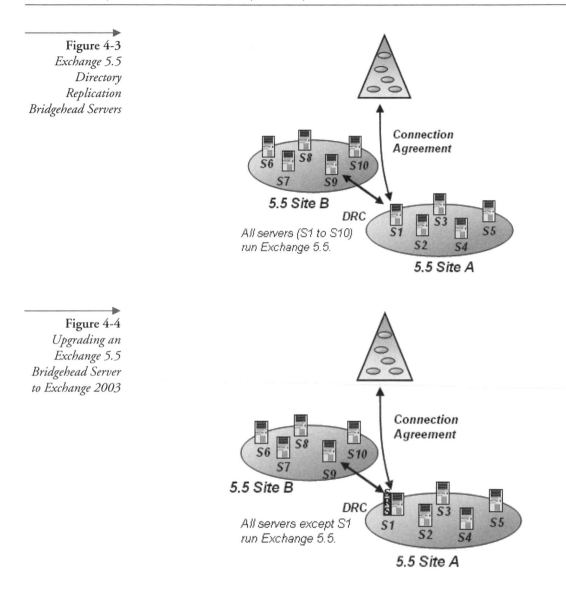

Figure 4-3
Exchange 5.5 Directory Replication Bridgehead Servers

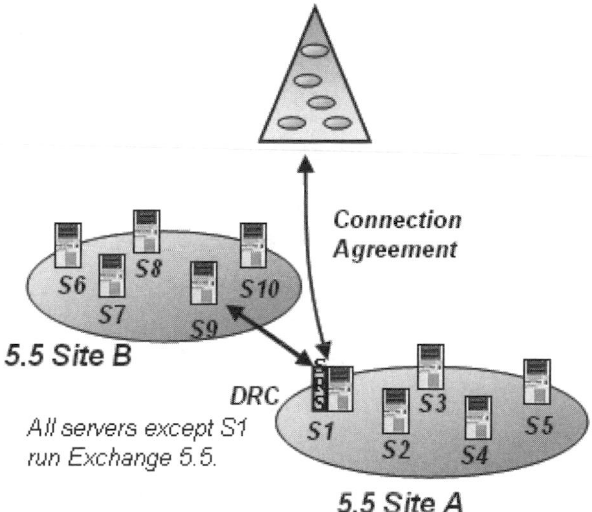

Figure 4-4
Upgrading an Exchange 5.5 Bridgehead Server to Exchange 2003

server S1 to Exchange 2003 would have implied rehoming the DRC to an alternative server in the other site, say S2.

You can see that with respect to intersite replication, the SRS is absolutely essential. Without it the management of DRCs would become a nuisance and would introduce all sorts of administrative overhead. The SRS proves its worth for management of CAs within a site, but coupled with managing connections between Exchange 5.5 bridgehead servers, it's essential.

4.6 What Takes Place during a Bridgehead Server Upgrade?

As server S1 gets upgraded to Exchange 2003, the Setup program modifies the existing local DIR.EDB database—the traditional Exchange 5.5 Directory Service—copies the new executables for the SRS from the installation CD-ROM, and creates several objects in the Configuration Naming Context of the AD.

Specifically, there is an instance of an object of class *msExchSiteReplicationService* to represent the SRS. An example of a default SRS object, which gets the name Microsoft DSA, is shown as a screenshot from ADSI Edit in Figure 4-5.

In this case (it's the first Exchange 2003 server in the site), the Setup program also creates a ConfigCA between the AD and the new SRS service installed locally. The SRS takes on the ownership of the DRC to server S9, and because the SRS object in the AD has a *legacyExchangeDN* attribute of:

```
/o=<OrgName>/ou=<Site>/cn=Configuration -
   /cn=Servers/cn=S1/cn=Microsoft DSA
```

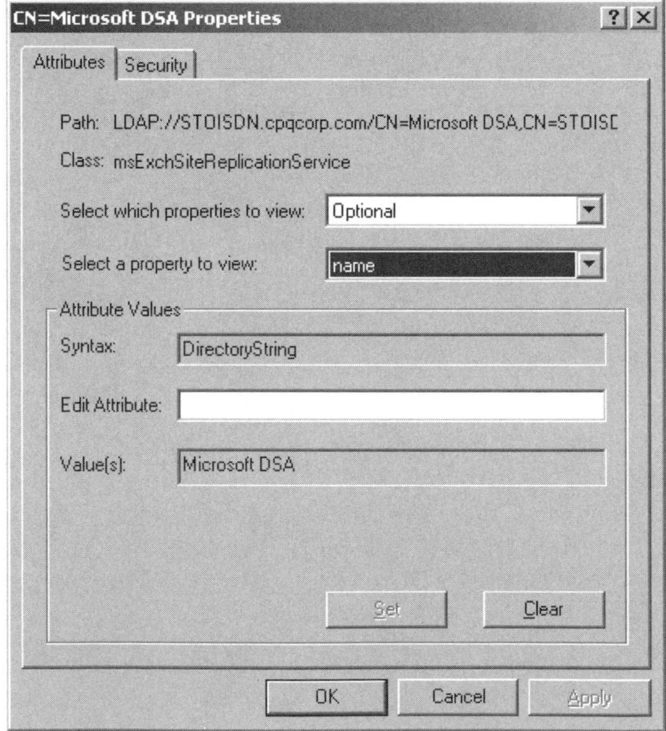

Figure 4-5 *The Default Active Directory Object for the Site Replication Service*

and is a mail-enabled object, it becomes the destination for replication messages from server S9. In fact, you can use any transport to send mail to the SRS object: Figure 4-6 shows the value of the *mail* attribute of the SRS. As you can see, it has a simple mail transfer protocol (SMTP) address, which means that any other Exchange 5.5 Directory Service can send directory information to it over an SMTP connector.

So let's review just where we are. The SRS is connected via a DRC to the bridgehead server S9 and via a ConfigCA to the AD. The ConfigCA is two-way, replicating configuration information for the Exchange 5.5 view of Site A from the SRS to the AD and back-replicating information for the AG A (the Exchange 2003 view of the site) from the AD to the SRS.

4.7 Site Replication Service Management

You'll find little exposed in the Exchange System Manager MMC snap-in to allow you to control the SRS: You can navigate to the *Tools* display, but when you right-click the SRS object, the lack of any real management options is striking. Basically, this service just runs and should cause you no management overhead whatsoever.

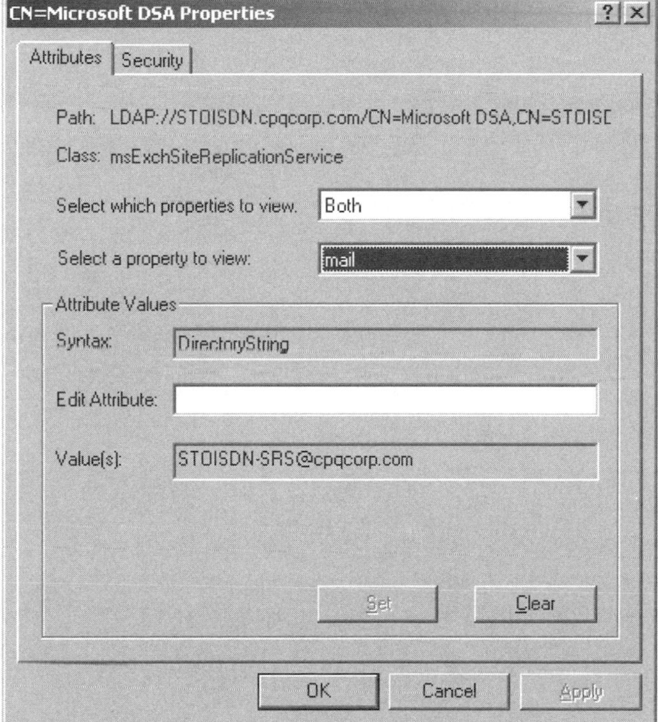

Figure 4-6 *Mail Attribute of the Site Replication Service Object*

But there is some system management effort you should bear in mind. I mentioned earlier that the SRS.EDB database is a direct descendant of the DIR.EDB database that was part of Exchange 5.5. Taking useful backups on an Exchange 5.5 server means backing up the Directory as well as the Information Store databases. In Exchange 2003, the directory is of course the AD, and presumably your day-to-day operational procedures facilitate the backup and restore of the AD. Specifically, on an SRS-enabled Exchange 2003 system, you should be sure to back up the SRS database as well. This is explicitly catered for from the Windows 2000 and Windows 2003 Backup Utility, as shown in Figure 4-7, and you should expect to see similar functionality appearing for your favorite third-party backup product soon.

Depending on the complexity and sophistication of your interoperability environment, you may choose to dedicate Exchange 2003 servers specifically for running the SRS. On such servers, be sure to host the SRS database (SRS.EDB and TEMP.EDB) on a dedicated disk volume as well as separate and distinct disk volumes for SRS database log files. Treat the SRS database the same as you would any other Exchange database volume. You can control the location of the SRS database, log files, and associated files by making changes to the following registry keys:

```
HKEY_LOCAL_MACHINE\System\CurrentControlSet\Services
  \MSExchangeSRS\Parameters
Value name: DSA Database File
Value type: STRING
Value data: <Path to the SRS.EDB file>
```

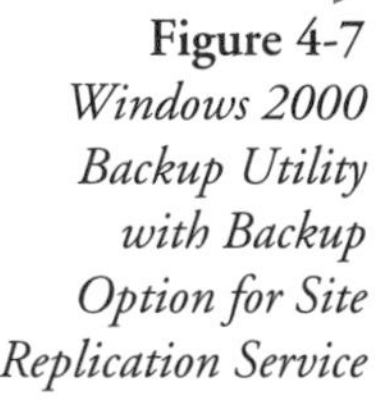

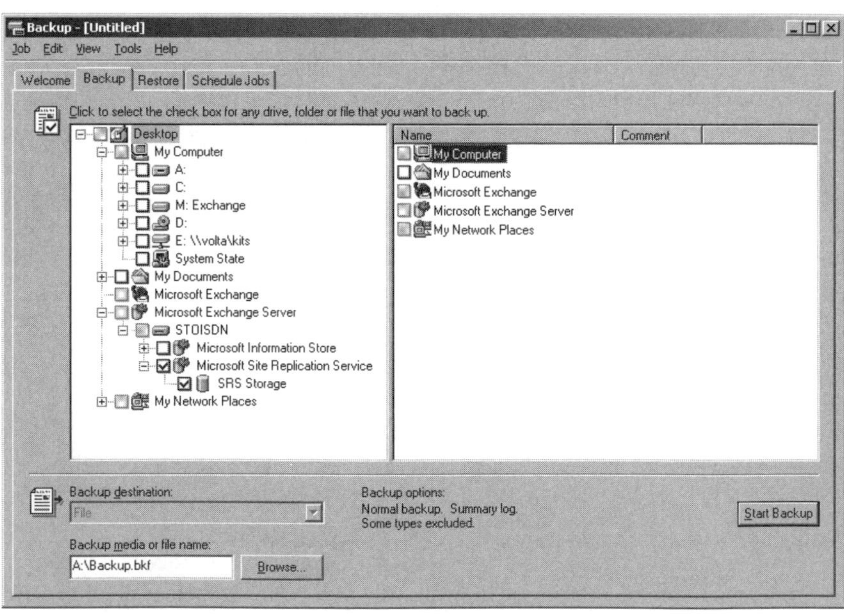

Figure 4-7
Windows 2000 Backup Utility with Backup Option for Site Replication Service

```
HKEY_LOCAL_MACHINE\System\CurrentControlSet\Services
  \MSExchangeSRS\Parameters
Value name: DSA Temporary File
Value type: STRING
Value data: <Path to the TEMP.EDB file>

HKEY_LOCAL_MACHINE\System\CurrentControlSet\Services
  \MSExchangeSRS\Parameters
Value name: DSA Working Directory
Value type: STRING
Value data: <Path to the Working Directory>

HKEY_LOCAL_MACHINE\System\CurrentControlSet\Services
  \MSExchangeSRS\Parameters
Value name: Database Log Files
Value type: STRING
Value data: <Path to the log files area>
```

You must restart the SRS after making any changes to these registry keys.

4.8 Site Replication Service Preference

When a completely new AG is created in an Exchange 2000 mixed-mode organization, an existing SRS from some other AG or site is selected to replicate this new AG to the Exchange 5.5 environment. Similarly, when a new Exchange 5.5 site is added to a mixed-mode Exchange organization, an existing SRS is selected to replicate the new site to the AD.

Before Exchange 2000 Service Pack 2, the decision logic for which SRS was selected was dictated by the alphabetical ordering of these AGs and site names. This process was performed by using an algorithm that compares a hash of the name of the AG and the name of each ConfigCA. The system administrator cannot control which SRS obtains or maintains ownership of the site's configuration naming context.

Each SRS in the organization runs its own separate instance of the SKCC. When the SKCC on one SRS obtains ownership of a configuration naming context, the SRS writes the Distinguished Name of the site or AG's configuration container onto the SRS's ConfigCA. Then, when the SKCC runs on other SRSs, the SKCC reads the site or AG's configuration Distinguished Name from the first SRS's ConfigCA and knows that the configuration naming context has been already claimed.

If the configuration naming context is a pure Exchange 5.5 site, the Distinguished Name of the configuration naming context is added to the *msExchServer2ExportContainers* attribute of the ConfigCA. If the naming context is a pure Exchange 2000 or Exchange 2003 AG, the naming context is added to the *msExchServer1ExportContain-*

ers attribute of the ConfigCA. If the naming context is a mixed AG, then the naming context is added to both the *msExchServer1ExportContainers* and the *msExchServer2ExportContainers* attributes of the ConfigCA because two-way replication is required for mixed AGs.

For example, consider the following mixed Exchange 5.5 and Exchange 2000 AGs:

- Auckland AG
- Brisbane AG
- Nice AG

If you want to add a new Exchange 2003 AG called Melbourne AG to the organization, the Nice AG SRS would be selected to replicate the new AG because Melbourne AG is alphabetically closer to Nice AG than the other values. Obviously this would result in an inefficient topology for replication of configuration information between the parts of the organization and accordingly unnecessary latency and delays.

To resolve this issue, Exchange 2000 Service Pack 2 and continuing into Exchange 2003 includes a *PreferredSRS* attribute that allows you to dictate which SRS is actually used in the selection logic. You can set *PreferredSRS* in the following locations for Exchange 2003, Exchange 2000, and Exchange 5.5:

- For new Exchange 2003 or Exchange 2003 AGs, enter PreferredSRS <SRS-short-Server-Name> in the *Administrative note* field of the AG object in the AD.
- For new Exchange 5.5 sites, type PreferredSRS <SRS-short-Server-Name> in the *Administrative note* field of the configuration object, underneath the site object in the Exchange 5.5 Directory Service.

The field should be populated with the short name (e.g., AUCKSRV01) of the server running Exchange 2003 on which an instance of the SRS database resides. All SRS servers should be running at least Exchange 2000 SP2 or higher before using the *PreferredSRS* attribute because earlier versions of Exchange 2000 do not recognize this parameter. Furthermore, the *PreferredSRS* setting does not rearbitrate existing AGs and sites; the setting only works for new groups or sites that are created after Exchange 2000 Service Pack 2 is applied.

4.9 Summary

Life could go on without the SRS. Although it is a useful component of Exchange 2003, it is neither critical to Exchange 2003's operation or to coexistence with

Exchange 5.5 servers. Admittedly, if the SRS didn't exist, administration of CAs and sequencing of server upgrades from Exchange 5.5 to Exchange 2003 might be just a little more complicated.

The SRS is not supported on a clustered Exchange system, so the first server you install into an Exchange 5.5 site must be a single-node system. For organizations wishing to avail themselves of the server consolidation benefits brought about by Exchange 2003, this is an inconvenience, but it's easily worked around by installing a small system into the site merely to act as a host for the SRS.

In its present form, the SRS supplements the functionality of the Active Directory Connector by always offering a source of Exchange 5.5 directory information. Any migration plans that you're drawing up now to move from Exchange 5.5 to Exchange 2003 will, in all likelihood, involve directory coexistence and ultimately the Active Directory Connector. As you finalize your plans, keep one eye on the SRS and use it as your friend when you define the placement of CAs, thus avoiding the need to modify and rehome them in the future. As Billy Joel says in his song, "Get it right the first time."

5

Public Folder Interoperability and Migration

5.1 Introduction

Even with Exchange 5.5, understanding and controlling Public Folder replication was always more of an art than a science. The landscape is more complicated with the advent of Exchange 2003 (specifically Exchange 2000) because mixed environments need to consider interoperability of Exchange 5.5 and Exchange 2003 Public Folder replication and ultimately the migration of Exchange 5.5 Public Folders to Exchange 2003.

There's no concept of a mixed-mode environment for Exchange 2000 and Exchange 2003. In such an environment, interoperability of Public Folders is simply identical to Public Folder implementation within a native Exchange 2000 organization or a native Exchange 2003 organization. In these cases, migrating Public Folder content from a server in an Exchange 2000 environment to a server in an Exchange 2003 environment is a matter of simply replicating the Public Folder content and rehoming the Public Folder. More or less the same holds true for an Exchange 5.5 environment, with the single added complication of dealing with replication of Public Folder e-mail addresses. The majority of this chapter discusses that particular interoperability requirement.

This chapter explains some of the core aspects of Public Folders in a mixed Exchange 5.5 environment, covering topics that will include Public Folder CAs, Public Folder Hierarchy replication, and permissions interoperability with groups and distribution lists.

5.2 Public Folder Connection Agreements

The Exchange 2003 Active Directory Connector provides a special type of CA for dealing with Public Folders in addition to the Configuration and Recipient CAs we've already discussed. The Public Folder CA replicates mail addresses for Exchange 5.5 Public Folders into the AD so that Exchange 2003 users have the capability to send e-mails directly to legacy Exchange 5.5 Public Folders just as they could do as native Exchange 5.5 users. Furthermore, it is common to find Public Folders added as a recipient to Exchange 5.5 Distribution Lists so that they provide an archive for all messages sent to the Distribution List. A Recipient CA will synchronize such a Distribution List as a UDG into the AD, but the Public Folder's mail address cannot be included in the UDG unless the mail address is specifically synchronized into the AD.

By default, all Public Folders in an Exchange 5.5 organization had mail addresses associated with them, and their directory entries were created in the *Recipients* container for the site unless you modified the *Public folder container* property on the *General* property page of the *Information Store Site Configuration*. Also, the Public Folder directory entries were hidden from the GAL. Figure 5-1 shows the *E-mail Addresses* property page of a Public Folder on my system. As you can see, it looks like any other mail-enabled object in the Exchange 5.5 Directory Service.

Primarily, Public Folder CAs synchronize the mail addresses of Exchange 5.5 Public Folders into the AD and, conversely, the mail addresses of Exchange 2000 and

Figure 5-1
E-mail Addresses Property Page for a Public Folder

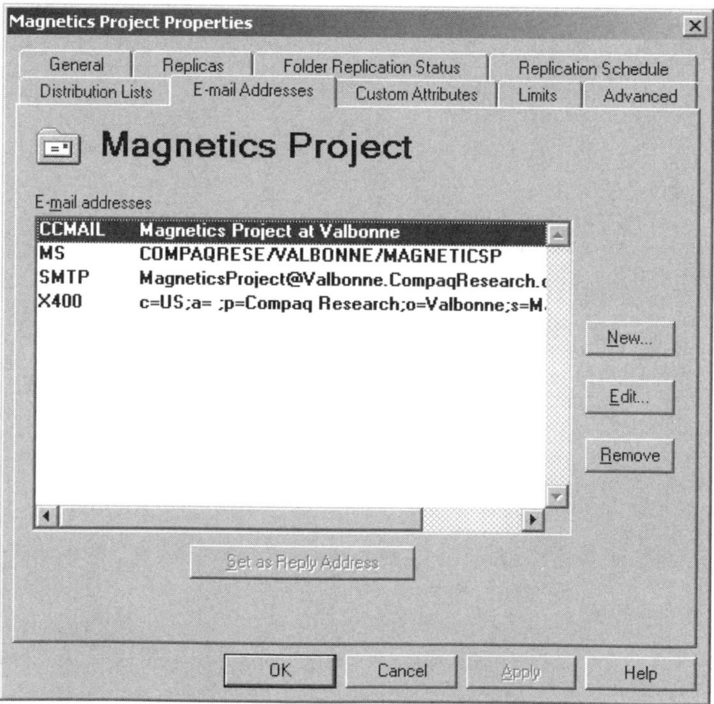

Exchange 2003 Public Folders in the Exchange 5.5 Directory Service. But there are other reasons why it's important to use one two-way Public Folder CA per Exchange 5.5 site.

If you attempt to administer a Public Folder created on Exchange 5.5 from the Exchange 2003 ESM snap-in and you haven't created an entry in the AD for that Public Folder using a Public Folder CA, the ESM console will generate errors. You see these errors because the properties of the Exchange 5.5 Public Folder indicate that it is mail-enabled and the ESM console attempts to look up the AD to retrieve the address properties. The properties cannot be retrieved if the object hasn't been synchronized to the AD and thus doesn't exist.

Similarly, the Exchange 5.5 Administrator program expects that any Public Folders it accesses have mail address properties, because this is the default behavior with Exchange 5.5 Public Folders. Accordingly, if you haven't implemented a Public Folder CA to synchronize mail addresses from an Exchange 2003 Public Folder into the Exchange 5.5 Directory Service, you cannot administer such an Exchange 2003 Public Folder with the Exchange 5.5 Administrator program.

Because Exchange 5.5 always expects to have e-mail addresses associated with Public Folders, running a DS/IS consistency checker instance on Exchange 5.5 can cause serious problems. The Exchange 5.5 public store will have knowledge of Exchange 2003 Public Folders (because the Public Folder hierarchy is replicated by default), but if it doesn't find an associated Exchange 5.5 Directory Service entry for that Public Folder, it will generate one. Effectively, this results in two separate e-mail addresses for the same Public Folder. Introducing a Public Folder CA in the future can then result in two separate directory entries (in both the Exchange 5.5 Directory Service and the AD), and this ultimately means that the Public Folder cannot receive mail.

5.3 Configuring Public Folder Connection Agreements

By using a specific CA for Public Folder mail addresses, Microsoft has been able to predefine much of the configuration that many of us typically find challenging with Recipient CAs. For example, there's no option to make Public Folder CAs one-way: they are two-way by default, and you can't change this setting. Other predefined options that you can't change include the settings on the *From Exchange* and the *From Windows* property pages: you can't specify the source or destination containers or Organizational Units on either page—they're grayed out—and the only objects you can synchronize are Public Folders, as shown in Figure 5-2, where the *From Exchange* properties are defined.

Figure 5-2
From Exchange Property Page on a Public Folder Connection Agreement

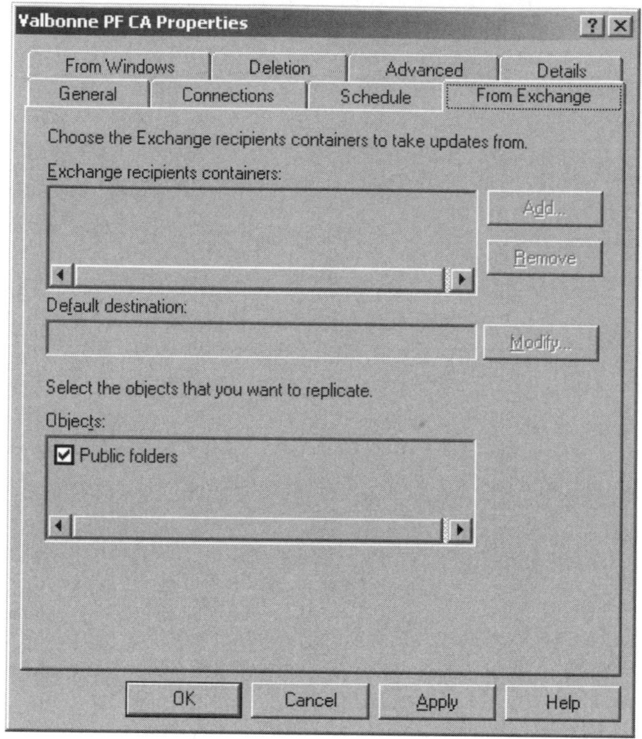

From Exchange 5.5 to Exchange 2003, you don't need to define the source container for Public Folder directory entries because the Active Directory Connector searches for Public Folder Directory Service objects in all containers down from the site level, although typically they will have been created in the *Recipients* container. Similarly, you don't need to define a target location for where the synchronized objects will be placed because these are by default created in the *Microsoft Exchange System Objects* container in the AD.

In the opposite direction, the Active Directory Connector searches only for Exchange 2003 Public Folder AD objects in the *Microsoft Exchange System Objects* container because all Public Folder directory objects are located here. The Active Directory Connector creates directory objects in the Exchange 5.5 Directory Service container specified by the *legacyExchangeDN* attribute of the Exchange 2003 Public Folder. The *legacyExchangeDN* attribute is set on an Exchange 2000 Public Folder by the Store when the Public Folder is created. When the Store process starts up, it queries the AD to determine the value of the attribute *msExchPfCreation* on the Administrative Group object in which it resides. This attribute will only be set if you have modified the location in which Exchange 5.5 Public Folder directory objects are created, as described previously, and is replicated from Exchange 5.5 via the

Configuration CA for the site. If the attribute is set, the Store uses this value for the *legacyExchangeDN* of the Public Folder; if it is not set, the *legacyExchangeDN* defaults to *Recipients*.

The *Microsoft Exchange System Objects* container is not by default part of the AD. This container only gets created in the AD when you run the Exchange 2003 Setup program with the /DomainPrep option. By implication, you'll also have had to run Exchange 2003 Setup with the /ForestPrep option to allow /DomainPrep to proceed.

Having much of the configuration predefined does simplify the process of setting up Public Folder CAs, of which you'll need one associated with each Exchange 5.5 site, but on the other hand, it also reduces flexibility. One organization I know of was planning to use a transition domain to temporarily house Active Directory Connector–created objects because they were rolling out Exchange 2000 before completing their Windows 2000 domain rollout and they needed a consistent GAL. The CAs create objects in the transition domain if the appropriate Windows 2000 domain isn't yet available. When the Windows 2000 domain is finally deployed, they use the *MoveTree* utility to relocate the Active Directory Connector–created objects from the transition domain to their rightful home. This approach works well for objects created using Recipient CAs, but unfortunately, *MoveTree* won't move the Public Folder directory objects created by a Public Folder CA. This means that they're stuck with the transition domain forever because they can neither move nor delete the Public Folder directory objects from the *Microsoft Exchange System Objects* container. Additionally, Public Folder CAs create AD objects in a flat manner in the *Microsoft Exchange System Objects* container: There's no way to group Public Folder directory objects into separate Organizational Units on a site-by-site basis.

5.4 Public Folder Permissions

Permissions on Public Folders are handled very differently between Exchange 5.5 and Exchange 2003. In Exchange 5.5, permissions on Public Folders are managed using ACLs on a folder. An ACL defines the access rights (e.g., read, create, edit, delete) that a particular user has on a Public Folder. In Exchange 5.5, the ACL isn't stored directly as a property of the Public Folder; instead each Public Folder has an *ACLID* property that points to a single entry in an *ACLID Table*. Each entry in the *ACLID Table* identifies the different access rights for the ACL, including the Public Folder owner, and in turn points to entries in an *ACL Members Table* that are effectively the Distinguished Names of Exchange 5.5 users. This is shown in Figure 5-3. When Public Folder replication takes place between Exchange 5.5 servers, the ACL information is packaged up into a property named *ptagACLData*, and the receiving Exchange 5.5 server will

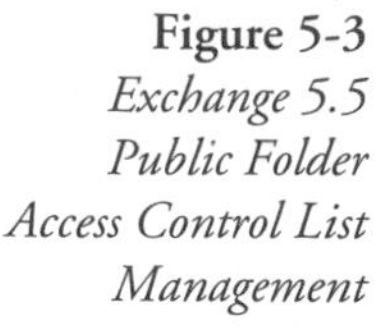

Figure 5-3
Exchange 5.5 Public Folder Access Control List Management

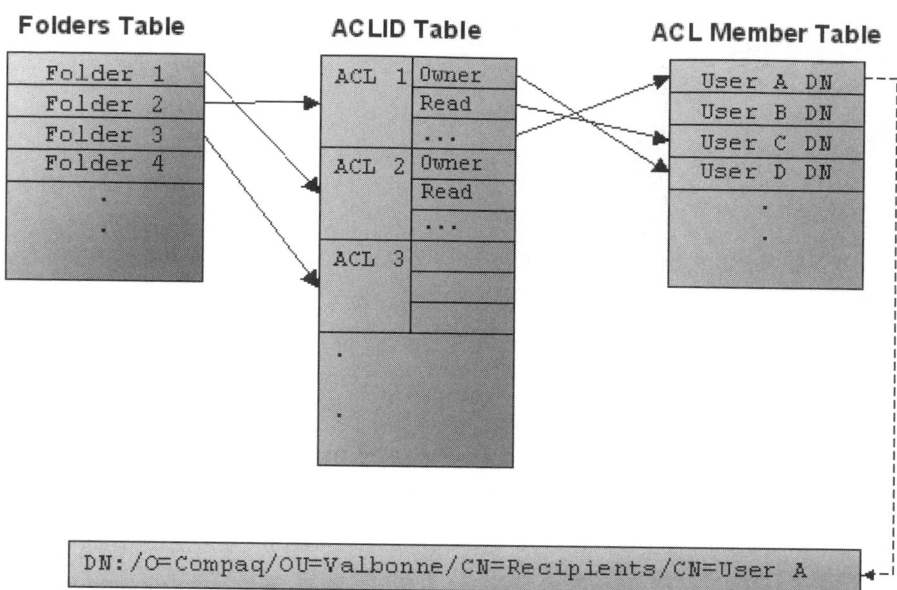

unpack the *ptagACLData* property and use the information to update its own ACL tables.

In Exchange 2003, permissions management is different. The Public Folder store in Exchange 2000 directly holds the ACL as a property of the Public Folder. The property, named *ptagNTSD*, contains the Windows 2000 or Windows 2003 SIDs of the users or groups that are included in the ACLs.

5.5 Exchange 5.5 and Exchange 2003 Public Folder Replication

Exchange 5.5 has the concept of a single Public Folder hierarchy or Public Folder Tree, whereas Exchange 2000 and Exchange 2003 offer the ability to use multiple Public Folder hierarchies. In Exchange 2003, we use the term MAPI Public Folder Tree—also known as a Top-Level Hierarchy (TLH)—to refer to that Public Folder Tree that is common to both Exchange 5.5 and Exchange 2003. In Exchange 2003, the MAPI Public Folder Tree is accessible from MAPI clients such as Outlook and Internet Message Access Protocol (IMAP) clients such as Outlook Express. Other Public Folder Trees, usually referred to as Application Public Folder Trees, are accessible only via HTTP-DAV clients such as Outlook Web Access. In Exchange 5.5, only the MAPI Public Folder Tree is available, and when we discuss Public Folder replication between Exchange 5.5 and Exchange 2003, this refers to replication of Public Folders in the MAPI Public Folder Tree. Application Public Folder Trees cannot be replicated to Exchange 5.5 because it has no concept of multiple Public Folder Trees. However, because Public Folder replication is simply e-mail based, where one Public Folder store e-mails another, it is possible to "backbone" Application Public Folder Tree traffic over Exchange 5.5 servers. In such circumstances an Exchange 5.5 Message Transfer Agent (MTA) will forward Public Folder replication updates from one Exchange 2003 Public Folder store ultimately to another.

All Public Folder stores contain a special Public Folder that holds the hierarchy information for the Public Folder Tree associated with that store. In Exchange 5.5, the Public Folder hierarchy was replicated by default (even if you disabled Public Folder replication) to all public stores in the organization. The same is true for a Public Folder Tree in Exchange 2003. Similarly, when you install an Exchange 2003 server into an Exchange 5.5 site, the Configuration CA identifies the Exchange 2003 Public Folder store associated with the MAPI Public Folder Tree to the existing Exchange 5.5 servers, and the Exchange 5.5 Public Folder hierarchy is replicated to the Exchange 2003 server.

Replicating Public Folders from Exchange 5.5 to Exchange 2003 is really not more complicated than replicating Public Folders from one Exchange 5.5 public store to another. You add the appropriate Exchange 2003 Public Folder store to the list of replicas for the Exchange 5.5 Public Folder, and the replication process takes care of replicating the Public Folder content as normal. In the opposite direction, you use the same technique, adding the Exchange 5.5 Public Folder store to the list of replicas for the Exchange 2003 Public Folder. This takes care of most Public Folder replication between Exchange 5.5 and Exchange 2003, with the exception of system Public Folders. Later in this chapter I'll discuss a utility introduced with Exchange 2003 that simplifies the process of migrating system Public Folder content from Exchange 5.5 to Exchange 2003.

The process used to replicate the Public Folder hierarchy is really no different from replicating the content of any other Public Folder, although with hierarchy replication, the content being replicated "describes" the hierarchy of the Public Folder Tree. Public Folder replication takes place by content being bundled up into discrete e-mail messages; the e-mail messages are sent to the Public Folder store, which holds the replica; and the messages are then unbundled and the content is applied to the Public Folder store. It's important to understand that you don't need to have a Public Folder CA in place for this replication to take place. A Public Folder CA creates directory entries with mail addresses for Public Folders, while Public Folder replication takes place by one Public Folder store e-mailing another. Creating a new Public Folder store in Exchange 2003 automatically associates a mail address with it, and this address is used in the replication process.

5.6 Permission Handling during Mixed-Version Replication

We've seen that the replication of Public Folder content between Exchange 5.5 and Exchange 2003 is relatively straightforward. However, mixed-version Public Folder replication becomes more interesting when ACLs are present on Public Folders.

In an Exchange 5.5 Public Folder ACL, the Distinguished Name is used to identify a user with permissions, whereas in an Exchange 2003 Public Folder ACL, the SID of a Windows 2000 or Windows 2003 object is used. Therefore, when an Exchange 5.5 Public Folder is replicated to an Exchange 2003 Public Folder Store, the ACL data must be converted. Exchange 5.5 sends ACL information for the Public Folder in the *ptagACLData* property when it sends an outbound replication message. When an Exchange 2003 Public Folder Store is to host a replica of an Exchange 5.5 Public Folder, it receives this ACL information but must promote the information into its own ACL storage property, *ptagNTSD*. The receiving Exchange 2000 Public Folder Store extracts the *ptagACLData* information into a temporary table, and for every Distinguished Name that is specified in the Exchange 5.5 version of the ACL, the Exchange 2003 Store looks up the AD to convert the Distinguished Name to an SID. This conversion process is only possible if a Recipient CA has already synchronized Exchange 5.5 mailbox information into the AD, and this part is critical. As a Recipient CA creates an object in the AD for an Exchange 5.5 mailbox, it writes the Distinguished Name of the Exchange 5.5 mailbox into the *legacyExchangeDN* attribute of the newly created Windows 2000 or Windows 2003 object. The Exchange 2003 Public Folder Store can thus build the new ACL by searching the AD for objects with a *legacyExchangeDN* that matches the *Distinguished Name* specified in the Exchange 5.5–style ACL and using the SID of the matching object. Once all of the Distinguished Names have been resolved to SIDs, the temporary tables are removed and the native Exchange 2003 *ptagNTSD* property is associated with the Public Folder. This process is shown in Figure 5-4.

If for any reason some of the Distinguished Names present in the Exchange 5.5 ACL cannot be found in the AD when the Exchange 2003 Public Store attempts to process the ACL, then several issues may occur, incurring differing levels of accessibility of the Exchange 2003 replica of the Public Folder. This is the case of so-called zombie users and is described as follows.

If the Recipient CA has been configured to create disabled user objects in the AD rather than enabled user objects, then the SID of the disabled user object is of little use with respect to enforcing permissions because no user will be logged into it. In this case, the disabled object is only present to provide a complete GAL. As the Active Directory Connector creates a disabled user object in the AD for an Exchange 5.5

Figure 5-4
Steps to Convert Exchange 5.5 Public Folder Access Control Lists to Exchange 2003 Access Control Lists

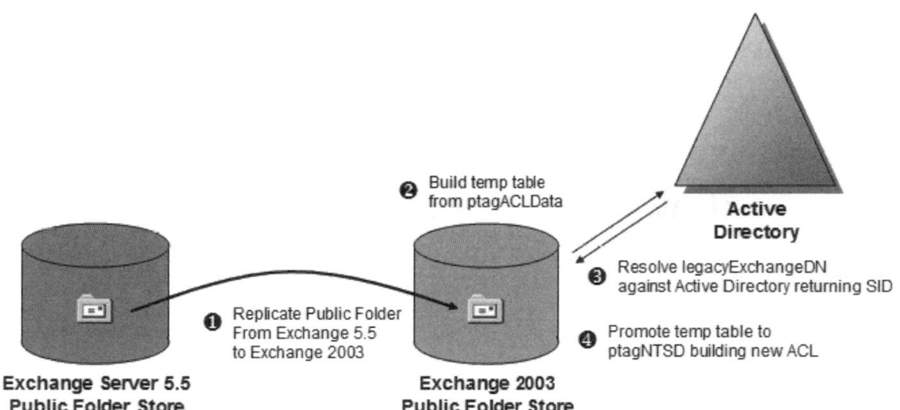

mailbox with a Windows NT4 account, the *msExchMasterAccountSID* attribute of the AD object is populated with the SID of the Windows NT4 account associated with the Exchange 5.5 mailbox. If a trust relationship exists between the Windows 2000 or Windows 2003 domain that holds the disabled user object and the Windows NT4 domain that holds the *Associated-Nt-Account*, then the SID of this Windows NT4 account will be used in the *ptagNTSD* property. The Windows NT4 account is the so-called *associated external account*.

If the AD contains disabled user objects with associated external accounts to represent the Exchange 5.5 mailboxes, then the trust relationship must exist between the domains for the Distinguished Name to SID conversion to take place. If no trust is in place or there are other problems accessing the associated external account, then the *ptagNTSD* property is not built and the Public Folder replica will be unavailable to Exchange 2000 users in the same manner as zombie users. You can draw an immediate conclusion from this behavior: careful implementation of Recipient CAs is absolutely critical for Exchange 5.5/Exchange 2000/Exchange 2003 Public Folder interoperability.

When replication in the reverse direction—from Exchange 2000/2003 to Exchange 5.5—takes place, the outgoing replication message from the Exchange 2000/2003 Public Folder Store will include the *ptagACLData* property so that the Exchange 5.5 server can correctly interpret any ACL information. In addition to providing the properties that the Exchange 5.5 Public Folder Store can understand, the outgoing replication message will also include the *ptagNTSD* property that Exchange 2000/2003 uses to replicate Public Folder ACL information natively. But because Exchange 5.5 servers can't understand this property, it is simply ignored by the Exchange 5.5 Public Folder Store. However, the property will be present on the Exchange 5.5 Public Folder replica. If any modifications are made to the Public Folder replica on the Exchange 5.5 Public Folder Store, the outgoing replication messages will include this property. Because Exchange 5.5 cannot enforce any security on this property, any Exchange 2000/2003 Public Folder Stores that receive replication messages from it will ignore the property.

5.7 Dealing with Zombie Users

Zombie users are user accounts that are not represented in the AD. Zombie users can affect the performance of an Exchange server by extending the ACL resolution process. Zombie users can be created in several ways, some of which stem from Public Folder interoperability. Zombie users may be created if the Exchange 2000 Server or Exchange Server 2003 replica of a Public Folder is not updated after a mailbox is deleted on the Exchange Server 5.5 server. If the user who is associated with that mailbox remains on the replicated ACL of the Public Folder, the user is now a zombie and cannot be resolved. Each time the Public Folder is used, Exchange tries to resolve the accounts that are listed on the ACL. This process causes slowdowns when zombie users are listed because the zombie user cannot be upgraded.

If the ACL is present on a heavily used Public Folder and there are ACL resolution issues, Exchange process threads may start to queue, waiting to use the resource that has been locked by the resolution process. After the threads gain access, they also try the same ACL upgrade that has already failed. This may cause the RPC thread pool to become used up, preventing any more clients from connecting to the Information Store. During the ACL resolution process, the immediate child folders of the requested Public Folder also have their ACLs resolved. Zombie users who reside on the ACLs of these child folders create the same resolution failure.

5.7.1 Zombie user processing with Exchange 2000

Different versions of Exchange 2000 through the various service packs up to Exchange 2003 handle the problem of zombie users in different ways. Exchange 2000 before Service Pack 1 dealt most severely with zombie users, but subsequent versions of Exchange have dealt more sensibly with the problem. For the purposes of completeness and clarity, I'll describe the various handling methods for zombie users that emerged over time.

Before Exchange 2000 Service Pack 1, if the AD lookup for any one of the Distinguished Names specified in the *ptagACLData* can't be resolved, then the entire list of users associated with the ACL does not get promoted into the *ptagNTSD* property. Effectively, the ACL is not applied to the replicated Public Folder, and no Exchange 2003 users have access rights to the Public Folder. Anonymous access to the Public Folder is also prevented. Access is blocked for all Exchange 2000 users apart from the

Public Folder owners, even if just one Distinguished Name can't be resolved, in case that single user has been explicitly denied access to the Public Folder but is a member of a group that has read access. Under such circumstances, the temporary files are retained and the Public Folder Store attempts to complete the promotion of *ptag--ACLData* permissions to the *ptagNTSD* property every time a client accesses the folder replica or when replication is attempted.

5.7.2 Zombie user processing with Exchange 2000 Service Pack 1

After Exchange 2000 Service Pack 1 is installed, the approach is more tolerant. If the user account is missing from the AD when the hierarchy replicates to an Exchange 2000 server, the Exchange 2000 server may no longer fail the ACL conversion and remove everyone except the owner, depending on whether the folder has had its ACL successfully upgraded in the past. If the Public Folder has never had its ACL completely and successfully upgraded previously, the behavior is the same as it is with a pre–Service Pack 1 version of Exchange 2000. That is, all users are removed whether they are zombie users or not, and no users, with the exception of the Public Folder owner, will be able to access the Public Folder. On the other hand, if the Public Folder has had its ACL completely and successfully upgraded before, any new zombie users on the Public Folder's ACL will not cause all users except the owners to be removed from the ACL. The zombie users only are ignored. The Store process will later try to add the zombie user to the ACL when the zombie user can later be identified in the AD.

5.7.3 Zombie user processing with Exchange 2000 Service Pack 3 and Exchange 2003

If Exchange 2000 Service Pack 3 has been installed along with the post–Service Pack 3 hotfix roll-up, or Exchange 2003 is in use, then zombie user processing can be somewhat more granular than that with Service Pack 1. With this configuration, the Exchange 2000 Public Store will skip zombie users and simply enforce permissions on Public Folders for those users and groups that are explicitly specified in the ACL and can be found in the AD. This behavior occurs when either of the following two conditions are in force. First, if the Exchange organization is in native mode, then any zombie users are skipped. This can be safely executed because there are no Exchange 5.5 servers in the organization and no Active Directory Connector, so replication problems caused by latency or other factors cannot be responsible for incomplete Exchange 5.5 Directory Service to AD replication. Second, all zombie users will be skipped if the Exchange organization is in mixed mode and the *Ignore zombie users* registry key is set, as discussed following.

You should use the *Ignore zombie users* registry key only when you are confident that the zombie users specified in the ACL are not the result of replication issues with the Active Directory Connector, such as latency. In such cases, you should let the normal behavior take effect and wait for subsequent Active Directory Connector replication to take place when the Exchange 2000 Public Store will attempt to reevaluate the ACL on subsequent access. After you set the registry key to ignore zombie users, every zombie user account that Exchange 2000 encounters is removed from the ACL. If the user is valid but is not in the AD at the time that the ACL was upgraded, the user is removed and you have to manually add the user to each ACL later. Simply retaining the zombie users in the ACL even in mixed mode is undesirable because even though access to the required Public Folder is available, the ACL can be continually reevaluated. In order to permanently avoid this situation, you might set the *Ignore zombie users* registry key. The registry key details are as follows:

```
HKEY_LOCAL_MACHINE\System\CurrentControlSet\Services
  \MSExchangeIS\ParametersSystem
Value name: Ignore zombie users
Value type: DWORD
Value data: <1 to ignore, 0 for normal behavior>
```

5.8 Exchange 5.5 Distribution Lists and Access Control Lists

Although it was possible to individually permission Exchange 5.5 mailboxes against Public Folders, it was much more common to control access to Public Folders using Distribution Lists because this made the administrative process easier. Adding users to a Distribution List with access permissions is much simpler than individually managing hundreds or thousands of users in an ACL.

With Windows 2000 and Windows 2003, the concept of the Exchange 5.5 Distribution List is superseded with the AD concept of a UDG, and both the Active Directory Connector and the Exchange 2000/Exchange 2003 upgrade process will in general convert Exchange 5.5 Distribution Lists into UDGs. Although a UDG offers the same functionality as a Distribution List in terms of mail address expansion, a UDG is not a security principal and therefore cannot be used in an ACL. To secure access to Public Folders using groups, Exchange 2000 and Exchange 2003 use a USG. A USG offers the same functionality as a UDG but additionally can be used in ACLs.

However, USGs can only exist in native-mode Windows 2000 or Windows 2003 domains. If you use Distribution Lists to protect Public Folders in Exchange 5.5 and wish to have a coexisting Exchange 5.5 and Exchange 2003 environment, you must ensure that any Windows 2000 or Windows 2003 domains that will hold USGs are in native mode. In fact, when you configure Recipient CAs to synchronize Distribution Lists, the Active Directory Connector will warn you if the target Windows 2000 or

Windows 2003 domain is not in native mode. This is a good reason to restructure Windows NT4 domains with new Windows 2000 or Windows 2003 domains rather than upgrade, although the complexity of your Windows NT4 environment will ultimately dictate the approach that you take.

The Exchange 2003 store process will convert UDGs (including nested UDGs) that the Active Directory Connector has created to become USGs under the following circumstances:

- When an Exchange 5.5 Public Folder is replicated to an Exchange 2003 server and a UDG is to be used in its ACL
- During an upgrade of an Exchange 5.5 Public Folder store where a UDG would be used in its ACL
- When a UDG is added to an ACL on a Public Folder

If the UDG to USG conversion process fails for any reason (e.g., the UDG is in a mixed-mode domain or the membership of a UDG hasn't been replicated), the Store process will retry the conversion the next time the folder is accessed by a client or if Public Folder replication occurs again from the Exchange 5.5 server with a modification to the ACL.

There are some circumstances where the Store will not attempt to convert a UDG in an ACL to a USG such as the following:

- If the UDG was previously converted to a USG but was then manually converted back to a UDG, a subsequent client access will not result in a conversion. If, however, the permission associated with the UDG is changed, the conversion will be retried.
- Nested UDGs will not be converted if their parent group is already a USG. Thus if a system manager manually converts a parent UDG to a USG but fails to convert the members, the store will not perform any further conversion. Furthermore, if a UDG is added as a member to a USG, the store will ignore this during the conversion process.
- If the *msExchDisableUDGConversion* attribute (on the Active Directory Organization object) is set to 2

5.9 Public Folder Deployment Guidelines

Public Folder implementation rules in Exchange 2003 are similar to those in Exchange 2000. Similarly, the process of moving Public Folders from one server to another within the same organization remains straightforward. In an organization that hosts multiple versions of Exchange (e.g., Exchange 5.5 and Exchange 2003), moving or rehoming a Public Folder from an Exchange 5.5 server to an Exchange 2003 server amounts to a Public Folder migration exercise. For user Public Folders (i.e., those that contain users' documents), the migration process is straightforward, but for system Public Folders (i.e., those that contain information relating to Offline Address Books, Schedule+ Free Busy information), a very slightly different process is required.

The remainder of this chapter describes some considerations for implementing your Public Folder infrastructure and the process that is normally employed to move or migrate user Public Folders, as well as other techniques that can be used for moving system Public Folders. Throughout the remainder of this chapter, just Exchange 2003 is frequently referred to as the destination server type, but the processes described are equally applicable to Exchange 2000 servers except where otherwise noted. Furthermore, the migration techniques described here relate only to intraorganizational migrations.

5.10 Planning and Understanding Public Folder Topologies

The degree to which Public Folders are used in your organization should determine where and how many Public Folder replicas you have. If your organization is a heavy consumer of Public Folders, then you should consider having Public Folder content near to those users. You may do so either by replicating Public Folders to multiple servers distributed across the network or ensuring that you have high-bandwidth, low-latency connections to a small number of core Public Folder servers and those clients that access them.

Plan to have at least one server hosting Public Folder content per Routing Group (RG) for frequently accessed Public Folders. For business critical Public Folder data you may elect to have multiple replicas of the content within a RG. Less frequently accessed content (reporting tools, such as those available for third-party vendors, should help you determine this) can be maintained on a single or small number of servers, not necessarily distributed across your network.

When an Outlook client requests some specific Public Folder content, the Information Store service on the client's home server determines where the requested Public Folder content is located. If the content is located on the same server or on another server in the same RG, then the client is directed to the Public Folder database on that server. If the content is not located on a server in the same RG, then a Public Folder referral must take place, where the client is directed to a remote server in some other RG that hosts the requested content. If only one such remote server exists in the organization, then the user is directed to that remote server. If multiple remote servers host the required content, then the Information Store service calculates the lowest-cost transitive route to the remote server using the costs associated with the Routing Group Connectors, SMTP Connectors, or X.400 Connectors that link the RGs. For example, as shown in Figure 5-5, if the client requests Public Folder content stored on Server C and Server D, Server C will be selected because of the lower cost to reach it.

If the "Do not allow public folder referrals" checkbox is checked on a connector, then that path to reach Public Folder content is ignored. If multiple remote servers have the same cost, then the client randomly selects one. If no route can be determined, then the client cannot access the Public Folder content.

The lowest-cost route calculated by the Information Store service is cached (within the Information Store process) on the user's home server for 60 minutes (this is not changeable, but the cache can be flushed by restarting the Information Store service), so that any subsequent request for access to that content can be efficiently serviced. Additionally, after the client has made its first contact with the required Public Folder server, it will persistently use that same Public Folder server for the 60 minutes' lifetime of the cache entry. This ensures a consistent view of Public Folder information.

5.11 Reintroducing Public Folder Affinity

With Exchange 5.5, there was no such lowest-cost transitive routing mechanism to determine where a client should be directed for specific Public Folder content. Instead,

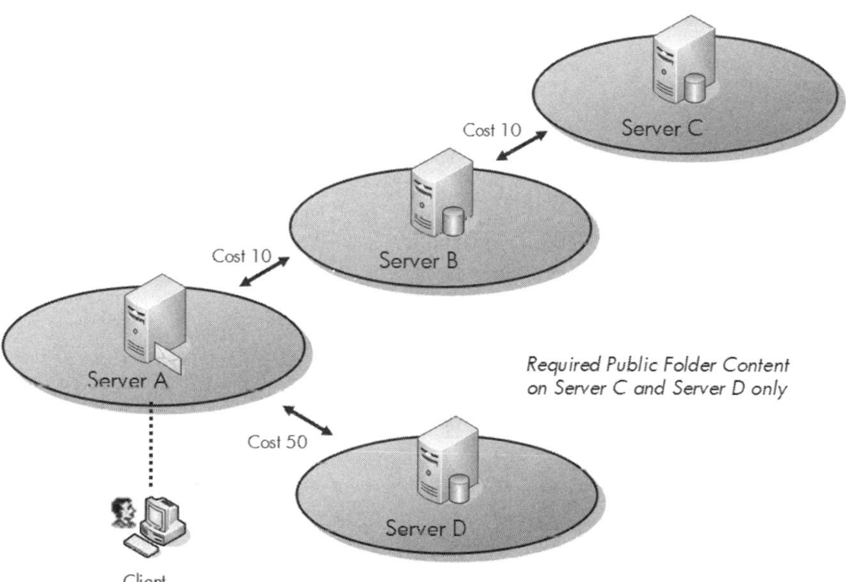

Figure 5-5 *Public Folder Referral Costs and Content Referral*

you explicitly defined a server for a particular Public Folder to which referrals would be directed. This Public Folder affinity capability was not present in Exchange 2000 but was re-introduced with Exchange 2003 to give administrators more flexibility for dealing with Public Folder referrals rather than relying on routing costs.

You can set Public Folder affinity costs on a server-by-server basis. For example, assume that I host specific Public Folder content on server OSBEX02 but not on my home mailbox server of OSBEX01. I can set the Public Folder Referrals property of the OSBEX01 server so that all Public Folder referrals are directed to OSBEX02. This is shown in Figure 5-6.

Little granularity can be implemented using this affinity mechanism. For instance, you cannot select specific affinity servers for specific Public Folders. Nor can you implement a fallback to using Public Folder referrals based on routing costs: It's a one or the other approach. However, you can define multiple affinity servers and associate a cost with each one, so that the lowest-cost affinity server is used for client referrals if it is available. If a specific affinity server is not reachable, then the next highest-cost one is selected.

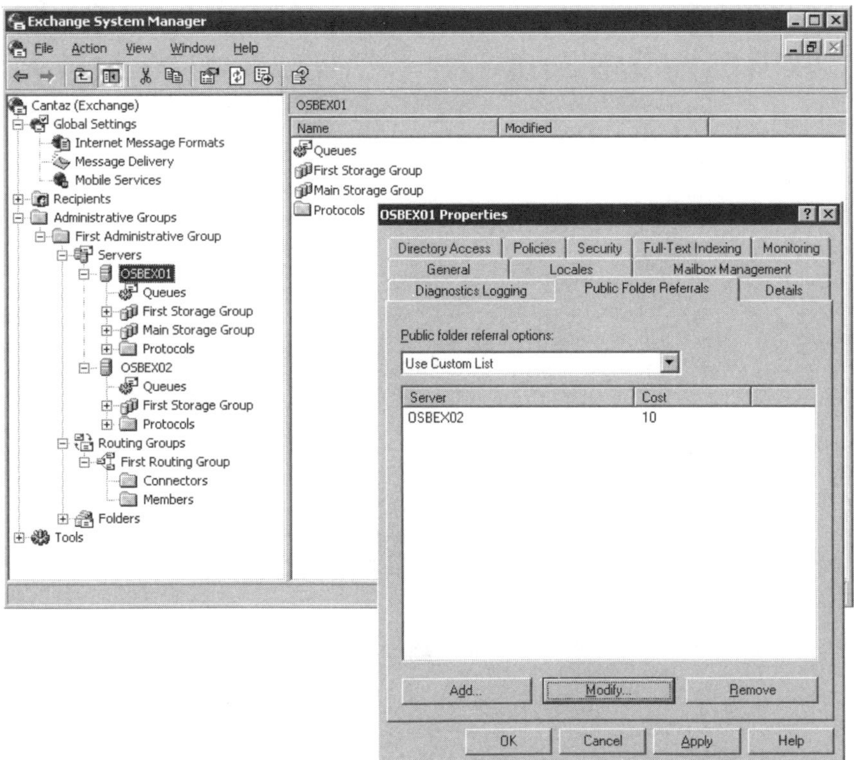

Figure 5-6 *Setting Public Folder Affinity Characteristics with Exchange 2003*

Entering server information into the Public Folder Referrals property tab results in the *msExchFolderAffinityCustom* attribute being set to 1, and the values you enter for the affinity servers are held in the *msExchFolderAffinityList* multivalued attribute. You can review these settings using ADSI Edit or LDP; both are to be found as properties of the following object in the AD:

```
CN=Configuration Container/CN=Services/CN=Microsoft Exchange
  /CN=<OrgName>/CN=Administrative Groups
  /CN=<SiteName>/CN=Servers/CN<ServerName>
```

Where

```
<OrgName> is the name of your Exchange Organization,
<SiteName> is the name of your Exchange Site, and
<ServerName> is the name of your Exchange server.
```

From a deployment perspective, it's obviously a small next step to use some simple programming to populate these values programmatically using a technique such as CDOEXM.

5.12 Getting Ready to Migrate Public Folders

If you are moving Public Folders from one Exchange 2003 server to another Exchange 2003 server in a non-migration scenario, then you need do little in terms of preparation beyond what is already in place in the environment. However, you must ensure that the new destination Exchange 2003 server has suitable disk capacity for the Public Folder database and any disk capacity that will be used by the transaction logs as the contents of the source Public Folders are moved. As a rule, aim to have at least 30% free space on the volumes that host both the Public Folder database and the volumes that host the transaction logs. Be aware that if you have a large amount of Public Folder content to move, you may see performance impacted on the source and destination servers as well as the intervening network links. With this in mind, you may wish to perform Public Folder moves during nonworking office hours. (Be watchful of the volume of log files generated with such moves.)

In a migration scenario where you are migrating Public Folders from an Exchange 5.5 server to Exchange 2003 server, you should have several prerequisites in place before starting to move Public Folders. First, you should ensure that the Windows 2000/2003 domain that holds any USGs to be associated with Public Folders to be held on the Exchange 2003 server is in native mode, as described earlier. Without a native-mode domain, USGs cannot be implemented to correctly enforce permissions on Public Folders. Second, check that all Recipient CAs are correctly in place from the Exchange 5.5 Directory Service to the AD and that all objects are replicating successfully. You can use the ExDeploy tools with Exchange 2003 to validate successful replication. Exchange 2003 is more forgiving of incomplete Active Directory Connector recipient replication than early versions of Exchange 2000, as described previously.

If you are migrating from Exchange 5.5, it is advisable to run the DS/IS Consistency Checker against those Exchange 5.5 Public Folders before migration. This is available from the *Consistency Adjuster* button on the *Advanced* tab when viewing the properties of an Exchange 5.5 server hosting Public Folders with the Exchange 5.5 Administrator program. This ensures that any ACLs on the Public Folders are maintained when Public Folder contents are replicated to the new Exchange 2003 server because users named on ACLs are consistent with actual valid users.

Migrating Public Folder content from an Exchange 5.5 or Exchange 2000 source server to a destination server running Exchange 2003 (or Exchange 2000) by simply replicating content and then removing the source server works well for most Public Folder data.

5.13 Moving User and System Public Folder Content

Rehoming user Public Folders to an Exchange 2003 system is straightforward, even if the Public Folders you wish to move exist on a legacy Exchange 5.5 server. Follow these steps:

1. From ESM, select your Exchange organization, then *Administrative Groups*, then your Administrative Group name, then *Folders,* and then *Public Folders*.
2. Select the desired Public Folder and then right-click and choose *Properties*.
3. Click on the *Replication* tab, select *Add,* and then add the additional servers from your organization on which you want the Public Folder replica to appear.
4. Click on the *Apply* button.
5. Right-click on the desired Public Folder again, select *All Tasks* and then *Propagate Settings*, select the *Replicas* checkbox, and then click *OK*.

Following this procedure, any required user Public Folders will be replicated to the destination servers. Once the Public Folder content has been fully replicated, you can remove the Public Folder from the original server if you wish. An example of this is shown in Figure 5-7.

You may also have to rehome several system Public Folders, typically from the first Exchange 5.5 server installed in the site. Again, you can perform this from the Exchange 2003 ESM utility:

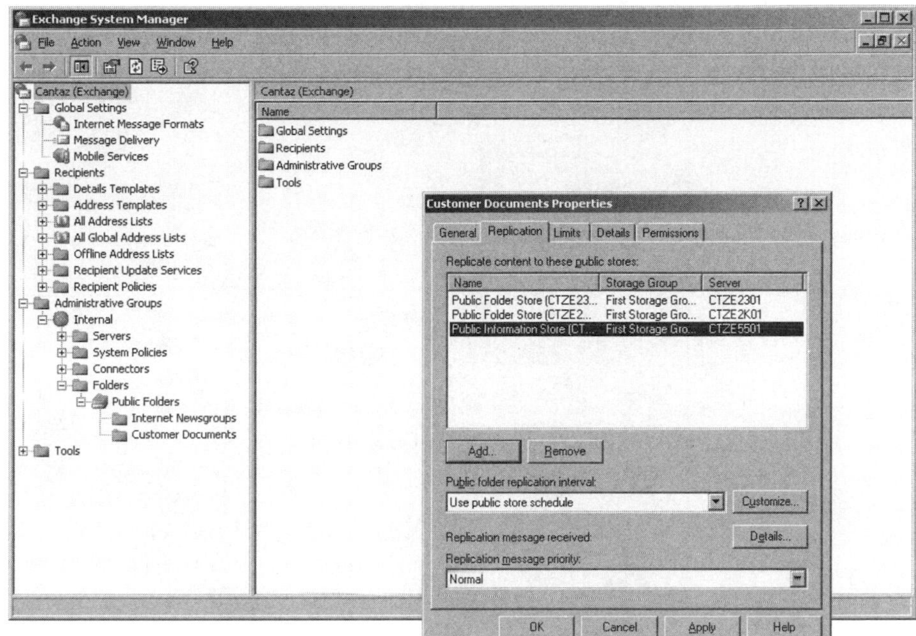

Figure 5-7
Creating User Public Folder Replicas

1. From ESM, select your Exchange organization, then *Administrative Groups*, then your AG name, then *Folders*, and then *Public Folders*.
2. Right-click *Public Folders* and then select *View System Folders*.
3. For each of:
   a. EX:/o= <Organization>/ou=<Site> (within the OFFLINE ADDRESS BOOK folder)
   b. OAB Version 2 (within the OFFLINE ADDRESS BOOK folder)
   c. OAB Version 3 and 3a
   d. EX:/o=<Organization>/ou=<Site> (within the SCHEDULE+ FREE BUSY folder)
   e. Organization Forms (within the EFORMS REGISTRY folder)
4. Select the appropriate object as specified above, right-click the object, and select *Properties*.
5. Select the *Replication* tab for each object and ensure that an Exchange 2003 Public Folder server has a replica of the system Public Folder. If not, add an Exchange 2003 Public Folder.

   An example of this is shown in Figure 5-8.

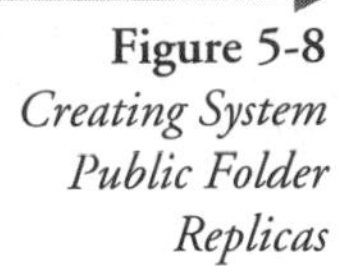

Figure 5-8 *Creating System Public Folder Replicas*

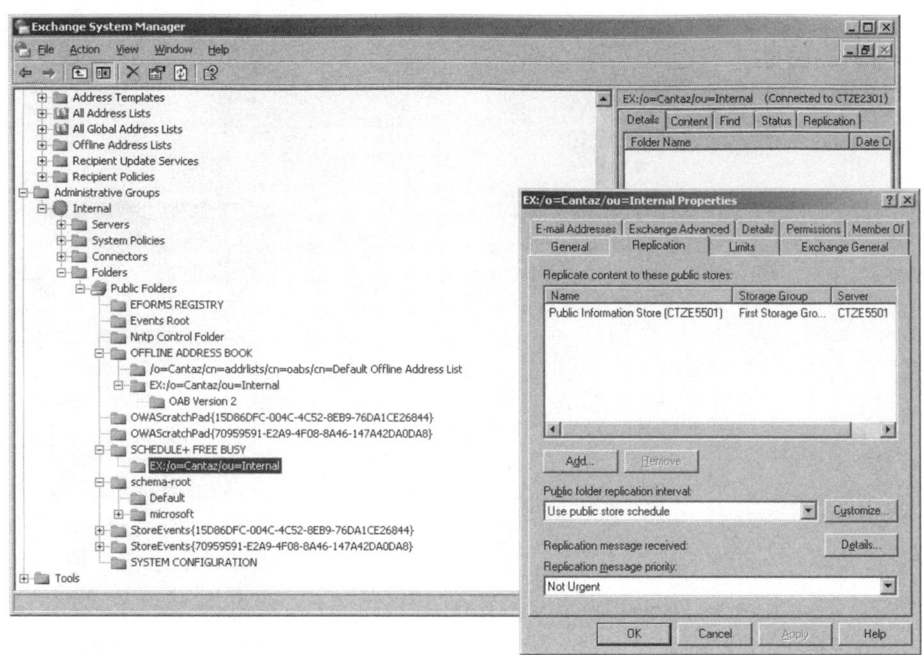

You may see additional system Public Folders, as shown in Figure 5-8, but these can be safely ignored because they are already homed on Exchange 2003 servers. Again, once the system Public Folders have been safely replicated, you may remove the original replica from the source server.

5.14 Using the Public Folder Migration Tool

Although the manual process works well to move both user and system Public Folders from an Exchange 5.5 server to an Exchange 2003 server (or from any Exchange server to any other Exchange server), it can be rather tiresome if you have a large number of top-level Public Folders to move. To automate and thus expedite the Public Folder migration process, Microsoft has supplied a utility with Exchange 2003 entitled the Public Folder Migration Tool, or more commonly known as pfMigrate.

pfMigrate (PFMIGRATE.WSF) is a command-line script that system administrators may use to create replicas of user and system Public Folders. It can be found on the Exchange 2003 CD-ROM in the \SUPPORT\EXDEPLOY folder. pfMigrate can only be used to create replicas on a new server within the same RG, and you must execute pfMigrate from an Exchange Administrator account with administrator permissions on the Public Folders that are being moved. You must use the /N parameter with the /A parameter, and in order to determine exactly how many Public Folders you need to move, you can first run pfMigrate with the /R parameter to generate a report. If neither the source server nor the target server is an Exchange 2003 system, then you must specify an Exchange 2003 server with /WMI parameter for Windows Management Instrumentation services. Also, note that pfMigrate only operates against the MAPI Public Folder Top-Level Hierarchy and cannot be used for other application Top-Level Hierarchy Public Folders. Nor can you specify any particular Public Folder or Public Folder tree to move—just a definite number of folders to move.

pfMigrate performs several functions, but ostensibly it can be used to create replicas of user Public Folders from a source server to a target server with the following syntax:

```
PFMIGRATE.WSF /S:CTZE5501 /T:CTZE2301 /A /N:10 /F:C:\pfMigrate.log
```

where

```
/S: defines the source server, /T: defines the target server,
/A indicates an add replica operation,
/N defines the number of Public Folders to move, and
/F defines the log file.
```

Once the user Public Folders have been replicated, you may delete any replicas off the source server using the following command:

```
PFMIGRATE.WSF /S:CTZE5501 /T:CTZE2301 /D /F:C:\pfmigrate.log
```

In this case, /D indicates a delete replica operation from the source server for any Public Folder that also has a replica on the server specified in the /T parameter. Once you've deleted any replicas, you may remove the server from the organization if you wish.

To move system Public Folders, use the following syntax:

```
PFMIGRATE.WSF /S:CTZE5501 /T:CTZE2301 /A /N:10 /SF /F:C:\pfmigrate.log
```

Note the /SF parameter. A resulting log file from a system Public Folder move operation is shown in Figure 5-9.

You can get a full description of pfMigrate's syntax by executing PFMIGRATE.WSF without any parameters on the command line.

5.15 Summary

Most of this chapter has described how ACLs are enforced for both individual users and groups when an Exchange 5.5 Public Folder is replicated to an Exchange 2003

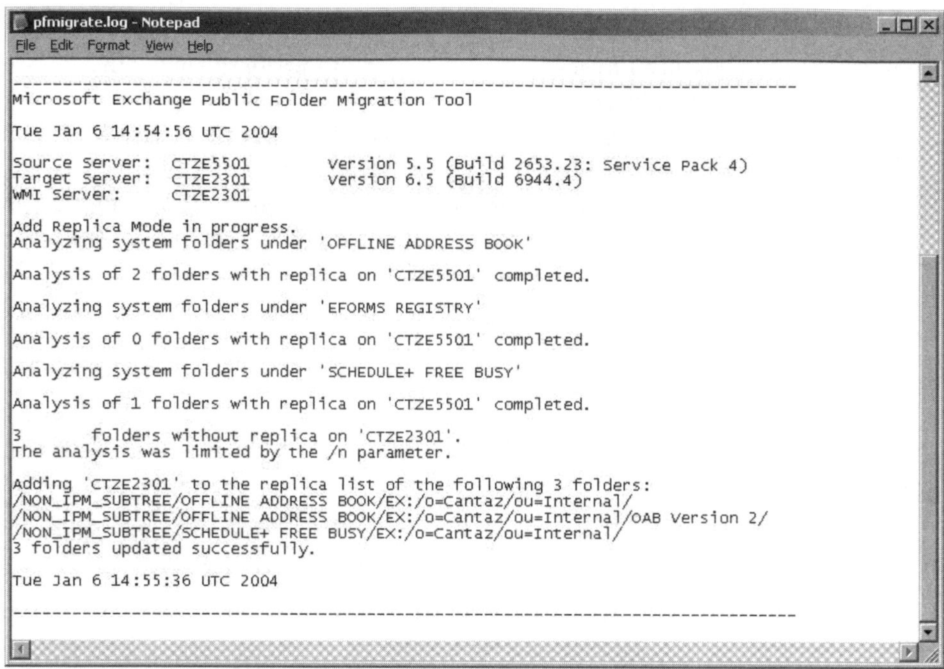
```
pfmigrate.log - Notepad
File Edit Format View Help
--------------------------------------------------------------------------------
Microsoft Exchange Public Folder Migration Tool

Tue Jan 6 14:54:56 UTC 2004

Source Server:   CTZE5501        Version 5.5 (Build 2653.23: Service Pack 4)
Target Server:   CTZE2301        Version 6.5 (Build 6944.4)
WMI Server:      CTZE2301

Add Replica Mode in progress.
Analyzing system folders under 'OFFLINE ADDRESS BOOK'

Analysis of 2 folders with replica on 'CTZE5501' completed.

Analyzing system folders under 'EFORMS REGISTRY'

Analysis of 0 folders with replica on 'CTZE5501' completed.

Analyzing system folders under 'SCHEDULE+ FREE BUSY'

Analysis of 1 folders with replica on 'CTZE5501' completed.

3       folders without replica on 'CTZE2301'.
The analysis was limited by the /n parameter.

Adding 'CTZE2301' to the replica list of the following 3 folders:
/NON_IPM_SUBTREE/OFFLINE ADDRESS BOOK/EX:/o=Cantaz/ou=Internal/
/NON_IPM_SUBTREE/OFFLINE ADDRESS BOOK/EX:/o=Cantaz/ou=Internal/OAB Version 2/
/NON_IPM_SUBTREE/SCHEDULE+ FREE BUSY/EX:/o=Cantaz/ou=Internal/
3 folders updated successfully.

Tue Jan 6 14:55:36 UTC 2004

--------------------------------------------------------------------------------
```

Figure 5-9
Log File Output from pfMigrate

Public Folder Store. Essentially the same process takes place when an Exchange 5.5 Public Folder Store is upgraded to become an Exchange 2003 Public Folder Store. In this case, the upgrade process analyzes existing Exchange 5.5–style ACLs and converts them to Exchange 2003–style ACLs by resolving the *legacyExchangeDN* against the AD to retrieve a SID.

Although it's important to create Public Folder CAs for the reasons described in the early part of this chapter, of the utmost importance is building a solid infrastructure to allow this kind of coexistence to take place. Careful attention to domains, trust relationships, the topology of Recipient CAs, and thoughtful account migration is indispensable.

Although Public Folders have not evolved significantly with Exchange 2003, several subtle changes have crept in with Exchange 2003 administration and even with some Exchange 2000 service packs. Overall, there should be no big shocks with Public Folder deployment and migration today, but at least some of the improvements should ease the pain associated with management of these often dreaded features. This chapter has aimed to tie together many of the loose ends of Exchange 2003 Public Folder migration.

6

Deployment and Interoperability Guidelines for the Active Directory Connector

6.1 Introduction

I often describe the Active Directory Connector as the lightsaber of Exchange 5.5 migration because it's extremely powerful and seems straightforward to implement; yet much like its fictional counterpart, the Active Directory Connector is actually a sophisticated tool that takes a good deal of mastery and careful use if it is to ultimately yield success.

As you migrate from Exchange 5.5 to Exchange 2003, it's unlikely that you will be able to migrate all Exchange 5.5 users in one single action. What's more likely, especially when you have thousands of users in your environment, is a long period of coexistence during which there will be a mixture of both Exchange 5.5 users and Exchange 2003 users. Correct deployment of the Active Directory Connector and appropriate CAs is key to facilitating this coexistence.

Much of the information described thus far about the Active Directory Connector relates to discrete aspects of Active Directory Connector functionality. This chapter ties those functionality aspects together and gives a complete picture of Active Directory Connector usage in a coexisting Exchange 5.5 and AD environment.

6.2 Why Native-Mode Windows 2000 or Windows 2003 Domains Are Best

Let's take a step back quickly and review some fundamentals. A Windows 2000 or Windows 2003 domain is said to be in *native mode* if it contains only Windows 2000 or higher DC. So long as you meet this requirement, you can have any mix of Windows NT4, Windows 2000, and Windows 2003 member servers in that domain that you like. A Windows 2000 domain is said to be in *mixed mode* if it contains any Windows NT4 DC.

In general, it's best for Exchange 2003 (and Exchange 2000) if you have as much (if not all) of your Windows 2000 or Windows 2003 infrastructure in place in native mode rather than mixed mode. There are a few reasons for this, but specifically with respect to the Active Directory Connector, it's important for the synchronization of certain types of Exchange 5.5 Distribution Lists.

When the Active Directory Connector synchronizes an Exchange 5.5 Distribution List over to the AD, it always creates a mail-enabled UDG as the synchronized object. Usually this represents no problem, because there are no restrictions on having UDGs in a mixed-mode domain. But the usage of the Exchange 5.5 Distribution List becomes important here. If you were using the Distribution List in Exchange 5.5 simply as a means of mail address expansion, then you can continue with the same model using a mail-enabled UDG in Windows 2000 or Windows 2003.

However, many organizations have other uses for Exchange 5.5 Distribution Lists. A very common practice is to use Distribution Lists as a means for enforcing permissions to the Public Folder tree structure. Instead of assigning permissions to individual mailboxes, the permissions would be assigned by using a Distribution List in the ACL on the Public Folder and simply adding/removing people to/from the appropriate Distribution List. This model works well and lends itself to a simpler and more efficient management technique.

Now here's the problem. In order to implement the same model in Exchange 2003, you have to use ACLs on the Public Folders that relate back to Windows 2000 or Windows 2003 groups. Windows 2000 and Windows 2003 offer two types of groups: Distribution Groups and Security Groups, which can exist in different modes—Domain Local, Domain Global, or Universal.

Distribution Groups can't be used in ACLs because they are not security principals: that is, they don't have a SID value associated with them in the AD. Security Groups, on the other hand, are security principals and are designed specifically for use in ACLs. The Active Directory Connector creates Universal Distribution Groups (ones that are visible across all domains in the forest and can have membership drawn from any domain in the forest) because these represent the most flexible group objects. (After all, the membership of Distribution Lists in Exchange 5.5 might have membership drawn from anywhere in the organization, and in Windows 2000 or Windows 2003, these user objects might be scattered across many domains.)

So with the Active Directory Connector creating UDGs, we find ourselves with a problem because we can't use this type of group to enforce permissions on Public Folders. Fortunately, Exchange 2003 will convert UDGs to USGs as described previously.

Of course, this conversion process only takes place if the UDG already exists in a native-mode domain. If the UDG is in a mixed-mode domain, then no conversion takes place. Similarly, only those UDGs that are used to permission Public Folders are converted to USGs; any other UDGs that are used simply for mail expansion are ignored during the conversion process.

So if you wish to host USGs, you must make sure that the CA you use is homing them into a native-mode domain. In fact, the Active Directory Connector MMC snap-in reminds you of this (see Figure 6-1) as you configure the agreement.

6.3 Scenarios that Require Multiple Connection Agreements

In the simplest cases, you can use just one bi-directional CA to replicate one or more legacy Exchange Recipient containers to a single AD Organizational Unit and one or more AD Organizational Units to a single Exchange container. Look at the example in Figure 6-2.

The objects contained in the AD Organizational Units are mapped to a single container on the target Exchange 5.5 server, and then the standard legacy Exchange directory replication model allows this container to be seen across all legacy Exchange sites. Similarly, any number of legacy Exchange containers can be mapped across to a single AD Organizational Unit that is replicated across the forest using the standard AD replication model. In more complex scenarios, a single CA is not sufficient. Fundamentally, there are two frameworks where multiple CAs are required.

Because legacy Exchange mailboxes may be synchronized across to the AD, you can use AD Management tools, such as the AD Users and Computers MMC snap-in, to manage legacy Exchange mailboxes. Managing legacy mailboxes from the AD means that you'll need to have a separate CA back to the Recipients container for the legacy Exchange site in which the mailbox is homed. In the Exchange 5.5 Directory

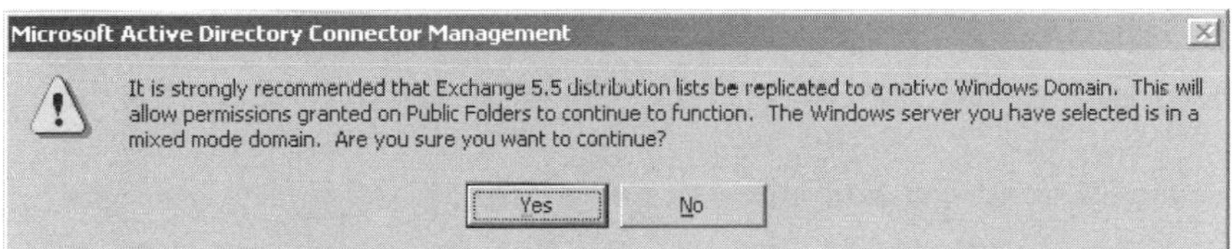

Microsoft Active Directory Connector Management
It is strongly recommended that Exchange 5.5 distribution lists be replicated to a native Windows Domain. This will allow permissions granted on Public Folders to continue to function. The Windows server you have selected is in a mixed mode domain. Are you sure you want to continue?
Yes
No

Figure 6-1 *Warning Message that Appears When You Are Synchronizing*

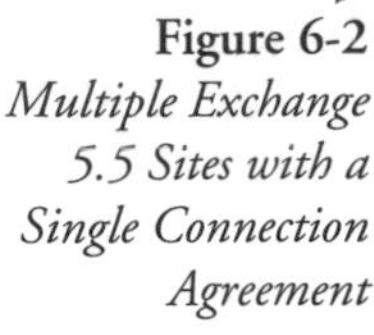

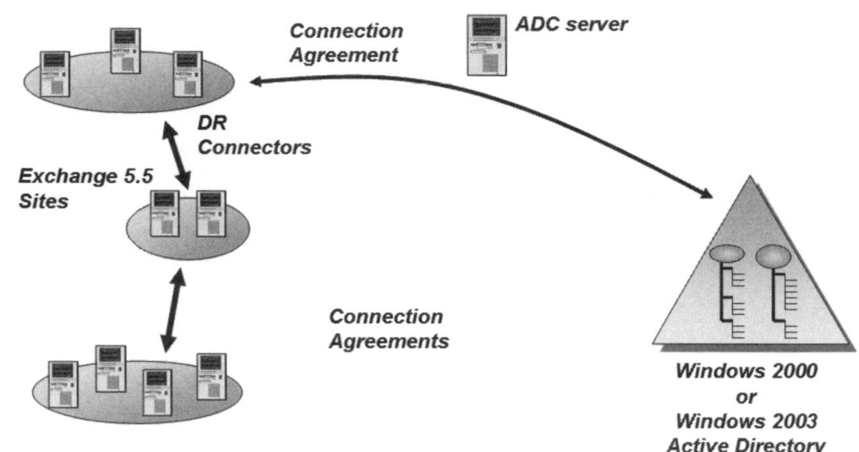

Figure 6-2 *Multiple Exchange 5.5 Sites with a Single Connection Agreement*

Service, objects outside the site in which they are homed are read-only, so a single CA to an arbitrary legacy Exchange site is not sufficient to allow write access to an object. Hence, in this scenario, one CA per legacy Exchange site is required. You can see an example of such a CA arrangement in Figure 6-3.

In terms of best practice, it makes a lot of sense to use like to manage like. This means that you should, if possible, use the Exchange 5.5 Administrator program to manage legacy Exchange objects and the AD Users and Computers snap-in to manage Exchange 2003 objects, for the most part. Although do note that the Exchange 2003 ESM utility now has several user management functions available. In fact, the Exchange 2003 installation menu allows you to install the Exchange 5.5 Administrator expressly for this purpose. Having said that, when Exchange 5.5 mailboxes are repli-

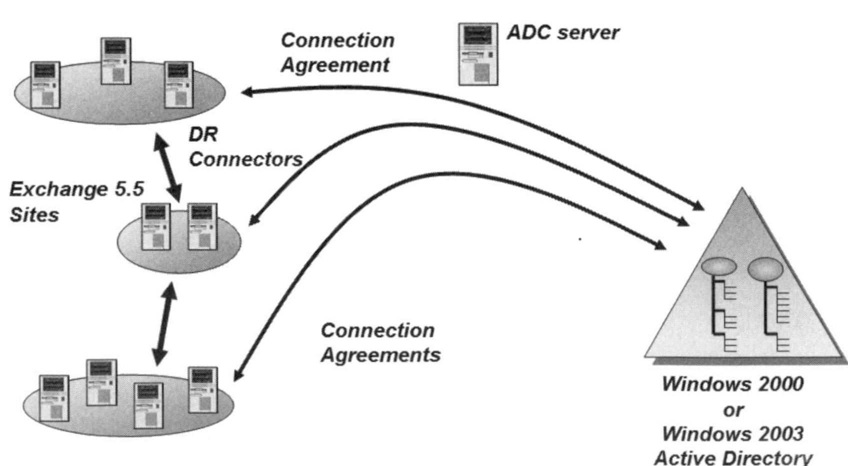

Figure 6-3 *Multiple Exchange 5.5 Sites with a Per-Site Connection Agreement Arrangement*

cated to the AD, this is now a potential single point of administration for those objects. In this case, using the AD Users and Computers tool to manage a legacy Exchange mailbox is desirable. The Exchange 5.5 Administrator program is still important, though, especially when it comes to managing distribution list membership with native Exchange 5.5 objects.

The other framework in which multiple CAs are required relates to many-to-many mappings. In general, a single CA allows one-to-one and many-to-one mappings of legacy Exchange containers to AD Organizational Units and vice versa. Many-to-one mappings are realized in two ways: (1) you select multiple containers on the same level at the source, and (2) container hierarchy is honored from the source. If you need to make many-to-many mappings, then a single CA is not sufficient, because only one target container or Organizational Unit can be specified on the CA. In this case, you'll need to use a separate CA for each target container or Organizational Unit, as shown in Figure 6-4.

When might you want to do this? Well, let's say you wanted to map users from three different legacy Exchange sites (say Antibes, Flayosc, and Mougins) across to three different Organizational Units (again called Antibes, Flayosc, and Mougins). You'd need three separate CAs to perform this type of mapping. If you are prepared to bundle all of the replicated objects into a single Organizational Unit in the AD, then a single CA will be sufficient.

6.4 Container Hierarchy Mapping

In general, a specific CA defines a many-to-one mapping of containers between directories. That is, when you define the source locations for a given CA, you can specify

Figure 6-4 *Mapping Arrangements for Legacy Exchange Containers*

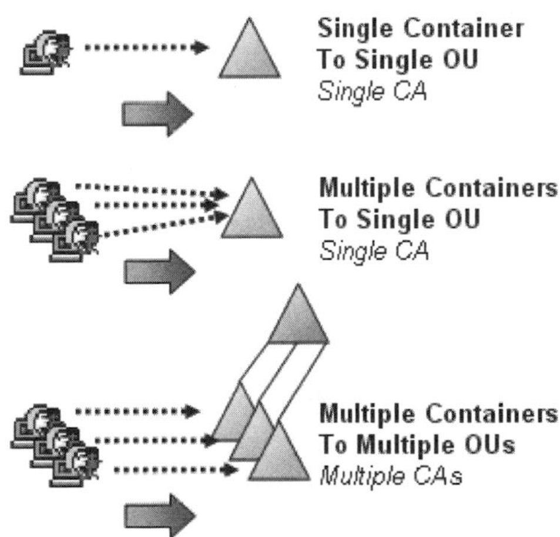

multiple containers from which you'll synchronize objects, but these objects must all be mapped into a single container in the target directory.

However, this many-to-one mapping doesn't mean that if you have multiple containers in your source directory and you want to retain the same structure that you need to have one CA per source container. Although the mapping function is many-to-one, the Active Directory Connector does allow container hierarchy to be synchronized across so it's possible to specify an entire Exchange 5.5 site hierarchy to synchronize to one Organizational Unit in the AD and have all objects within that site synchronized across with the hierarchy intact. This approach is typical in most deployments. You'll often find at least a single CA from each site in the Exchange 5.5 organization mapping to an Organizational Unit in the AD.

6.5 Moving Synchronized Objects between Containers

It's interesting to note what happens when a synchronized object is moved between different containers. For example, Figure 6-5 shows a two-way CA in place between the *Recipients* container of an Exchange 5.5 site and the *Temporary Objects* Organizational Unit in the AD. When an object is synchronized from the Exchange 5.5 *Recipients* container, any changes made to the object in either directory will be synchronized to the other. Consider that we move the synchronized object to another location in the AD, a container entitled *Final Objects.*

Note that no CA maps the Exchange 5.5 *Recipients* container to the AD *Final Objects* container. Despite this lack of a CA to the alternative container, if a change is made to the object in the Exchange 5.5 Directory Service, then this change is replicated to the synchronized object in the AD, even though it is now located in a different container. From a visual perspective, it's as if there is an invisible one-way CA from the *Recipients* container in Exchange 5.5 to the *Final Objects* container in the AD. In fact, no matter where you relocate such an object in the AD, the CA linking the *Recipients* container to the *Temporary Objects* Organizational Unit tracks the moved object using

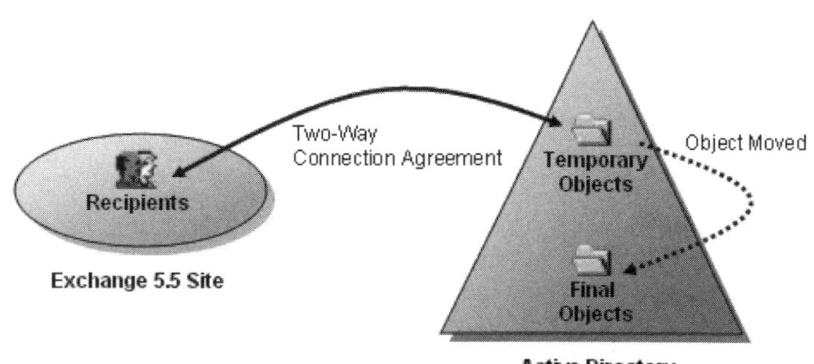

Figure 6-5 *Two-way Connection Agreement and Moved Object*

the Windows 2000 or Windows 2003 GUID and will always replicate Exchange 5.5 changes to the AD.

The converse, however, is not the case. Any changes made directly to the synchronized object in the AD *Final Objects* container are not replicated back to the original object in the Exchange 5.5 Directory Service. For these modifications to be replicated, an additional CA is required, one-way in this case, mapping the *Final Objects* to the *Recipients* container in the Exchange 5.5 Directory Service, as shown in Figure 6-6.

In the reverse scenario, there is no real concept of an object moving between Exchange 5.5 containers and retaining the synchronization integrity. Moving an object between containers in the Exchange 5.5 Directory Services implies a change to the object's Distinguished Name, and this results in a completely different synchronization match.

6.6 Using Multiple Active Directory Connectors

Depending on the complexity and geographic distribution of your environment, you may decide to use just one Active Directory Connector hosting multiple CAs, or you may decide to deploy an Active Directory Connector in major geographic regions around the globe (e.g., one in the Americas, one in Europe, and one in Asia Pacific). From a directory synchronization standpoint, it's easier to conceptualize synchronization if you centralize all synchronization activity to just one location. The downside of this is that directory replication latency comes into play, and as synchronization takes place between the directories in the central location, you have to wait for the Exchange 5.5 Directory Service replication interval and the AD replication schedules to kick in before you can be sure that the updated objects have been distributed across your organizations.

Distributing Active Directory Connectors implies that you will use a set of CAs per Active Directory Connector that will synchronize Exchange 5.5 containers and AD

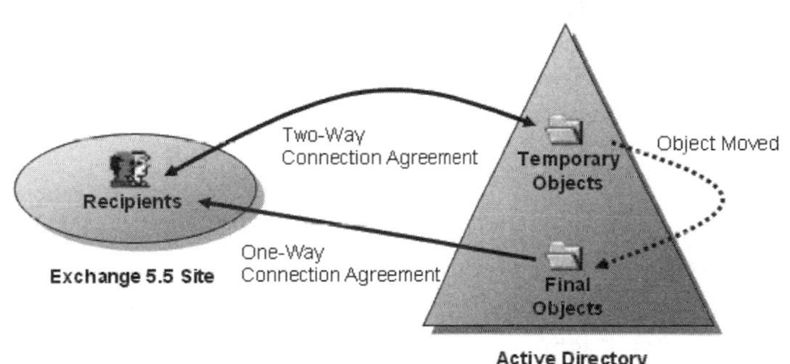

Figure 6-6 *Required Connection Agreements to Ensure Complete Synchronization*

Organizational Units close to you and in a timely fashion. Although you can have multiple CAs synchronizing the same set of objects (more about this later), it's best if you tolerate or optimize your directory replication settings rather than introducing more complexity into the synchronization environment.

6.7 Exchange 5.5 Back-Replication

While we're on the subject of what gets synchronized with CAs, it's interesting to discuss a little unexpected replication that you might see in your Exchange 5.5 environment when you start to deploy and enable the Active Directory Connector.

Let's take a simple example. Assume that I have a large Exchange 5.5 environment, distributed globally with multiple sites, hundreds of Exchange 5.5 servers, and tens of thousands of users. Over the weekend, my Exchange 5.5 Administrators have been out for a few drinks or taken a break during Bible study, and they've decided that on Monday they'd like to come in and start experimenting with the Active Directory Connector. They plan to bring up an Active Directory Connector and use a one-way CA from the *Recipients* containers in the headquarters location to bulk-load user objects into the AD. For the sake of this example, let's assume that the company is based in Chicago and this location has 10 Exchange 5.5 servers, each with 1,000 users.

Now, there's no real Windows 2000 or Windows 2003 infrastructure in place in my fictional company, but the Exchange 5.5 Administrator people are a forward-looking bunch, and they just want to get familiar with the technology because they know that some day soon they'll be asked to start planning for the move to Exchange 2003. What better way to understand how it all works than to start playing with the tools, so they bring up a small test lab with a couple of Windows 2000 or Windows 2003 servers on it, which aren't visible out on the corporate network.

So this is what the Administrators think is going to happen: They'll configure a one-way CA from Exchange 5.5 to the AD, add in the 10 *Recipients* containers, which are all homed in the *Chicago* site, enable the CA, and they'll start to see the AD get populated with 10,000 user objects, based on the 10,000 mailboxes in the *Chicago* site. They're pretty confident that this is a safe test because the only traffic they expect to see is object synchronization coming from the *Chicago* site into their test Windows 2000 or Windows 2003 environment.

6.7.1 Exchange 5.5 connection agreement attribute modifications

But what really happens here is just a little bit different and not a little surprising! What they'll see occur is a wave of Exchange 5.5 replication take place across the hundreds of

Exchange 5.5 servers that exist worldwide. Every one of the 10,000 Chicago-based mailboxes gets re-replicated across the whole Exchange 5.5 environment. Clearly this comes as a surprise to my Administrators. They only created a one-way CA to the AD, so they didn't expect to see anything change on the production Exchange 5.5 environment.

So what causes all of this 5.5 replication? Well, it breaks down like this: As the Active Directory Connector synchronizes each of the 10,000 Exchange 5.5 mailboxes, it modifies an attribute on the object in the Exchange 5.5 Directory. The *ADC-Global-Names* attribute gets updated to reflect the fact that the Active Directory Connector has synchronized this object. You may ask where this attribute has come from. It gets added to the Exchange 5.5 Directory Schema when you upgrade a single Exchange 5.5 server to Service Pack 3. (You can see the attribute as shown by the Raw Mode Administrator tool in Figure 6-7.)

Now dust off your Exchange 5.5 books (maybe even the ones written by the individual referenced in Figure 6-7). Remember that when you make any change to an Exchange 5.5 object, the *Object-USN* and *Object-DSN-Signature* attributes get updated, which means that the object will take part in Exchange 5.5 intrasite or intersite directory replication.

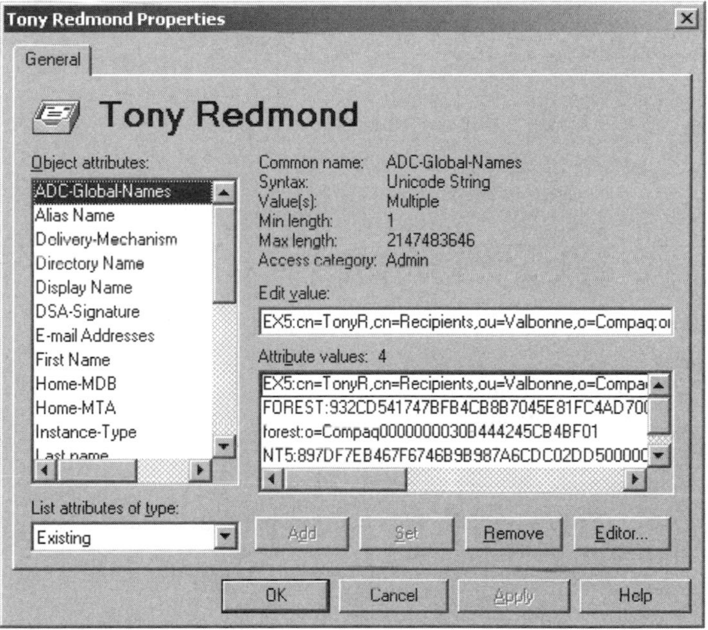

Figure 6-7
A View of the Raw Properties from the Exchange 5.5 Administrator

So what's the lesson here? If you're going to do some testing (and you should be doing some sooner rather than later), make sure you use a separate test lab that is not connected to the production environment to avoid these unexpected anomalies.

At a basic level, for each Exchange directory object changed on a server, approximately 5 KB of data is sent to all other servers within the site. For replication between sites, each object compresses to about 1 KB.

6.7.2 The insulation site concept

One approach I've seen several companies use for prototype and development activity is to use the concept of the Exchange 5.5 insulation site. Based on what we've just discovered in the previous section, it would seem that we would avoid this problem of source Exchange 5.5 objects being modified if we could access them and synchronize them into the AD in a read-only fashion at source. Unfortunately, there is no setting on a CA that we can use to ensure that Exchange 5.5 attributes are not modified when replication takes place.

However, remember that Exchange 5.5 objects are read-only outside their home site. In the previous scenario, if the administrators created a new site and had no users homed within that site, but the site contained only mailboxes replicated in from other sites, then all of those mailboxes would effectively be read-only. If CAs were directed to this insulation site, then no modifications would be written to the mailbox objects and no back-replication would occur.

6.8 Connection Agreement Deployment Models

The deployment approach that you take for your CAs is closely related to the state of your migration from Windows NT4 to Windows 2000 or Windows 2003. If you have already deployed Windows 2000 or Windows 2003 in the domains that host your user accounts, then the CAs will be able to match Exchange 5.5 mailboxes with Windows 2000 or Windows 2003 user objects. If you have not already upgraded your Windows NT4 domains to Windows 2000 or Windows 2003 domains, then the CAs will create new Windows 2000 or Windows 2003 objects to provide a GAL and allow Exchange 2003 to determine how to route mail to Exchange 5.5 mailboxes.

Although I cannot describe all possible deployment configurations for your CAs, the next three sections describe the fundamentals of most approaches.

6.8.1 The simple domain and connection agreement model

We commence by looking at a relatively straightforward environment that comprises a single Windows NT4 domain named BALMORAL and two Exchange 5.5

sites named USA and Europe in an organization named OSBORNE, as shown in Figure 6-8.

Also shown in Figure 6-8 is the relationship between the Windows NT4 account for the user COLGAN and her Exchange 5.5 mailbox. These two entities are bound together because the primary Windows NT Account attribute (known in LDAP as the *Assoc-NT-Account*) of Aoife Colgan's mailbox references the SID of the Windows NT4 account COLGAN, '12345' as an example in this case. At this point, all that is in place is the normal operating environment of Windows NT4 and Exchange 5.5: there are no Active Directory Connector or Exchange 2003 servers in place.

For this environment, when the BALMORAL Windows NT4 domain is upgraded in place to Windows 2000 or Windows 2003, access to Exchange 5.5 mailboxes is still possible because during an in-place domain upgrade, SID values for objects remain unchanged. Having upgraded the domain, the next step in the migration process is to install an Active Directory Connector server and configure some CAs. The CAs should be defined as two-way CAs between each Exchange 5.5 site and the Users Organizational Unit in the AD, as shown in Figure 6-9. In the example shown, I've directed the Exchange 5.5 end of the CA to the *Recipients* container in the Exchange 5.5 site. It's equally appropriate to direct this end of the CA to the *Site* container of the Exchange 5.5 site and thus synchronize object from all containers within the site to the AD.

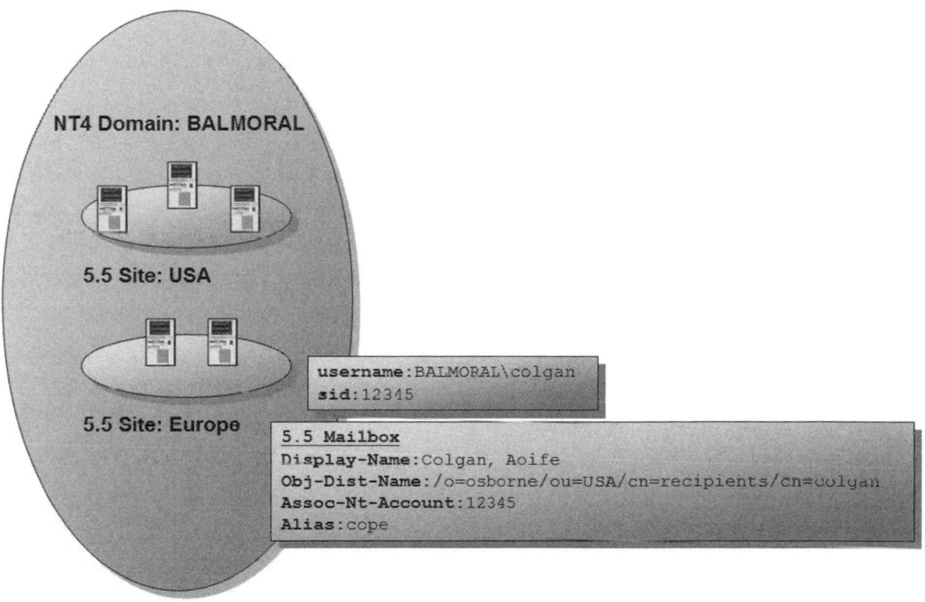

Figure 6-8 *Single Windows NT4 Domain and Exchange 5.5 Environment*

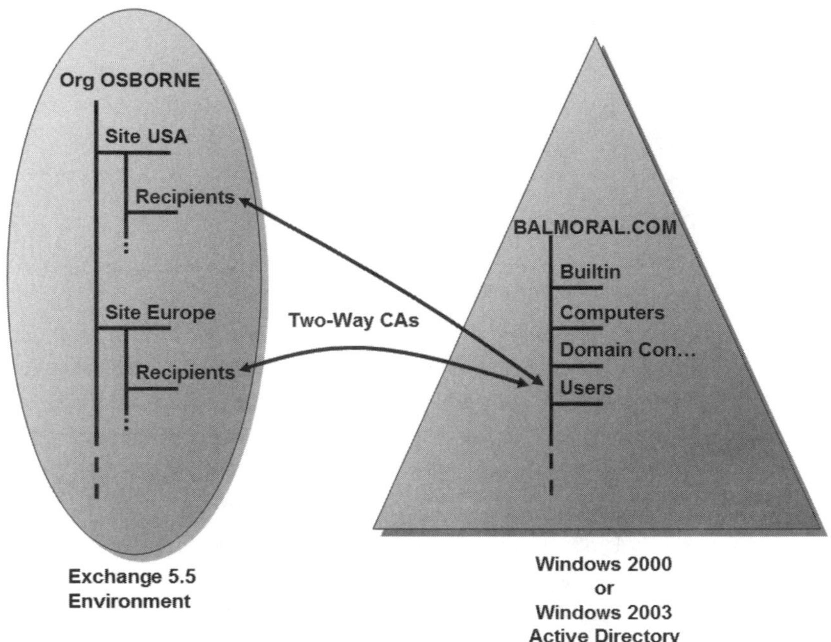

Figure 6-9 *Connection Agreements from Exchange 5.5 Sites to Users Organizational Unit*

When the Active Directory Connector synchronization cycle starts, it will match the *Assoc-Nt-Account* SID value from each Exchange 5.5 mailbox with the SID of the corresponding user object in the AD. Thus no new user objects are created in the AD and the Active Directory Connector merges mailbox attribute information from the Exchange 5.5 Directory Service into each AD user object.

As you then introduce Exchange 2003 servers into the Exchange 5.5 environment and move user mailboxes from Exchange 5.5 stores to Exchange 2003 stores, the attributes of existing user objects are updated to reflect the new location of the mailbox. No new user objects are created in the AD for the new Exchange 2003 mailboxes.

6.8.2 Connection agreements to final organizational unit topology

Although many smaller organizations may be faced with the migration of a single domain in conjunction with Exchange 5.5, larger organizations typically have more complex environments. The domain model shown in Figure 6-10 is typical of that being deployed today by many large organizations. In this environment, in line with most customer environments, the bulk of the user accounts, computer accounts, group objects, and so on are found in the child domains of americas.balmoral.com, emea.balmoral.com, and asiapacific.balmoral.com. Little is held in the root domain,

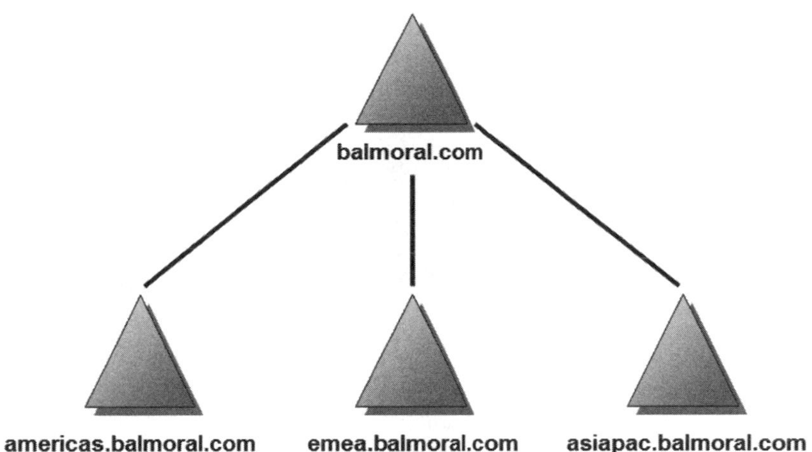

Figure 6-10 *Windows 2000 or Windows 2003 Domain Model*

balmoral.com, which serves primarily as a placeholder for the domain tree. However, it is common to find a few administrator accounts or groups held in the root domain.

As far as the deployment of the Active Directory Connector and the Exchange migration strategy is concerned, it is unimportant how you come to deploy a final Windows 2000 or Windows 2003 environment. Organizations that have several Windows NT4 domains may choose to perform in-place upgrades of their domains and restructure them into a topology similar to that in Figure 6-10. Other organizations that have many hundreds of domains may choose a different approach. For example, at Hewlett-Packard, or more precisely in the pre-merger Compaq environment, we had some 23 account domains and more than 17,000 different resource domains. Clearly, performing in-place upgrades of this environment would have posed some significant challenges, and accordingly we chose to build a brand-new domain structure like that in Figure 6-10.

For the following example, let's assume that we've already migrated all Windows NT4 accounts to Windows 2000 or Windows 2003 accounts and that these accounts are deployed in the domain model shown in Figure 6-10. Using the OSBORNE Exchange 5.5 organization as an example, let's assume that this organization consists of 17 Exchange 5.5 sites distributed globally. What combination of CAs can we use to synchronize Exchange 5.5 mailbox information with AD objects? If we can assume that all mailboxes held in an Exchange 5.5 site map directly to user objects in one particular domain, then we can use a single CA from each Exchange 5.5 site to an Organizational Unit in the AD, as shown in Figure 6-11. In our example, we assume that the Dublin, Berlin, Nice, and Madrid sites all contain user mailboxes that can be mapped into the emea.balmoral.com domain. With one CA per Exchange 5.5 site, the Active Directory Connector processes mailboxes from each Exchange 5.5 site

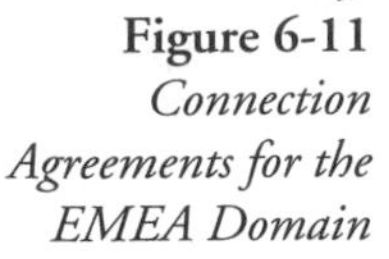

Figure 6-11 *Connection Agreements for the EMEA Domain*

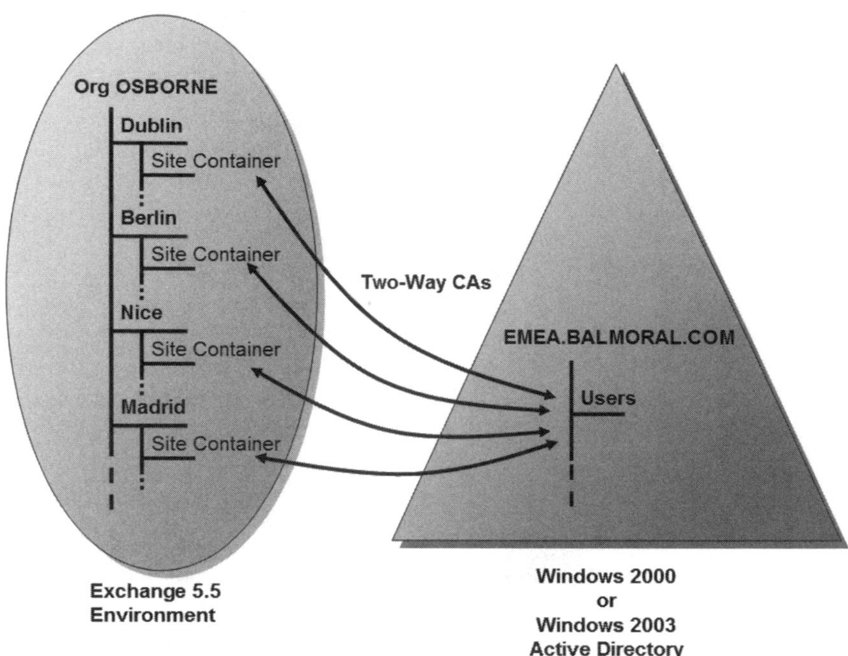

and matches them against the user objects in the Windows 2000 or Windows 2003 domain.

This approach can be used for each of the other Exchange 5.5 sites because mailboxes from each site can be synchronized into a particular Windows 2000 or Windows 2003 domain, as shown in Figure 6-12. We use one CA per site to synchronize objects into an appropriate domain in the AD.

Even if you haven't already migrated your Windows NT4 accounts to Windows 2000 or Windows 2003 accounts, this approach can still work well. Of course, no user objects will be found in the destination domain, so no matching will take place. In this case the Active Directory Connector will create new user objects (depending on your CA configuration), which can later be matched against using Windows NT4 migration tools.

However, using a single CA from each Exchange 5.5 site to an Organizational Unit in the AD may impose some deployment restrictions. There are three points that you must consider:

1. Mailboxes (or custom recipients or distribution lists) in an Exchange 5.5 site must map to user objects in an Organizational Unit in a single domain. If you have Exchange 5.5 directory objects that must map to different Organizational

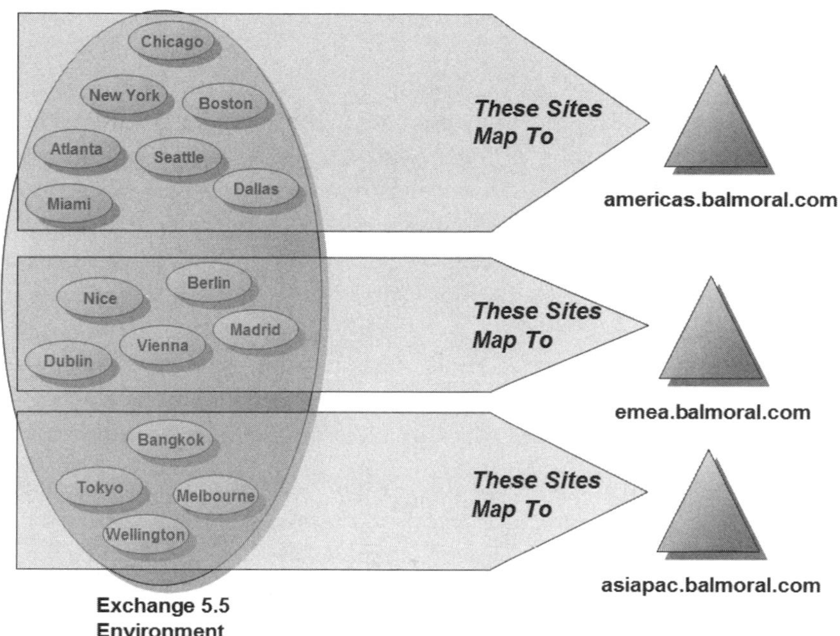

Figure 6-12 *Mapping Exchange 5.5 Sites To Specific Windows 2000 Or Windows 2003 Domains*

Units in the target domain, then you'll need one CA per target Organizational Unit.

2. If you have a mix of mailboxes in an Exchange 5.5 container that must be synchronized to different Organizational Units, you'll need to use either an LDAP search filter or a matching rule to select only those objects that you want to synchronize.

3. If you don't wish to synchronize the container hierarchy associated with an Exchange 5.5 site, you'll need to use multiple CAs.

6.8.3 Connection agreements to temporary organizational unit topology

Many organizations wish to deploy Exchange 2003 in advance of migrating their entire Windows NT4 environment to Windows 2000 or Windows 2003. When all Windows NT4 objects have been either upgraded or migrated to Windows 2000 or Windows 2003 objects, introducing the Active Directory Connector merely matches Exchange 5.5 mailboxes with Windows 2000 or Windows 2003 user accounts. However, if you haven't moved any Windows NT4 objects to Windows 2000 or Windows 2003, then the AD is effectively empty, at least insofar as its usefulness as a Global Address List for Exchange 2003.

So in a mixed environment, where you have Exchange 2003 users functioning alongside Exchange 5.5 users and you have not migrated Windows users, the Active Directory Connector must create objects in the AD to represent the Exchange 5.5 mailboxes and thus provide a complete and consistent Global Address List. Many organizations will tend to use a temporary Organizational Unit structure in the AD to hold the Active Directory Connector–created objects. Separating the Active Directory Connector–created objects, which are typically disabled user objects, from real Windows 2000 or Windows 2003 user objects that have been migrated from Windows NT4 has the following benefits:

1. The separation allows system managers to easily differentiate between user accounts that have been migrated and those that have been created by the Active Directory Connector merely because of their difference in location.
2. It's common to find specific access control and Group Policy Object (GPO) settings on the Organizational Unit structure where the real Windows 2000 or Windows 2003 users accounts reside, and in general it's not desirable to have these settings apply to Active Directory Connector–created objects, which are just temporary in nature.
3. From a CA perspective, using the temporary structure allows you to define the minimum number of CAs (one per site) to represent all Exchange 5.5 mailboxes.
4. Using just one CA per site means that you recreate the container hierarchy from the Exchange 5.5 site only in the temporary Organizational Unit structure. As you migrate Windows NT4 accounts to Windows 2000 or Windows 2003 accounts, your migration tools should match against the Active Directory Connector–created objects, and then you can move the final users' accounts to their rightful location in the final Organizational Unit structure.

Assuming the same domain environment already described in section 6.8.2, you should expect to use an Organizational Unit hierarchy similar to that shown in Figure 6-13.

The Organizational Unit hierarchy shown here relates to just the emea.balmoral.com domain, but the same Organizational Unit hierarchy would exist in the other child domains for this AD forest. Also note the special Accounts Organizational Unit that acts as a parent for the Resources, Users, and Groups Organizational Units. This allows you to structure the representation of objects in the AD much more flexibly than using the standard Users and Groups Organizational Units. (Note that the default Users and Groups Organizational Units still exist in the domain but do not contain any objects and for the sake of clarity are not shown in Figure 6-13.)

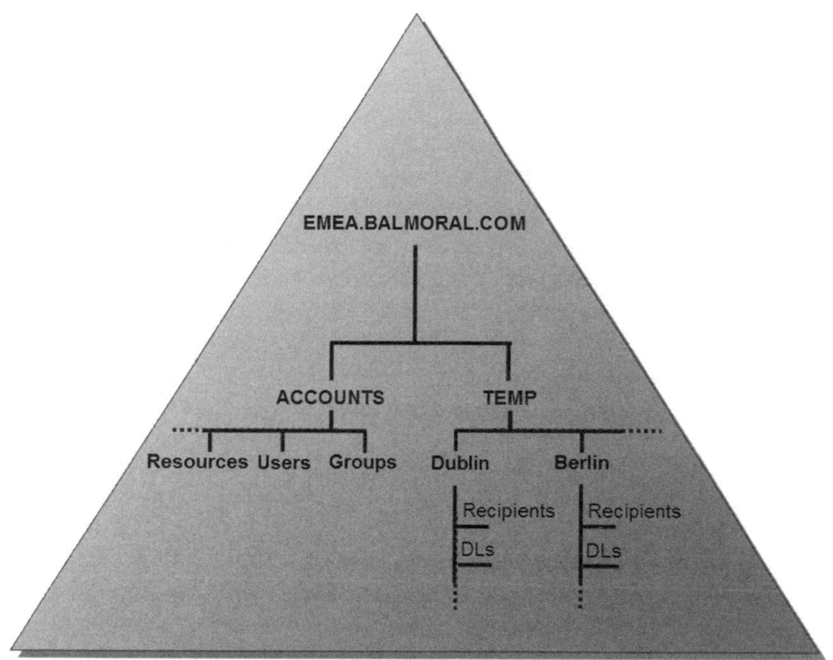

Figure 6-13 *Organizational Unit Hierarchy with Temporary Migration Organizational Unit*

With this model, let's step through the migration process for users associated with this domain. Assuming that no native Windows 2000 or Windows 2003 objects exist, effectively we have an empty AD. We then use the Active Directory Connector to create disabled user objects in the TEMP Organizational Unit. A two-way CA from each Exchange 5.5 site (in our case this would be Dublin, Berlin, Nice [not shown], and Madrid [not shown], yielding four CAs in total) would create sub-Organizational Units in the TEMP Organizational Unit reflecting the container hierarchy from the respective Exchange 5.5 sites. The mail-enabled objects created thus provide entries in the Global Address List for any Exchange 2003 users. As Windows NT4 accounts are migrated to Windows 2000 or Windows 2003 accounts, the migration tool should detect the matching Active Directory Connector–created object already present in the TEMP Organizational Unit and merge the objects together. This results in one object that can be moved to its final location in the Users sub-Organizational Unit of the ACCOUNTS Organizational Unit.

Using this model requires some sophistication with CAs, as shown in Figure 6-14, which represents the CAs required for the Nice and Madrid Sites. (Dublin and Berlin have been omitted from the figure for the sake of clarity.) The two-way CAs between the Exchange 5.5 sites and the Dublin and Berlin Organizational Units in the TEMP Organizational Unit are sufficient to synchronize objects bidirectionally between Exchange 5.5 and the AD for as long as the Active Directory Connector–created

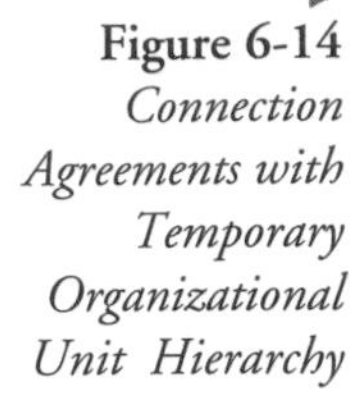

Figure 6-14 *Connection Agreements with Temporary Organizational Unit Hierarchy*

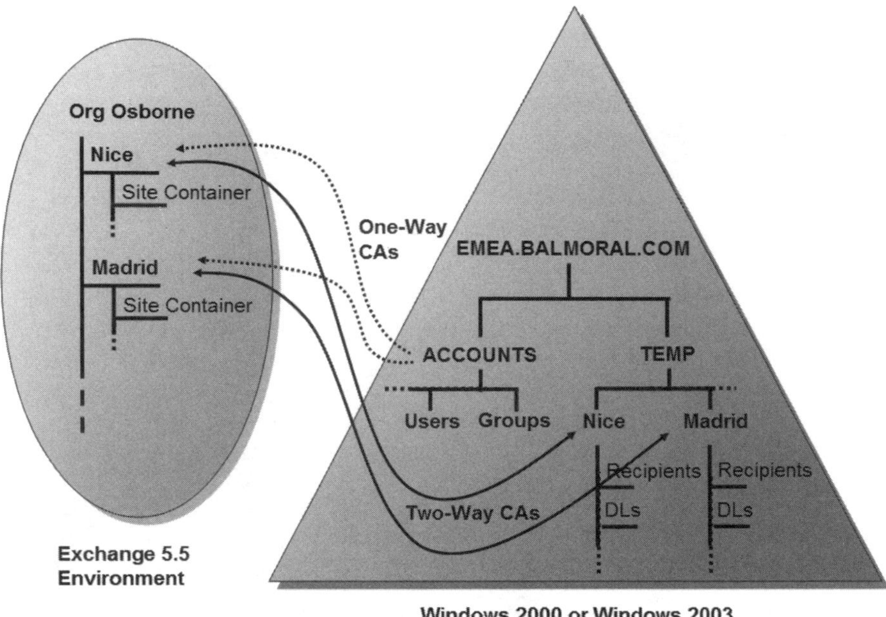

objects exist. As Windows NT4 accounts are migrated to Windows 2000 or Windows 2003, the migration tool (or the AD Cleanup Wizard) merges the Active Directory Connector–created objects with the migrated objects, and the newly merged objects are moved to the ACCOUNTS Organizational Unit. Any changes made to the Exchange 5.5 mailboxes will still be replicated to the newly merged objects because the two-way CAs in place between the Exchange 5.5 sites and the TEMP Organizational Unit can still access the newly merged object, even though the object is now in a different location in the AD. (The CA uses the *ADCGlobalNames* attribute and the Windows 2000 or Windows 2003 GUID to track the objects.) However, the two-way CAs are only capable of replicating changes from Exchange 5.5 to the AD for these newly merged and relocated objects: they can't replicate changes from AD to Exchange 5.5. To replicate these changes made directly to the objects in the AD requires additional: one-way CAs from the ACCOUNTS Organizational Unit back to each Exchange 5.5 site.

This CA topology should be applied to every Exchange 5.5 site in the organization. Effectively, every Exchange 5.5 site will require a two-way CA to the TEMP Organizational Unit and a one-way CA from the ACCOUNTS Organizational Unit back to the Exchange 5.5 site. For this environment, 16 Exchange 5.5 sites require a total of 32 CAs (16 two-way and 16 one-way).

6.9 Deploying Active Directory Connectors

As previously mentioned, you may find it desirable to deploy multiple Active Directory Connector servers in some circumstances. In the scenario described in the previous sections with a globally distributed deployment of Exchange 5.5 sites and domains, it is not surprising that you should use more than one Active Directory Connector server.

An Active Directory Connector hosts a CA that synchronizes data over an LDAP connection typically between separate Exchange 5.5 and AD servers. There is little sense in deploying an Active Directory Connector in Boston that hosts a CA whose endpoints connect to an Exchange 5.5 server and a Global Catalog server both located in Bangkok. It's more appropriate to home the CA on an Active Directory Connector closer to the endpoints. This reduces the overhead of Active Directory Connector synchronization over wide-area connections and relies on the inherent replication mechanisms within the Exchange 5.5 Directory service and the AD.

Determining the quantity and locations of required Active Directory Connector servers is largely a matter of understanding the underlying network, Exchange 5.5 topology, and Windows 2000 or Windows 2003 site and domain models. In the example scenario we've been working with, we'll consider that the environment has a solid hub-based network infrastructure. The network backbone topology is shown in Figure 6-15 and consists of six core network locations joined by high-speed links, that we can assume to be on an asynchronous (ATM) backbone. Each core network location acts as a hub for outlying locations that are connected into the network using lower-speed lines that are typically in the range of 64 kbps to 512 kbps. Each network location is also an Exchange 5.5 site.

With such a topology, and bearing in mind the CA deployment requirements that we've already discussed, it makes sense to position Active Directory Connector servers at each of the core network locations. This results in six Active Directory Connector servers each hosting several CAs, one for each Exchange 5.5 site close to the network hub.

Table 6-1 shows how each of the CAs are hosted on the various Active Directory Connector servers.

Using Active Directory Connector servers at distributed locations means that you can share the load of synchronization across multiple systems. Furthermore, it means that you can distribute the network traffic across all of the network. As new objects and modifications to existing objects are synchronized into the AD, these changes will be replicated across the network within the AD. Similar replication takes place for those new objects and changed objects in the Exchange 5.5 Directory Service. Because the

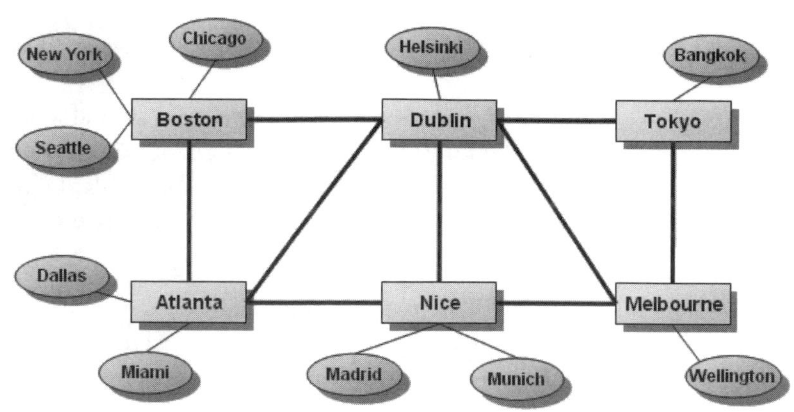

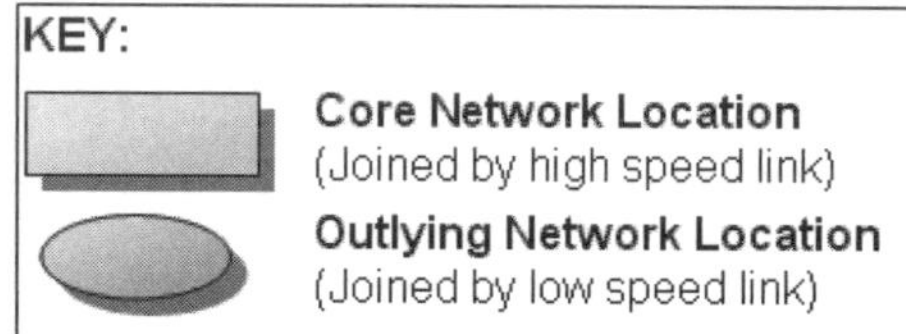

Figure 6-15 *Network Topology and Exchange 5.5 Environment*

Table 6-1 *Active Directory Connector Server Locations and Hosted Connection Agreements*

Active Directory Connector Location	Connection Agreements
Boston	Boston GC to Boston Exchange 5.5 Server
	New York GC to New York Exchange 5.5 Server
	Chicago GC to Chicago Exchange 5.5 Server
	Seattle GC to Seattle Exchange 5.5 Server
Atlanta	Atlanta GC to Atlanta Exchange 5.5 Server
	Dallas GC to Dallas Exchange 5.5 Server
	Miami GC to Miami Exchange 5.5 Server
Dublin	Dublin GC to Dublin Exchange 5.5 Server
	Helsinki GC to Helsinki Exchange 5.5 Server
Nice	Nice GC to Nice Exchange 5.5 Server
	Madrid GC to Madrid Exchange 5.5 Server
	Munich GC to Munich Exchange 5.5 Server
Tokyo	Tokyo GC to Tokyo Exchange 5.5 Server

Table 6-1 (continued)

Active Directory Connector Location	Connection Agreements
	Bangkok GC to Bangkok Exchange 5.5 Server
Melbourne	Melbourne GC to Melbourne Exchange 5.5 Server
	Wellington GC to Wellington Exchange 5.5 Server

endpoints of the CAs are targeted to Exchange 5.5 servers and GC servers at multiple locations, the replication traffic is balanced. And because synchronization is taking place between systems near to the users, there's less impact from replication latency. Users close to the data that is being synchronized are more likely to use it than are users located farther afield.

6.10 Network Impact from Active Directory Connector Synchronization

Synchronization of data between the Exchange 5.5 Directory Service and the AD takes place over LDAP. Unless you have co-located your Exchange 5.5 Directory Service on the same system as your GC, the synchronization process will incur some network overhead merely to move the data from one system to another over the CA.

Table 6-2[1] gives some indication of the network impact associated with Active Directory Connector synchronization between systems. For the most part, these figures are based on the synchronization traffic resulting from a change to a single attribute (telephone number) on the directory object.

What conclusions can we draw from this data?

- When no modifications are made to either the Exchange 5.5 Directory Service or the AD, there is little network load associated with the Active Directory Connector. What little traffic is generated results from the Active Directory Connector querying the directory systems to determine if any objects need synchronized.
- Changes made to objects in the AD generate less overall network load than changes made to objects in the Exchange 5.5 Directory Service.

1. I'm indebted to Paul Bowden from the Exchange Product Group at Microsoft for the data in this table, based on early testing with the Active Directory Connector.

Table 6-2 *Network Load Associated with Active Directory Connector Synchronization*

Activity	Active Directory Connector to GC	GC to Active Directory Connector	Active Directory Connector to 5.5	5.5 to Active Directory Connector	Total
No objects to synch	19 KB	14 KB	5 KB	3 KB	41 KB
1 change in AD	24 KB	91 KB	9 KB	8 KB	132 KB
2 changes in AD	24 KB	98 KB	11 KB	12 KB	143 KB
3 changes in AD	24 KB	101 KB	14 KB	15 KB	154 KB
1 change in 5.5 Directory Service	33 KB	103 KB	10 KB	8 KB	154 KB
2 changes in 5.5 Directory Service	37 KB	111 KB	10 KB	10 KB	168 KB
3 changes in 5.5 Directory Service	43 KB	115 KB	12 KB	12 KB	182 KB

- Network load associated with synchronization from the AD to the Exchange 5.5 Directory Service appears to grow linearly with 11 KB overhead for each object that is synchronized.
- Network load associated with synchronization from the Exchange 5.5 Directory Service to the AD appears to grow linearly with 14 KB overhead for each object that is synchronized.

Clearly, the first time you initiate synchronization between the Exchange 5.5 Directory Service and the AD, you can expect to see a significant amount of network traffic generated. This load may be substantial and potentially detrimental to the stability of your network if you immediately attempt to synchronize many tens of thousands of objects at one time. Remember that a lot of other network traffic must be taken into account. Not only is network load associated with synchronization over the Active Directory Connector between the Exchange 5.5 Directory Service and the AD, but also with the inherent replication mechanisms of these two directory services. As you synchronize new objects into the AD, more network load is generated as the AD replicates this data to all of its GC servers throughout the forest. Similarly, objects synchronized into the Exchange 5.5 Directory Service are replicated to all Exchange 5.5 servers within the organization. Nor should you neglect the effects of back-replication within the Exchange 5.5 Directory Service because objects are modified in the Exchange 5.5 Directory Service as they are synchronized into the AD. (This also occurs in the AD, but it is less significant because the AD uses attribute-based replication, whereas the Exchange 5.5 Directory Service uses object-based replication.)

To avoid a potentially crushing tsunami of replication, you should phase in the synchronization activity. Although you may configure all of the CAs on the various Active Directory Connectors at the same time, you should only activate them sequentially. With the example environment outlined in the previous sections, you can limit the effects of network overload by activating the CAs on each particular Active Directory Connector server over a period of days. For example, you could activate all CAs on the Boston Active Directory Connector on Monday, wait for network traffic to stabilize, then activate all CAs on the Atlanta Active Directory Connector on Tuesday, and so on.

Obviously, the approach you take and the activation interval you use depends on the nature of your particular environment. Whatever approach you take, you should use a test lab environment to understand and characterize your environment's behavior before you deploy for real in your production environment. Forewarned is forearmed.

6.11 Summary

At first glance, the Active Directory Connector appears to be a straightforward tool: Simply point one end of a CA to an Exchange 5.5 server and the other end to the AD, and the result is a single homogeneous directory. Although this is partly true, quite a few refinements need to be applied to have an Active Directory Connector function correctly in your environment.

In this chapter, I've touched on many of the less intuitive aspects of the Active Directory Connector to build a foundation of understanding that will be indispensable when you come to deploy it in a real-life production environment. I've tried to move forward from just describing the details of the Active Directory Connector's operation. Rather, my intention was to build on that fundamental knowledge and describe how the Active Directory Connector can be put to work in real-life environments.

Obviously, it is impossible to exhaust every possibility for deployment in a book such as this one, but the major scenarios described here are based on real working environments in use by some large multinational organizations. Each of these organizations has taken a significantly different approach to interoperability and migration. One organization is afforded the luxury of waiting until a Windows deployment has been completed, and as you have seen, the Active Directory Connector and CA configuration is reasonably straightforward. On the other hand, one of the other organizations has been tasked with aggressively deploying Exchange 2003 or Exchange 2000 before the Windows deployment has been completed. This results in a more sophisticated AD model and a more intricate Active Directory Connector and CA implementation.

All approaches are equally valid and provide the same level of interoperability and high-fidelity directory synchronization between Exchange 5.5, the AD, and ultimately Exchange 2003 or Exchange 2000. All you need to do is decide which approach is most appropriate for your organization and set about implementing it.

7

Moving from Exchange 5.5 to Exchange 2003

7.1 Introduction

Building a solid Windows infrastructure merely provides a robust platform for a new Exchange 2003 deployment. But what of the work required to evolve your existing Exchange 5.5 environments up to the brave new world that is Exchange 2003? Concerning ourselves with the Exchange 5.5 to Exchange 2003 migration aspect, this is not just an upgrade of a few binaries; this is the reengineering of a whole infrastructure. We're presented with almost myriad challenges: (1) providing mail coexistence between Exchange 5.5 and Exchange 2003; (2) providing synchronization services between the Exchange 5.5 and the AD; and (3) how to move Exchange 5.5 mailboxes to Exchange 2003 mailboxes. Of course, we haven't even mentioned Public Folder infrastructures, business applications built on top of Exchange 5.5, and other third-party products that may have potentially been integrated into your Exchange environment. And if that wasn't enough, we also need to be concerned with the effort that's required to upgrade the underlying infrastructure that Exchange 2003 will run on. In all likelihood, you'll probably have Windows NT4 deployed for account domains and resource domains for Exchange 5.5 servers, and these domains will need to be upgraded to Windows 2000 or Windows 2003.

As you can see, moving up to Exchange 2003 isn't just about upgrading a single software product: It's about building a new infrastructure and doing so in a smooth and transparent way so that none of your existing users has an interruption to service. It's not impossible to do, and in the remainder of this chapter, we'll explore the different tools and techniques that are critical in order for your deployment to be successful.

7.2 Exchange 5.5 Migration Fundamentals

We should adhere to several guiding principles with regard to moving from Windows NT4 and Exchange 5.5 to Windows 2000 or Windows 2003 and Exchange 2003. Any migration activity should be low in risk and easy to recover from in case something goes wrong. We should impact the users as little as possible (e.g., service interruption, rebuilding desktop systems). Finally, the effort required to complete the migration to Windows 2000 or Windows 2003 and Exchange 2003 should be as little as possible.

We need to decide on an approach that can be taken to get us to the end zone. Two main approaches exist (although there are variants of each one) when migrating: Either we upgrade existing Exchange 5.5 servers to Exchange 2000 and then subsequently to Exchange 2003, or we establish an integrated coexisting environment by placing new Exchange 2003 servers in the Exchange 5.5 environment and moving users over to the new infrastructure. Irrespective of which approach you take, you still need to provide good interoperability between the Exchange 5.5 and Exchange 2003 infrastructures for the duration of the migration. Within a single Exchange organization, this coexistence is shown diagrammatically in Figure 7-1.

In Figure 7-1, we've integrated a new Exchange 2003 infrastructure into an existing Exchange 5.5 environment. This is done by creating an Exchange 2003 server (either by upgrade from Exchange 5.5 through Exchange 2000 and then upgrade to Exchange 2003 or fresh Exchange 2003 installation) in an existing Exchange 5.5 site or a completely separate AG. With this link in place, and the associated Active Directory Connector connections and mail connections to support it, we can have more or less seamless interoperability between Exchange 5.5 and Exchange 2003. If integration isn't achieved at this level, then you essentially end up with a separate Exchange 2003 organization (different from the Exchange 5.5 organization)— the so-called interorganizational migration. In such a case, you're faced with the age-old problem of interorganization interoperability, such as directory synchronization (made easier using the Active Directory Connector), mail connectivity, and perhaps most important, Public Folder interoperability.

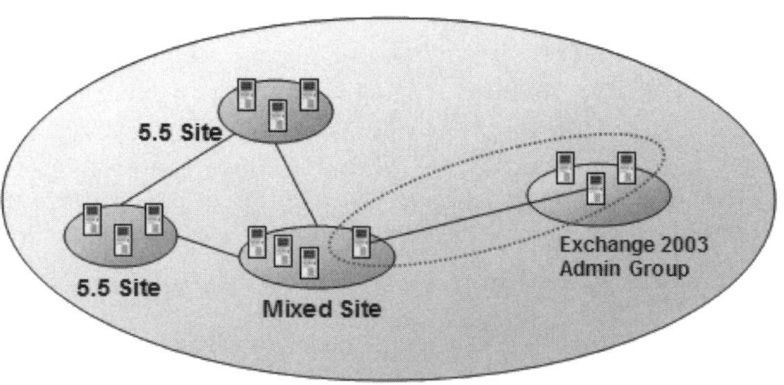

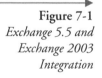

Figure 7-1 *Exchange 5.5 and Exchange 2003 Integration*

There are pros and cons associated with upgrades or Exchange organizational restructuring using fresh installs. Upgrading existing servers uses existing hardware but affects service levels because systems are unavailable for the duration of the upgrade. Adding new Exchange 2003 servers to the existing Exchange 5.5 sites results in new hardware being required, but user impact is reduced because users can just be moved from one server to another in a short period. Whichever approach you take, the best way to get there is to ensure that you've completed a move to Windows 2000 or Windows 2003 for account domains. If you haven't fully completed this exercise, then although you can still migrate to Exchange 2003, it becomes much more complex.

7.3 Making a Clean Break from Exchange 5.5

Before any migration project is embarked upon, it's important to understand just what level of interoperability and coexistence requirements you will need in your environment. Coexistence and migration mean different things to different people, but basically, we have two points: a start point and an endpoint. The start point represents the Exchange 5.5 environment while the endpoint represents a pure Exchange 2003 environment. Ideally, if we could move from the start point to the endpoint in an infinitesimally small period of time, then the problem of coexistence approaches zero. However, the resources required to make such a journey are hard to come by, and in most cases, some level of sustained coexistence is required in support of a migration project.

An alternative exists. We can still make the move from start point to endpoint using some quantity of time but ignore the problem of coexistence altogether. In real terms, this means that we begin a deployment of Exchange 2003 alongside an existing or legacy Exchange environment, but we make no effort to do the following:

- Allow new Exchange 2003 users to communicate with legacy Exchange users
- Move mailbox data from legacy Exchange servers to new Exchange 2003 servers
- Replicate Public Folders from legacy Exchange servers to Exchange 2003 servers
- Maintain group membership, Distribution Lists, or Public Folder access controls
- Maintain third-party product integration or business applications

This is certainly the easiest migration to make because we have no coexistence factors to consider. I've heard more and more people suggest the "clean break" or greenfield migration approach, especially with the sophistication of some of today's third-party migration tools. But I don't believe that this is the best way forward. Most organizations have too much invested in their existing infrastructures to just let them die gracefully. What's more likely is that some form of coexistence will be required during a period of migration. Typically, this kind of coexistence takes the form of mail and directory interoperability coupled with a plan to migrate data from the legacy Exchange environment to the new Exchange 2003 environment.

Even with the definition of greenfield implementation, most organizations consider this only to be a completely new organization that is built separate and distinct from the existing Exchange organization. This does not mean that organizations do not want to provide directory synchronization, mail exchange, mailbox migration, and possibly Public Folder interoperability. In general, even with such greenfield deployments, they do require these services. These interorganizational migrations are discussed later in this book.

7.4 Exchange 5.5 Migration Terminology Refresher

We use several key terms repeatedly when talking about migrating from Exchange 5.5 to Exchange 2003. Some of the terms we've introduced already and explained in passing, but they are critically important to understanding the nature of migration and the behavior that you'll see as users are moved. It's important then that we fully describe them here.

- **Distinguished Names:** We'll discuss Distinguished Names a lot. There are essentially two types: Distinguished Names that we meet in the Exchange 5.5 Directory Service and Distinguished Names that we meet in the AD. Objects in the Exchange 5.5 Directory Service are uniquely identified by their Distinguished Name, whereas objects in the AD are uniquely identified by their GUID.

  An Exchange 5.5 Directory Service example might be:

  ```
  /o=Balmoral/ou=Sales/cn=Recipients/cn=DariaC
  ```

  An AD example might be:

  ```
  cn=DariaC, cn=Users, dc=Balmoral, dc=com
  ```

- **legacyExchangeDN:** Under certain circumstances (e.g., when synchronizing legacy Exchange 5.5 Directory Service objects with AD objects), it's important that an object that has been migrated from the Exchange 5.5 Directory Service be able to *remember* how it was uniquely identified in the Exchange Directory Service. The *legacyExchangeDN* attribute holds this information and acts as a link back to the Exchange object.
- **Security Identifier (SID):** SIDs uniquely identify objects in the Windows NT4 SAM account database. So, clearly, there are two unique representations of

objects in Windows NT4 and Exchange 5.5. The SID is important because it's used as the primary mechanism to enforce security controls in NT4.

- **sIDHistory:** In a fashion similar to the *legacyExchangeDN* attribute, it's often important that an object migrated from the Windows NT4 SAM database to an AD object *remembers* its SID from its Windows NT4 lifetime. The *sidHistory* attribute performs this function, and the ClonePrincipal API utility used by the Windows 2000 or Windows 2003 migration scripts and tools populates this AD attribute when a new security principal is created in Windows 2000 or Windows 2003. You should note that upgrading a Windows NT4 domain to Windows 2000 or Windows 2003 does not populate the *sIdHistory* attribute.
- **msExchMasterAccountSID:** The Active Directory Connector, when creating security principals in the AD, does not populate the *sidHistory* attribute, but it will inspect it when trying to match objects. Instead, the Active Directory Connector stores legacy SID information (which links the Exchange 5.5 mailbox object to a Windows NT4 account) in this attribute and, importantly, some migration tools and the AD Cleanup Wizard use this attribute for object-matching purposes.

7.5 The Importance of sID History During Exchange 5.5 Migration

A SID is a unique value used by both Windows NT4 and Windows 2000/Windows 2003 to identify an account or a group. The most important use for SIDs with respect to migration is the construction of ACLs and the protection of Windows resources during a period of migration. The ability to create a new Windows 2000 or Windows 2003 account from a source Windows NT4 account and placing the source account's SID on the destination account's *sIDHistory* list is critical for any Windows migration.

Many large organizations execute migration projects from Windows NT4 to Windows 2000 or Windows 2003 that are gradual and take place over time. For those organizations that restructure their Windows NT4 environment to a new Windows 2000 or Windows 2003 environment, some particular circumstances are applicable. New Windows 2000 or Windows 2003 user objects are created for existing Windows NT4 users. Because a SID is unique to an account, when a user receives a new Windows 2000 or Windows 2003 account, they will be using a new SID. Resources are typically migrated over time, as existing Windows NT4 resource domains and resources in Windows NT4 account domains are migrated in a structured manner. This means that a user's account may have been moved to Windows 2000 or Windows 2003 before any of the resources that he or she requires access to have been moved from Windows NT4. Because the original Windows NT4 account's SID exists in the destination account's *sIDHistory*, this provides the user with the ability to access legacy resources until the migration process moves the resources into the Windows 2000 or Windows 2003 domains. Typically at that point, the migrated resources have their ACLs updated to reflect the new Windows 2000 or Windows 2003 accounts.

7.6 Exchange 5.5, Windows Migrations, and the ClonePrincipal Toolkit

The ClonePrincipal toolkit is a group of VBScript and DLLs that provide the ability to migrate accounts and groups from a Windows NT4 domain to a Windows 2000 or Windows 2003 domain, adding the SID of the source account or group to the *sidHistory* attribute of the destination account or group. This allows the destination account or group to effectively masquerade as the source (or cloned) account. This functionality is implemented via an application programming interface (API) that was originally developed by Microsoft to support the migration of accounts to a Windows 2000 environment.

The ClonePrincipal toolkit is used by several other tools to facilitate the migration of Windows NT4 accounts to Windows 2000 or Windows 2003. Specifically, Microsoft's ADMT uses the ClonePrincipal logic as the basis of its operation. Several third-party tools have also been developed based on this API. Although the tools are certainly useful and enhancements to the basic functionality, the ClonePrincipal tool is still useful in its own right. Its operation relies on scripts and DLLs, and subsequently, it's possible to customize it or write your own migration scripts and procedures.

The ClonePrincipal toolkit is part of the Windows 2000 Support tools, which are installed from the Support\Tools folder on the Windows 2000 distribution media. The installation will copy the required files to \Program Files\Support Tools and will register the CLONEPR.DLL.

The following list, taken from Microsoft's Clone Principal User's Guide, describes the core components:

- **CLONEPR.DLL:** COM object with methods to support ClonePrincipal operations
- **SIDHIST.VBS:** Sample script that adds the SID of a source account to the *sIDHistory* of a destination account in a different forest
- **CLONEPR.VBS:** Sample script that clones a single security principal
- **CLONEGG.VBS:** Sample script that clones all of the Global Groups in a domain

- **CLONEGGu.VBS:** Sample script that clones all of the Global Groups and Users in a domain
- **CLONELG.VBS:** Sample script that clones all of the Local Groups in a domain
- **CLONEPR.DOC:** ClonePrincipal documentation

With modern-day migrations, it's more likely that you will use some of the third-party products that are available from companies such as Quest, Bindview, or NetIQ. These third-party tools all have excellent reputations for migrating legacy Windows accounts to either Windows 2000 or Windows 2003.

7.7 Requirements for Writeable Access to sIDHistory

Several configuration actions must be taken before you can use the ClonePrincipal tool, or any migration tool based on it, to write to the *sidHistory* attribute. Specifcally, you must ensure that the following tasks have been performed:

- You must set the *TcpipClientSupport* registry value. On the source primary DC, create and set the following registry key:

  ```
  HKEY_LOCAL_MACHINE\System\CurrentControlSet\Control\Lsa
  Value name: TcpipClientSupport
  Value type: DWORD
  Value data: 1
  ```

  Then, reboot the source domain controller. This registry value makes the Security Account Manager listen on the transmission control protocol (TCP) transport. ClonePrincipal will fail if this registry value isn't set on the source DC.

- You must enable auditing in the source and destination domains. In the destination Windows 2000 or Windows 2003 domain, perform the following tasks:

  1. In the *AD Users and Computers* MMC snap-in, select the destination domain *Domain Controllers* container.
  2. Right-click on *Domain Controllers* and then choose *Properties.*
  3. Click on the *Group Policy* tab.
  4. Select the *Default Domain Controllers Policy* and select *Edit.*
  5. Under *Computer Configuration\Windows Settings\Security Settings\Local Policies\Audit Policy*, double-click on *Audit Account Management.*
  6. In the *Audit Account Management* window, select both *Success* and *Failure* auditing. Wait 15 minutes for the policy auditing change to take effect or reboot.

In the source Windows NT4 domain, perform the following tasks:

1. In *User Manager for Domains*, click the *Policies* menu and select *Audit.*
2. Select *Audit These Events.*
3. For *User and Group Management*, select *Success* and *Failure.*
4. In *User Manager for Domains*, click the *User* menu and select *New Local Group.*
5. Enter a group name composed of the source domain NetBIOS name appended with three dollar signs (e.g., BALMORAL$$$). Ensure that there are no members for the group.

- Finally, ensure that a trust relationship exists from the source domain to the destination domain.

7.8 Running Exchange 5.5 on Windows 2000 Servers

As part of the journey to Exchange 2003, many organizations will first update their complete Windows NT4 infrastructure, both account domains and resource domains, to Windows 2000 or Windows 2003. Particularly if you intend to do in-place upgrades of Exchange 5.5 servers to Exchange 2003, it is an absolute requirement that at some stage you have Exchange 5.5 running on a Windows 2000 server and then Exchange 2000 running on a Windows 2000 server. Remember that neither Exchange 5.5 nor Exchange 2000 is supported on Windows 2003 member servers.

Apart from in-place upgrades, there's no requirement that you must have Exchange 5.5 running on Windows 2000 servers. If you don't wish to upgrade servers in place, but instead want to perform a restructuring migration, then you don't need to upgrade an Exchange 5.5 server from Windows NT4. The restructuring approach allows you to move users from Exchange 5.5 servers running Windows NT4 to Exchange 2003 servers running on either Windows 2000 or Windows 2003. This approach is in line with the guiding principle of minimal effort.

If you do wish to upgrade in place, be sure to get existing Exchange 5.5 servers deployed with at least Exchange 5.5 SP3, but preferably SP4, deployed before you start the process of upgrading the operating system from Windows NT4 to Windows 2000. This approach provides an opportunity to flatten Windows NT4 domains into a more manageable model and eliminate potentially a wealth of resource domains that you may have had. If you had Exchange 5.5 servers running on Windows NT4 Backup Domain Controllers (BDCs), you now have an opportunity to fold them back into Windows 2000 Master Account Domains as member servers. It's important that you do this because it simplifies topology and administration and from a stepped approach makes a subsequent migration to Windows 2003 simpler. Although, if you have a large environment running Exchange 5.5 on Windows NT4, a restructuring approach makes much more sense because there is less work to perform.

In the Exchange 5.5 and Windows NT4 environment, it was a best practice to either have Exchange 5.5 running on a BDC for a resource domain or at least have a BDC logically close by. In moving to Windows 2000 and Windows 2003, it's desirable to get the domain into native mode as quickly as possible. It's easy to do this with Windows NT4 member servers because they can exist in a Windows 2000 or Windows 2003 native-mode domain. However, Windows NT4 DCs can't exist in a Windows 2000 or Windows 2003 native-mode domain, so it's imperative to have these servers upgraded to Windows 2000 or Windows 2003 quickly. Although there's no great technical challenge associated with this move, it is yet another hurdle that you have to jump over before you can begin your Exchange 2003 migration in earnest.

In general it's a matter of best practice to eventually run Exchange 2003 on member servers, not DCs or GC servers. And I've already described earlier in this book that Exchange 2003 is in fact only supported on GC servers under restricted circumstances. During this upgrade period, it's best if you can avoid running Exchange 5.5 on Windows 2000 DCs. However, if you do have Exchange 5.5 running on a Windows 2000 DC, remember that there will be some contention for access to the LDAP port 389, so you will need to take the appropriate action to reassign Exchange 5.5's LDAP port, as described earlier.

Deploying a Windows 2000 platform for your Exchange 5.5 environment can be done in several ways. The most straightforward method is to perform in-place upgrades of the operating system, but you need to balance this with the complexity of your overall infrastructure. One approach that has proved successful with several organizations has been to install a completely new operating system platform on sometimes brand-new hardware. Exchange 5.5 databases can be saved onto a backup medium, the server reinitialized, Exchange 5.5 reinstalled, and then the databases restored to the new server. This also allows organizations that have invested effort in designing a standard operating system platform an opportunity to apply this new platform to existing Exchange 5.5 systems.

7.9 Exchange 5.5 to Exchange 2003 Migration Approaches

You can take several approaches when it comes to moving from an Exchange 5.5 deployment to Exchange 2003. Primarily, we'll look at three different deployment scenarios: (1) upgrading to Exchange 2003; (2) restructuring approach after Windows

2000 or Windows 2003 deployment; and (3) the accelerated restructuring approach before completing a Windows 2000 or Windows 2003 deployment.

7.9.1 The Exchange 5.5 to Exchange 2003 upgrade approach

You cannot perform an in-place upgrade from an Exchange 5.5 server to an Exchange 2003 server. Even if you attempt to do so, the Exchange 2003 Setup program will instruct you that it cannot proceed. This is different from the process that you could have used to upgrade an Exchange 5.5 server to Exchange 2000, where an in-place upgrade was possible.

The alternative, and only recommended, method for migrating an Exchange 5.5 server to Exchange 2003 is to use the Move Mailbox Wizard approach. Essentially, this approach involves installing an Exchange 2003 server into the same Exchange 5.5 site as the Exchange 5.5 server from which you want to migrate mailboxes. You then move all mailboxes from the Exchange 5.5 server onto the Exchange 2003 server, ultimately decommissioning the Exchange 5.5 server when all mailboxes have been moved off. One of the requirements that must be in place before any such Exchange 2003 servers can be installed into the Exchange 5.5 site is that an Active Directory Connector environment must already be in place. This is the same approach that can also be used for Exchange 5.5 to Exchange 2000 migration.

Exchange 2000 servers can be directly in-place upgraded to Exchange 2003, so if you really must perform an in-place upgrade on an Exchange 5.5 server—possibly because you don't have enough extra or new hardware to use the Move Mailbox Wizard approach—then you can perform an in-place upgrade from Exchange 5.5 to Exchange 2000 followed by another in-place upgrade from Exchange 2000 to Exchange 2003. This is not recommended. though, given the time required to perform such a series of operations and the impact of lack of service availability on users. However, in some cases it may be absolutely the only approach you can take. Remember that after such a series of upgrades, it is of the utmost importance to take new backups of the Exchange databases. You should really perform two backups in this scenario: one immediately after the upgrade from Exchange 5.5 to Exchange 2000 and another after the upgrade from Exchange 2000 to Exchange 2003.

Although upgrading from Exchange 5.5 in place to Exchange 2000 and then to Exchange 2003 is one of the most intuitive means by which to get Exchange 2003 deployed, it is also the most complicated, time-consuming, and least appealing approach. This section covers what's involved in upgrading an Exchange 5.5 server to Exchange 2000. Building on this, and covered later in this book, we'll discuss upgrading an Exchange 2000 server to Exchange 2003. Let's look at the process of getting to Exchange 2000 in the first instance.

7.9.1.1 Exchange 5.5 to Exchange 2000 upgrade assumptions

With this approach there are two stages of upgrade that must be performed: first an upgrade from Exchange 5.5 to Exchange 2000 and then from Exchange 2000 to Exchange 2003. The most important assumption associated with the classic Exchange 5.5 to Exchange 2000 upgrade approach is what needs to be done to the Windows NT4 accounts. You can't have an Exchange 2000 mailbox unless you have a Windows 2000 or Windows 2003 account. So you must have completed your migration from Windows NT4 account domains to Windows 2000 or Windows 2003 account domains before you start upgrading an Exchange 5.5 server that hosts mailboxes. (An Exchange 2000 mailbox can be associated with either a Windows 2000 or a Windows 2003 user object.) You must also have taken the steps to get Exchange 5.5 running on a Windows 2000 server so that the upgrade can proceed, specifically running Exchange 5.5 SP3, or preferably SP4.

7.9.1.2 Exchange 5.5 to Exchange 2000 upgrade process

Before starting the upgrade process, you must have an Active Directory Connector in place. This is required at the very least for the automatic configuration of a ConfigCA as a server in an Exchange 5.5 site becomes a first Exchange 2000 server in the site. Furthermore, you need the Active Directory Connector to host any Recipient CAs that are required to represent Exchange 5.5 mailboxes, custom recipients, and Distribution Lists in the AD.

Upon running the Setup program, you are confronted with the options to upgrade the existing Exchange 5.5 server to Exchange 2000 (as shown in Figure 7-2). Exchange 2000 uses a different database structure than Exchange 5.5, so in addition to the time required just to upgrade the binaries, the total upgrade time depends on the size of the Information Store databases. The Setup process upgrades the Information Store databases at the rather impressive rate of around 25 GB per hour, although this depends largely on the configuration of your system, and especially the configuration of disk spindles and IO controllers you use on the server. During setup, the databases are not upgraded completely. Instead, only a minimum part of the Information Store is upgraded, and the remainder of it is upgraded as background thread that runs as soon as Exchange 2000 starts up. (As an interesting historical aside, the original behavior was to perform a minimal upgrade of the database while Setup was executing and then only upgrade the parts of the Information Store on demand by the user. However, this plan was short-lived, when the first usability tests revealed that the load on the system was somewhat more than expected, to say the least, when newly upgraded users all logged on at the same time!)

While this background thread is running, there is a slight performance penalty, a loading on the IO system of around 5%. The duration of the background thread

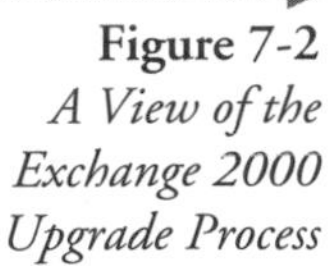

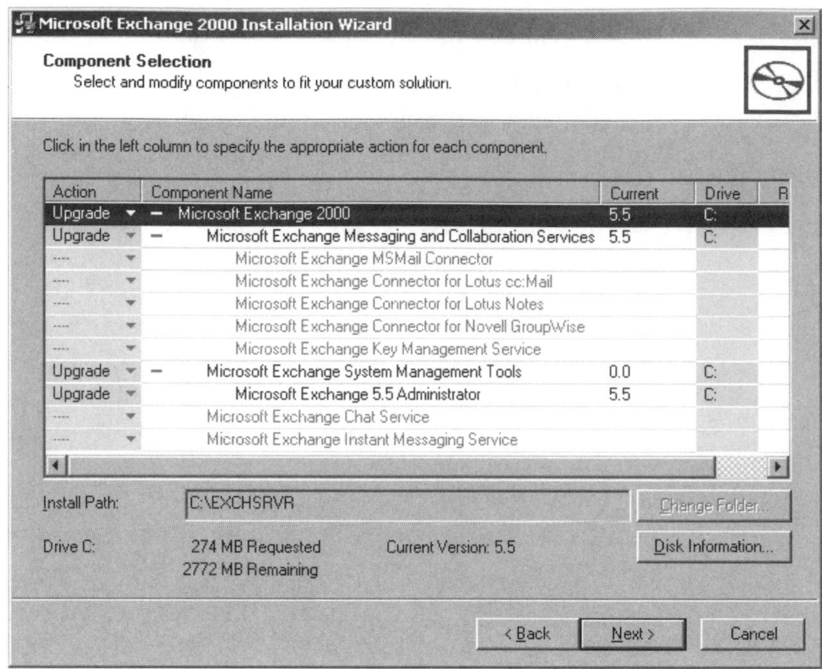

Figure 7-2
A View of the Exchange 2000 Upgrade Process

operation is similar to the time required by Setup, again around 25 GB per hour. Rather than suffer this slight penalty, you can force a total database upgrade to take place. To do this you should dismount the databases once Exchange 2000 starts up and execute the following command from a command window:

```
ESEUTIL /F name
```

7.9.1.3 Exchange 5.5 to Exchange 2000 upgrade internals

Let's look at the simple case of what happens when a single Windows NT4 and Exchange 5.5 server are upgraded to Windows 2000 and Exchange 2000. We begin with a Windows NT4 SAM entry for the user and an Exchange 5.5 Directory Service entry, as shown in Figure 7-3.

After an upgrade from Windows NT4 to Windows 2000, users still get access to their Exchange 5.5 mailboxes because the access information has been preserved through the in-place Windows NT4 upgrade. That is, the *Assoc-NT-Account* that points to the Windows NT4 SID is consistent because the same SID is available after the upgrade. An object's Windows NT4 SID does not change when the domain is upgraded to Windows 2000. Immediately following the Windows NT4 upgrade, we'll be left with a new Windows 2000 account, with details as shown in Figure 7-4. Notice

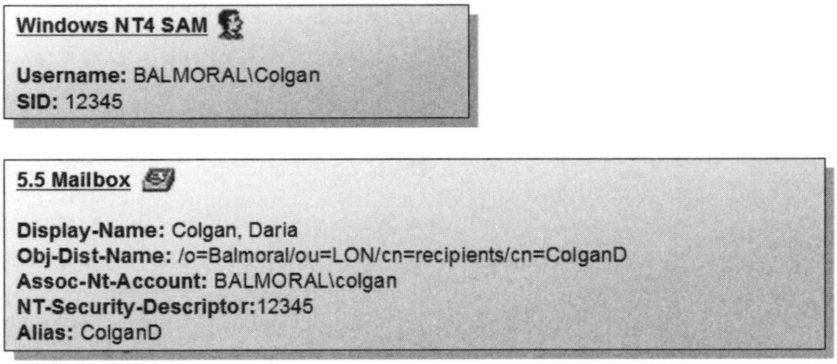

Windows NT4 SAM

Username: BALMORAL\Colgan
SID: 12345

5.5 Mailbox

Display-Name: Colgan, Daria
Obj-Dist-Name: /o=Balmoral/ou=LON/cn=recipients/cn=ColganD
Assoc-Nt-Account: BALMORAL\colgan
NT-Security-Descriptor: 12345
Alias: ColganD

Figure 7-3 *Windows NT4 and Exchange 5.5 Information Before Upgrade*

that the Distinguished Name is 'colgan' and is consistent with the SAM Account Name of the Windows NT4 account.

Following the account domain upgrade, the Active Directory Connector should be installed and the appropriate CAs put in place and activated to map the Exchange 5.5 mailbox to the new Windows 2000 account. After running the CA, the Windows 2000 account will be updated to reflect the Exchange 5.5 mailbox, but specifically you should notice that the Distinguished Name changes after Active Directory Connector synchronization. This is evidence that the Exchange 5.5 mailbox details have been merged with the AD object and some of the new values that you should expect to see are shown in Figure 7-5.

The important concern here is access to the Exchange 5.5 mailbox. There is no interruption to access to the mailbox because the down-level account name has remained the same.

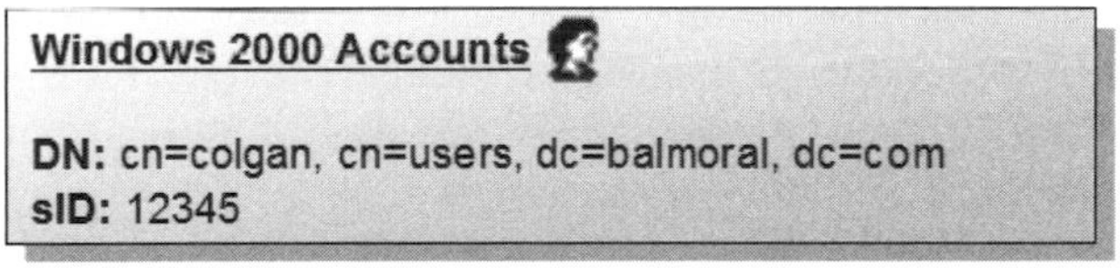

Windows 2000 Accounts

DN: cn=colgan, cn=users, dc=balmoral, dc=com
sID: 12345

Figure 7-4 *Windows 2000 Account Details After Upgrade*

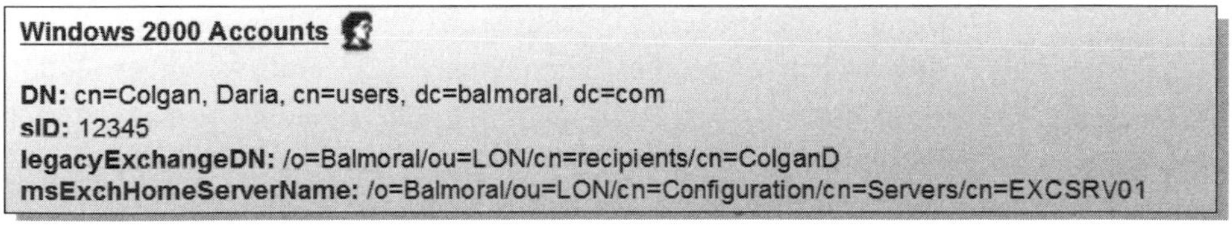

Windows 2000 Accounts

DN: cn=Colgan, Daria, cn=users, dc=balmoral, dc=com
sID: 12345
legacyExchangeDN: /o=Balmoral/ou=LON/cn=recipients/cn=ColganD
msExchHomeServerName: /o=Balmoral/ou=LON/cn=Configuration/cn=Servers/cn=EXCSRV01

Figure 7-5 *Updated Windows 2000 Account Details Following Active Directory*

Following the Active Directory Connector synchronization, the Exchange 2000 Setup program can be executed and the Exchange 5.5 server is upgraded to Exchange 2000.

7.9.1.4 Exchange 2000 to Exchange 2003 upgrade

Remember, though, that after this process a subsequent upgrade from Exchange 2000 to Exchange 2003 must be performed. From an operating system perspective, the Windows 2000 platform should be upgraded to Windows 2003 after the upgrade from Exchange 2000 to Exchange 2003 has been completed.

7.9.1.5 Exchange 5.5 to Exchange 2003 upgrade benefits and drawbacks

Performing in-place upgrades means that you reuse your existing hardware, so it's attractive from this perspective. Also, if your environment is reasonably straightforward and requires little modification, this is the natural approach to take because it requires little in the way of restructuring or external migration tools. Additionally, account passwords remain intact. The in-place upgrade, even with the multistage process of stepping through Exchange 2000 on the way to Exchange 2003, is attractive to small organizations and those with budget constraints. On the other hand, the existing hardware on which you are running Windows NT4 and Exchange 5.5 may not be suitable for Windows 2000 or Windows 2003 or Exchange 2003. If that's the case, and you need to upgrade hardware, then you'll have to cover the extra cost in any event.

But perhaps the biggest drawback is the service interruption. Servers must be taken offline to perform a complex number of upgrades: first Windows NT4 to Windows 2000, then Exchange 5.5 to Exchange 2000, then Exchange 2000 to Exchange 2003, and then Windows 2000 to Windows 2003. And do bear in mind that backups should be taken at all intervals during the upgrade procedure so that you can recover something usable if a disaster occurs during a subsequent phase of the upgrade. Even if you do this during nonworking office hours, it is a major disruption and can take a significant period of time. In addition, because the upgrade process has server granularity, if something goes wrong, it can take considerable time to recover from it, restore backup tapes, and get your users up and running again.

7.9.1.6 Upgrading Exchange 5.5 clusters to Exchange 2003

Upgrading a cluster is not a straightforward task. You must perform the first phase of the upgrade process to reach Exchange 2000 running on Windows 2000 and then subsequently upgrade to Exchange 2003 and Windows 2003. Upgrading a nonclustered system is more or less a self-contained process after you double-click on SETUP.EXE. However, upgrading a cluster is a less self-contained process. Instead, we must use one of two approaches: (1) a cluster server rebuild process along the same lines as the disaster recovery process for Exchange 5.5 or (2) we must introduce a new Exchange 2000 cluster into the same site and move users onto it. Let's look at the disaster recovery–style option first.

With the disaster recovery mode of upgrade, we essentially save off the existing Exchange 5.5 databases, reinitialize[1] the existing server (i.e., reinstall the operating system and Exchange 2000 from scratch), and build a new Exchange 2000 cluster. When we have the new cluster built using existing hardware, we can restore the old cluster databases onto the new cluster, and after the databases have been upgraded, we wind up with a new Exchange 2000 cluster. This approach is somewhat convoluted, but it is well documented and should be relatively straightforward. As an in-place upgrade, it suffers from the fact that the server is taken out of service for a period of time, probably a few days while it's backed up, rebuilt, and then restored, so this represents a considerable impact on user service levels. The upgrade steps for an Exchange 5.5 cluster are as follows:

1. Back up all user and configuration data on the cluster.
2. In *Cluster Administrator*, bring the Exchange 5.5 Cluster group offline.
3. From *My Computer*, go to H:\Exchsrvr, where H is the letter of the shared cluster drive, and rename the MDBDATA directory. (Choose a new name such as MDBTEMP.) If you do not rename this directory, the directory will be removed in step 4.
4. Remove Exchange 5.5 Server (and all the Exchange 5.5 system files) from both nodes by running Exchange 5.5 Setup and selecting *Remove all* on the *Installation Options* screen.
5. From *My Computer*, go to H:\exchsrvr, where H is the letter of the shared cluster drive, and change the directory that you renamed in step 3 back to MDBDATA.
6. Install Exchange 2000 on both nodes of the cluster. (Follow the procedure for Exchange 2000 cluster installation outlined in the file \DOCS\C20_CLUSTERING.RTF on the Exchange 2000 installation CD.) Do not install both nodes at the same time. After you complete installing the first node, restart that node and then begin installation on the other node.

1. A certain Exchange Program Manager who shall remain nameless described this much more eloquently to me some time ago, employing the phrase "torch the existing box" in place of the somewhat more mundane "reinitialize the existing server."

7. Create a resource group in the same cluster group that the Exchange 5.5 virtual server was in, but do not bring the group online. (See the previously referenced document for information on creating a resource group.)
8. From *My Computer*, go to H:\Exchsrvr\MDBDATA, where H is the letter of the shared cluster drive.
9. In the MDBDATA directory, delete all of the files except for PRIV.EDB and PUB.EDB. Rename these files PRIV1.EDB and PUB1.EDB, respectively.
10. In *Cluster Administrator*, right-click the resource group, and then click *Bring Online*. As the databases come online for the first time, Exchange 2000 recognizes that they are in Exchange 5.5 format and immediately initiates a process to upgrade them to Exchange 2000/2003 format.

The alternative upgrade approach is along the lines of the general restructuring approach that we can use for any type of Exchange 5.5 server. We'll discuss that approach in more detail later, but essentially it allows us to install a brand-new cluster into the same site that the Exchange 5.5 cluster is in and simply move users from the old cluster to the new one. This approach has many attractions, not least of which is that we get an opportunity to use new hardware, which is particularly important for Exchange 2000 clustering, but also there is significantly less impact on server availability to the users.

With either of these approaches, bear in mind that the first Exchange 5.5 server in a site that you upgrade to Exchange 2000 must run the SRS. And because the SRS cannot run on a cluster, if you wish to upgrade an Exchange 5.5 cluster to become an Exchange 2000 cluster, you must previously have installed or upgraded a nonclustered Exchange 2000 system into that site.

With an upgrade to Exchange 2000 on Windows 2000 completed, you then need to perform an upgrade to Exchange 2003. The upgrade path is more or less mandatory here: you must upgrade each node in the cluster from Exchange 2000 to Exchange 2003, and only then can you upgrade the operating system to Windows 2003. Exchange 2000 clustering is your friend, and the concept of rolling upgrades becomes critical. With either active/active or active/passive clustering, the approach to take is to fail-over services to one node in the cluster and then perform the Exchange upgrade on the unused node. Ideally, you should upgrade to Exchange 2003 on both nodes first, and only then consider upgrading the operating system to Windows 2003, but it is okay to upgrade the unused node to both Exchange 2003 and Windows 2003 in one step and then reintroduce this node back into the cluster in an active capacity. You should seek to minimize the time when you have asymmetrical versions of Exchange and Windows on cluster nodes.

7.9.2 The restructuring approach with Exchange 5.5 to Exchange 2003 migration

As an alternative to the upgrade approach, it's possible to build a new Exchange 2003 environment alongside, but integrated with, the existing Exchange 5.5 environment. This approach, just like the upgrade approach, relies on Exchange 5.5 intraorganizational coexistence with Exchange 2003 servers.

7.9.2.1 *Exchange 5.5 to Exchange 2003 restructuring assumptions*

One of the biggest assumptions we make with this approach—and in fact, the most important factor related to its relative ease as a migration mechanism—is that the migration of account domains from Windows NT4 to Windows 2000 or Windows 2003 is complete. If the migration isn't completed, then the restructuring scenario becomes complicated from an AD perspective and essentially turns into the Accelerated Restructuring Approach that is described later.

Of course, with a restructuring approach—much like the approach you might take for Windows restructuring—you need to invest in at least some new hardware on which to run the parallel Exchange 2003 environment. This does not mean that you need to replace every single Exchange 5.5 server system with new hardware for Exchange 2003. You may do this, or you may take an opportunity to consolidate server systems and replace several Exchange 5.5 systems with a single Exchange 2003 server, perhaps even a cluster. This *Pacman* approach is appealing because it builds on the strengths of Exchange 2003. Alternately, you may be able to reuse old Exchange 5.5 hardware with a *Moving Train* or *Leapfrog* approach. That is, kick-start the restructuring operation by introducing a new Exchange 2003 server on new hardware, move Exchange 5.5 users onto this new server, thus freeing up the old hardware on which Exchange 5.5 was running for recycling, perhaps for the next Exchange 2003 server.

7.9.2.2 *Exchange 5.5 to Exchange 2003 restructuring process*

In terms of Exchange 2003 restructuring, what you do not want to do is build a new Exchange 2003 organization that is separate from the existing Exchange 5.5 organization. This does not offer a coexistent environment or rich interoperability. What we do wish to build is a new Exchange 2003 environment that is integrated into the existing Exchange 5.5 environment. The simplest way to do this is to select that you'll join an existing Exchange 5.5 site during the first Exchange 2003 server installation. Selecting this option prompts you on the next setup screen to specify the name of an Exchange 5.5 server in the site that you wish to join, and subsequently RPC communications take place and configuration information is read from the Exchange 5.5 Directory

Service and written into the AD configuration naming context. The installation process uses a temporary CA to read this copy of the configuration information from Exchange 5.5 to the AD, so you must already have an Active Directory Connector configured somewhere in your organization.

With the restructuring approach, you install the new Exchange 2003 server into an existing Exchange 5.5 site: a site that must have at least one Exchange 5.5 Service Pack 3 (or preferably Service Pack 4) server. Such a site is often referred to as a *mixed-vintage site*, because it hosts both legacy Exchange 5.5 servers and new Exchange 2003 servers. (The same expression holds true for Exchange 2000 servers in the site.) The site should not have previous versions of Exchange in it (i.e., Exchange 4.0 and Exchange 5.0) because such versions render the environment unsupported, although evidence suggests that such environments are functional. But do note that previous versions of Exchange 5.5 without Service Pack 3 are supported.

Before an Exchange 2003 server can be installed into an Exchange 5.5 site, you must already have an Active Directory Connector available. You'll need the Active Directory Connector there to support CAs for the recipient containers and Organizational Units that you wish to synchronize, but just as important, the installation process associated with the first Exchange 2003 server creates a ConfigCA so that configuration information can be synchronized between the Exchange 5.5 and Exchange 2003 environments. During installation, Setup chooses the first Active Directory Connector returned to it by a DC in order to home the ConfigCA. If you have multiple Active Directory Connectors (e.g., one in each major geographic area), then it's possible that you may find an *Americas* Active Directory Connector being used to host a ConfigCA for a site in Europe. There's no way to control this during installation, but you should review the placement of ConfigCAs after installation and rehome remote ConfigCAs to local Active Directory Connectors if they've been homed incorrectly, thus improving configuration information synchronization performance.

The beauty of the mixed-vintage site is that you have Exchange 2003 servers in Exchange 5.5 sites operating seamlessly and transparently to your users. Within the site, the Exchange 2003 server looks much like any other Exchange 5.5 server when viewed from the Exchange 5.5 Administrator program, and similarly, Exchange 5.5 servers can be viewed from the Windows 2003 Exchange System Manager (ESM) MMC snap-in and appear pretty much like any other Exchange 2000 server. (Examples of these views are shown in Figure 7-6 and Figure 7-7.)

Although the servers are visible from both management interfaces, you should not cross the streams when it comes to server management. That is, you should use the Exchange 5.5 Administrator program to manage Exchange 5.5 servers and use the ESM utility to manage Exchange 2003 servers. Hybrid management practices are not

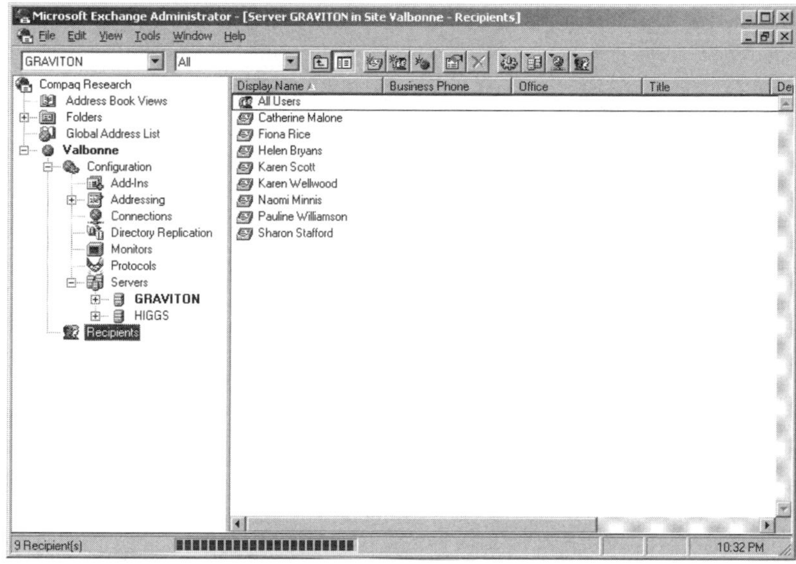

Figure 7-6 *Exchange 5.5 Administrator Program Showing Mixed-Vintage Site (Server HIGGS runs Exchange 2003)*

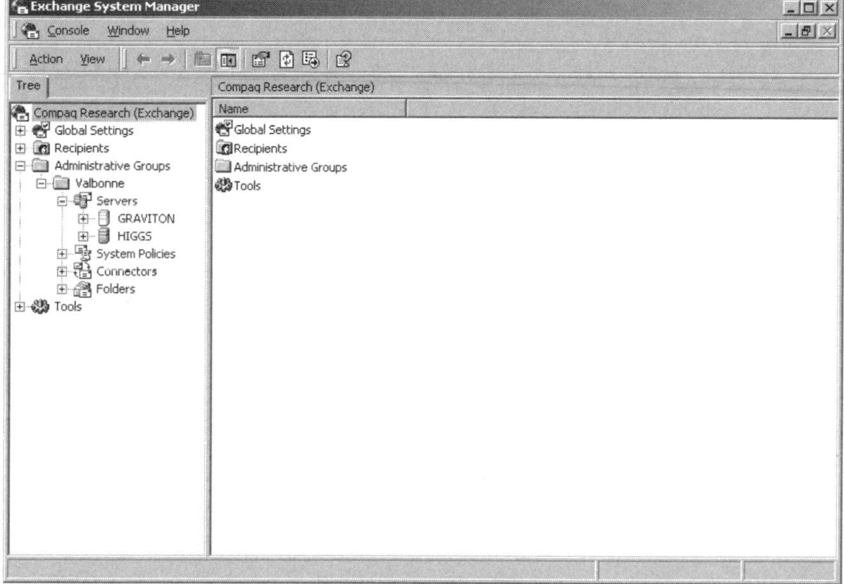

Figure 7-7 *Exchange System Manager Showing Mixed-Vintage Site (Server GRAVITON runs Exchange 5.5)*

recommended. If you need any further encouragement for this, you should look at the Exchange 2003 installation process: it explicitly offers an option to install the Exchange 5.5 Administrator program so that you can manage Exchange 5.5 servers in mixed-vintage sites.

Within a mixed-vintage site, legacy Exchange servers and Exchange 2003 servers communicate using RPCs for MTA-to-MTA communication, Site Replication Service–based intrasite replication, and Exchange 5.5 Administrator communications.

In an Exchange 2003 mixed-mode organization, Exchange 5.5 sites map directly to Exchange 2003 AGs (individual servers can't be moved between AGs and RGs until the Exchange 2003 organization is running in native mode). Sites are represented as a fixed AG/RG pair. You can see this mapping of Sites and AG/RG pairs by looking at Figure 7-6 and Figure 7-7. The Valbonne Site as viewed from the Exchange 5.5 Administrator program is shown as an AG from the ESM.

Although Exchange 5.5 server to Exchange 2003 server communication within a mixed-vintage site takes place using RPCs, if there are multiple Exchange 2003 servers in the site, they communicate with each other using native SMTP transport, as they would do in a normal Exchange 2003 RG. Additionally, one of the Exchange 2003 servers in a mixed-vintage site acts as the Routing Group Master and generates the Link State Table to provide optimized routing information to the other Exchange 2003 servers in the site (AG/RG pair). The Routing Group Master generates information on how to connect to other Exchange 5.5 servers based on what it receives via the ConfigCA.

Having built a closely integrated mixed-vintage site, there's now a straightforward mechanism to move user mailboxes from Exchange 5.5 to Exchange 2003: It's called point-and-click! You can use the Windows 2000 or Windows 2003 AD Users and Computers MMC snap-in or the ESM snap-in to select the Exchange 5.5 mailbox (which is associated with a Windows 2000 or Windows 2003 user object), right-click and select Exchange Tasks and then Move Mailbox Wizard, and then select the appropriate database on the new Exchange 2003 server to which the mailbox should be moved. (Figure 7-8 shows a screenshot from part of this process.)

Mailbox move performance, which relies on MAPI for its operation, is affected by the throughput that you can glean from the IO subsystem on both the source and target Exchange servers. As a rough guideline, on my single-disk test systems, a 115 MB mailbox took approximately nine minutes to move. Thus the effective transfer rate was about 12 MB per minute. Faster disks, controllers, high spindle count, low workload on the servers, and the network should all contribute to speedier migrations. Transfer rates of 4 gb per hour are common. The Move Mailbox Wizard is described in more detail later in this book.

Single-instance storage is not preserved across moves, even if the mailboxes are moved from the same source Exchange 5.5 information store. However, this may not be too important to you because many organizations, especially larger ones, have observed poor single-instance sharing ratios. Moves between any Exchange 5.5 server

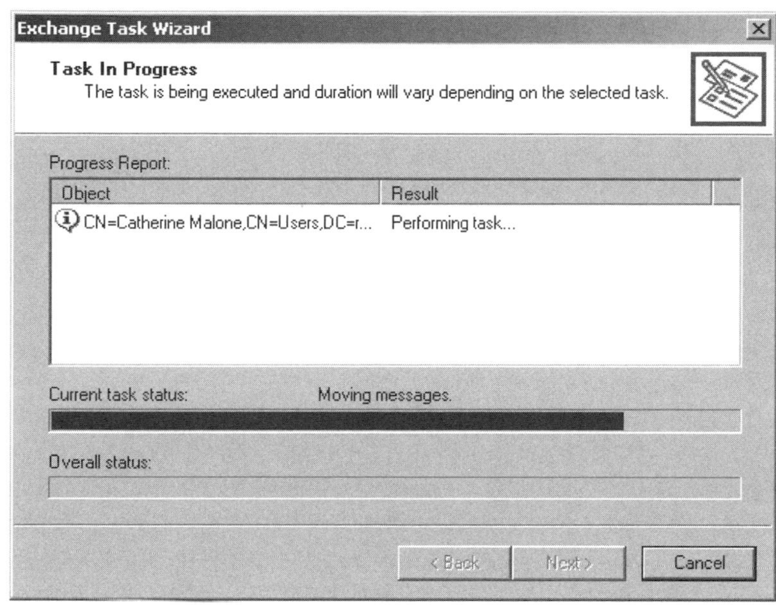

Figure 7-8 *Active Directory Users and Computers Move Mailbox Wizard*

to any Exchange 2000 server (and back to Exchange 5.5 if required) are supported within a site or AG/RG pair. However, moving a mailbox from an Exchange 5.5 server in one site to an Exchange 2000 server in another AG/RG pair is not supported. That is, mailbox moves between mixed-vintage sites are not supported in Exchange 2000 mixed mode; you must be in native mode before you can move Exchange 2000 mailboxes between servers in different AGs or RGs.

Although moving mailboxes from Exchange 5.5 servers to Exchange 2003 servers is a convenient way to migrate data, there are some restrictions on its operation. If the Exchange 5.5 server is running on a GC server while Exchange 2003 (or Windows 2000, for that matter) is running elsewhere in the forest, you cannot move mailboxes from the Exchange 5.5 server. The attempt to do so results in MAPI error 80040111-0286-00000000. To allow the migration of mailboxes from this server, you must reconfigure the server so that it is no longer a GC server. (But obviously another GC server in the forest must be available.)

7.9.2.3 Exchange 5.5 to Exchange 2003 restructuring internals

Let's look at the process of restructuring and what happens when Windows NT4 accounts are migrated to Windows 2000 or Windows 2003 in advance of an Exchange 5.5 mailbox move. We start with a Windows NT4 account and Exchange 5.5 mailbox, as shown in Figure 7-9.

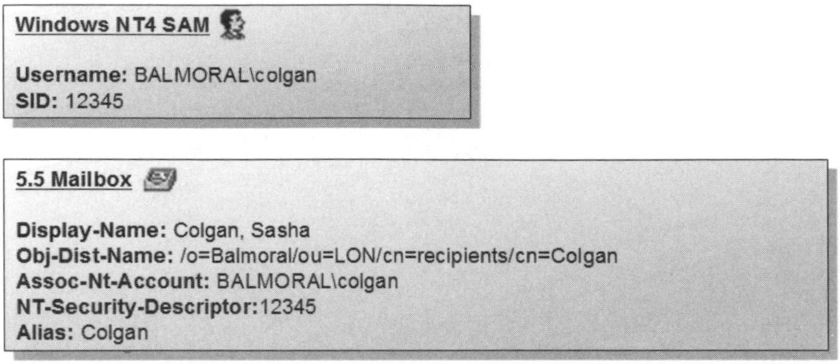

Figure 7-9 *Windows NT4 and Exchange 5.5 Mailbox Information Before Account Migration*

Windows NT4 SAM

Username: BALMORAL\colgan
SID: 12345

5.5 Mailbox

Display-Name: Colgan, Sasha
Obj-Dist-Name: /o=Balmoral/ou=LON/cn=recipients/cn=Colgan
Assoc-Nt-Account: BALMORAL\colgan
NT-Security-Descriptor:12345
Alias: Colgan

Account migration takes place before any Exchange mailboxes are moved, so Windows 2000 or Windows 2003 accounts are created to host the Exchange 2003 mailboxes. In the Upgrade Approach, we assumed that Windows NT4 account domains were upgraded in place. However, for the purposes of this example, we'll assume that Windows NT4 account domains are not upgraded, but instead Windows NT4 accounts are migrated using the ClonePrincipal technique into a new Windows 2000 or Windows 2003 account domain. This account migration process can disable the existing Windows NT4 accounts, or they can remain enabled and in use. However, it makes sense to disable the old accounts and use the new Windows 2000 or Windows 2003 accounts. Because we're creating new accounts, the new Windows 2000 or Windows 2003 user objects get a new SID. Using appropriate migration tools, such as Microsoft's ADMT, Bindview's Direct Migrate, Quest's DM Suite, or NetIQ's One Point Suite means that the *sidHistory* attribute will be set on the new object to reflect its relationship to the old Windows NT4 account, as shown in Figure 7-10. This yields a new relationship between the Exchange 5.5 mailbox and the account used to access it: now a Windows 2000 or Windows 2003 account is used.

Access to Exchange 5.5 mailboxes is preserved because down-level account names and the *sidHistory* attribute are maintained in the new account. When the first Active Directory Connector synchronization cycle occurs, the Exchange 5.5 mailbox can be successfully matched against the Windows 2000 or Windows 2003 account using the *sidHistory* attribute. (You must explicitly configure the global Active Directory Connector policy so that matching occurs based on *sidHistory* values.) The Windows 2000 or Windows 2003 account information is merged with information from the Exchange 5.5 mailbox directory entry, resulting in an updated Windows 2000 or Windows 2003 object, as shown in Figure 7-11.

Following the Active Directory Connector synchronization, you can install Exchange 2003 servers into Exchange 5.5 sites and subsequently move Exchange 5.5 mailboxes to information stores on Exchange 2003 servers.

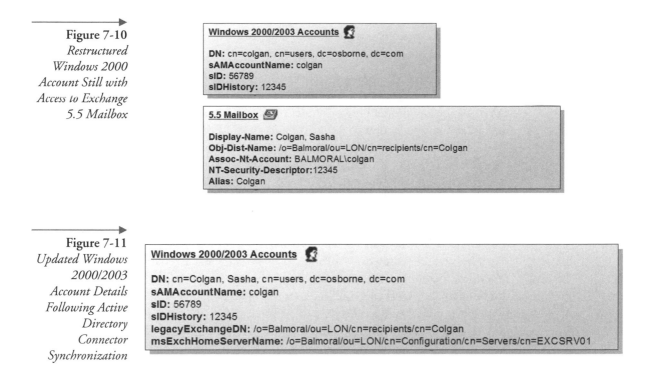

Figure 7-10 *Restructured Windows 2000 Account Still with Access to Exchange 5.5 Mailbox*

Windows 2000/2003 Accounts

DN: cn=colgan, cn=users, dc=osborne, dc=com
sAMAccountName: colgan
sID: 56789
sIDHistory: 12345

5.5 Mailbox

Display-Name: Colgan, Sasha
Obj-Dist-Name: /o=Balmoral/ou=LON/cn=recipients/cn=Colgan
Assoc-Nt-Account: BALMORAL\colgan
NT-Security-Descriptor: 12345
Alias: Colgan

Figure 7-11 *Updated Windows 2000/2003 Account Details Following Active Directory Connector Synchronization*

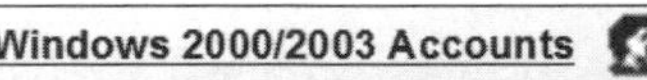

DN: cn=Colgan, Sasha, cn=users, dc=osborne, dc=com
sAMAccountName: colgan
sID: 56789
sIDHistory: 12345
legacyExchangeDN: /o=Balmoral/ou=LON/cn=recipients/cn=Colgan
msExchHomeServerName: /o=Balmoral/ou=LON/cn=Configuration/cn=Servers/cn=EXCSRV01

7.9.2.4 Using ExDeploy for Exchange 5.5 to Exchange 2003 restructuring

For a guided, handheld approach to migration from Exchange 5.5, you can use the ExDeploy tools. Essentially ExDeploy defines a process for the tasks that you must perform in order to complete such a migration. ExDeploy defines three phases for migration from Exchange 5.5.

The ExDeploy tools are to be found on the Exchange 2003 installation CD-ROM in the \support\ExDeploy directory. Double-click on the exdeploy.chm file to start the wizard. This is a compiled help file that identifies the steps you must carry out. Note that when you start the ExDeploy tool, you are presented with various options for how you wish to proceed. You should choose the set of procedures that relate to Exchange 5.5 to Exchange 2003 migration. Be sure not to run ExDeploy from a network share: doing so will result in ExDeploy not functioning correctly.

Before you begin, it is important that the account from which you execute the ExDeploy tools has the necessary permissions. To actually run the ExDeploy tools, the account must have Domain Administrator and Exchange 5.5 Administrator permissions. For subsequent operations you will need Enterprise, Schema, Domain, and Local Machine Administrator permissions to run Forestprep; Domain and Local Machine Administrator permissions to run Domainprep; Domain and Local Machine

Administrator permissions to install the Active Directory Connector; and Full Exchange and Local Machine Administrator to install Exchange 2003.

The first phase comprises several steps basically defining the infrastructure prerequisites for a migration to take place and then a set of basic connectivity tests that you can run to ensure proper network functionality. To perform these tasks you must connect to an existing Exchange 5.5 server and an AD GC server. The connectivity tests, DCDiag and NetDiag, confirm DC connectivity and a functioning domain name service (DNS). DCDiag and NetDiag have been described earlier in this book. Additionally, this phase contains the DSScopeScan toolset, which contains several individual tools that check the consistency and integrity of the Exchange 5.5 environment, particularly in regard to server names and versions, connector counts, and user counts.

The second phase runs through several; standard Exchange 2003 installation processes, including Forestprep and Domainprep. Executing the Domainprep action doesn't actually go off and run Domainprep in all domains. You'll still have to do this in all of the domains that require Domainprep, and if you wish you can run the ExDeploy wizard on a server in each domain to have this performed. Also included in the second phase is a series of tests that collectively comprise the OrgPrepCheck tool group, which performs some basic checking on the Exchange 5.5 organization after the Forestprep and Domainprep tools to ensure that schema extensions and the appropriate groups and policies are in place and that the organization is ready for an upgrade to Exchange 2003. We are still in the preparatory phase of Exchange 2003 installation, and before any Exchange 2003 servers can be installed, we must have the Active Directory Connector installed and configured. The second phase facilitates this installation and directs you to the Active Directory Connector Tools wizard, which can ease the burden of configuring CAs in less complex environments.

The actual installation of Exchange 2003 takes place with the third phase when some final DNS checks are performed and the installation of Exchange 2003 servers is facilitated. A screenshot from ExDeploy Phase 3 is shown in Figure 7-12. With Exchange 2003 servers successfully in place, you can use the Move Mailbox Wizard to actually move mailbox content from Exchange 5.5 servers to Exchange 2003 servers.

It is important to understand that you don't actually need to use the ExDeploy tools in order to start an Exchange 5.5 migration to Exchange 2003. You can perform these activities independently of using ExDeploy. And in reality, ExDeploy offers no more than a guiding hand through the process that is really only appropriate for small organizations with perhaps just a couple of servers and/or sites. For larger, more complex environments, you really need to develop your own set of processes to prepare for migration.

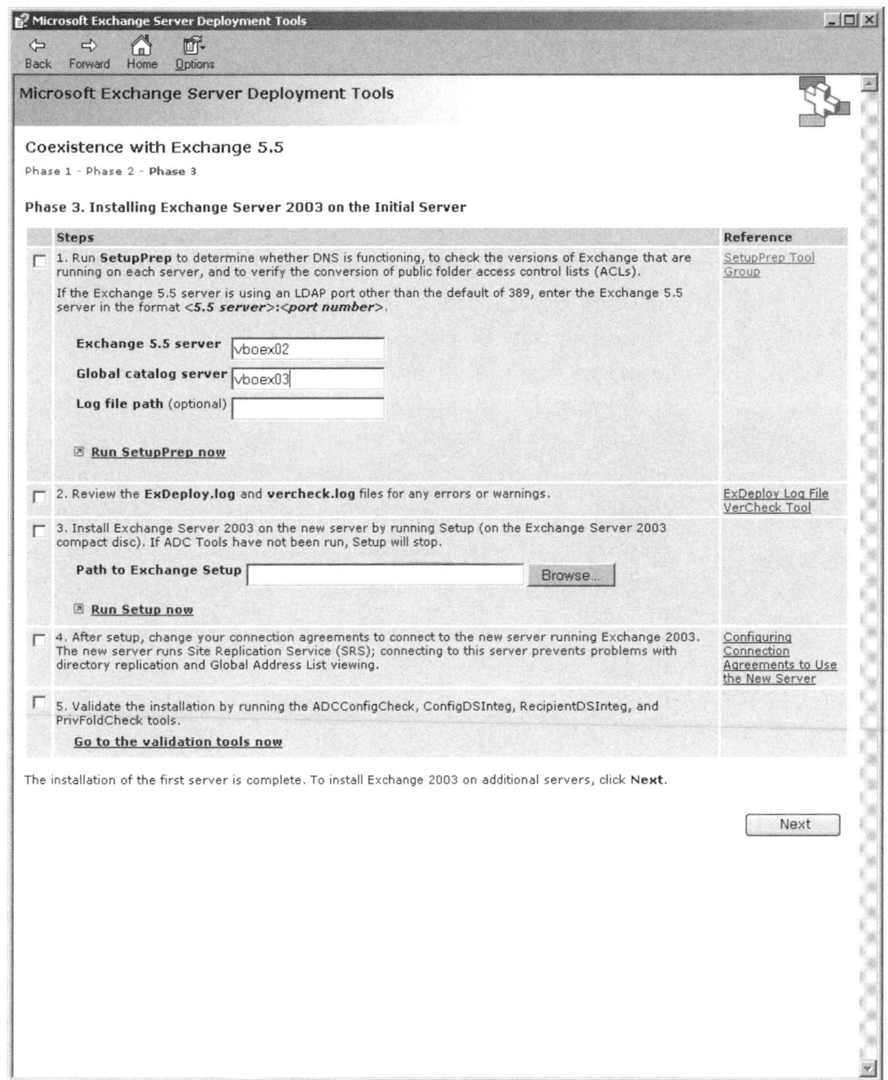

Figure 7-12 *ExDeploy Exchange 5.5 Migration Phase 3*

With the initial checks carried out and with the appropriate Active Directory Connector CAs in place, you can now continue with tasks as defined in the ExDeploy Wizard. The next tasks are the SetupPrep tools. These tasks include the OrgNameCheck tool, which searches for and identifies any illegal characters in the Exchange 5.5 organization name and site names and server names. Any characters used in these constructs must conform with the RFC-821 specification. In general, brackets are the biggest offender in most organizations. Logging information is written to the

OrgNameCheck.log file and the ExDeploy.log. Additionally, the OrgCheck and PubFolderCheck tools are run. These tools perform the following functions:

- OrgCheck validates schema extensions and checks that the domain groups exist, the appropriate security descriptors are assigned, the Exchange configuration container is in place, and a GC server is available in the same or an adjacent site to Exchange 2003 server.
- PubFoldCheck is the Public Folder DS/IS Consistency Checker. Its default actions create a new Directory Service entry if a Public Folder entry is found in the Information Store without a preexisting Exchange 5.5 Directory Service entry; delete a Directory Service entry if a corresponding Public Folder object is not found in the Information Store; rehome Public Folders to a local Exchange 5.5 server if the Public Folder is homed in an unknown site; and remove invalid users from Public Folder permissions. Note that PubFoldCheck will only perform these actions if the inconsistencies detected are older than one day. (Do exercise caution before running PubFoldCheck because it can cause serious consequences and potential data loss.)

At this point in the installation, Setup checks that the Active Directory Connector Tools checks have been performed. If not, the installation will not proceed. However, if the checks have been successfully performed, but error messages were written to the log files, then although an error message is displayed (twice in fact), the installation of Exchange 2003 can proceed normally.

Following the preinstallation checks, you should then proceed to install the Exchange 2003 server into the existing Exchange 5.5 site. This should proceed without incident, and when the server has been installed, you can set about moving mailboxes over to the new server from the Exchange 5.5 server. You may also run the final set of postinstallation tasks from ExDeploy that confirm that the installation has proceeded correctly. These tasks are ADCConfigCheck, ConfigDSInteg, RecipientDSInteg, and PrivFoldCheck, and all write to the ExDeploy.log logfile.

7.9.2.5 Exchange 5.5 to Exchange 2003 restructuring benefits and drawbacks

The restructuring approach has the lowest impact when it comes to migration to Exchange 2003. In place of the extended time required to upgrade a server to Windows 2000 or Windows 2003 and then subsequently upgrade to Exchange 2003, during which time user mailboxes are unavailable, you can build the new Exchange 2003 server alongside the existing Exchange 5.5 service and move users either one at a time or using scripts written with Collaboration Data Objects for Exchange Management

(CDOEXM). From a user perspective, there is little interruption to service, only the time required to move users from one server to another.

The migration granularity, this time on a mailbox as opposed to a server with the upgrade approach, also presents significantly less risk in case something goes wrong. Furthermore, if your new deployment is leveraging the server consolidation aspect of Exchange 2003, then the restructuring approach offers a simple way to consolidate hardware systems and reuse hardware by virtue of the *Pacman* and *Moving Train* approach that was described previously.

Although the restructuring approach is desirable for many reasons, it can be expensive because a parallel infrastructure of some description must be in place. However, it's likely that your hardware will need to be improved for Windows 2000 or Windows 2003 and Exchange 2003 anyhow, so this point may be moot. Similarly, the *Moving Train* approach allows existing hardware to be reused, so the costs may not be that prohibitive. If you are familiar with Exchange 5.5 to Exchange 2000 migration, then there is very little that's new with Exchange 5.5 to Exchange 2003 migration. The same principles and tools are used today as yesterday. Furthermore, migrating from Exchange 5.5 is straightforward because it's simply a matter of creating an interoperability environment with the Active Directory Connector and then using the Move Mailbox Wizard to move data: there's no decision to be made about upgrading or moving!

7.9.3 The accelerated restructuring approach for Exchange 5.5 to Exchange 2003

The conventional restructuring approach assumes that Windows NT4 account domains are migrated to Windows 2000 or Windows 2003 domains before deploying Exchange 2003, but specifically before deploying the Active Directory Connector. This assumes that some form of CA topology, like that specified in Chapter 6 earlier in this book, is used to allow the Active Directory Connector to match Exchange 5.5 mailboxes with Windows 2000 or Windows 2003 accounts.

However, many organizations strive to deploy Exchange 2003 urgently, and in many cases the deployment of Windows 2000 or Windows 2003 is only in support of Exchange 2003. In such circumstances, it's common to see deployments of the Active Directory Connector and Exchange 2003 in advance of a complete migration of Windows NT4 account domains to Windows 2000 or Windows 2003 domains. In support of even a single Exchange 2003 user, an infrastructure must be in place to create a GAL in the AD, and accordingly the appropriate CAs must be deployed. If organizations wish to deploy Exchange 2003 with urgency, but can't wait to complete the migration from Windows NT4 to Windows 2000 or Windows 2003, then the accelerated restructuring approach is a natural fit.

7.9.3.1 Exchange 5.5 to Exchange 2003 accelerated restructuring assumptions

The assumptions associated with the accelerated restructuring approach basically negate the good practice associated with both the upgrade and the restructuring approaches. In both of those approaches, you ensured that all account domain migration from Windows NT4 to Windows 2000 or Windows 2003 had been completed. If this is done, any form of migration is relatively pain-free.

The basic premise of the accelerated restructuring approach is that this account domain upgrade is either not completed before you start to move to Exchange 2003, or it is started at the same time and runs in parallel to an Exchange 2003 migration. Effectively, it's the sequencing of when Active Directory Connector synchronization is run in relation to account domain migration that's important. Put the Active Directory Connector in place any time before you've completed your account domain migration and Exchange 2003 migration becomes more challenging.

7.9.3.2 Exchange 5.5 to Exchange 2003 accelerated restructuring process

With the accelerated restructuring approach, during the midpoint of the migration we find ourselves with a mix of Windows NT4 and Windows 2000 or Windows 2003 users, along with a mix of Exchange 5.5 and Exchange 2003 mailboxes. Although this kind of migration is the most complex, it's equally likely that it will be the most common for sizable organizations.

The major complication with the accelerated restructuring approach is the risk of AD object duplication. With the other approaches, the Active Directory Connector was always able to match an Exchange 5.5 mailbox to an existing Windows 2000 or Windows 2003 user account, but with the accelerated restructuring approach, an unmigrated Exchange 5.5 user will have two account identities. There will be a Windows NT4 account associated with the Exchange 5.5 mailbox and a Windows 2000 or Windows 2003 user object (or potentially a contact) in the AD. The potential problem arises when the Windows NT4 account is migrated to Windows 2000 or Windows 2003. In this circumstance, we rely on intelligence in the account migration tools to recognize that an object already exists in the AD referencing this user. In that case, the migration tools should merge information from the Windows NT4 user object with the existing Windows 2000 or Windows 2003 object already created by the Active Directory Connector.

Simply creating a new account in Windows 2000 or Windows 2003 may not be appropriate because this process will not carry across any Windows NT4 account history (so permission structures will be lost). Similarly, just using an object already created by the Active Directory Connector may not be appropriate because there is no *sidHistory* associated with an Active Directory Connector–created object, so again, permission structures are lost.

The leading Windows 2000 or Windows 2003 migration tools seem to be able to deal with the situation relatively well. For example, the tools from Microsoft, Bindview, Quest, and NetIQ all help with varying degrees of sophistication to merge legacy Windows NT4 accounts with Windows 2000 or Windows 2003 account objects (probably created by the Active Directory Connector). At an early stage in your deployment project, you should evaluate the characteristics for each of these tools and choose the one that most suits your needs and your environment. Of course, the Active Directory Connector allows you to create mail-enabled Contacts (as well as enabled or disabled user objects) in the AD to represent Exchange 5.5 users, but because these Contacts aren't security principals, it's more difficult to merge with them at Windows NT migration time.

If you use migration tools that aren't intelligent enough to detect an existing account and merge with it, or you just create new users, then you may well end up with a live user account as a result of the account domain migration and a user account or contact as a result of previous Active Directory Connector synchronization. In this case you'll need some way to rationalize the duplicate objects and merge them together. In such cases, you'll need to use the AD Cleanup Wizard, as described in section 7.10.

7.9.3.3 Exchange 5.5 to Exchange 2003 accelerated restructuring internals

Let's look at a typical sequence of events that you might expect to see with the accelerated restructuring migration. We do not assume that there is an object in the AD that references the Exchange 5.5 mailbox, but we do assume that the Active Directory Connector will create a security principal (either an enabled or disabled user object, but not a contact) when synchronization takes place. We begin with a Windows NT4 account and an Exchange 5.5 mailbox like that shown in Figure 7-13.

As a matter of best practice, you should configure the Active Directory Connector's CAs to create disabled user accounts for an Exchange 5.5 mailbox if it can't match it against an existing Windows 2000 or Windows 2003 account. The disabled user object gets a new SID in Windows 2000 or Windows 2003 and of course has a new Distinguished Name. The AD Distinguished Name and *samAccountName* is built from the Exchange 5.5 mailbox display name, as described in sections 3.14 and 3.15.

Windows NT4 SAM

Username: BALMORAL\colgan
SID: 12345

5.5 Mailbox

Display-Name: Colgan, Miles
Obj-Dist-Name: /o=Balmoral/ou=LON/cn=recipients/cn=Colgan
Assoc-Nt-Account: BALMORAL\colgan
NT-Security-Descriptor: 12345
Alias: ColganM

Figure 7-13 *Windows NT4 and Exchange 5.5 Mailbox Before Account Migration*

The primary Windows NT4 account SID is saved in the *msExchMasterAccountSID* attributes. Remember that the *sidHistory* attribute is not populated by the Active Directory Connector. In addition, the legacy Exchange 5.5 Distinguished Name is stored in the *legacyExchangeDN* attribute. This results in an Active Directory Connector–created AD object like that shown in Figure 7-14.

Typically, the next step is to migrate the Windows NT4 account to a Windows 2000 or Windows 2003 account. Using the proper migration tools, you'll avoid object duplication. Such tools should check on the *msExchMasterAccountSID* (and previously on the *samAccountName* but no longer with Exchange 2003). But in the worst case, you may end up creating another security principal in the AD. For example, using the ClonePrincipal API scripts to migrate the Windows NT4 account will result in a new object being created for this user with a new Distinguished Name, a new SID, and the old SID being placed in the *sidHistory* attribute. This results in two objects in the AD now referencing the same person, as shown in Figure 7-15.

Notice the different SID values for these objects, and also pay particular attention to the Distinguished Names for each one. The Display Name for the Active Directory Connector–created object (uppermost in Figure 7-15) has an RDN of 'ADC_271E828E1828459E045' built by the Active Directory Connector, while the migrated Windows NT4 account has an RDN of 'colgan' built from the Windows NT4 account name.

Windows 2000/2003 Accounts

DN: cn=ADC_271E828E1828459E045, cn=users, dc=balmoral, dc=com
sAMAccountName: ADC_271E828E1828459E045
sID: 56789
msExchMasterAccountSID: 12345
legacyExchangeDN: /o=Balmoral/ou=LON/cn=recipients/cn=Colgan
msExchHomeServerName: /o=Balmoral/ou=LON/cn=Configuration/cn=Servers/cn=EXCSRV01

Figure 7-14 *Active Directory Connector–created Disabled User Object*

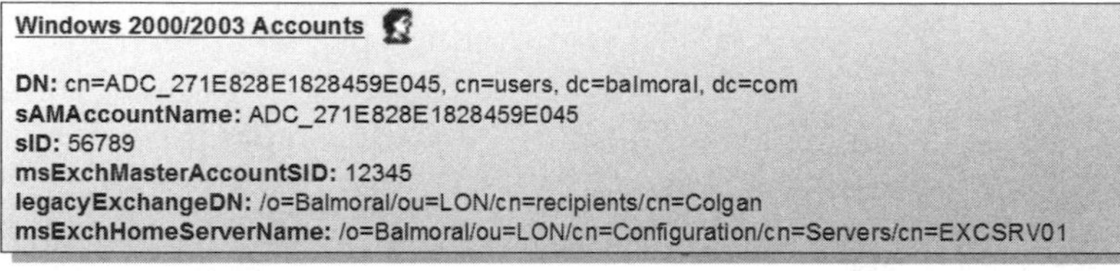

Windows 2000/2003 Accounts

DN: cn=ADC_271E828E1828459E045, cn=users, dc=balmoral, dc=com
sAMAccountName: ADC_271E828E1828459E045
sID: 56789
msExchMasterAccountSID: 12345
legacyExchangeDN: /o=Balmoral/ou=LON/cn=recipients/cn=Colgan
msExchHomeServerName: /o=Balmoral/ou=LON/cn=Configuration/cn=Servers/cn=EXCSRV01

Windows 2000/2003 Accounts

DN: cn=colgan, cn=users, dc=balmoral, dc=com
sAMAccountName: colgan
sID: 13579
sIDHistory: 12345

Figure 7-15 *Two User Objects in Active Directory Referencing the Same Person*

Before you can proceed, it is common practice at this stage to run the AD Cleanup Wizard to merge both the security principals for Miles Colgan together into a single AD object. When the AD Cleanup Wizard operates, the source (disabled) object attribute information is always merged into the target (live) object attribute information, resulting in a single enabled security principal. This results in an enabled user account similar to that shown in Figure 7-16.

Notice that the Display Name information for this merged object has reverted back to that for the migrated user account. When the Active Directory Connector next initiates a synchronization cycle, it will update the object's Display Name with the Exchange 5.5 mailbox's Display Name, like that in Figure 7-17.

The final step in this process is to migrate the Exchange 5.5 mailbox to an Exchange 2000 mailbox. You can do this using the Move Mailbox functionality of the AD Users and Computers snap-in or ESM tools in the same way as you would

Windows 2000/2003 Accounts

DN: cn=colgan, cn=users, dc=balmoral, dc=com
sAMAccountName: colgan
sID: 13579
sIDHistory: 12345
msExchMasterAccountSID: 12345
legacyExchangeDN: /o=Balmoral/ou=LON/cn=recipients/cn=Colgan
msExchHomeServerName: /o=Balmoral/ou=LON/cn=Configuration/cn=Servers/cn=EXCSRV01

Figure 7-16 *Merged Active Directory User Object Details*

Windows 2000/2003 Accounts

DN: cn=Colgan, Miles, cn=users, dc=balmoral, dc=com
sAMAccountName: colgan
sID: 13579
sIDHistory: 12345
msExchMasterAccountSID: 12345
legacyExchangeDN: /o=Balmoral/ou=LON/cn=recipients/cn=Colgan
msExchHomeServerName: /o=Balmoral/ou=LON/cn=Configuration/cn=Servers/cn=EXCSRV01

Figure 7-17 *Active Directory Connector–updated Merged Active Directory User Object Details*

for a conventional restructuring operation. Alternately, you could upgrade existing Exchange 5.5 servers first to Exchange 2000 and then to Exchange 2003 in a more hybrid fashion. Either way, the real complexity in this approach relates to manipulation of data in the AD.

7.9.3.4 Exchange 5.5 to Exchange 2003 accelerated restructuring benefits and drawbacks

The only benefit associated with the accelerated restructuring approach is that it facilitates a timely and rapid move to Exchange 2003 because there is no need to wait on the completion of an account domain migration from Windows NT4 to Windows 2000 or Windows 2003.

This is its greatest strength and its greatest weakness. The synchronization model is more complex and can result in duplicate object creation in the AD unless you use the appropriate migration tools. To avoid any cleanup headaches, using migration tools is a must. Although there may be some cost associated with these tools, it's likely that they will save much pain in the long run.

7.10 Active Directory Account Domain Cleanup Wizard

The AD Account Domain Cleanup Wizard is an invaluable tool in any Exchange 2000 migration toolbox. In the simplest of environments where Windows NT4 account domains associated with Exchange 5.5 mailboxes are upgraded to Windows 2000 or Windows 2003, your risk of exposure to AD Cleanup Wizard should be minimal. Similarly, in larger environments, where sophisticated third-party migration tools are used correctly to perform account and mailbox migration, it is again unlikely that you'll need to use AD Cleanup Wizard.

Nevertheless, AD Cleanup Wizard is a powerful tool, and there are many scenarios in which its use will be mandatory. In the remainder of this chapter, we explain the operation of AD Cleanup Wizard and just how it can be used to make account and mailbox migration as clean as possible.

7.10.1 Why more isn't necessarily better

Many circumstances can cause duplicate objects to exist in the AD. Migrating from Exchange 5.5 is typically the most common, and the reasons for duplication are more or less obvious. Let's look at an example.

In this scenario, you've used the Active Directory Connector to create disabled user objects in the AD corresponding to your Exchange 5.5 mailboxes. The next step in most environments is to migrate Windows NT4 accounts to Windows 2000 or

Windows 2003 accounts. But many migration tools can't match an Active Directory Connector–created disabled user object with the Windows NT4 account that's being migrated. In such a case, you end up with two user objects in the AD: a disabled user object created by the Active Directory Connector and a live user object created by your migration tool.

Simply deleting one or the other of the objects is not an option because they both hold important information. The Active Directory Connector–created disabled user object contains information about the user gleaned from the Exchange 5.5 Directory Service, such as job title, office location, telephone number, and e-mail addresses. A relevant example for the user Richard Bijaoui is shown in Figure 7-18. Similarly, the user object created by the migration tool lacks these attributes (shown in Figure 7-19) but does contain important information about the user's Windows 2000 group membership (shown in Figure 7-20) and other security attributes, such as the *sidHistory*. Your mantra for migration should be to merge directory information, but all you've done here is partition the information for a single user into two distinct objects.

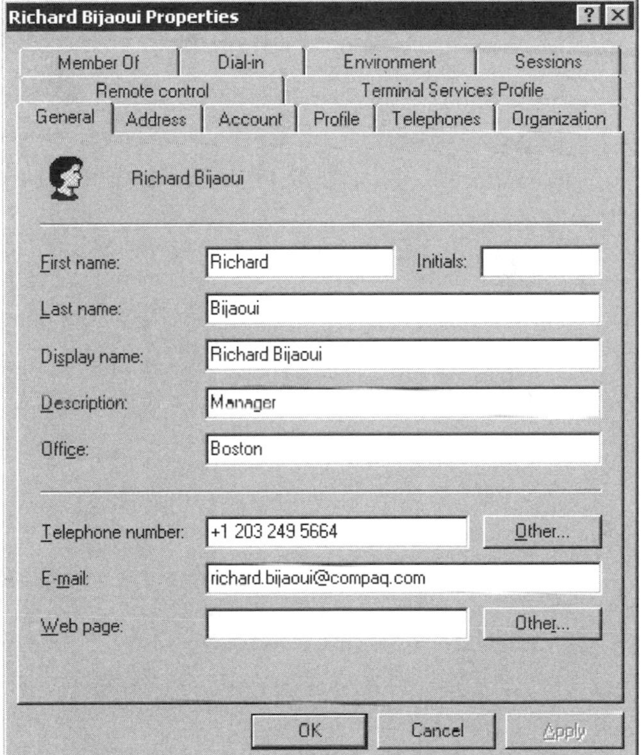

Figure 7-18
Properties for the Disabled User Object Created by the Active Directory Connector

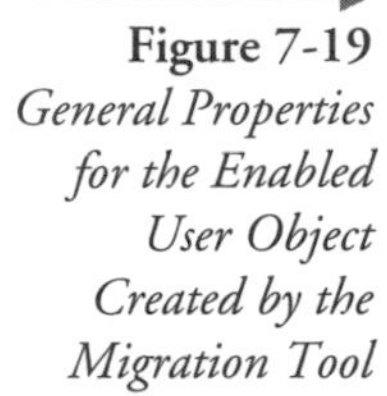

Figure 7-19 *General Properties for the Enabled User Object Created by the Migration Tool*

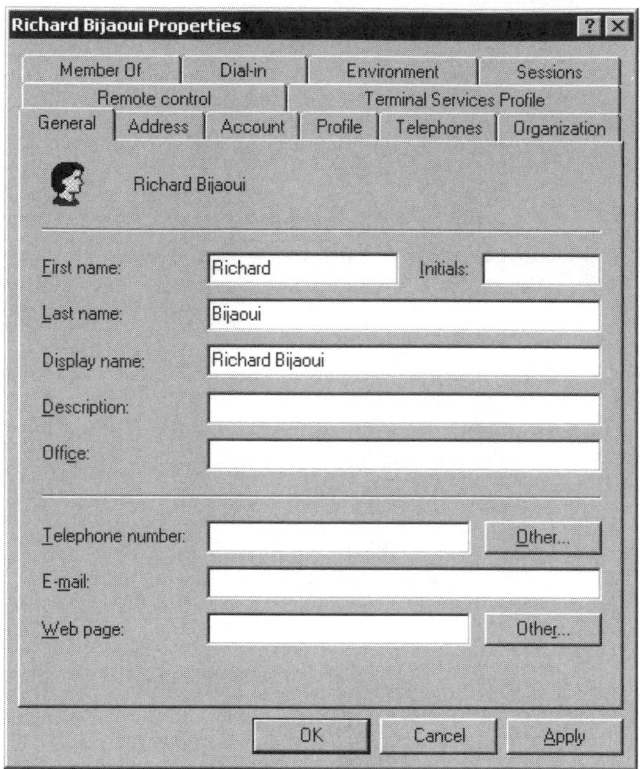

7.10.2 Merging two objects into one object

Because two representations of a single user are of little use, you should merge information from both of these objects into a single object. You use the AD Cleanup Wizard for this task.

In our example, the disabled user object has been created in an Organizational Unit called *Temporary Migrated Users* (Figure 7-21), while the enabled user account has been migrated from NT4 into the Users Organizational Unit in the AD (Figure 7-22). Accordingly, when you kick off the AD Cleanup Wizard, you should limit the search scope only to a well-defined set of containers, in this case *Temporary Migrated Users and Users* (Figure 7-23). It's sensible to do this because it reduces the likelihood of the AD Cleanup Wizard selecting inappropriate accounts for merging. Performance is a factor here, too. Rough performance testing shows that it takes around 40 minutes to search through a forest with 10,000 user objects, so limiting your search to particular areas of the forest should give speedier results. This phase of AD Cleanup only focuses on identifying accounts that the Wizard thinks should be merged; it doesn't actually proceed to merge the account data.

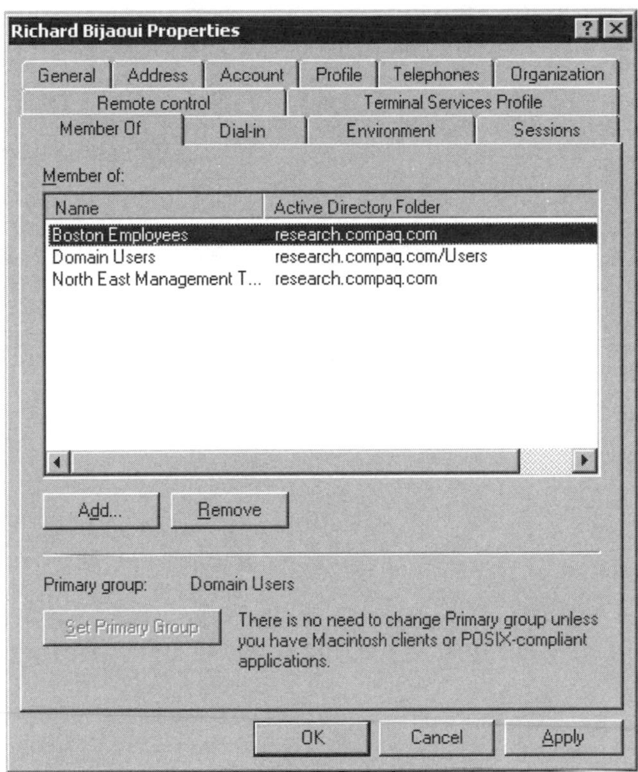

Figure 7-20 *Group Membership Properties for the Enabled User Object Created by the Migration Tool*

The AD Cleanup Wizard uses different matching rules as it attempts to tie up different types of objects. Matching a disabled user object against an enabled user object—which is the case here—the Wizard tries to match the *msExchMasterAccountSID* attribute of the disabled user against either the *objectSID* or *sidHistory* of the enabled user.

Let's see why this is the case (refer to Figure 7-24). When the Active Directory Connector creates a disabled user object, the disabled object is assigned a new SID because it's a new security principal in the Windows 2000 domain. The existing Exchange 5.5 mailbox is associated with an NT4 account (which itself has a SID), and the NT4 account is identified using the Exchange 5.5 Directory Service attribute *Assoc-NT-Account* (the primary Windows NT account). To preserve the linkage back to this Windows NT4 account, the Active Directory Connector populates the disabled user object's *msExchMasterAccountSID* attribute with the value of the *Assoc-NT-Account* attribute.

Subsequently, when the Windows NT4 account is migrated into Windows 2000, the new enabled user object receives a new SID (it's a new security principal), but the SID of the NT4 account is placed into the *sidHistory* attribute. So now we have a

Figure 7-21 *Disabled User Object Created by the Active Directory Connector Homed into Temporary Migrated Users*

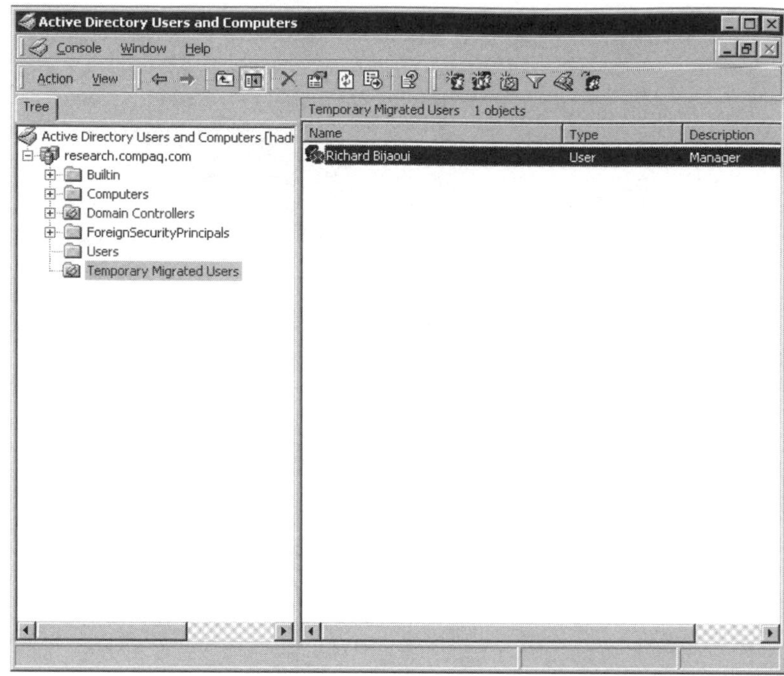

Figure 7-22 *Enabled User Object Created by Migration Tools in the Users Organizational Unit*

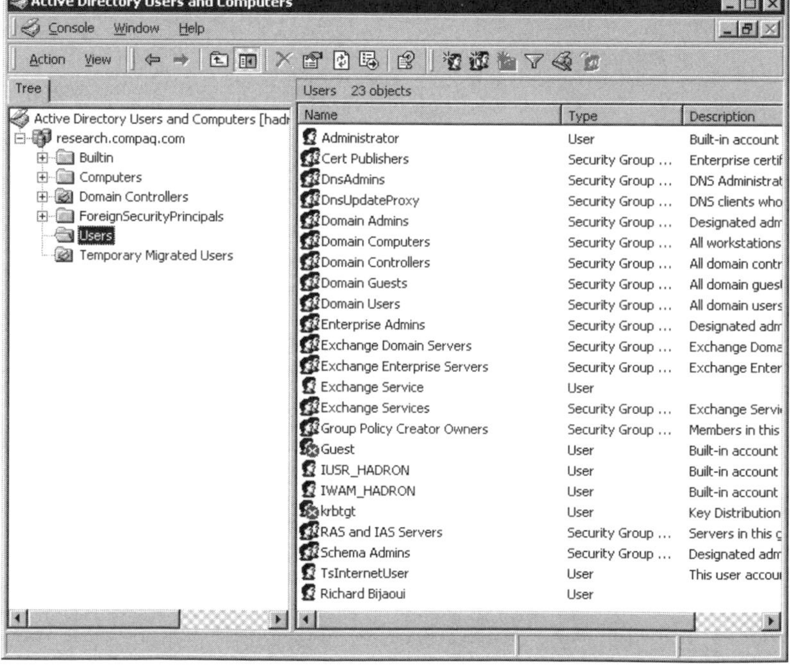

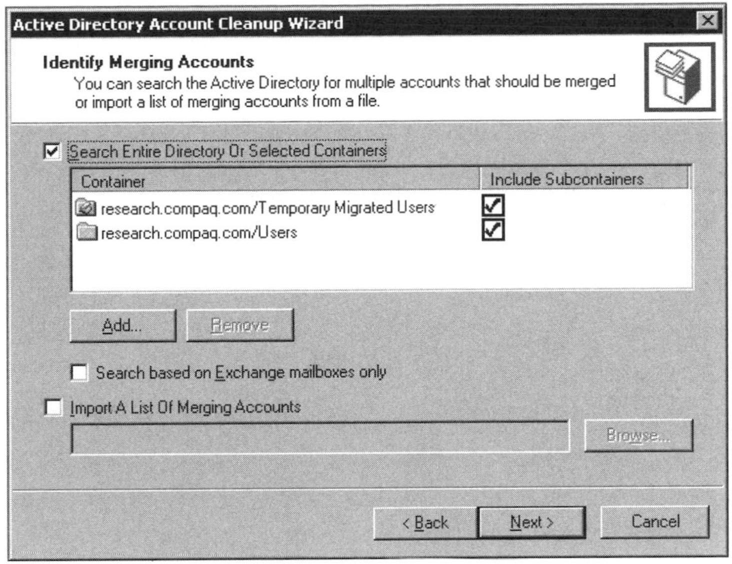

Figure 7-23 *Active Directory Cleanup Wizard Search Scope*

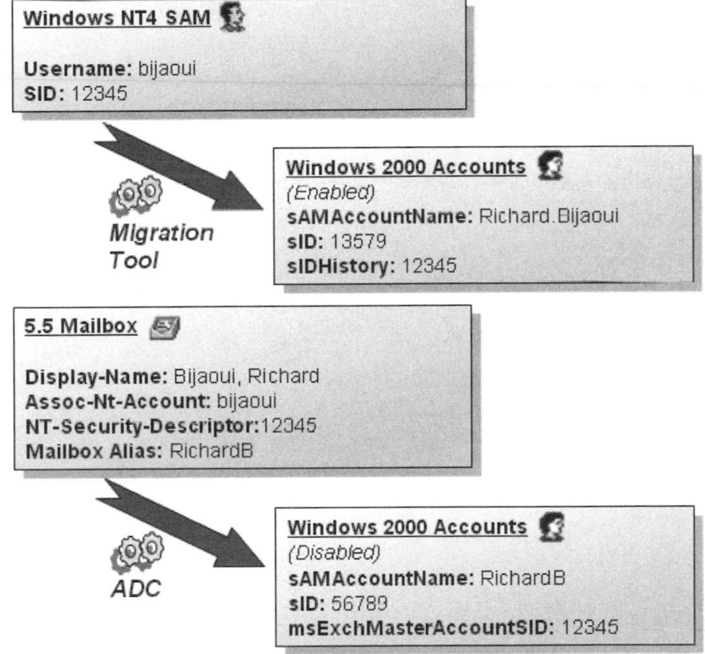

Figure 7-24 *SID Relationships Between Account Objects*

means to link both the disabled and enabled user objects: the *msExchMasterAccount-SID* and *sidHistory* attributes share the same value.

In our example, the AD Cleanup Wizard selects both accounts for user Richard Bijaoui and displays them before asking you to confirm—you need to confirm twice—that you really want to merge them. Merging accounts is a one-shot operation. Once you've merged objects together they can't be unmerged, so you need to be certain that these accounts are valid merge candidates. For any particular merge pair, you can look at some key attributes of the objects (Figure 7-25) before you commit to merging them.

When the merge is completed, the attributes from the disabled user object are merged into the enabled user object, and only one object remains in the AD.

7.10.3 Other merge operations

As well as merging disabled user objects into enabled user objects, you can also merge a contact into an active user object provided only one of those objects is mail-enabled (i.e., has an Exchange mail alias).

However, matching with contacts is not an exact science. The matching that we see with disabled user objects and enabled user objects is much more exact because the matching is based on SIDs. Matching with a contact is based on names and conse-

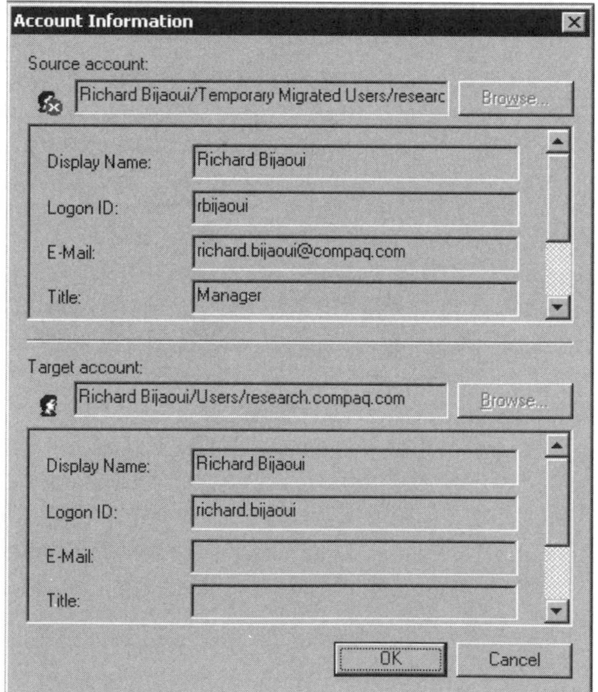

Figure 7-25 *Account Information for Merge Candidates*

quently is less precise. When you match on a number (i.e., a SID value), it's simpler and more likely to be accurate because there's less chance for confusion. As you can see in Figure 7-24, the match is clearly defined on the value 1234.

Contacts don't have SID values, or *sIDHistories*, because they are not security principals. If you want the AD Cleanup Wizard to merge a contact with a user object, searching is performed using the common name (*cn*) and/or display name (*displayName*) attributes. For example, you may have a contact with a display name of Steve Balladelli. This will be matched against an enabled user object and judged to be a merge candidate if either the display name or common name of the user object matches Steve Balladelli. In addition to matching on names, AD Cleanup will also match the Exchange 5.5 mailbox alias (*mailNickname*) against the Windows NT4 login ID (*samAccountName*), although this is less useful today with the new Active Directory Connector behavior of Exchange 2003.

This flexibility of matching on common name terms, mailbox aliases, and account names is a great benefit for contact-based merge operations. Often, naming information isn't consistent between Exchange 5.5 and NT4, and in our example, if the Exchange mailbox was named for Steve Balladelli but the NT4 account was named for Steven Balladelli, a match would not exist based on common and display name operations. Using a match based on alias and login ID provides a useful alternative mechanism if naming standards are inconsistent. (Of course, many environments don't have synergy between their Exchange 5.5 alias names and login account names!)

7.10.4 What the Active Directory Connector creates in the Active Directory

Versions of the Active Directory Connector that were available with Windows 2000 and previous betas and release candidates of Exchange 2000 allowed you to synchronize an Exchange 5.5 mailbox to a contact, a disabled user, or an enabled user object in the AD. Although this provided great flexibility, it was also dangerous. In the event of duplicate objects in the AD, if you'd used the Active Directory Connector to create contacts, matching would, as we've seen, be less precise and potentially fraught with problems.

The Active Directory Connector that ships with Exchange 2003 is less flexible, but in essence, is better. Now the Active Directory Connector only lets you create either disabled user or enabled user objects, not contacts; the problem of matching based on names for the most part goes away.

However, there is an exception to this rule. The restriction on contacts only applies to intraorganizational CAs, whereas interorganizational CAs can create contacts. An intraorganizational CA links an Exchange 5.5 organization that shares the same name as an Exchange 2003 organization (i.e., a mixed-vintage organization). Conversely, an interorganizational CA synchronizes Exchange 5.5 mailbox data from one (or many) organizations into a differently named Exchange 2003 organization. For example, the Exchange 2003 organization may well be called FOO, but you may wish to synchronize in objects from an Exchange 5.5 organization named BAR. To do this, you must use an interorganizational CA.

7.10.5 Manual merges

Occasionally, you may have a requirement to force a merge operation to take place. Consider an example where a new account is created in Windows 2000 for the user Paul Laahs. Because this is a new account and not a migrated one, there's no SID History associated with it. If the Active Directory Connector then creates a user object for Paul Laahs's Exchange 5.5 mailbox, no matching can take place on sidHistory by the Active Directory Connector, and thus a duplicate account is created. Correspondingly, when AD Cleanup runs, it won't detect a match because these are two user objects and user object matching is only performed using SIDs, not names.

Hopefully, scenarios such as this will be rare, but when they do happen you have to manually select the two duplicate objects using the *Add* button on the *Review Merging Accounts* window. This is a powerful feature of the AD Cleanup Wizard, but remember that merging objects is a one-time operation that can't be undone. Make sure the objects really represent the same person before you merge them.

7.10.6 Command-line operation

The AD Cleanup Wizard has a useful command-line interface to it as well as its GUI. The various options and commands are shown in Table 7-1, and you can get full descriptions of these qualifiers in the online help within the ESM tool.

Using the command line allows you to script AD Cleanup Wizard operations so that they can be performed automatically and potentially unattended. For example, you may have a migration process that runs at appropriate times to bring Windows NT4 accounts over to Windows 2000 or Windows 2003. If this were a scripted task, you could execute a script that performs AD Cleanup Wizard operations immediately after it to ensure AD integrity.

Running the command-line version of AD Cleanup Wizard explicitly splits a merge operation into two phases. The first phase performs a search on the AD for duplicate objects and creates a file that contains merge candidates. You must then explicitly run the AD Cleanup Wizard command again to process the merge candidate data file and merge the objects. Obviously this is done for safety, but the ability to generate a report of potential duplicate objects from a script is a useful feature that any

Table 7-1 *Active Directory Cleanup Command-Line Qualifiers*

Option	Description
/?	Displays a list of available options.
/S	Searches the entire Active Directory forest for Active Directory Connector–created duplicate objects (i.e.,, those objects that have *msExchMasterAccountSID* attribute set) and creates a file called MergeFileName.CSV in the working directory.
/C	Used in conjunction with /S to specify a file containing a list of containers in the Active Directory to be searched, for example:
	Active Directory Cleanup Wizard /S /C:E:\MyFiles\Containers.CSV
/X	Extends the /S operation to include more than just Active Directory Connector–created duplicate objects.
/M	Performs a merge using the merge candidates listed in MergeFileName.CSV
/O	Specifies and alternative file containing merge candidates, for example:
	Active Directory Cleanup Wizard /M /O:E:\MyFiles\Candidates.CSV
/L	Specifies the location of the Active Directory Cleanup Log file, for example:
	Active Directory Cleanup Wizard /S /L:E:\MyFiles\MyLog.LOG

organization in the midst of a migration project should use. As a good management practice, you might consider running such a script every night and analyzing the results the next morning.

7.10.7 When you do and don't need to use Active Directory Cleanup Wizard

You've seen some of the rules for automatic detection of merge candidates. These are mainly based on SIDs and naming structures. You can infer two things from this: the importance of using good migration tools and the need for good naming standards.

Migrating all of your Windows NT4 accounts to Windows 2000 or Windows 2003 first usually minimizes the requirement for using the AD Cleanup Wizard. All of the major migration tools (e.g., AD Migration Tool from Microsoft, Direct Migrate from Bindview, DM Suite from Quest, and One Point Suite from NetIQ) rely on the ClonePrincipal API from Microsoft. This allows the *sIDHistory* to be populated into the migrated account, and subsequently, the Active Directory Connector will match on it. Thus no potential for duplicate objects exists.

It's unlikely that you'll be able to wait for a complete migration of your Windows NT4 domains before you put the Active Directory Connector in place, so the likelihood of object duplication is very real. However, many of the third-party migration tools are becoming more Exchange aware and are capable of matching the SID of a Windows NT4 account that is being migrated to Windows 2000 against the *msExchMasterAccountSID* of an existing Active Directory Connector–created object. This reduces the need to run the AD Cleanup Wizard. Similarly, some of the tools are also becoming good at matching on name terms. So the need to have Windows NT4 account naming data in line with naming data from Exchange 5.5 becomes important, too. Any effort spent on sanitizing your existing environment (e.g., tying up names such as Rich and Richard, or Steve and Steven) will reduce headaches during migration.

7.11 Summary

If you are familiar with Exchange 5.5 to Exchange 2000 migration, then there is very little that's new with Exchange 5.5 to Exchange 2003 migration. The same principles and tools are used today as yesterday. Furthermore, migrating from Exchange 5.5 is straightforward because it's simply a matter of creating an interoperability environment with the Active Directory Connector and then using the Move Mailbox Wizard to move data: There's no real decision to be made about upgrading or moving!

The possibility of discovering duplicate objects in your AD during or after a migration to Exchange 2003 is a very real one. The AD Cleanup Wizard provides an invaluable way to detect and merge these troublesome duplicates while preserving attribute and access control information as well as ensuring the integrity of groups and distribution lists.

Of course, the AD Cleanup Wizard is not all-powerful. It can't merge objects between forests, nor can it merge enabled objects in different domains within the same forest (you must move them into the same domain first). It can't merge two objects that both have Exchange mailboxes associated with them: that's an entirely different problem! And it can't merge two objects that are both mail-enabled: which mail address would it choose? Although it reduces many migration headaches, the Cleanup Wizard should not be used as an excuse for sloppy Exchange 5.5 and Windows NT4 account data synergy or carefree migration practices. Take the time up front before any migration activity to clean up your existing sources of data to reduce the likelihood of duplicates or, in the worst case, to increase the likelihood of the AD Cleanup Wizard finding a match. By selecting the right migration tools for the job and carefully planning your move to Exchange 2003, you may get away with never having to use the AD Cleanup Wizard at all. Prevention is always better than cure.

8

Moving from Exchange 2000 to Exchange 2003

8.1 Introduction

Exchange 2000 to Exchange 2003 migration is a relatively straightforward process and certainly nowhere near as complicated as the migration from Exchange 5.5 to either Exchange 2000 or Exchange 2003. Moving from Exchange 2000 to Exchange 2003 can be achieved in one of two ways: either (1) by performing an in-place upgrade on the Exchange 2000 server or (2) by installing a new Exchange 2003 server in the same Administrative Group as the Exchange 2000 server and using the Move Mailbox Wizard to move mailboxes onto the new platform. This chapter describes the various processes in some degree of detail, but ultimately the approach that you take is determined by the complexity of your environment and other factors, such as available resources and budget.

8.2 Exchange 2000 to Exchange 2003 Migration Approaches

One of the most important details to bear in mind about Exchange 2000 is that it is ***not*** supported on a Windows 2003 server. However, do note that Exchange 2000 is supported running on a Windows 2000 member server in a Windows 2003 DC environment. The corollary to this is that Exchange 2003 is supported on a Windows 2000 platform so long as that platform is running Windows 2000 Service Pack 3 or higher and either Windows 2003 DCs or Windows 2000 Service Pack 3 DCs are available. This dependency mandates a particular in-place upgrade strategy for Exchange 2000 to Exchange 2003 migration.

There are essentially two approaches you can take: either (1) perform an in-place upgrade on an Exchange 2000 server or (2) install a new Exchange 2003 server into an existing Exchange 2000 AG and then use the Move Mailbox Wizard to move mailboxes from existing Exchange 2000 servers to the new Exchange 2003 server. Either approach is valid, and the use of one approach over the other is really determined by your particular environment. For small environments with a minimal number of servers and restricted hardware budgets, in-place upgrades work well. The servers you are upgrading should be capable of sustaining the user load, although if the servers were suitable for Exchange 2000, then they will most likely also be suitable for Exchange 2003. The granularity of this form of migration is poor—all users on a server are migrated—and it is more risky, with the possibility of a failure during the upgrade and a need to restore the system from backups.

Introducing new Exchange 2003 servers into the existing Exchange 2000 environment is also a valid migration approach. I like this approach because it has a high degree of granularity: You move individual users or groups of users at any one time. With such a scenario, if something goes wrong, it is easier to recover from. Obviously, though, it requires extra hardware, so depending on your budget this may or may not be an attractive approach. Remember that you don't need to replace every existing Exchange 2000 server with a new Exchange 2003 server: you can always recycle the Exchange 2000 servers that you've just decommissioned.

Whatever approach you decide to implement, it is imperative that you perform backups of any Exchange server databases that will be affected during the process before you start any upgrade activity or begin to move mailboxes. Do note that you do not need to be in Exchange 2000 native mode (even though the ExDeploy Wizard states that you are upgrading from Exchange 2000 native mode) to perform any migration to Exchange 2003. It is also important to note that you must rerun the new Exchange 2003 Forestprep and Domainprep tools again, even though you ran them for the initial Exchange 2000 deployment, as you would do for a greenfield implementation of Exchange 2003.

8.2.1 Exchange 2000 to Exchange 2003 in-place upgrade guidelines

If you do wish to perform in-place upgrades, then you must first upgrade the Exchange 2000 server to Exchange 2003, and only then can you upgrade the Windows 2000 operating system to Windows 2003. No other sequence of upgrade events can take place, although you may use the Move Mailbox Wizard approach for Exchange 2000 to Exchange 2003 migration directly to another server without performing any in-place upgrades.

In any event, once you have Exchange 2003 on a Windows 2000 server, then the process of upgrading the Windows 2000 system to Windows 2003 is straightforward, and in fact Exchange 2003 behaves proactively during the upgrade process. The

Exchange 2003 system ensures that the Windows WWW service is not disabled during the upgrade (which would otherwise take place by default) because Windows 2000 to Windows 2003 upgrades tend to disable services as a security measure. Additionally, it makes the appropriate changes to IIS 6.0 that an Exchange 2003 installation on top of Windows 2003 would otherwise effect, namely switching to Worker Process Isolation Mode and enabling the appropriate Exchange Internet Server Application Program Interface (ISAPI) for normal operation, including RPC over hypertext transfer protocol (HTTP) and Outlook Web Access (OWA).

8.2.2 Using the ExDeploy tools for Exchange 2000 to Exchange 2003 migration

Migration from Exchange 2000 to Exchange 2003 is somewhat simpler than migration from Exchange 5.5 to Exchange 2003, or from Exchange 5.5 to Exchange 2000 for that matter. You can choose to make matters straightforward by using the Exchange 2003 ExDeploy tools. ExDeploy can be found on the Exchange 2003 installation CD-ROM in the \support\ExDeploy directory. Double-click on the exdeploy.chm file to start the wizard. Choose the set of options that describe Exchange 2000 to Exchange 2003 migration and you'll be presented with the options as shown in Figure 8-1.

You don't need to use ExDeploy to perform any such migration though. ExDeploy is merely a set of prompts that describe the migration process, and in reality it is really only useful if you have a simple environment with just a handful of Exchange 2000 servers that need to be upgraded. If you have a broader, more complex environment, then consider the conventional approach to upgrade, perhaps briefly reviewing the ExDeploy suggestions to help with your plans.

8.2.3 Exchange 2003 upgrade restrictions

Although most Exchange 2000 servers can simply be upgraded in place to Exchange 2003, certain Exchange 2000 servers cannot be. Specifically, if you have any Exchange 2000 servers running the Instant Messaging service, Chat, or Key Management Service, these services must be removed before any in-place upgrade can take place. If you absolutely must retain them, you can keep the servers in place and just use the Move Mailbox Wizard to move user mailboxes onto other Exchange 2003 servers.

If you currently use the Front-End/Back-End server model for OWA or IMAP, for example, then you must be sure to migrate the Front-End servers before you attempt to migrate any Back-End servers. This holds true whether or not you attempt to upgrade a Back-End server in place or even install a new Back-End server. If you

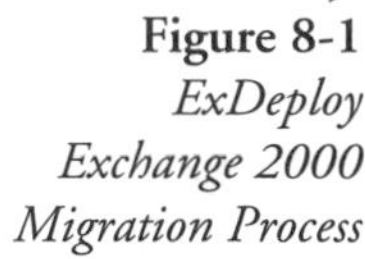

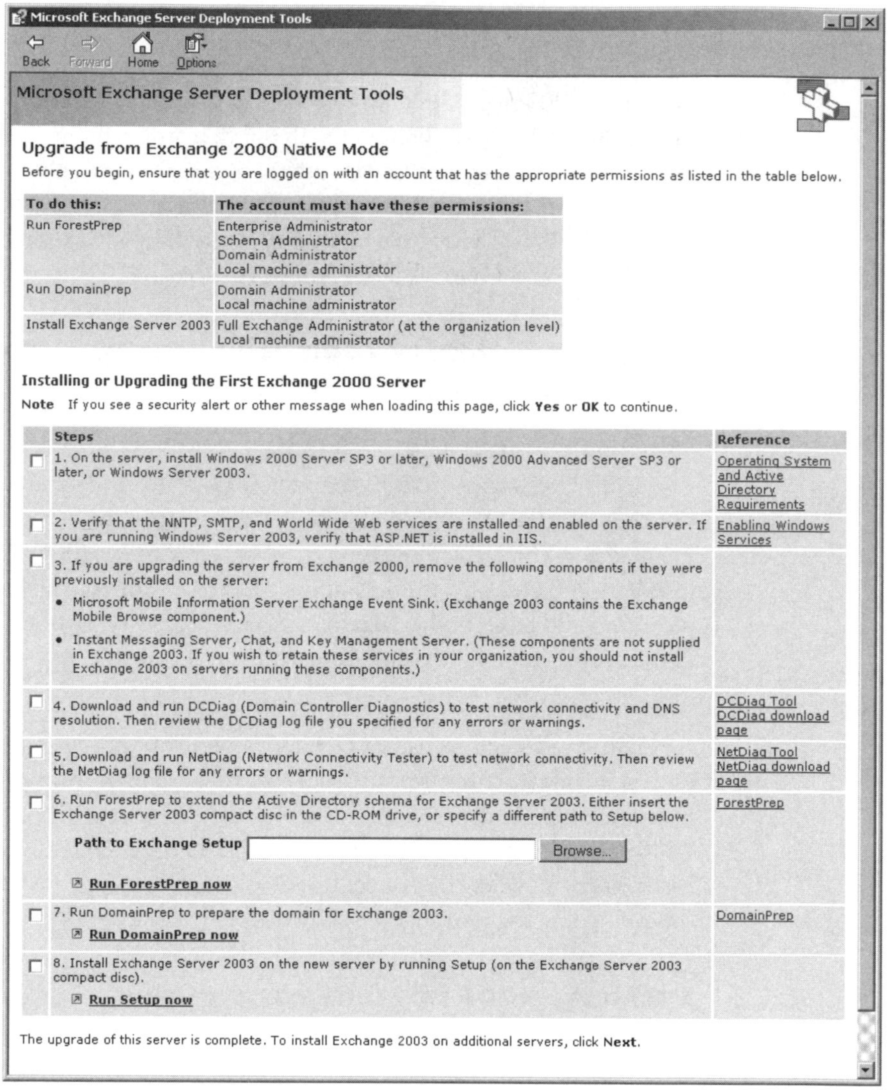

Figure 8-1
ExDeploy Exchange 2000 Migration Process

Microsoft Exchange Server Deployment Tools

Back Forward Home Options

Microsoft Exchange Server Deployment Tools

Upgrade from Exchange 2000 Native Mode

Before you begin, ensure that you are logged on with an account that has the appropriate permissions as listed in the table below.

To do this:	The account must have these permissions:
Run ForestPrep	Enterprise Administrator Schema Administrator Domain Administrator Local machine administrator
Run DomainPrep	Domain Administrator Local machine administrator
Install Exchange Server 2003	Full Exchange Administrator (at the organization level) Local machine administrator

Installing or Upgrading the First Exchange 2000 Server

Note If you see a security alert or other message when loading this page, click **Yes** or **OK** to continue.

Steps	Reference
1. On the server, install Windows 2000 Server SP3 or later, Windows 2000 Advanced Server SP3 or later, or Windows Server 2003.	Operating System and Active Directory Requirements
2. Verify that the NNTP, SMTP, and World Wide Web services are installed and enabled on the server. If you are running Windows Server 2003, verify that ASP.NET is installed in IIS.	Enabling Windows Services
3. If you are upgrading the server from Exchange 2000, remove the following components if they were previously installed on the server: • Microsoft Mobile Information Server Exchange Event Sink. (Exchange 2003 contains the Exchange Mobile Browse component.) • Instant Messaging Server, Chat, and Key Management Server. (These components are not supplied in Exchange 2003. If you wish to retain these services in your organization, you should not install Exchange 2003 on servers running these components.)	
4. Download and run DCDiag (Domain Controller Diagnostics) to test network connectivity and DNS resolution. Then review the DCDiag log file you specified for any errors or warnings.	DCDiag Tool DCDiag download page
5. Download and run NetDiag (Network Connectivity Tester) to test network connectivity. Then review the NetDiag log file for any errors or warnings.	NetDiag Tool NetDiag download page
6. Run ForestPrep to extend the Active Directory schema for Exchange Server 2003. Either insert the Exchange Server 2003 compact disc in the CD-ROM drive, or specify a different path to Setup below. **Path to Exchange Setup** Browse... **Run ForestPrep now**	ForestPrep
7. Run DomainPrep to prepare the domain for Exchange 2003. **Run DomainPrep now**	DomainPrep
8. Install Exchange Server 2003 on the new server by running Setup (on the Exchange Server 2003 compact disc). **Run Setup now**	

The upgrade of this server is complete. To install Exchange 2003 on additional servers, click **Next**.

attempt to perform either of these actions for Back-End servers, the upgrade or installation will terminate with the error message, as shown in Figure 8-2.

8.2.4 Exchange upgrades and the front-end/back-end server model

In order to experience the new, improved Exchange 2003 OWA interface and functionality, both Front-End servers and Back-End servers must be running Exchange

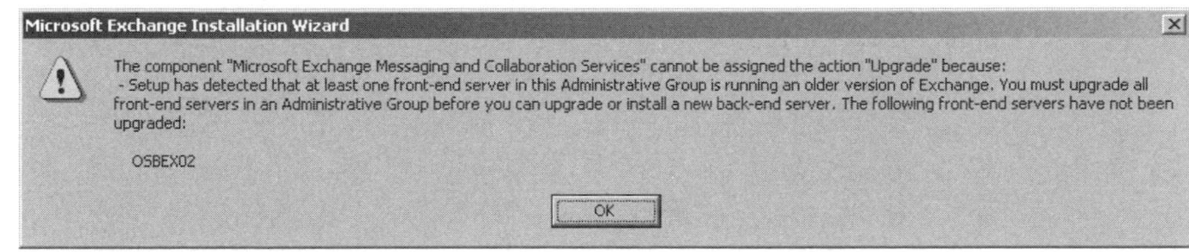

Figure 8-2 *Error Dialog Displayed for Back-End Server Upgrade with Front-End Server Not Upgraded*

2003. Any other combination of Front-End and Back-End servers will result in the legacy Exchange 2000 OWA functionality. This can be summarized as follows:

- Exchange 2000 Front-End/Exchange 2000 Back-End: Exchange 2000 OWA
- Exchange 2003 Front-End/Exchange 2000 Back-End: Exchange 2000 OWA
- Exchange 2000 Front-End/Exchange 2003 Back-End: Unsupported
- Exchange 2003 Front-End/Exchange 2003 Back-End: Exchange 2003 OWA

If only the Front-End server is running Exchange 2003 and the Back-End server is still running Exchange 2000, then the new Exchange 2003 OWA forms-based authentication cannot be used, even though the Exchange 2000 OWA interface is still presented. Even with this configuration, however, session timeouts are handled much better if all servers involved are running Exchange 2003.

8.2.5 Upgrading Exchange 2000 in-place to Exchange 2003 procedure

The actual process of upgrading from Exchange 2000 is relatively uneventful: a mere matter of putting the CD-ROM in the drive and running setup. Providing all prerequisites have been met, you should be faced with little complication. There are some important points to bear in mind, though, once the upgrade has actually finished.

During an in-place upgrade from Exchange 2000 to Exchange 2003, there are no actual changes to the structure of the Exchange databases. (With other versions of Exchange, this was the case during upgrade and often resulted in potentially long upgrade times, directly proportional to the size of the databases.) Immediately after the upgrade, however, you will see some significant activity from the STORE.EXE process and the EXSCHEMA.EXE process. This activity, which consumes only moderate amounts of CPU resources, takes place because the OLEDB schema requires some postupdate changes. The overhead from this OLEDB schema update should not significantly impact the overall performance of the system, nor should user access be in any way compromised. In fact, the entire process should take no more than about 10 or 15 minutes. Despite the lack of changes to the database, it is always good practice to take full backups of the Exchange 2003 databases immediately after the upgrade, and this is highly recommended.

If you are running Full Text Indexing services on any Exchange 2000 servers that are being upgraded to Exchange 2003, the Full Text Indexes require a complete rebuild after the upgrade completes. For general reasons of performance, it is not wise to run the Full Text Index rebuild during normal hours of system operation when there are users logged on to the system. Similarly, immediately after an upgrade to Exchange 2003, you may have other critical tasks that you wish to perform, such as backing up the databases. For this reason, the Exchange 2003 upgrade procedure indefinitely pauses the rebuild of any Full Text Indexes so there is no interface to postupgrade tasks. As a system administrator, you should schedule the Full Text Index complete rebuild to take place as soon as is practical immediately after the upgrade.

8.3 Mixed Exchange 5.5/Exchange 2000 migrations to Exchange 2003

Another migration scenario we must consider is that of mixed Exchange migration (i.e., migrating an existing mixed Exchange 5.5 and Exchange 2000 environment to Exchange 2003). Fortunately, the migration of this type of environment is really no different from the processes we need to use for each of the individual migration strategies.

In such a mixed environment, the Active Directory Connector will already be in place to provide directory synchronization between the Exchange 5.5 Directory Service and the AD. Bear in mind that any existing Exchange 2000 servers will only be running on Windows 2000 servers (because Exchange 2000 is not supported on a Windows 2003 server) but that the AD may or may not be implemented within a Windows 2003 forest/domain environment. Similarly, Exchange 5.5 must be running on Windows 2000 or earlier servers because it is not supported on Windows 2003 servers. Whatever the mix of operating systems in the environment, any existing Active Directory Connector servers must be upgraded to the Active Directory Connector versions supplied with Exchange 2003.

With the upgraded Active Directory Connector servers in place, you may proceed to move users to Exchange 2003. For Exchange 2000 servers, you can perform in-place upgrades as described here or you can use the Move Mailbox functionality. For Exchange 5.5 servers, you must use the Move Mailbox functionality.

8.4 The Exchange 2003 Move Mailbox Wizard

Microsoft's only supported method of migrating directly from Exchange 5.5 servers to Exchange 2003 servers in an intraorganizational migration is to use the Move Mailbox Wizard, and the recommended method of getting from Exchange 2000 servers to Exchange 2003 servers is also by using the Move Mailbox Wizard. The Move Mailbox Wizard is not a new component of Exchange 2003: It has been around from Exchange 2000 days, but it has been significantly enhanced to make it a much more attractive and efficient tool for moving mailboxes from legacy Exchange servers to Exchange 2003. This section describes its use and new features.

8.4.1 Using the Move Mailbox Wizard

The Move Mailbox Wizard can only be used with an intraorganizational migration, not with an interorganizational migration. This means that you must be moving mailboxes between servers within the same Exchange organization. Furthermore, the Exchange 2003 version of the Move Mailbox Wizard, just like its Exchange 2000 predecessor, can only move mailboxes between servers within the same Exchange 5.5 site or AG, while the Exchange organization is in mixed mode. (Note that when in mixed-mode an Exchange 5.5 site corresponds to an Exchange 2000/2003 AG.) However, this restriction applies only to the basic version of Exchange 2003. If you are using Exchange 2003 Service Pack 1, then mailboxes can be moved between sites, although you must perform some discrete tasks to support this mode of operation. You can move mailboxes between any combination of Exchange 5.5, Exchange 2000, and Exchange 2003 servers. This is shown in Figure 8-3.

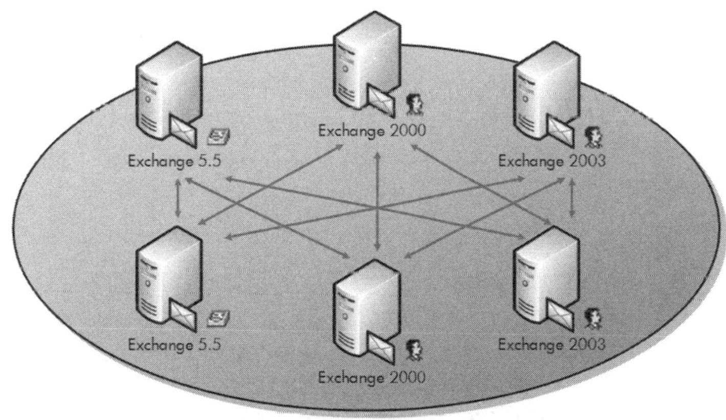

Figure 8-3 *A Single Site/Administrative Group Mailbox Move Summary*

Otherwise, if you are not using Exchange 2003 Service Pack 1 for your Exchange 2003 servers, you must upgrade the Exchange organization to native mode (such that you only have Exchange 2000 or Exchange 2003 servers in your organization) so that you may move mailboxes between servers and across AG. In this scenario you may move mailboxes between any combination of Exchange 2000 and Exchange 2003 servers.

Because the Exchange 2003 Move Mailbox Wizard is more functional than its predecessor, you may wish to use it to move mailboxes between just Exchange 5.5 and Exchange 2000 servers, even if you have no Exchange 2003 servers in your environment. To use the Exchange 2003 Move Mailbox Wizard like this, you must first run the Exchange 2003 Forestprep in your AD forest. Do this by executing the SETUP.EXE /FORESTPREP command from the \SETUP\I386 folder on the Exchange 2003 installation CD-ROM. Make sure you run this command on a server in the same Windows domain as your Schema Operations Master server. Then run Setup again, this time on the server or workstation you will use as the console for your administrative operations. Choose the option to install only the Exchange Management components. Note that this server or workstation needs only to be running Windows 2000 (or Windows 2003 or Windows XP) and does not require any local installation of Exchange server.

8.4.2 Exchange 2003 Move Mailbox operation

The Move Mailbox Wizard operates by making a MAPI connection to the source server, reading contents of the source mailbox, and writing that same content to a mailbox on the target server. With the move operation complete, the content of the source mailbox is removed from the source server and the user's AD object attributes are updated, so that the user's mailbox is now shown to be homed on the target server rather than the source server. Effectively the mailbox has been moved. You can select just a single mailbox for processing or you can select multiple mailboxes for processing.

The Exchange 2000 version of the Move Mailbox Wizard, however, was less than perfect in terms of performance and scalability. Although you could select multiple user objects using the AD Users and Computers tool, the user objects were processed in a purely sequential fashion. For example, if you selected five users, the move mailbox operation for User 2 would not commence until the move mailbox operation for User 1 had completed; the move mailbox operation for User 3 would not commence until the move mailbox operation for User 2 had completed, and so on. The Exchange 2003 Move Mailbox Wizard is now multithreaded, with up to four threads per Move Mailbox Wizard session. Using our previous example with five users introduced above, the move mailbox operations for User 1 through User 4 would take place in parallel. In general this yields better performance, simply because a single large mailbox does not act as a bottleneck and block the move of other smaller mailboxes. If four threads are not sufficient, you can run multiple instances of the Move Mailbox Wizard even on the same server or workstation and from the same instance of either ESM or AD Users and Computers. You can see multiple mailboxes being moved at the same time in Figure 8-4.

Furthermore, most well-configured production Exchange servers capable of supporting hundreds or thousands of normal MAPI (Outlook) clients would not be overly stressed with a single move mailbox operation, despite the intensity of the operation (i.e., a large number of MAPI operations condensed into a small amount of time). Usually there would be sufficient capacity on the system, especially in terms of the disk IO subsystem and on the network, to allow multiple threads to execute. Thus, running the new Exchange 2003 Move Mailbox Wizard is just plain smarter! Observed performance figures on the server environment that hosts my production mailbox shows that a single thread executed at a transfer rate of about 500 MB per hour. However, I know of another environment on ProLiant 800s and a Smart Array 5304 controller where transfer rates of around 2 GB per hour and higher were observed. My production environment had the source and target servers co-located on the same 100 Mbps LAN and the servers at either end had typical RAID0+1 IO subsystems. Depending on the configuration of your systems and the intervening network, you should expect to see transfer rates in the range of about 500 MB to 4 GB per hour, although don't expect the performance improvement to scale linearly with an increase in threads.

Figure 8-4
Moving Multiple Mailboxes at the Same Time

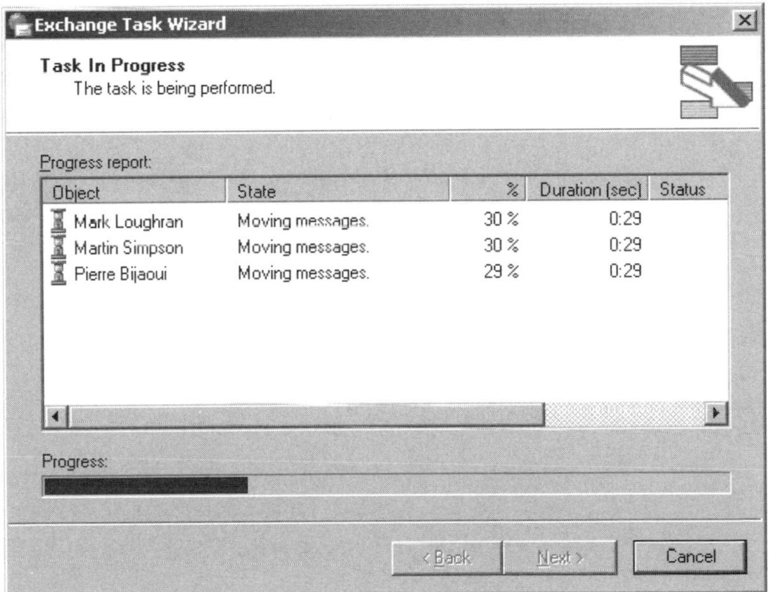

8.4.2.1 Mailbox bloat during Move Mailbox operations

Do also watch out for increases in the amount of space that a mailbox will take following a Move Mailbox operation. Real-life experience of performing these operations within my production environment would suggest that some form of mailbox "bloat" takes place during such an operation. The likely cause for this kind of behavior is most probably the breaking down of Single Instance Storage (SIS) as mailboxes are moved between systems. Microsoft claims that the Move Mailbox Wizard strives to maintain SIS wherever possible, but it is certainly true that some environments have seen significant decreases in their SIS ratios following such mailbox moves. Of course, the real value of SIS is questionable in any event: Many organizations say that they observe very low SIS ratios, so they really are not overly perturbed about the possibility of the SIS ratio decreasing from an already low value, and as a consequence the storage requirement increasing. As a matter of good system management practice, it is advisable to increase mailbox limits (even temporarily) on any accounts that you plan to move from either Exchange 5.5 or Exchange 2000 servers to Exchange 2003. Doing so might help prevent a flood of calls to the help desk on the morning following the bulk move operation if users can't send mail.

Another important consideration is the increase in transaction log space required. As mailboxes are moved, the operations will generate very many MAPI transactions, and as such, sufficient extra capacity should be in place to cater for the extra log files, especially if a large number of mailboxes are being moved.

8.4.2.2 The Move Mailbox Wizard and Exchange System Manage Console

Also of note with the new Exchange 2003 Move Mailbox Wizard is its location. Previously, the Move Mailbox Wizard was only accessible from the AD Users and Computers MMC snap-in, because moving user mailbox data was perceived primarily as a user function. Although the Move Mailbox Wizard is still available within AD Users and Computers with Exchange 2003, it is now also exposed on the ESM MMC snap-in, so that it can now be interpreted as a function of Exchange management. This dual homing of the Move Mailbox Wizard makes sense when you consider the fact that a system manager may often wish to look at properties of the Exchange databases as a prelude to actually moving users: With the Move Mailbox Wizard available from ESM, all of the information a system manager might require is now available in the same place (see Figure 8-5).

To move mailboxes, use either AD Users and Computers or ESM and then navigate to list the relevant users in the details pane. Select the user or users to be moved, right-click your selection, and then click Exchange Tasks. In Exchange Task Wizard, select the Move Mailbox option and then click Next. Then use the server drop-down

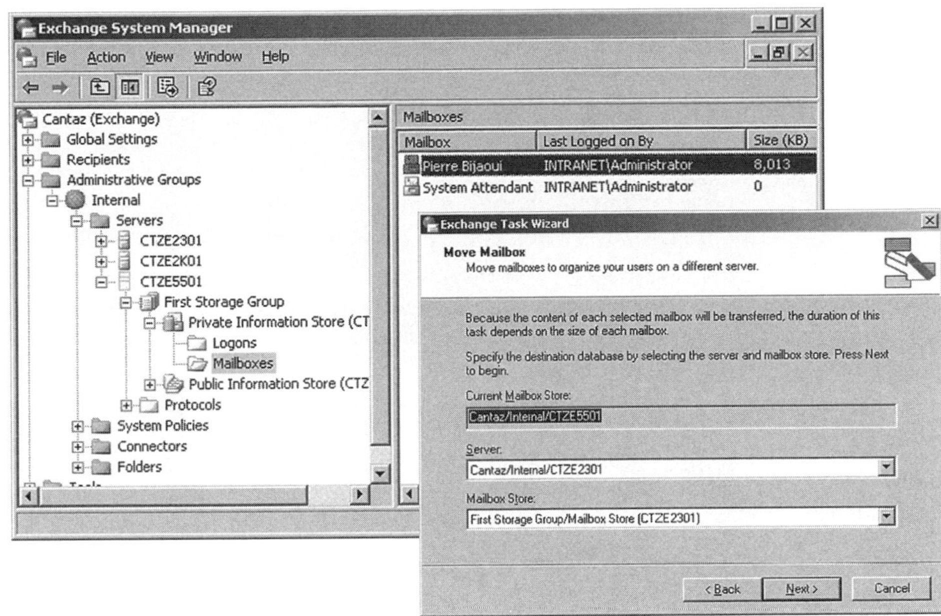

Figure 8-5 *Move Mailbox Wizard Exposed from Exchange System Manager*

list to specify the target server, and then in the Mailbox Store drop-down list, select a mailbox store. Then click Next.

8.4.2.3 Scheduling Move Mailbox operations

Obviously you don't ever want to perform lots of user Move Mailbox operations during normal working hours. Therefore, with the Exchange 2000 version of the Move Mailbox Wizard, you had to perform the move operations manually and during non-working office hours. This is inconvenient and inappropriate for two reasons: (1) if you do perform moves during working hours, it places load on the system and potentially impacts performance for other users; and (2) performing the Move Mailbox operations out of hours typically means that you must be present on the system either at night or over the weekend to do the pointing and clicking. In this day and age, we should all be looking to technology to perform its long-awaited promise: enriching our lives rather than forcing us to work harder and spending more of our precious time cooped up in computer rooms, offices, or working from home when we should be spending time with our families. Exchange 2003 now does its little bit for humankind: it is now possible to schedule the Move Mailbox Wizard to run at a particular time of day and run unattended. You simply select the mailboxes to be moved, identify to where they will be moved, and define the time that you wish for the Move Mailbox operation to start.

As well as simply selecting a start time for Move Mailbox operations, you can also define an end time, thus ensuring that if you have a large number of mailboxes to move and the entirety of the operations has not completed, you can terminate the outstanding move operations at a particular time. For example, let's say you selected 100 mailboxes to be moved starting at 1:00 a.m. You might define 8:00 a.m. as the end time for this operation, so that if only 50 mailboxes had been successfully moved by 8:00 a.m., the mailbox move currently being processed is abandoned and any pending mailbox moves are also abandoned. Thus the system performance is not compromised when users begin logging on at 8:30 a.m. You can see the scheduling options exposed in Figure 8-6.

If you defer the start time for a Move Mailbox operation, you must keep the Move Mailbox Wizard session open and allow it to count down to the start time of the operation, as shown in Figure 8-7. You cannot configure a start time for the operation and then exit the Wizard. It was possible to perform unattended Move Mailbox operations before with the Exchange 2000 version Move Mailbox Wizard functionality. However, it was not possible to do this directly from the user interface, and the only way of automating this activity was by using some scripts and a batch job scheduler such as WinAT. Furthermore, the complexity of the scripts would obviously increase if you wished to have move operations terminate at a particular time.

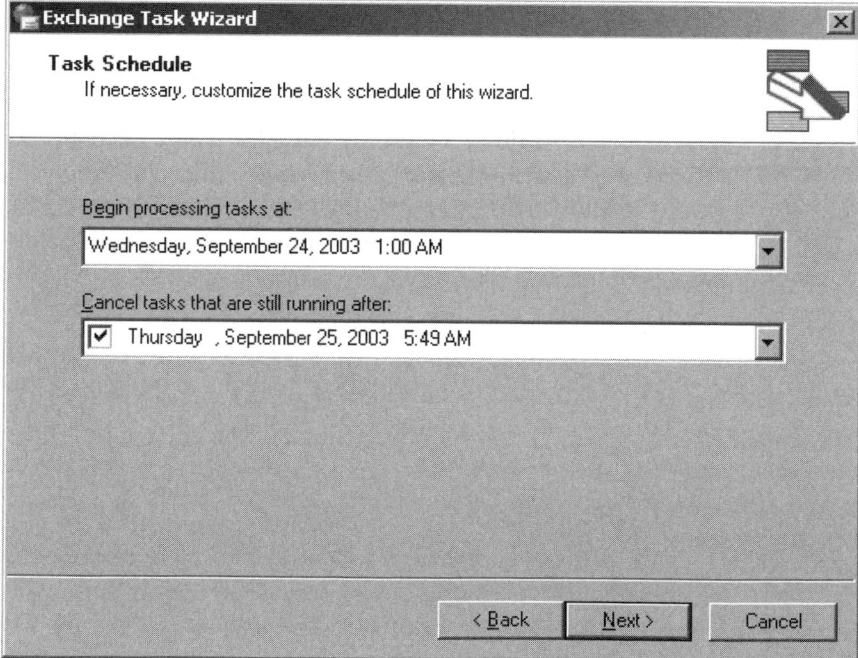

Figure 8-6 *Scheduling Options for the Move Mailbox Wizard*

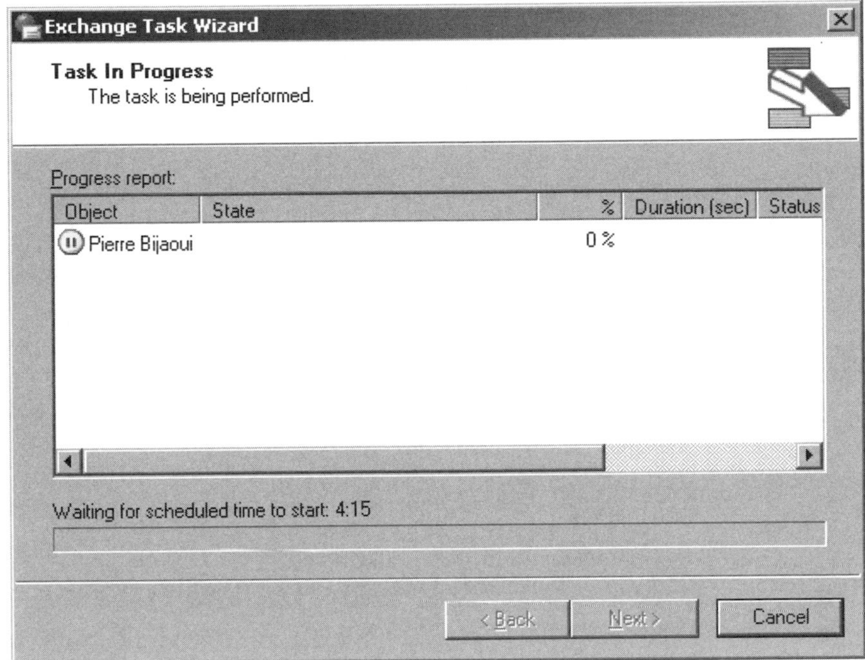

Figure 8-7 *Scheduling the Start Time for a Move Mailbox Operation*

8.4.2.4 Move Mailbox Wizard and corrupted items handling

The Exchange 2000 version of the Move Mailbox Wizard did not deal well with corrupt data in user mailboxes. If a corrupt message was detected during the Move Mailbox operation, the entire operation was abandoned and the mailbox was not moved. Any pending mailbox moves would be abandoned as well.

The Exchange 2003 version of the Move Mailbox Wizard is much more intelligent when it comes to dealing with errors. You can define the action you would like the Move Mailbox Wizard to take if an error is detected during the move operation. You can configure the Move Mailbox Wizard so that corrupted items that cannot be read from the source server are simply skipped and logged as errors. For example, if you specify a threshold of 10 corrupted items, then the Move Mailbox Wizard will delete up to 10 corrupted items during the Move Mailbox operation and still successfully move the mailbox. It is important that you back up the source database before you start any Move Mailbox operations because any corrupted items that are encountered and ignored by the Move Mailbox Wizard are permanently deleted. If the threshold level for corrupt data items is not exceeded when the move operation is taking place, the mailbox is moved successfully and any corrupted items are permanently deleted from the source and ultimately the target mailbox. If the threshold value is exceeded during the operation, then that particular operation is canceled and the mailbox is not moved from the source server. Note, however, that any corrupted data items that were previously deleted before the threshold value was exceeded will already have been permanently deleted and are unrecoverable.

Alternately, if you do not wish to tolerate any problem items during the move operation, you can have processing of that mailbox terminate immediately, and the Move Mailbox Wizard will then move on to processing the next mailbox.

The mechanics of how Move Mailbox Wizard functions for each mailbox are as follows. First, the Move Mailbox Wizard connects to both the source and target servers using MAPI. Then the folder hierarchy is read from the source server and re-created on the target server. A MAPI transfer is then initiated, which moves messages from the source server to the target server. If the read of an item fails, it is retried; if it fails again, it is dropped from the processing list and the Move Mailbox Wizard either continues processing this mailbox or abandons it as determined by the configuration settings.

8.4.2.5 Status reports and Move Mailbox reports

The Move Mailbox Wizard will display information about pending moves, moves currently in progress, failed moves, and completed moves. Timing information with regard to schedule information and elapsed times for moves is also displayed. Whenever a Move Mailbox session is completed, Move Mailbox Wizard will produce a detailed report of the move. This report can be analyzed offline or incorporated into other reporting or administrative systems. These reports are defined in extensible markup language (XML), so the rendering of the data can be manipulated by use of a custom XML style sheet.

8.4.2.6 Planning Move Mailbox operations

If you are moving large numbers of mailboxes, you should structure the moves in a well-defined process. Follow this approach:

1. Size the target servers to ensure that you have enough space for new data and the transaction logs.
2. Back up your source and target servers before any moves.
3. Try the migration process with a handful of large mailboxes to ensure that the process is correct.
4. Move the real mailboxes.
5. Run a full backup on the target server to make sure that transaction log files are truncated.
6. Reallocate any storage that was put in place temporarily for the process.

8.4.2.7 Automating Move Mailbox operations

In a previous life I was a reasonable C and Visual Basic programmer, but as the years moved on I left that world behind, unable (and for the most part unwilling) to keep up with the fast-paced development trends requiring C++, C#, Active X, COM, and so on. So these days, I'm by no means a "real programmer."

However, Microsoft has really stepped up to the bar to make Exchange 2000 and Exchange 2003 management operations, among other things, easily accessible for even rudimentary programmers like myself. Using coding techniques based on Collaboration Data Objects (CDO) and Collaboration Data Objects for Exchange Management (CDOEXM), it's relatively straightforward to write utilities that will process Exchange mailboxes and move their contents to Exchange 2003 mailbox stores. For example, the following text shows a simple Visual Basic Script code extract that you might use as the basis of a program to migrate an Exchange 5.5 or Exchange 2000 mailbox to an Exchange 2003 mailbox server.

```
Private Function MoveMailbox(UserDN As String,
               TargetMBStoreDN As String)

     Dim objPerson As New CDO.Person
     Dim objMailbox As CDOEXM.IMailboxStore

     objPerson.DataSource.Open "LDAP://" & UserDN

     Set objMailbox = objPerson
     objMailbox.MoveMailbox "LDAP://" & TargetMBStoreDN
     objPerson.DataSource.Save
     Set objPerson = Nothing
End Function
```

This code operates as follows:

- The Distinguished Name of the user to be moved and the Distinguished Name of the target Exchange 2003 mailbox store are passed as parameters to the function.
- The data source (i.e., the Exchange 5.5 or Exchange 2000 mailbox) associated with the user is instantiated.
- The *MoveMailbox* method is called against the instantiated mailbox, specifying the target for the Move Mailbox operation.

This code extract works by moving one mailbox at a time—you pass the details through as parameters to the function. However, you could augment this kind of functionality to process multiple mailboxes by using LDAP queries. For example, you might execute the following command:

```
MoveMailboxes.vbs
  "&(surname=M*)(extensionAttribute10=E55)"
  "Users MailBoxStore"
```

Such a command, assuming the existence of a script similar to that outlined as follows, would cause all objects in the AD, possibly created by the Active Directory Connector, whose surname attribute begins with M and have the value of Extension Attribute 10 set to E55, to be moved from Exchange 5.5 mailbox stores to Exchange 2003 mailbox stores.

```
' Set parameters to call arguments
'
strLDAPQueryFilter = WScript.Arguments (0)
strTargetStore = WScript.Arguments (1)
'
' Get the Domain details needed to process the users
'
Set objRoot = GetObject("LDAP://RootDSE")
strDefaultDomNC = objRoot.Get("DefaultNamingContext")
Set objRoot = Nothing
'
'Get the actual list (array) of users to move
'
Set objResultList = ADSearch("LDAP://" & strDefaultDomNC,
        strLDAPQueryFilter,
        "ADsPath",
        "subTree",
        False)
'
' Process each element
'
For intIndex = 1 to (objResultList.Count)
  strUserADsPath = objResult (intIndex)
  MoveMailbox (strUserADsPath, strTargetStore)
Next
```

This code operates as follows:

- An LDAP search filter representing all users that will be moved and the Distinguished Name of the target Exchange 2003 mailbox store are passed as parameters to the script.
- The domain within which we are processing is determined because we need this to search the AD.
- The AD is searched, returning those objects that match the LDAP search filter.
- Each element returned from the AD search is processed—each is a Distinguished Name representing a user to be moved—and these are passed to the *MoveMailbox* function described at the beginning of this section.

These code extracts are pretty simplistic and lack robust coding techniques, such as integrity checking, logging, and event handling, but they do illustrate the power of CDO programming combined with Exchange 2000. There's much you can do, and when you have large numbers of users to migrate, automating the Move Mailbox functionality, which is ordinarily available with just the AD Users and Computers or ESM user interface, is very powerful.

8.5 Summary

Migrating from Exchange 2000 to Exchange 2003 is relatively straightforward. Once again, the main complexity is with the underlying infrastructure and ensuring that your migration from Windows 2000 to Windows 2003 is in sync with your plans for Exchange. Just make sure you have at least Windows 2000 SP3 DCs in place for the Exchange 2003 servers. Actually migrating Exchange 2000 servers to Exchange 2003 is simple. You either perform an in-place upgrade or you use the Move Mailbox Wizard to move the data from legacy Exchange 2000 servers. There's no extra complexity required with account migration or directory synchronization as there is with Exchange 5.5. Bearing that in mind, there's really very little to stop you from making the move to Exchange 2003 right away.

There's little doubt that the new Move Mailbox Wizard is much improved over the previous version: Its multithreaded and scheduling capabilities are a huge step forward. It is a valuable tool for moving users from Exchange 2000 servers to Exchange 2003 servers and an indispensable tool for moving users off Exchange 5.5 servers. It still has its limitations, though: it can't move mailboxes between Exchange 5.5 sites while in mixed mode and it is an intraorganizational tool only. If your requirements fall into any of these latter scenarios, you need to consider other approaches such as ExMerge or the Exchange Migration Wizard, or third-party tools from companies such as Bindview, NetIQ, or Quest.

9

Interorganization Migrations

9.1 Introduction

Using the techniques described already for mailbox migrations, you are restricted to performing moves within a single organization—these techniques cannot be used for interorganization moves. With the large numbers of acquisitions and divestitures that many organizations seem to incur these days, the problem of migrating from multiple and distinct Exchange 5.5 organizations to a single Exchange 2003 organization is a common one. For interorganization interoperability and migration projects, there are several challenges to be overcome, notably:

- Directory synchronization
- Mail flow
- Mailbox content migration
- Public Folder interoperability

Mail flow is probably the easiest problem to overcome with interorganization environments. SMTP is usually the simplest approach, but care must be taken if a shared SMTP address space is to be used across multiple separate Exchange organizations. Often X.400 is a good mechanism to use here to avoid mail routing issues, but a centralized hub-and-spoke architecture can be used even with SMTP.

9.2 Deciding on an Interorganization Migration Approach

Several tools and utilities are available for this kind of migration, and the most commonly used one has for some time been the Mailbox Merge Wizard (formerly known as ExMerge). However, the Mailbox Merge Wizard only deals with actually moving mailbox data, not the other associated problems with interorganization migration.

Other tools you should consider for use within environments such as this include the Active Directory Connector with interorganization CAs, which will perform directory synchronization, but do note that although you can use interorganization CAs, such CAs will not synchronize Exchange 5.5 Distribution List membership to the AD: Distribution Lists are represented as contacts in the target AD. Other solutions you might consider for directory synchronization include Microsoft's Information and Identity Server (MIIS) and HP's LDAP Directory Synchronization Utility (LDSU).

Public Folder synchronization is a prickly subject, and the only free piece of software available for this is the Microsoft Inter-Organizational Replication Tool. This tool consists of two communicating components that you can install on Exchange servers in different Exchange organizations to replicate Public Folder contents between the organizations. The tool can be used between pairs of Exchange servers even of different versions (from Exchange 5.5 up to Exchange 2003). This tool is primarily used to synchronize the contents of the Schedule + Free/Busy Public Folders between different Exchange organizations. Although the Inter-Organizational Replication Tool has had a bad reputation in the past, the newly updated version now available with Exchange 2003 has been markedly improved and is much more stable than previous versions.

9.3 Using the Exchange Server Migration Wizard

The Exchange Server Migration Wizard is installed automatically with Exchange 2003 and now includes support for straightforward migration of mailboxes from Exchange 5.5 organizations, Exchange 2000 organizations, and Exchange 2003 organizations into an Exchange 2003 organization as long as the source Exchange organization is different from the target Exchange 2003 organization (i.e., you cannot use this wizard for intraorganization moves).

9.3.1 Exchange Server Migration Wizard operation

The Exchange Server Migration Wizard works in conjunction with the Active Directory Connector. As always, you can set up interorganization CAs from, as in this example, an Exchange 5.5 organization named Starfish to an Exchange 2003 organization named Razorbucks. The Exchange 2003 Active Directory Connector (actually the Exchange 2000 Service Pack 1 Active Directory Connector) allows you to create full-fledged user objects in the AD with an interorganization CA, as shown in Figure 9-1.

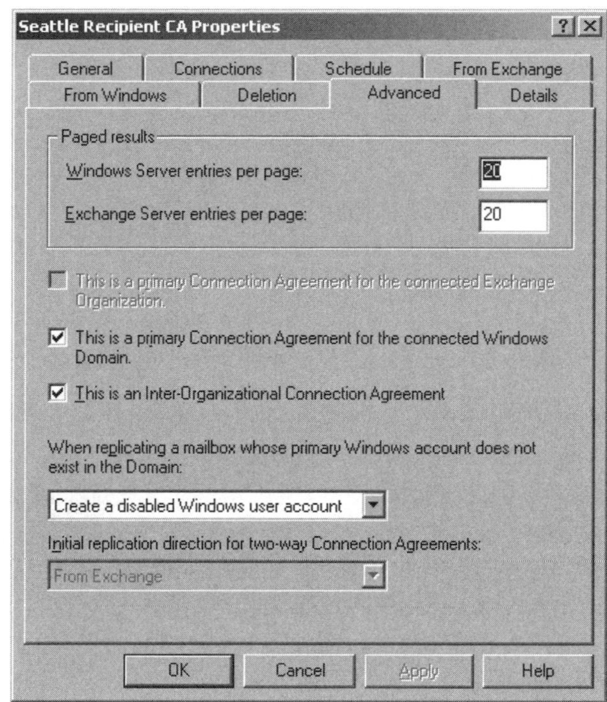

Figure 9-1 *Interorganization Connection Agreement Creating a Disabled User Object in the Active Directory*

Shortly after you invoke the Exchange Server Migration Wizard (from *Start Menu/Programs/Microsoft Exchange/Migration Wizard*) and click away the first few less interesting screens, you can choose the Exchange 2003 server and Exchange 2003 database to which you'd like your Exchange 5.5 mailboxes moved. This list gets prepopulated because the Exchange 2003 server enumerates the data from the AD Configuration Naming Context (where most Exchange 2003–related information is held).

After selecting the target location, you must specify the source server on which the Exchange 5.5 users reside. Here's the first gotcha. When you enter the server name of the Exchange 5.5 server, be sure to enter the NetBIOS version of the computer name. In my case, the Exchange 5.5 server name was PULSAR. Entering the fully qualified domain name of pulsar.research.compaq.com didn't seem to work, despite a perfectly functioning DNS.

Here's the second gotcha. The Exchange Server Migration Wizard uses LDAP from the Exchange 5.5 Directory Service to enumerate all users on that server that are available for migration, and if, as was my case, you are running your Exchange 5.5 LDAP service on a nonstandard port (I was using 390 because my Exchange 5.5 server was running on a Windows 2000 DC), you must explicitly specify the port number with the server name. Thus, as shown in Figure 9-2, I used pulsar:390 after a little desperation. As it turns out, this is documented in the online help, but to be honest, why Microsoft couldn't just have used another data entry field on the form where you can explicitly specify the port number escapes me. (They do it on the Active Directory Connector! And because subsequent operation of the wizard uses MAPI RPCs, why didn't they just connect to the Exchange 5.5 server over MAPI and read the LDAP port number that's actually in use?)

The Exchange Server Migration Wizard will then present a list of Exchange 5.5 mailboxes that you can select for migration. After selecting the appropriate Exchange 5.5 mailboxes, you must then select the location in the AD where you would like the Exchange Server Migration Wizard to either create new Windows 2000 or Windows 2003 accounts for the mailboxes being moved or where you would like it to search for Windows 2000 or Windows 2003 accounts that already exist, as shown in Figure 9-3. This dialog box appears very similar to that presented when configuring a CA and selecting the target locations in the AD for the search and creation of Windows 2000 or Windows 2003 accounts. (You probably created these using an interorganization CA earlier to provide a complete GAL.)

When selection of the appropriate configuration information is completed, the Exchange Server Migration Wizard then presents a summary of the Windows 2000 or Windows 2003 account-matching or creation activities it expects to perform. In this example, as shown in Figure 9-4, my interorganization CA had already created a Windows account in the *Users* container, and the Exchange Server Migration Wizard matched this account with the associated Windows NT account of the mailbox being moved.

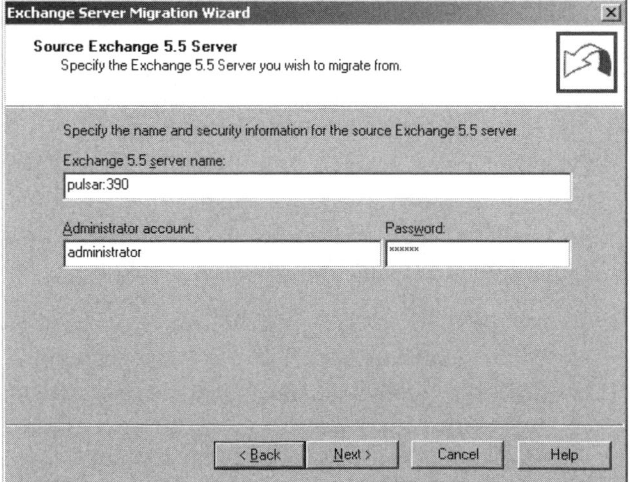

Figure 9-2
Specifying the Migration Wizard Source Exchange 5.5 Server

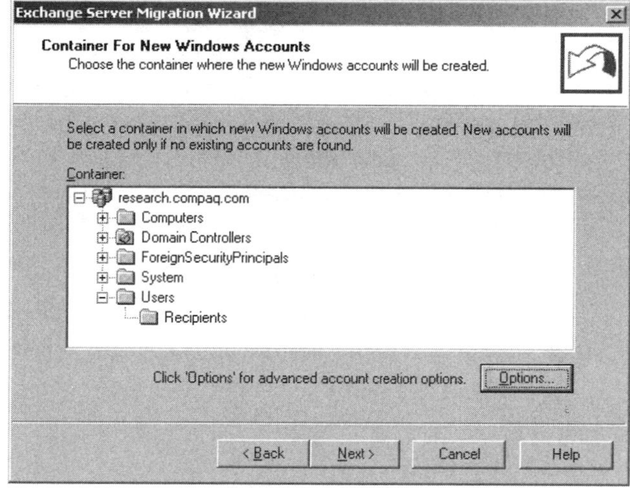

Figure 9-3 *Selecting the Locations in the Active Directory for Migrated Exchange 5.5 Mailboxes*

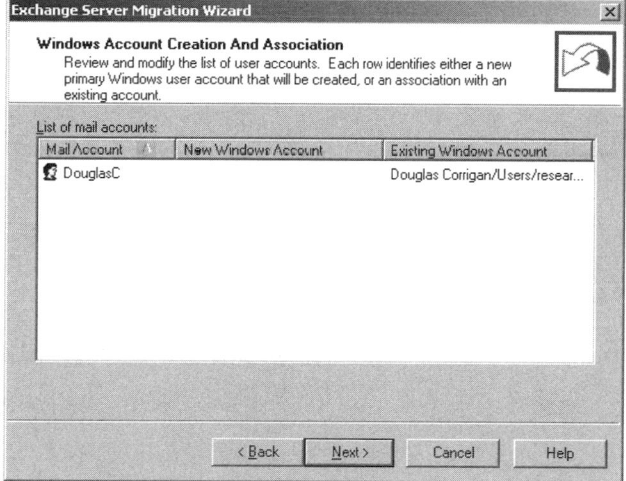

Figure 9-4 *Summary of Account Creation/Matching Behavior*

The Exchange Server Migration Wizard's matching functionality is similar to the matching activity that the *Active Directory Cleanup Wizard* and other migration tools employ, allowing matching on user objects and contacts using SMTP addresses, rectifying or avoiding the creation of duplicate Windows 2000 or Windows 2003 accounts by matching the ID of the Exchange 5.5 mailbox's associated Windows NT account with either the object SID or *sidHistory* attribute of the existing Windows 2000 or Windows 2003 user object. If a match is found, the Exchange Server Migration Wizard need not create a new Windows 2000 or Windows 2003 user.

Then we're ready to get to the actual process of migration. Having specified the source Exchange 5.5 server, the mailboxes to be migrated, and the target Exchange 2003 database to host the migrated accounts, the wizard uses RPC-based MAPI connections from the source server to migrate the mailbox directly into the appropriate mailbox store in Exchange 2003. The data migration performance you see during this migration is roughly equivalent to the performance you see using the *Move Mailbox Wizard* from AD Users and Computers or ESM.

For the 143 messages migrated during the move operation shown in Figure 9-5, it took 2 minutes 26 seconds; roughly about 18 MB of data per minute, given that the mailbox in question contained just over 40 MB. It goes without saying that this figure depends largely on the hardware configuration of your systems. Generally, the more spindles and the faster the disks and controllers you have, the better the performance. My figures may seem a little on the conservative side, but bear in mind that this test was carried out on relatively old single-disk systems.

9.3.2 Other points to note on the Exchange Server Migration Wizard

There are a few other points to consider when using the Exchange Server Migration Wizard. A few of them caught me by surprise during my tests and are worthy of mentioning just for completeness. First, when you are running the Exchange Server Migration Wizard and migrate mailboxes from Exchange 5.5 to Exchange 2003, you don't actually move the mailboxes. The original Exchange 5.5 mailbox remains intact on the Exchange 5.5 server, so in effect you're copying the mailbox data. The impact of

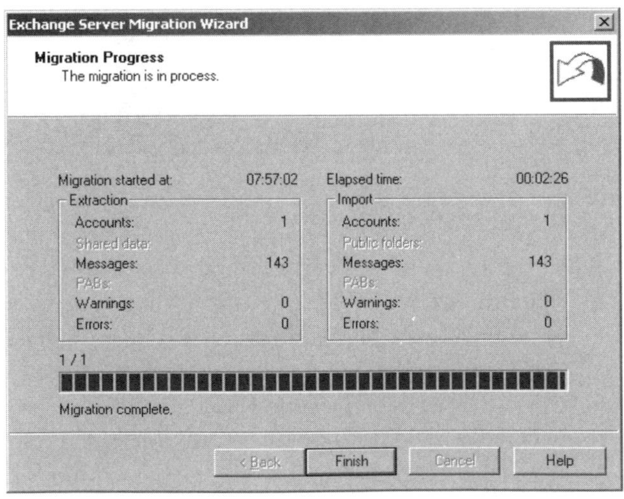

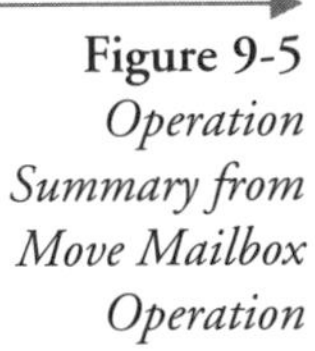

Figure 9-5 *Operation Summary from Move Mailbox Operation*

this warrants some careful consideration. You may have some significant postmigration cleanup to carry out on the Exchange 5.5 environment unless you have a solid mail routing and directory synchronization infrastructure in place. Without one, SMTP mail, for example, may still be routed to the old Exchange 5.5 mailbox and remain blissfully unaware of its new intended location in Exchange 2003.

If the Exchange 2003 Information Store service on the target server is not running when you attempt the migration, unsurprisingly the migration attempt will fail. However, no checking for the active service or that the Exchange 2003 databases are mounted is carried out. You are allowed to run through the migration exercise, only to wait forever as the migration status reports "Migration in progress," but nothing happens. I found this out and traced the reluctance of the Exchange 2003 Information Store service to start to be a result of a time skew of several hours between my Exchange 2003 server and its GC server.

9.4 Partial Organization Migrations

Usually, when you upgrade an Exchange 5.5 organization to Exchange 2003, it's typically a single organization upgrading in its entirety. However, often a single Exchange 5.5 organization consists of several different operating companies, agencies, or divisions that wish to move to Exchange 2003 and Windows 2000 or Windows 2003 at different rates. In such circumstances, it's often the case that Exchange 5.5 sites map cleanly to the operating companies. This section outlines a straightforward approach for upgrading those sites (and thus the separate companies, agencies, or divisions that will be referred to as entities hereafter) to Exchange 2003 essentially in isolation from the rest of the environment. Effectively, such partial organization migrations are just a form of interorganization migration and warrant discussion here. Often these forms of migration represent a simple and cost-effective way to break off part of a legacy Exchange 5.5 organization and move to Exchange 2003 without incurring the cost of expensive third-party Exchange migration tools.

9.4.1 Differing Exchange 5.5 to Exchange 2003 partial migration approaches

One of the most obvious approaches to the problem of an Exchange 5.5 entity wishing to move to Exchange 2003, while other entities in the same organization do not, is to split that entity off from the rest of the organization and then proceed to migrate it to Exchange 2003 in a normal intraorganization fashion.

Splitting a site off from an Exchange 5.5 organization is a relatively straightforward process: You remove the Directory Replication Connectors between the site that you wish to remove and the rest of the Exchange organization, then you let the directory information from the other Exchange 5.5 sites disappear from the local Exchange Directory Service. When the Directory Service has been purged, the local Exchange 5.5 site is removed from the Exchange organization and becomes a separate Exchange 5.5 organization in its own right. However, if you split a site off from the Exchange 5.5 organization before moving to Exchange 2003, then you must implement some mechanism to synchronize the Directory Service from the original Exchange 5.5 organization to the new one so that a complete and consistent GAL can be maintained. To do this you'll need to use a tool such as HP's LDSU or Microsoft's MIIS tools. Figure 9-6 shows the relationship between two Exchange 5.5 sites in the same organization, and Figure 9-7 shows the relationship between those same two sites after Site B has been partitioned off from the rest of the Exchange organization.

Other approaches are valid, too. There are numerous interorganization tools available. You could install a brand-new Exchange 2003 server into its own Exchange organization and use the standard Microsoft tools to move users from the Exchange 5.5 server in Site A to the new Exchange 2000 organization. This involves the following steps:

1. Use the Active Directory Connector and interorganization CA between the Exchange 5.5 organization and the Exchange 2003 organization to replicate Exchange 5.5 directory information. However, remember that interorganization CAs replicate Exchange 5.5 Distribution Lists as contacts in the AD.

Figure 9-6
An Exchange 5.5 Organization with Two Sites

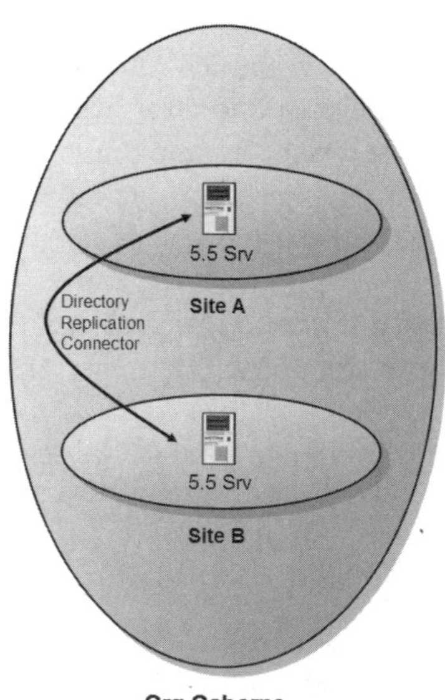

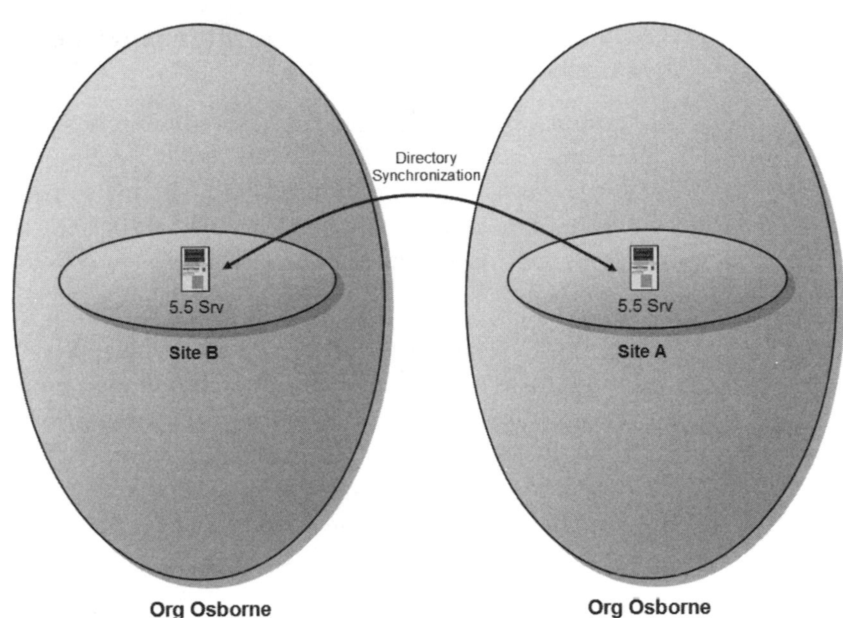

Figure 9-7 *Site A Removed from Osborne Exchange Organization and Requiring Directory Synchronization*

2. Move mailbox data from servers in the Exchange 5.5 site to the Exchange 2003 server using the Exchange Server Migration Wizard. However, note that the Exchange Migration Wizard does not remove the Exchange 5.5 mailboxes that it migrates.
3. Use the Exchange Inter-Organization Replication Tool to replicate Public Folder content from appropriate Exchange 5.5 servers to the Exchange 2003 server.

This out-of-the-box approach using the standard Microsoft tools is not ideal because of the problems outlined with Distribution List replication, mailbox migration, and Public Folder replication. Several third-party vendors, such as NetIQ and Quest, have supplementary tools for this aspect of interorganization migration that provide directory replication functionality (better Distribution List handling), mailbox move functionality (post-move cleanup and rollback functionality), and complete Public Folder replication tools with permissions.

Although all of these tools are versatile, they are most useful when multiple separate Exchange 5.5 organizations are merging into one Exchange 2003 organization. We are more concerned with an Exchange 5.5 organization that is breaking up (or at least one part of it is), and although the tools can be used in this situation, they are not required.

9.4.2 Evolving intraorganization migrations to interorganization migrations

One reason why intraorganization migrations are desirable is because the directory replication, mailbox moves, and Public Folder replication is straightforward. Thus the first approach outlined of breaking a site off to become a separate Exchange 5.5 organization and then performing an intraorganization is useful, although we are faced with the initial problem of Exchange 5.5 to Exchange 5.5 directory synchronization.

However, we can implement a variation of this approach for an all-around simpler migration that bypasses this directory synchronization problem. Let's assume that the entity represented by Site A (as shown in Figure 9-6) wishes to move to Exchange 2003, but the rest of the Exchange organization does not (or cannot). Rather than split Site A off into a separate organization in the first instance, we can immediately start an intraorganization migration to Exchange 2003 in Site A. We do this through the following steps:

1. Running Forestprep and electing to join the existing Exchange 5.5 organization
2. Installing an Exchange 2003 server into Site A (where a Configuration CA is automatically created within the site)
3. Setting up a Recipient CA from an Exchange 5.5 server in Site A to an AD GC server providing the GAL to the Exchange 2003 organization

The first steps in this migration are shown in Figure 9-8. In this example, the intraorganization CA within Site A can serve multiple functions. You can use it to synchronize only objects within Site A, such as mailboxes, custom recipients, or Distribution Lists, and rely on an external synchronization mechanism (e.g., LDSU or MIIS) to synchronize objects from Site B to provide a complete Global Address List for Exchange 2003 users.

Rather than use an external directory synchronization process, you can use another Recipient CA within Site A to replicate objects from Site B into the Exchange 2003 GAL. It's important to provide a complete GAL, but it's more important that objects in Site B aren't modified or touched in any way—we'll be separating from Site B in the future, and we want no residual impact on Site B objects. (The Active Directory Connector replication process modifies the source Exchange 5.5 objects that it replicates.) However, if we use a Recipient CA within Site A to replicate objects from Site B, no modification to the Site B objects takes place because those objects are read-only in Site A. However, this approach causes problems when we finally separate Site A from Site B: when this takes place, Site A will have no knowledge of Site B objects and thus will be no use as a source of directory synchronization.

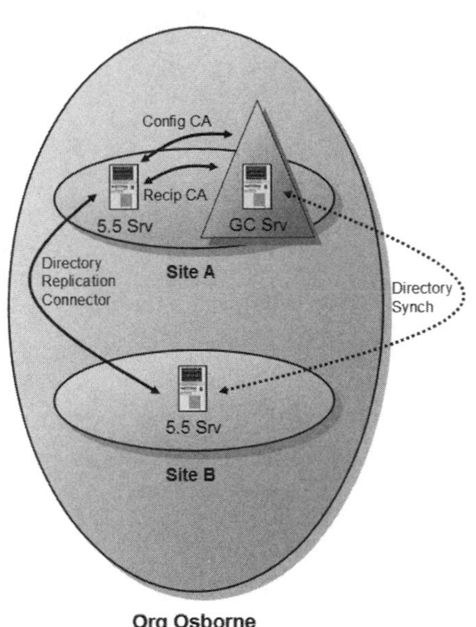

Figure 9-8 *Site A Beginning an Intraorganization Migration*

The scenario shown in Figure 9-9 is better. When Site A is subsequently separated from the rest of the Exchange 5.5 organization, the interorganization CA with the Exchange 5.5 endpoint in the Insulation Site will always be a source of Exchange 5.5 Directory Service information. And we use the insulation site rather than connecting directly to a server in Site B—if we did this, then the Active Directory Connector would modify the source objects. Objects in the insulation site will be read-only.

Installing the Exchange 2003 server into Site A is the first step in the migration of Site A to a separate Exchange 2003 organization. When all Exchange 5.5 mailboxes have been moved onto Exchange 2003 servers, as shown in Figure 9-10, we are ready to move Site A out of the Exchange 5.5 organization. Separating the Exchange 2003 Site/AG A from the rest of the Exchange 5.5 organization is accomplished by removing the DRC between Site B's bridgehead server and the SRS server in Site A.

When the DRC between the two sites is removed, Site A effectively becomes its own Exchange 2003 organization in mixed-mode, as shown in Figure 9-11.

Any Public Folders that should only exist for the entity represented by Site A must be homed onto a Site A server before the separation takes place, and no Public Folder replicas must exist on Site B servers. (Note that Public Folders cannot be shared between the two organizations with this migration approach, but you may wish to use third-party tools to achieve this goal.) Be sure that no Distribution Lists that existed in Site A had membership drawn from Site B. If so, then the integrity of those Distribution Lists (now represented as UDGs in the AD) will be compromised. Similarly, make

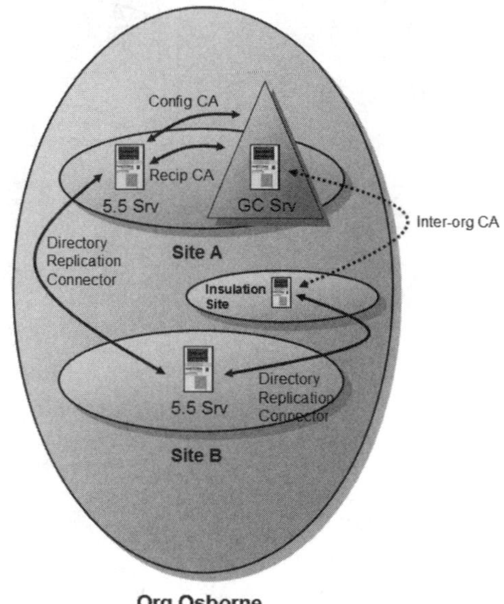

Figure 9-9 *Site A Intraorganization Migration with Insulation Site*

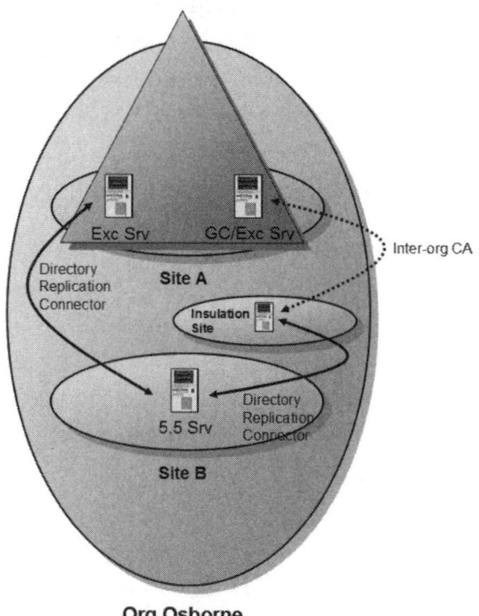

Figure 9-10 *All Servers in Site A Become Exchange 2003 Servers*

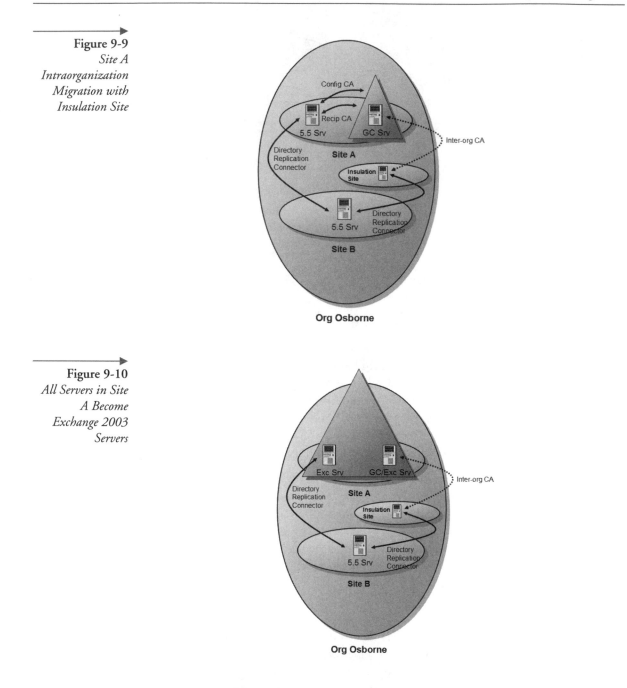

sure that no Public Folders homed in Site A have ACLs that comprise objects from Site B. If so, when the separation takes place, access to those Public Folders could be blocked because the ACLs cannot be resolved.

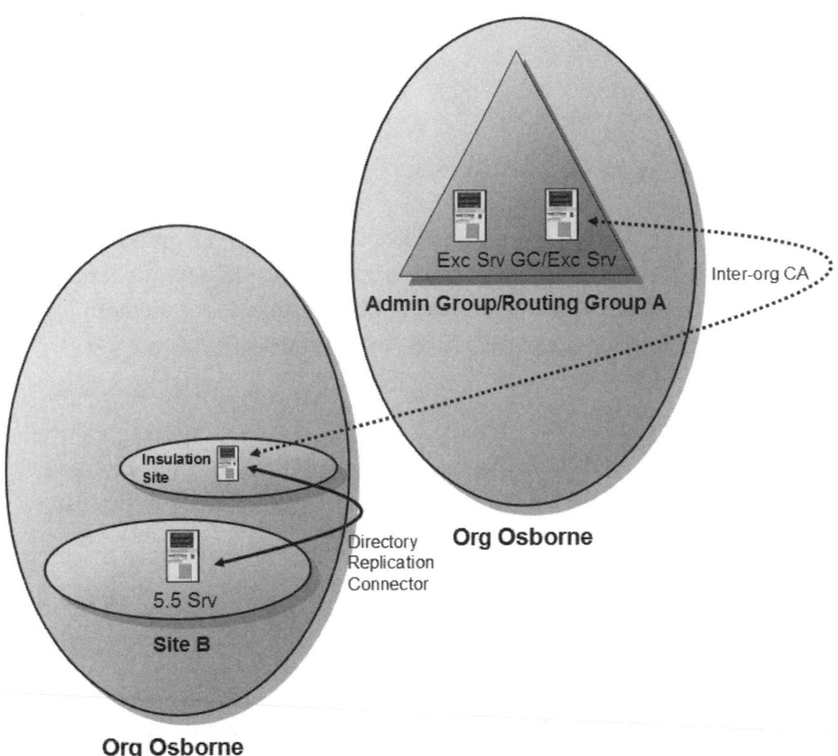

Figure 9-11 *Exchange 2003 Site Separated into a Separate Organization*

9.5 Third-Party Tool Approach to Interorganization Migration

This section outlines an approach to interorganization migration using third-party migration tools. There are several third-party tools in the marketplace, and in this section I have based the migration approach on one of those market-leading tools. In general the third-party tools all take more or less the same approach to migration, and I've outlined the general approach by way of an example here. (The generalized approach is based on the migration approach for Aelita's Exchange Migration Wizard, now owned by Quest.)

9.5.1 The need for third-party tools and interorganization migrations

Quite a few companies have collected other Exchange organizations over the years by means of various mergers and acquisitions. Other companies have been forced to use separate Exchange organizations as a result of various organizational and political constraints. Many of these companies are on the verge of making big changes to their Exchange messaging environments. They know it's time to move to the latest version of Exchange and it's also time to overhaul those existing—and often sub-optimal—Exchange organizational structures. Consolidation is the buzzword, but consolidation has many faces. There's the concept of consolidating multiple Exchange organizations into fewer organizations; consolidating multiple Exchange sites into fewer sites; and consolidating many servers into fewer again servers. Almost all of these forms of consolidation result in fundamental changes to the topology of an existing Exchange organization. Changes to the topology of an Exchange organization usually spell interorganization migration.

Coupled with the fact that in the United States and Europe, 43% and 39%, respectively, of Exchange shops are running Exchange 5.5[1] third-party migration tools, designed for interorganization migration from Exchange 5.5 to Exchange 2000/2003, they are a great addition for any company's migration toolkit.

This section describes the use of generalized third-party migration tools and especially directory synchronization, as well as the remaining features of such an approach, specifically mailbox migration, Public Folder migration, and calendar/scheduling migration.

9.5.2 Interorganization migrations

The fundamental decision any company has to make when setting out to move from Exchange 5.5 to Exchange 2000/2003 is whether to perform an intraorganization migration or an interorganization migration.

9.5.2.1 *Intraorganization migration characteristics*

Intraorganization migrations have the following characteristics:

- Can only be used to upgrade a single Exchange 5.5 organization
- Offer high-fidelity directory synchronization (via the Active Directory Connector) between the Exchange 5.5 Directory Service and the AD
- Offer high-fidelity Public Folder interoperability between Exchange 5.5 servers and Exchange 2000/2003 servers
- Provide mailbox move operations and in-place server upgrade capabilities.
- Provide RPC-based interserver message transfer

1. Exchange Development Group, June 2003.

- Inherit the Exchange 5.5 administration model because the Exchange 5.5 site topology is translated to the Exchange 2000/2003 AG model

In general, if you have a straightforward, single Exchange 5.5 organization and you wish to move to Exchange 2000/2003 and you are happy with these characteristics, then intraorganization migrations make sense.

9.5.2.2 Interorganization migration drivers

However, there are many reasons why you may wish to avoid the intraorganization migration and opt for an interorganization approach:

- You have more than one Exchange 5.5 organization and you wish to consolidate the organizations into one (or at least fewer) Exchange 2000/2003 organizations.
- Even with a single Exchange 5.5 organization, you do not wish to inherit the Exchange 5.5 administrative model but wish to restructure into a new topology.
- You do not wish to preserve any configuration from the Exchange 5.5 organization into the new Exchange 2000/2003 organization but wish to start again with a clean sheet.
- You would like the capability to run the new Exchange 2000/2003 organization in parallel with the legacy Exchange 5.5 organization and have mailbox contents kept in sync between the two organizations to allow for a quick cutover and, if required, an easy rollback.

If any of these requirements strike a chord, then third-party migration tools have myriad features well-suited to your migration and consolidation project.

9.5.3 Third-party migration tools features

Third-party migration tools offer several key features, including the following:

- Synchronization functions for the GAL and for Public Folder contents (including users' calendar data) from multiple Exchange 5.5 organizations to Exchange 2000/2003
- Unattended, rules-based, compressed, gradual transfer of mailbox contents with multiple source/target pairs from Exchange 5.5 to Exchange 2000/2003
- Automatic client MAPI profile reconfiguration

However, other problems still remain, including reconfiguration of Offline Stores files (OSTs) and Offline Address Books, although it's likely that products will evolve to fix these problems in the future.

9.5.3.1 *Sample migration and consolidation topologies*

From a topology perspective, there are many potential scenarios we might consider; a few examples are shown in Figure 9-12.

9.5.4 Getting started with third-party migration tools for interorganization migration

Irrespective of the nature of your interorganization migration, you must adhere to some general guidelines when it comes to embarking on a migration project. Third-party migration tools generally implement a console/agent architecture with a single central Console acting as the management interface to all migration projects underway. The system running the Console is typically also used as the Database repository, where configuration information is stored and maintained. Several agents on the other source and target systems are used to perform the various streams of data synchronization and migration (i.e., directory synchronization, mailbox synchronization, Public Folder synchronization, and Calendar synchronization). You use the Console to set up and maintain the various synchronization instances. This is shown graphically in Figure 9-13, although do note that it is possible to have multiple source and target systems, even in different Exchange organizations.

9.5.4.1 *General third-party migration tools system requirements*

There are several prerequisites for the systems hosting the console/database, source, and target systems, as follows:

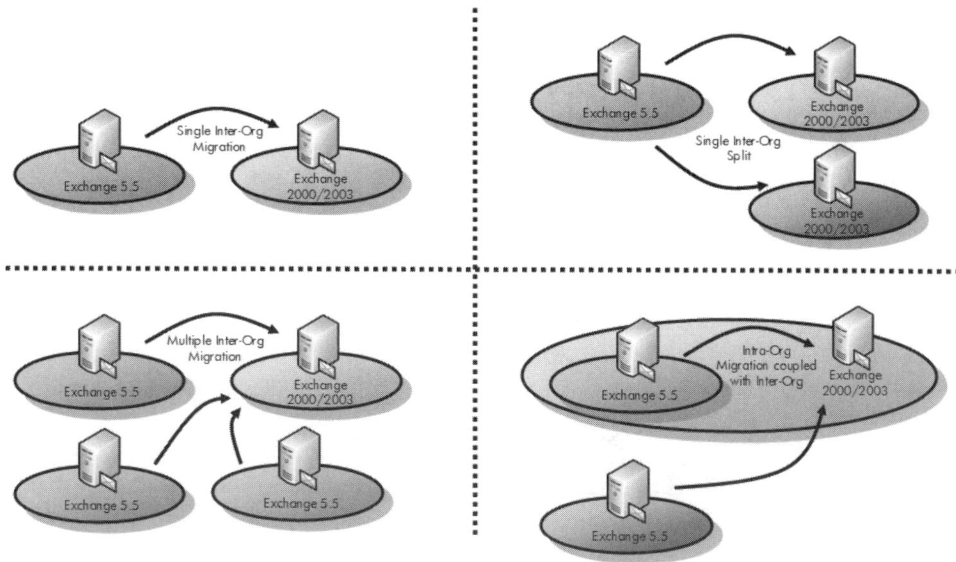

Figure 9-12
Sample Migration Scenarios Using Third-Party Migration Tools

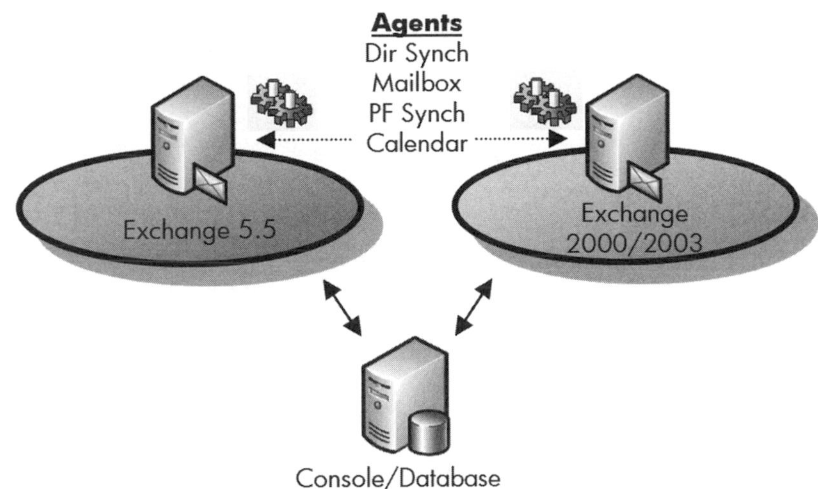

Figure 9-13 *Third-Party Migration Tools Console/Agent Architecture*

- *Console/Database system:* Windows 2000 preferably with Service Pack (SP) 4 or higher Collaboration Data Objects (CDO) Library V1.2 available either by installing Outlook 2000 or Exchange 5.5 (the CDO Library is available with Outlook XP, but if you use Outlook XP, then you must configure the Outlook Template Security Settings as described in the Installation Guide), SQL Server 2000 preferably with SP3 or Microsoft SQL Server Desktop Engine (MSDE), both of which provides the minimum version, V2.6, of Microsoft Data Access Component (MDAC) required
- *Source systems:* Windows NT4 SP5 (preferably SP6A) or Windows 2000 (preferably SP4), Exchange Server 5.5 SP4, Internet Explorer 4.01 SP2 (or higher)
- *Target systems:* Windows 2000 SP2 (or higher) or Windows 2003 Exchange Server 2000 SP1 (preferably SP3) or Exchange Server 2003

9.5.4.2 Installation process

Initial configuration of the third-party migration tools Console is straightforward: You simply install the Console from the installation CD-ROM and select the option to create a new database to act as the project (the container for all migration instances) repository. You'll then be presented with the Console interface and you begin the process of defining the Exchange source and target organizations that will participate in the migration activity. The Console interface is shown in Figure 9-14.

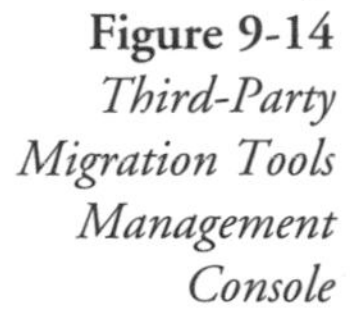

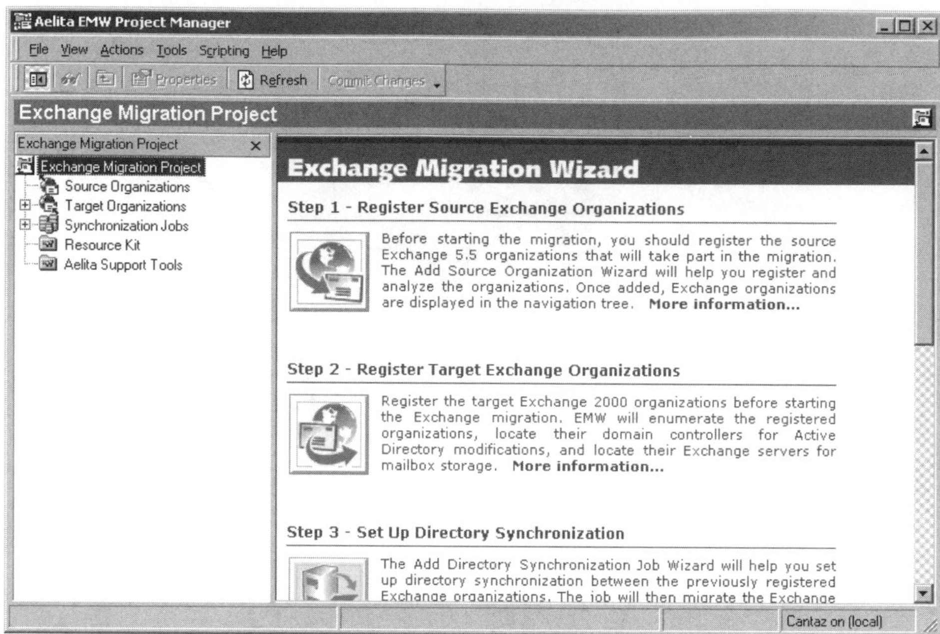

Figure 9-14 *Third-Party Migration Tools Management Console*

9.5.5 Configuration for interorganization migrations

9.5.5.1 Adding source organizations

The first step in configuration of the migration environment is to add the source servers. Click on *Step 1 – Register Source Exchange Organizations* or right-click on *Source Organizations* and select *Add Source Organizations*. You will be presented with the dialog boxes, as shown in Figure 9-15.

You should enter the NetBIOS name of a server in the Exchange 5.5 organization. The Console application will then make an LDAP connection to that source server and read the entire organization's configuration information. Remember that if you are running your Exchange 5.5 Directory Service on a Windows 2000 DC, then the LDAP service will be running on a port other than 389. All of the information about the organization's topology, sites, servers, and so on will then be presented in the Console window. You can repeat this activity for each source Exchange 5.5 organization from which you wish to migrate or consolidate.

9.5.5.2 Adding target organizations

You repeat the process for any and all target Exchange organizations in your environment. The same process takes place: You specify a single server in the organization, the

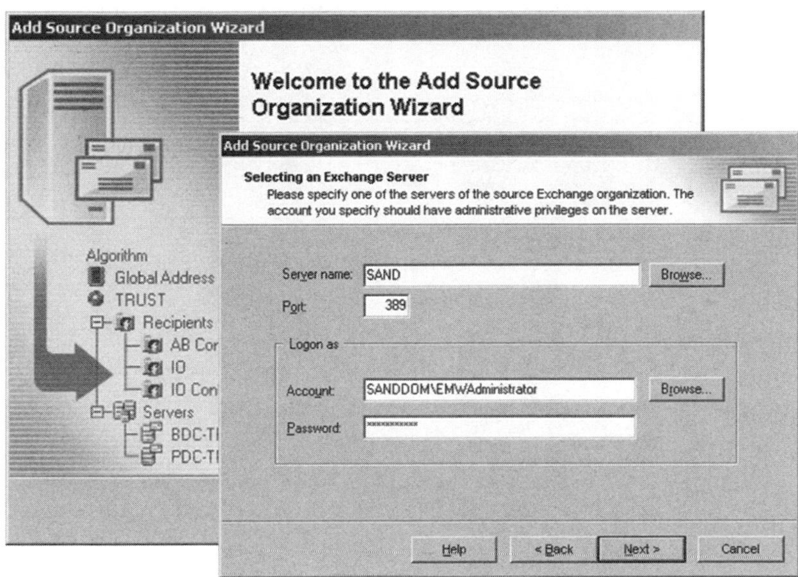

Figure 9-15
Adding Source Organizations

LDAP port, and credentials for access. A resulting Console view for my environment with two legacy Exchange 5.5 organizations is shown in Figure 9-16.

9.5.6 Synchronizing directories

The synchronization options from source organizations to target organizations are flexible. You first need to install and create a Directory Synchronization Agent, which must be installed on a Windows 2000 or Windows 2003 server. You can choose any Windows 2000 or Windows 2003 server in your environment to host the Agent: it need not be a server that is already an Exchange 5.5 server, Exchange 2000 server, or Exchange 2003 server.

The Agent hosts one or more Directory Synchronization Jobs, which specifies an instance of synchronization between Exchange 5.5 and Exchange 2000/2003 (or more specifically an AD). You must have at least one Job per Exchange 5.5 site because an Exchange 5.5 site defines a writeable boundary to the Exchange 5.5 Directory Service. Thus if you have two legacy Exchange 5.5 organizations with four sites each, and you are consolidating these two organizations into a single Exchange 2000/2003 organization, you will require eight Directory Synchronization Jobs, all of which might be homed on a single Directory Synchronization Agent. Depending on the load expected in your environment, you might have to use multiple Directory Synchronization Agent servers. This is shown graphically in Figure 9-17.

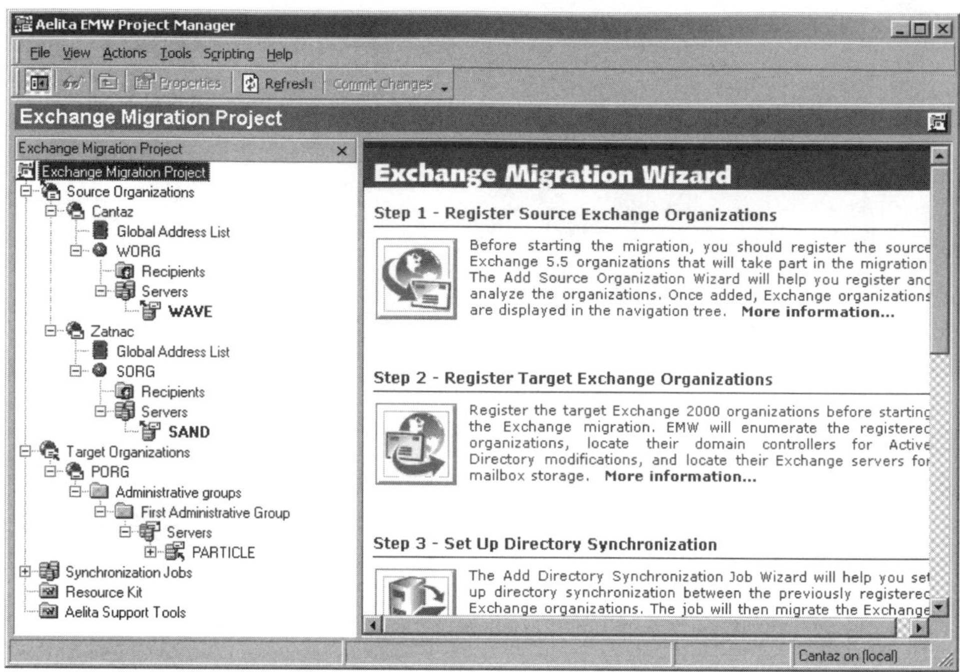

Figure 9-16 *Console View Showing Source and Target Organizations*

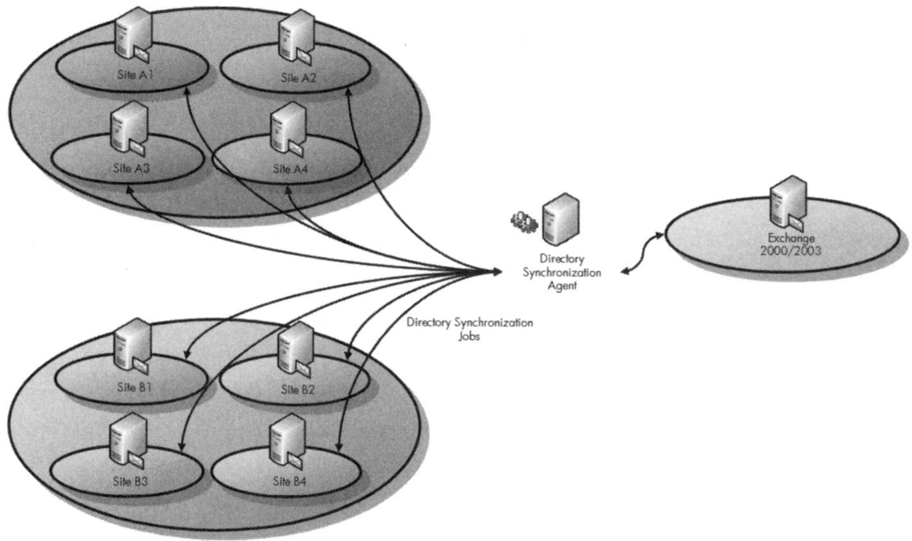

Figure 9-17 *Multiple Directory Synchronization Jobs Homed on a Directory Synchronization Agent*

As a matter of best practice it makes sense to select a Windows 2000 or Windows 2003 server to host the Agent that is nearby (in physical network terms) to both the

Exchange 5.5 server and the AD DC that it will communicate with for a particular Job. This reduces latency and other wide-area connection delays. For this reason, you may elect to use more than one Agent (accordingly on more than one server). You don't need a separate server on which to host the Agent: you might co-locate it on an Exchange 5.5 bridgehead server or on a DC, but do bear in mind that if you home multiple Jobs on the Agent, this will produce load on the server.

Setting up the Directory Synchronization Agent is straightforward: you specify the server on which it is to run along with credentials with which to run the service. Then you proceed directly to setting up some Directory Synchronization Jobs. Remember that although you enter into the configuration of the first Job automatically, you must explicitly create a Job for every Exchange 5.5 site.

You run through the following essential steps when doing this:

1. Specify the Exchange 5.5 server name (you can select from a list of servers already populated into the Console when you created the source organization), port number for access to the Exchange 5.5 Directory Service, and the account with which to run.
2. Specify similar information for the AD DC associated with the target Exchange 2000/2003 organization.
3. Third-party migration tools will automatically create a mailbox for every user that they synchronize into the target organization, so you must specify the actual Exchange 2000/2003 server and mailbox store in which you wish to see the mailbox created. This is done as a precursor to eventual mailbox migration.
4. Specify the Mail Redirection type: third-party migration tools use hidden Custom Recipients on Exchange 5.5 and hidden Contacts on Exchange 2000/2003 so that mail is always routed to the correct mailbox during the migration phase. For example, if a user on Exchange 2000/2003 sends mail to a user that has not yet been migrated from Exchange 5.5, then the mail destined for that user's Exchange 2000/2003 mailbox is redirected to the hidden contact on the Exchange 2000/2003 system and finally relayed to the Exchange 5.5 mailbox and vice versa. This redirection technique gives you more flexibility when it comes to defining the mail transfer points between your Exchange organizations during migration. You can elect to use either X.400 or SMTP transport for these redirection recipients. In my configuration, as shown in Figure 9-18, I've used SMTP and fairly obvious addressing structures to indicate the nature of the mail system. Depending on the configuration of SMTP namespaces within your company, you may use several modified SMTP address spaces—as in my example—or you may just use X.400 as the interconnect.

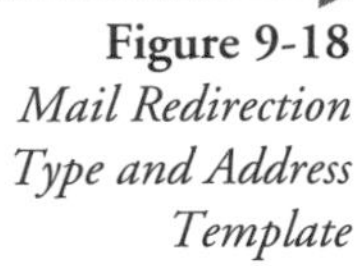

Figure 9-18
Mail Redirection Type and Address Template

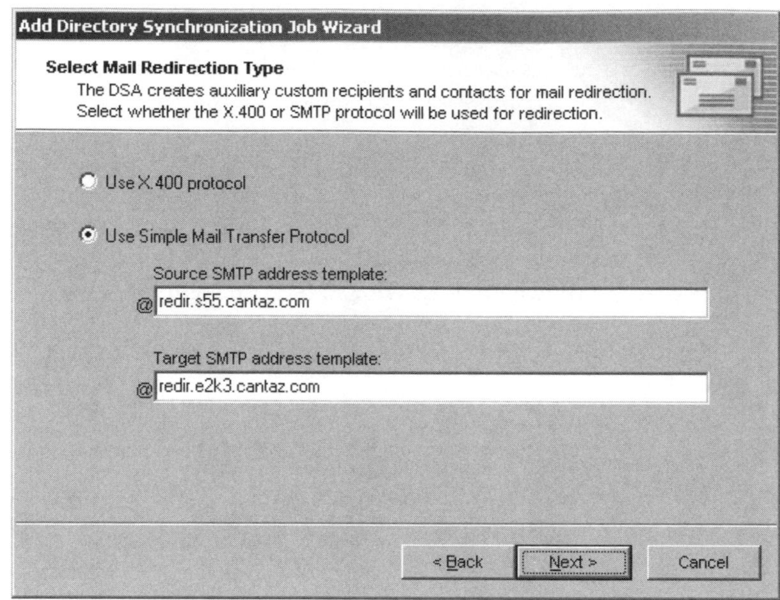

5. Specify the Exchange 5.5 container and the Exchange 2000/2003 AD Organizational Unit to hold the Redirection objects.

Further options are available to define the type of objects that you will synchronize (e.g., mailboxes, Distribution Lists, Custom Recipients), the source containers from which you will synchronize, and to specify LDAP search filters to provide further selective granularity on what will be synchronized. You may then also choose Conflict Resolution Settings to indicate which change to an object is authoritative if an object changes in both directions. Finally, you can set the schedule for synchronization: either continuous or at intervals.

The configuration options available when setting up a Directory Synchronization Job expose the real power of third-party migration tools when it comes to merging and splitting organizations. In the simple case of a merge operation, you specify the recipient containers from each source Exchange 5.5 organization and direct them to one (or more) Organizational Units in the single target Exchange 2000/2003 organization. Figure 9-19 shows such an arrangement, with the recipient containers for the respective Exchange 5.5 organizations identified.

And conversely it is just as simple to split a source Exchange 5.5 organization and migrate users to separate Exchange organizations, as shown in Figure 9-20, where users from two different containers in Exchange 5.5 get migrated to different target Exchange organizations.

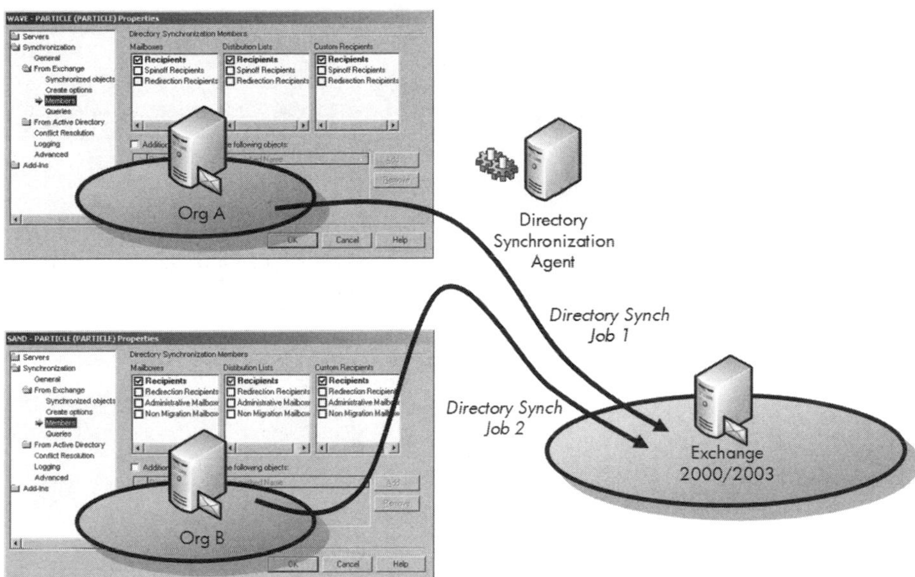

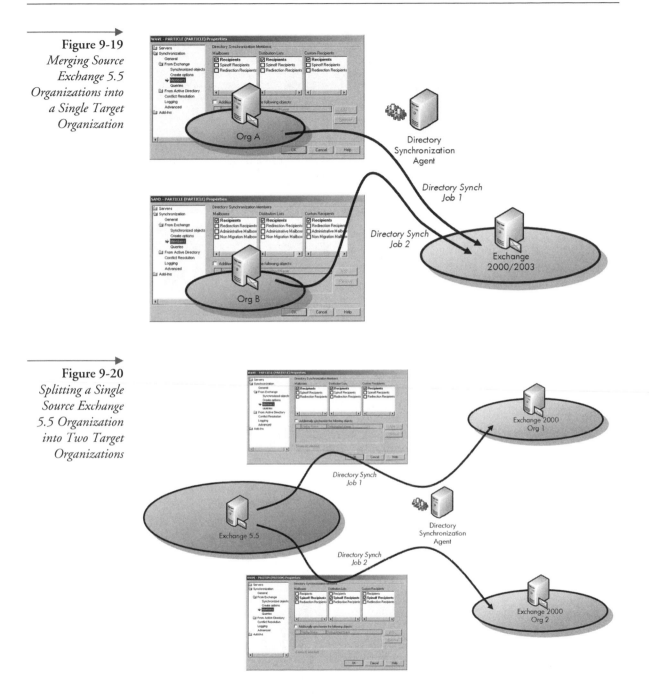

Figure 9-19 *Merging Source Exchange 5.5 Organizations into a Single Target Organization*

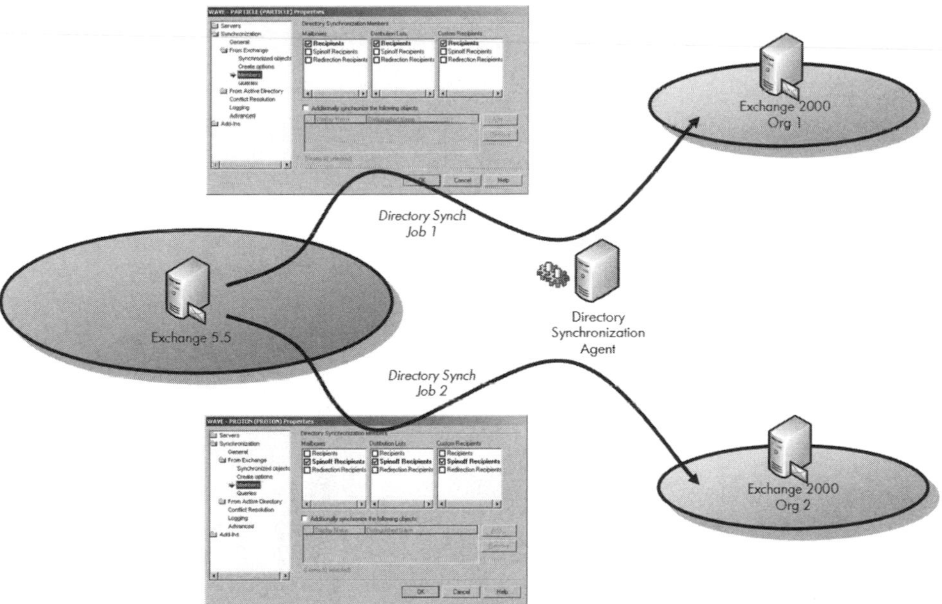

Figure 9-20 *Splitting a Single Source Exchange 5.5 Organization into Two Target Organizations*

As synchronization takes place (either continuously or at intervals as determined by your configuration), you can check the Console (see Figure 9-21) to get an update

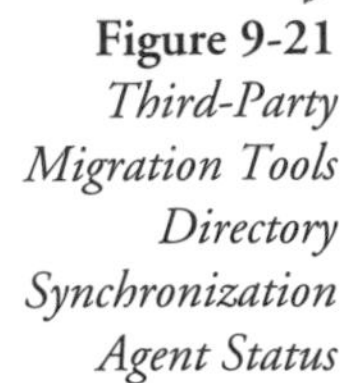

Figure 9-21 *Third-Party Migration Tools Directory Synchronization Agent Status*

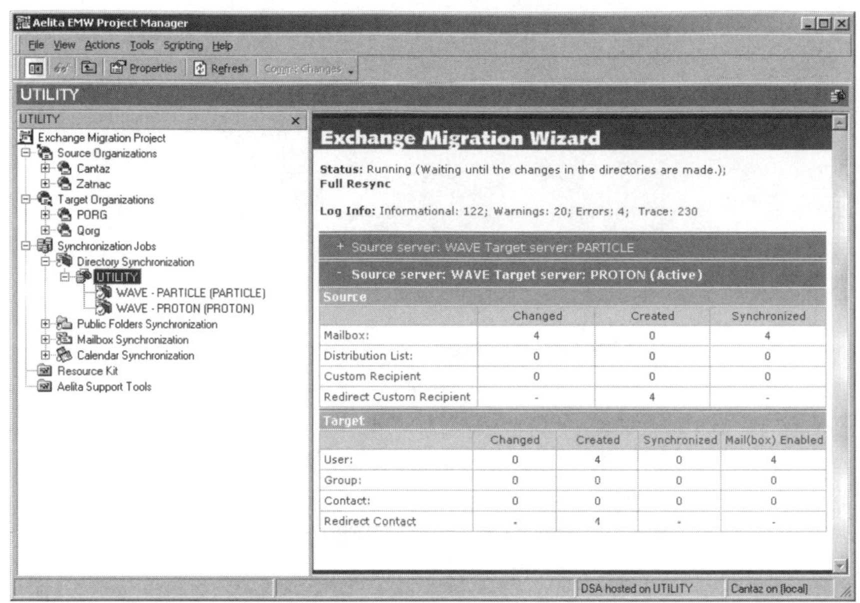

on the status of synchronization. Detailed logging information is also provided: Right-click on the Agent, select Log, and the log information is displayed, as shown in Figure 9-22.

This functionality represents the core features of migration consolidation (and divestiture) activities using third-party migration tools. There are several other features

Figure 9-22 *Directory Synchronization Job Log File Excerpt*

```
EMWDSA.LOG - Notepad
File Edit Format Help
Trace    0          objSearch.Filter = '(rdn=Microsoft\20System\20Attendant)'
Informational   0         Initiating full resynchronization from the Exchange directory to the Active Directory.
Trace    -2147218431      Enumerating changed mailboxes in the Exchange directory.
Trace    0          Object 'cn=SherylS,cn=Recipients,ou=WORG,o=Cantaz' was enumerated.
Trace    0          Object 'cn=AmyA,cn=Recipients,ou=WORG,o=Cantaz' was enumerated.
Trace    0          Object 'cn=BarbaraB,cn=Recipients,ou=WORG,o=Cantaz' was enumerated.
Trace    0          Object 'cn=CeliaC,cn=Recipients,ou=WORG,o=Cantaz' was enumerated.
Trace    0          Object 'cn=Administrator,cn=Recipients,ou=WORG,o=Cantaz' was enumerated.
Trace    0          Object 'cn=DeborahD,cn=Spinoff Recipients,ou=WORG,o=Cantaz' was enumerated.
Trace    0          Object 'cn=EleanorE,cn=Spinoff Recipients,ou=WORG,o=Cantaz' was enumerated.
Trace    0          Object 'cn=FelicityF,cn=Spinoff Recipients,ou=WORG,o=Cantaz' was enumerated.
Trace    0          Object 'cn=GraceG,cn=Spinoff Recipients,ou=WORG,o=Cantaz' was enumerated.
Informational   -2147220459     Object cn=SherylS,cn=Recipients,ou=WORG,o=Cantaz already participates in another direct
Informational   -2147220459     Object cn=AmyA,cn=Recipients,ou=WORG,o=Cantaz already participates in another directory
Informational   -2147220459     Object cn=BarbaraB,cn=Recipients,ou=WORG,o=Cantaz already participates in another direc
Informational   -2147220459     Object cn=CeliaC,cn=Recipients,ou=WORG,o=Cantaz already participates in another directo
Informational   -2147220459     Object cn=Administrator,cn=Recipients,ou=WORG,o=Cantaz already participates in another
Trace    0          The DSA is trying to change the password of the 'Deborah Danker' user account (directory name is 'CN=De
Trace    0          The 'Deborah Danker' user account (directory name is 'CN=Deborah Danker,CN=Users,DC=qorg,DC=research,DC
Informational   0         New password of the 'Deborah Danker' user account (directory name is 'CN=Deborah Danker,CN=User
Informational   0         Active Directory User 'CN=Deborah Danker,CN=Users,DC=qorg,DC=research,DC=cantaz,DC=com' was suc
Trace    0          The DSA is trying to change the password of the 'Eleanor Eastman' user account (directory name is 'CN=E
Trace    0          The 'Eleanor Eastman' user account (directory name is 'CN=Eleanor Eastman,CN=Users,DC=qorg,DC=research,
Informational   0         New password of the 'Eleanor Eastman' user account (directory name is 'CN=Eleanor Eastman,CN=Us
Informational   0         Active Directory User 'CN=Eleanor Eastman,CN=Users,DC=qorg,DC=research,DC=cantaz,DC=com' was su
Trace    0          The DSA is trying to change the password of the 'Felicity Firestone' user account (directory name is 'C
Trace    0          The 'Felicity Firestone' user account (directory name is 'CN=Felicity Firestone,CN=Users,DC=qorg,DC=res
Informational   0         New password of the 'Felicity Firestone' user account (directory name is 'CN=Felicity Firestone
Informational   0         Active Directory User 'CN=Felicity Firestone,CN=Users,DC=qorg,DC=research,DC=cantaz,DC=com' was
Trace    0          The DSA is trying to change the password of the 'Grace Goodman' user account (directory name is 'CN=Gra
Trace    0          The 'Grace Goodman' user account (directory name is 'CN=Grace Goodman,CN=Users,DC=qorg,DC=research,DC=c
Informational   0         New password of the 'Grace Goodman' user account (directory name is 'CN=Grace Goodman,CN=Users,
Informational   0         Active Directory User 'CN=Grace Goodman,CN=Users,DC=qorg,DC=research,DC=cantaz,DC=com' was succ
Informational   0         Active Directory User 'CN=Deborah Danker,CN=Users,DC=qorg,DC=research,DC=cantaz,DC=com' is now
Informational   0         Contact 'CN=Aelita EMW Redirector (A7A84825-42F6-4EC9-A47F-89183CE9102D),OU=Redirection Recipie
Informational   0         Custom Recipient 'CN=Aelita EMW Redirector (10B8702E-4961-4F29-B784-94BCED915277),cn=Redirectic
```

of these tools, which are secondary to the business of migration but useful nonetheless and deserve mention:

- As Windows 2000/2003 user objects are created, most third-party migration tools can automatically set random/complex passwords on those accounts optionally write the password values to the synchronization log file, or allow a standard administrator-defined password to be used for all new accounts.
- After initial synchronization, only changes to existing objects are synchronized, but you can revert back to a full synchronization at any time by selecting the *Full Synchronization* option on the Job properties page.
- The *Restore Redirection* option on the Job's properties pages can be used to validate that all redirection Custom Recipients and Contacts are in place.
- By default, permissions from Exchange 5.5 mailboxes are synchronized to the Exchange 2000/2003 environment.

Third-party migration tools generally use extension attributes in Exchange 5.5 to store supplemental information. The extension attributes typically hold values that indicate whether an object should be synchronized to the target directory, similar to an LDAP search filter.

9.5.7 Interorganization mailbox migration

Providing interoperability by means of interorganization mail connections—which are straightforward to do for any environment—and directory synchronization only provides the first part of the interorganization migration. The next challenge comes with actually moving mailbox contents from a server in a source Exchange 5.5 organization to the target Exchange 2000/2003 organization.

Microsoft provides the Move Mailbox Wizard for intraorganization moves, and the Exchange Server Migration Wizard and ExMerge can also be used. The latter tools work for interorganization moves, but they are both one-shot tools and provide no ongoing or gradual mailbox synchronization. This is another area where third-party migration tools usually excel.

Much like the directory synchronization, mailbox synchronization is implemented using agents, three in this case: the Mailbox Source Agent (MSA), the Transmission Agent (TA), and the Mail Target Agent (MTA). This is shown graphically in Figure 9-23.

The MSA resides on the source Exchange 5.5 server, which monitors the synchronization status of mailboxes. You need one MSA per Exchange 5.5 server. Each mailbox is queried for changes since the last synchronization, the changes are written to locally stored PST files for each mailbox and then compressed in a single file, known as

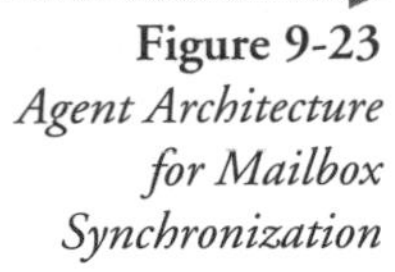

Figure 9-23
Agent Architecture for Mailbox Synchronization

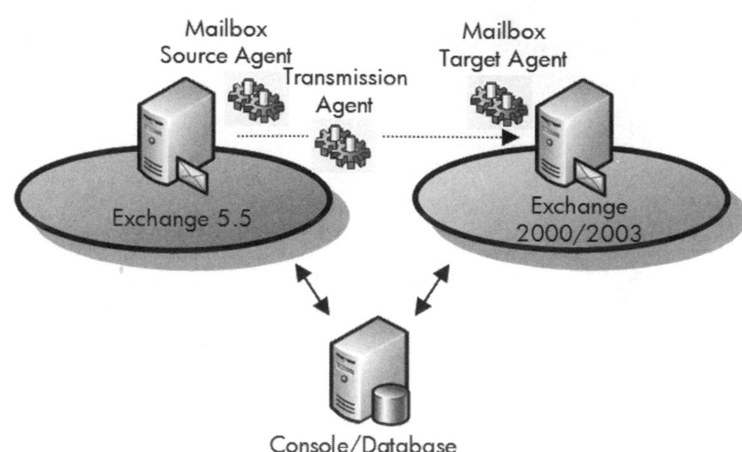

the PRV file. The MSA then transfers the aggregate PRV file to the TA, also installed on the Exchange 5.5 server, which transfers mailbox information to the target Exchange 2000/2003 server. If there are multiple target servers to receive data, then there will be multiple PRV files. The TA will send the appropriate PRV file directly to the required target server. On the target server, the MTA accepts the data, decompresses it, and transfers it to the destination mailboxes.

The whole mailbox synchronization process uses compressed data files (which is another advantage over the default Microsoft tools) so that the actual transmission on the wire is kept to a minimum. This is useful in many consolidation scenarios because servers distributed over the wide area network (WAN) are often being consolidated to centralized locations. (This trend is becoming more widespread with the advent of Outlook 2003's cached working mode, which makes centralized, consolidated Exchange data centers with outlying remote clients all the more attractive and effective.) You can explicitly choose whether to use compression, and if you do, you can choose the compression level. No compression incurs more network traffic but is faster; high compression incurs less network traffic but is slower.

Right-clicking the Mailbox Synchronization item in the Console and selecting *Add Mailbox Synchronization Job* will set up all of the requisite agents on the source and target servers. Each Job identifies the single source Exchange 5.5 server and the single target Exchange 2000/2003 server. Although you are prompted to define the Storage Group and Mailbox Store on which the mailboxes are to be synchronized, you should select those Storage Groups and Mailbox Stores that correspond with those already identified during the Directory Synchronization phase.

The Collections feature exposes the real power of mailbox synchronization and consolidation. A Collection is a group of mailboxes that will be synchronized together.

Each Collection retains its own settings and priority. You can define when the migration for a particular Collection will take place. A Synchronization Job can handle multiple Collections. A Collection will only begin processing if all higher-priority Collections have fully completed their processing.

When you run through the Mailbox Synchronization Job Wizard, you initially define whether you want to use Collections at all and some general settings around Collections (i.e., an initial first Collection, one Collection per target server mailbox store, or simply distributing a fixed number of mailboxes into an arbitrary Collection name). This is shown in Figure 9-24.

Electing to use Collections means that you have much granularity in selecting which mailboxes will be moved at any given time. With the Wizard you can add individual mailboxes to a given Collection or you can select any number of Exchange 5.5 recipient containers as the source, as shown in Figure 9-25. You can add additional Collections to a Job at any time through the Console interface. With this interface you configure additional settings such as the Collection priority and start and end times. By default, the synchronization is set to start immediately, but you can define exactly when you would like synchronization to start for each Collection. And by default, the synchronization process is active for about four weeks from the default start time. Again, you can change this as required. You may also add mailboxes to a collection using an external file (e.g., CSV formatted), which is useful if the Exchange migration is part of a wider migration project in your environment and you must align your Exchange migration with other migration activities.

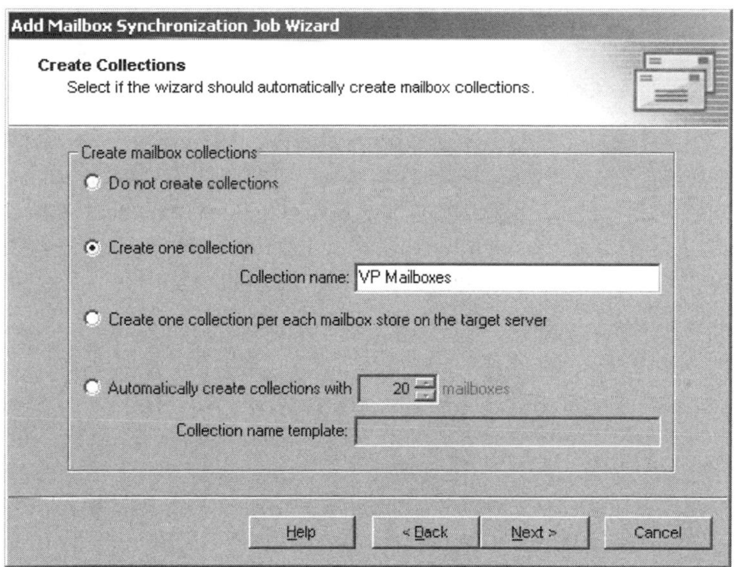

Figure 9-24 *Creating Mailbox Collections with the Mailbox Synchronization Job Wizard*

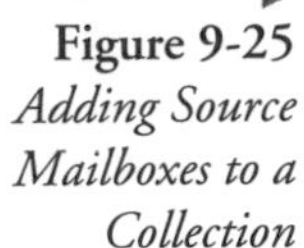

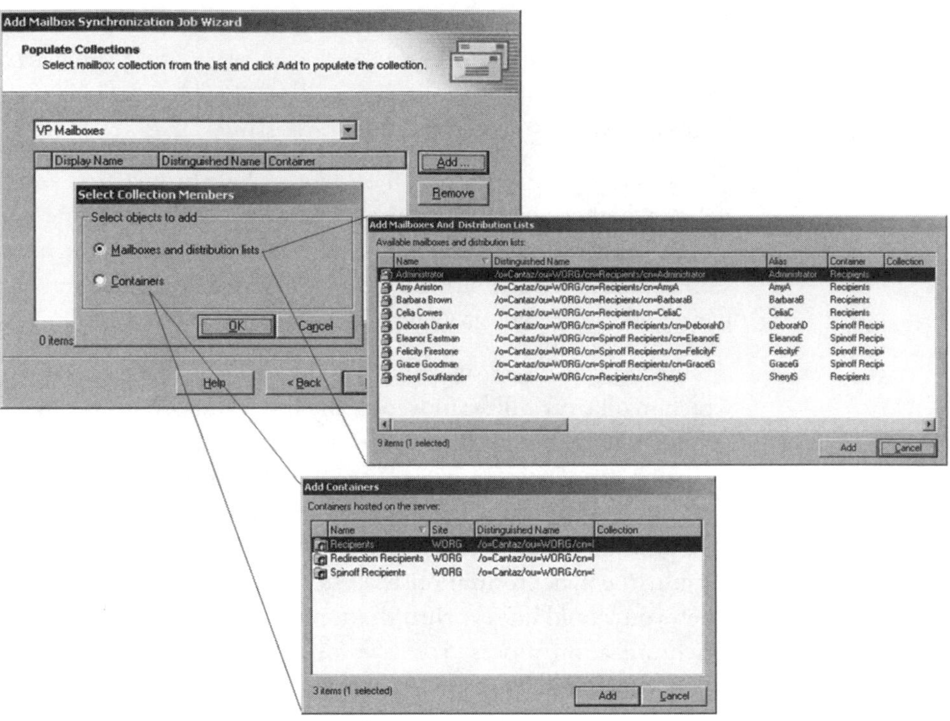

Figure 9-25 *Adding Source Mailboxes to a Collection*

All of this means that you need to carefully plan and schedule your entire migration and consolidation strategy, and in fact, schedule the whole process well in advance of any actual migration activity. With this approach you can gradually migrate users at the pace that suits you and imposes the least amount of load on the network and other end systems.

Getting the mailbox contents in sync between the source Exchange 5.5 organization and the target Exchange 2000/2003 organizations is just one step in the mailbox migration process. The next stage is to decommission the Exchange 5.5 mailbox and have the Exchange 2000/2003 mailbox become the primary mailbox for the user. This process is known as mailbox switching.

Behind the scenes, the mailbox switching process is relatively trivial. Two things happen. On the Exchange 5.5 server, the user's mailbox is modified so that an alternate recipient is defined for the mailbox. Any mail now sent to that mailbox is redirected to the alternate recipient. The specified alternate recipient is actually the redirection custom recipient created when directory synchronization took place. Thus any mail delivered to the redirection custom recipient is relayed to the Exchange 2000/2003 mailbox in the target organization. In the target organization the redirection on the

Exchange 2000/2003 mailbox to the redirection contact is removed. Figure 9-26 shows the alternate recipient modification to an Exchange 5.5 mailbox.

Switching can be performed manually by selecting users already synchronized and associated with a particular Synchronization Job, right-clicking, and choosing the option to switch. Multiple mailboxes may be selected and switched at the same time. Third-party migration tools can be configured so that when mailboxes are switched, suitable messages are sent to user mailboxes informing them that they have been migrated.

Collections can also be configured so that fully synchronized user mailboxes are automatically switched. This is done by setting the properties on the Collection. Some heavily used mailboxes may never become fully synchronized at a given point in time so long as mail continues to be delivered into the source mailbox. For this reason, you can automatically have mailboxes switched even if they are slightly out of sync. You specify the threshold (in KB) that you will tolerate, and immediately after the mailbox is switched, any unsynchronized content is brought across to the target server.

Note also that mailboxes can be unswitched by simply toggling the switched setting, so that users incurring problems with their new Exchange 2000/2003 mailbox can be simply and quickly moved back to Exchange 5.5.

With an interorganization migration, users' MAPI profiles are invalidated when a user is moved to an Exchange server in a new organization. Third-party migration tools

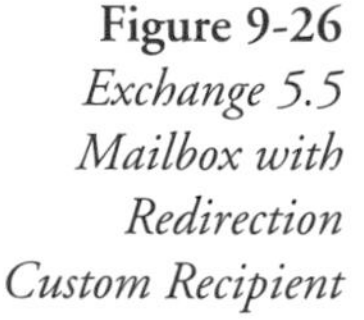

Figure 9-26
Exchange 5.5 Mailbox with Redirection Custom Recipient

usually provide a Profile Updating Utility that is integrated with the mailbox switching process. The utility can be run from a logon script and recognizes a flag set by the mailbox switch process. Thus, the move is relatively transparent to the end user.

9.5.8 Public folder synchronization

Consolidation of servers and organizations involves more than just consolidating mailboxes. It's likely that Public Folders must be consolidated to a central server as well. Third-party migration tools provide a mechanism for Public Folder synchronization in a fashion similar to the synchronization utilities we've already discussed.

Unlike mailbox synchronization where the activity is unidirectional (from Exchange 5.5 to Exchange 2000/2003) changes to Public Folder content may take place in either environment, so the synchronization must be bidirectional. Access to Public Folders is critical too, so all permissions and Access Control List structures on the Public Folders are maintained during the synchronization process.

In general, you should ensure that Public Folder synchronization is in place before you actually switch users over to the new environment. Doing so means that any Public Folders that the user might need access to are already in place.

The Public Folder synchronization architecture is very similar to that used for mailbox synchronization. The architecture is implemented using agent source, transmission, and target agents. However, because Public Folder synchronization can be bidirectional, six agents must be used: a Public Folder Source Agent (PFSA) and a Transmission Agent (TA) on the Exchange 5.5 server with a corresponding PF Target Agent (PFTA) on the Exchange 2000/2003 server, as well as a PFSA and TA on the Exchange 2000/2003 server along with a PFTA on the Exchange 5.5 server. This is shown graphically in Figure 9-27.

For full interoperability, bidirectional synchronization should be used, but for a simpler migration, synchronization can be unidirectional. The same rules that apply for compression of data for mailbox synchronization apply for Public Folder synchronization.

When you set up a Public Folder Synchronization Job, you define a pair of source and target servers: one Exchange 5.5 server and one Exchange 2000/2003 server. You need one Public Folder Synchronization Job for each Exchange 5.5 site in which you have Exchange servers that host Public Folder stores.

In much the same way that you can group specific mailboxes into Collections for mailbox synchronization, the same concept applies for Public Folder synchronization. You can define a number of Collections, assigning priorities for each one. Within each Collection you can define the source and target Public Folders that you wish to

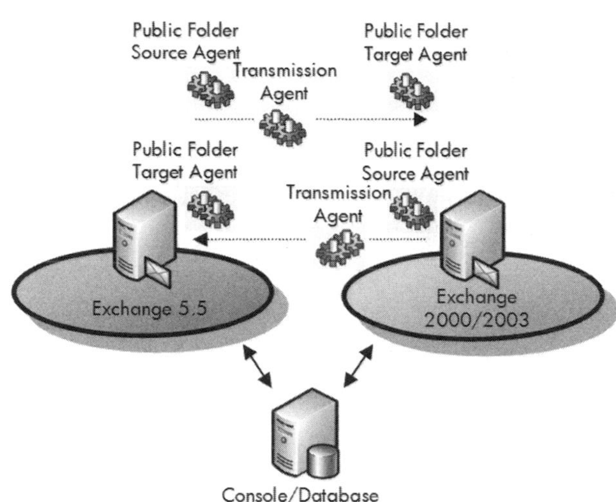

Figure 9-27 *Agent Architecture for Public Folder Synchronization*

synchronize. A high-priority Collection must have finished processing before a lower-priority Collection can commence. Thus you may wish to place critical shared project documentation Public Folders into a high-priority Collection, over a Public Folder that deals with, say, the Chess Club. Collections can be configured to run for a specified period or can be terminated as soon as the target Public Folders have been brought up to synchronization with the source. This latter approach is useful if the aim is to perform a one-shot Public Folder migration rather than ongoing interoperability.

Public Folder replication does not need to be on a one-to-one basis. You can modify the Public Folder hierarchy on the target Exchange 2000/2003 organization and consolidate multiple Exchange 5.5 Public Folders to a single Public Folder on the Exchange 2000/2003 side. If you do follow this approach, though, think carefully about the implications of bidirectional synchronization.

Again the implementation and flexibility of this agent model and the ability to select particular Public Folders means that this is a powerful tool for consolidating multiple organizations and collapsing their respective Public Folder structures. Conversely, the same flexibility is equally adept at splitting a single organization's Public Folder hierarchy out to multiple target organizations.

9.5.9 Calendar and Schedule+ Free/Busy information

Calendar information for any given user is stored in the private Calendar folder for that user in their mailbox store on their Exchange 5.5 server. Free/Busy information for all users within an Exchange 5.5 site is stored in a hidden Public Folder called Schedule+ Free Busy. Replication of that Public Folder within an Exchange organization means that all users in the organization can see the Free/Busy status for a given user. Within the site, when changes are made to the user's calendar that affect the Free/Busy settings of that user, the Schedule+ Free Busy Public Folder is automatically updated.

For the purposes of interorganization migration and consolidation, third-party migration tools provide a Calendar synchronization service that synchronizes Calendar information between servers. You must create a Calendar Synchronization Job that defines the source and target mailbox servers between the two organizations. You need one Calendar Synchronization Job for every Exchange 5.5 server and Exchange 2000/2003 server pair. A Calendar Synchronization Agent (CSA) installed on the Exchange 5.5 server performs the synchronization. Synchronization may be either unidirectional (from Exchange 5.5) or bidirectional. Bidirectional synchronization is especially important when mailbox delegation is in use. This is shown in Figure 9-28.

In reality, this relationship is the same as that for mailbox synchronization. If you are migrating all users from a single Exchange 5.5 server to a new Exchange 2000/2003 server, then you require one Job. If you are splitting an Exchange 5.5 organization into two Exchange 2000/2003 organizations and thus have one server in each target organization, then you require two Jobs (one Job from the server in the Exchange 5.5 organization to the server in the first Exchange 2000/2003 organization and one Job from the server in the Exchange 5.5 organization to the server in the second Exchange 2000/2003 organization).

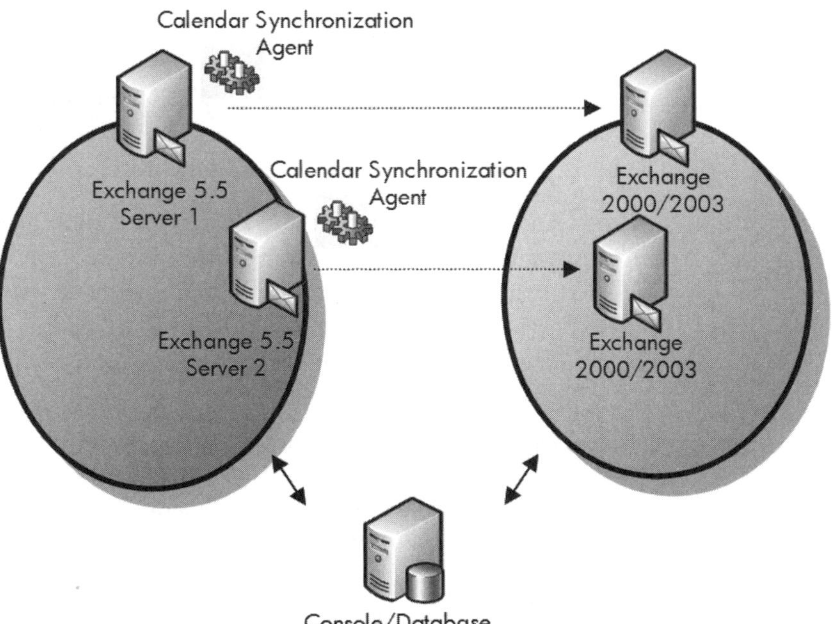

Figure 9-28 *Calendar Synchronization Architecture*

As Calendar information is synchronized from a user's Exchange 5.5 Calendar folder to their Exchange 2000/2003 Calendar folder via the Calendar Synchronization Agent, the calendars of all users across all organizations gradually come in sync. At the same time, within the target organization, the Schedule+ Free Busy Public Folder is updated to reflect the Calendar information for all users. Thus, Free/Busy information is updated *automatically* between organization and as a by-product of Calendar synchronization. That said, in large organizations with many users and many servers in a site, the time to process many Calendar folders may result in unacceptable latency in updates to the Schedule+ Free Busy Public Folder in the target organization. If this is the case, and the need for near-real-time synchronization of the Schedule+ Free Busy Public Folder is great, then you can optionally configure one of the CSAs to directly update the Public Folder continuously.

There should be a close similarity between the topology of the Mailbox Synchronization Jobs and the Calendar Synchronization Jobs. (If users' mailboxes are synchronized from Server A to Server B, then their calendars should be synchronized from Server A to Server B as well.) Therefore, when you define a Calendar Synchronization Job between two servers, there is an option to select the same mailboxes for calendar synchronization as were defined for mailbox synchronization. The appropriate dialog box is shown in Figure 9-29.

9.5.10 Other consolidation and interorganization migration considerations

Several other areas need to be considered with any migration project:

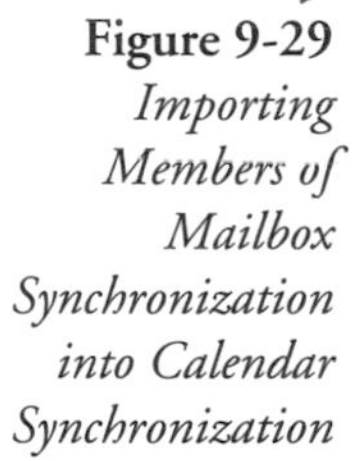

Figure 9-29 *Importing Members of Mailbox Synchronization into Calendar Synchronization*

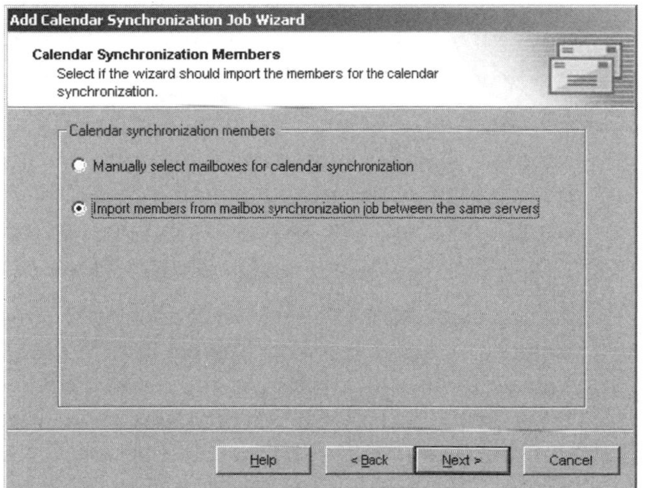

- Large migrations often require a certain amount of scripting and customization to take place. Third-party migration tools can integrate scripts written in languages such as VBScript into the Console. Objects may be selected through the Console and the scripts executed and applied to the selected objects.
- Add-ins to modify the default behavior of directory and mailbox synchronization agents can be developed and integrated into third-party migration tools.
- E-mail notifications can be sent to administrators when certain migration tasks have been performed (e.g., migration statistics, migration adherence to schedule).
- Additional third-party components such as the Statistics Collection Agent and the Reporting Console can be integrated into the project to provide comprehensive reports at regular intervals on the current status of the environment and the migration progress.
- Define the tasks that need to be performed once the users from the source organizations have been completely migrated to the target organizations. This will include shutting down any redundant and still-active synchronization jobs, decommissioning old servers, cleaning up the active migrated mailboxes, and removing redundant redirection recipients.

9.6 Summary

This chapter has outlined many different approaches that can be taken to the not-so-straightforward task of moving from Exchange 5.5 or Exchange 2000 to Exchange 2003 in an interorganization mode. Whether you take this approach and opt for interorganization migrations, whether by using the free Microsoft tools or by using third-party tools, is entirely a matter of choice and largely influenced by factors that will be inherent in your environment.

Certainly there is a place for interorganization migrations, but in most cases this approach should be confined to those environments where a diversity in organizational structures mandates it. Although the mailbox migration described here is relatively trivial, there are many factors to consider, including Public Folder interoperability, directory synchronization, mail routing, MAPI profile integrity, and so on.

You can take many different approaches when one part of an Exchange 5.5 organization wishes to move to Exchange 2003 but others don't. If the Exchange 5.5 sites map cleanly to the entities wishing to move, then either the hybrid of a site split followed by an intraorganization migration or an intraorganization followed by a site split can be used, the latter being the most flexible approach and the approach described in the majority of this chapter. Such intraorganization migrations are highly desirable: They afford a simple mechanism for directory synchronization, especially with Distribution Lists, mailbox moves, and importantly, Public Folder replication. In environments where no clear demarcation between entities and sites, Public Folders, and Distribution Lists can be made, then you must resort to using third-party migration tools.

Interorganization migrations are becoming increasingly common. Consolidation of servers, sites, and organizations are similarly becoming prevalent. Faced with such challenges, there is little doubt that the out-of-the-box Microsoft tools are insufficient for the tasks at hand. And as such, there is little doubt that third-party tools are a necessity. The first challenges to be resolved relate to directory synchronization between organizations. Third-party migration tools cover all aspects of migration: directory synchronization, mailbox synchronization, Public Folder synchronization, and Calendar synchronization. Not only do they perform the basic tasks for these migrations, but they have a rich set of functions that facilitate well-paced, gradual, step-by-step, unattended migrations. The degree of flexibility with all of the tools means that they can be used for all scenarios from the simple one-to-one Exchange 5.5 to Exchange 2000/2003 migration right up to the most sophisticated and complex multiorganizational consolidations and divestiture scenarios involving all flavors of Exchange 5.5, Exchange 2000, and Exchange 2003. Improvements to the tools over subsequent releases of the various products will allow even greater flexibility with the ability to migrate and consolidate from Exchange 2000 and Exchange 2003 organizations.

10

Deploying Exchange for External Access

10.1 Introduction

Enterprise Exchange 2003 users will typically use Outlook 2003 (or earlier versions) as their client of choice when inside the corporate environment and accessing their Exchange mailboxes. When such users require access to their mailboxes from outside the corporate environment, several different approaches can be employed. These approaches can include dial-up connections or tunneled/Virtual Private Network (VPN) sessions using the Routing and Remote Access Service (RRAS). More commonly though, users are often turning to OWA to provide a means to access their Exchange mailboxes.

For a user to get access to an Exchange mailbox from a Web browser somewhere on the Internet, a connection needs to be established from the Web browser to typically an Exchange 2003 Front-End server within the corporate environment using HTTP. The Exchange 2003 Front-End server will then proxy the HTTP connection to the appropriate Exchange 2003 Back-End server. Several approaches can be used for this task, each with varying degrees of complexity, cost, and security. This chapter discusses perhaps the most common means of implementing this architecture and reviews several significantly more secure approaches that achieve the same goal.

10.2 Using Exchange 2003 Front-End Servers in the DMZ

For reasons of security, it is unwise to open a corporate firewall to allow access from Web browser clients straight through to Front-End and Back-End servers on the internal part of the network. Why is it unwise? Basically because you have to open your firewall such that any computer on the Internet can connect over either HTTP or HTTP over Secure Sockets Layer (SSL) directly to Front-End servers on your internal network. There's no packet filtering and a clear path and view of your environment, and malicious attacks on your Front-End servers can be relatively easily mounted. Once access to the Front-End servers is achieved, there are barriers between them and the rest of the corporate network.

The common practice that has emerged to mitigate against this security issue involves placing the Front-End servers in the DMZ and Back-End servers in the internal part of the network. Ostensibly, this appears to be a reasonable approach to take because access from Internet Web browsers to Front-End servers comes in through the relatively open part of the external-facing firewalls, whereas the connections from the Front-End servers to the Back-End servers and AD servers is more tightly controlled through the internal-facing part of the network. This is shown in Figure 10-1.

Although this architecture appears secure, it can be argued that it is far from secure because a significant number of "holes" must be created in both the external-facing and, most significantly, the internal-facing firewalls.

Table 10-1 defines the open ports that are required for the traffic from the Internet through the external-facing firewall to the DMZ.

Both basic HTTP and HTTP over SSL (HTTP-SSL) should be enabled, because both can be used to access your mailbox. Of course, using SSL is the preferred mecha-

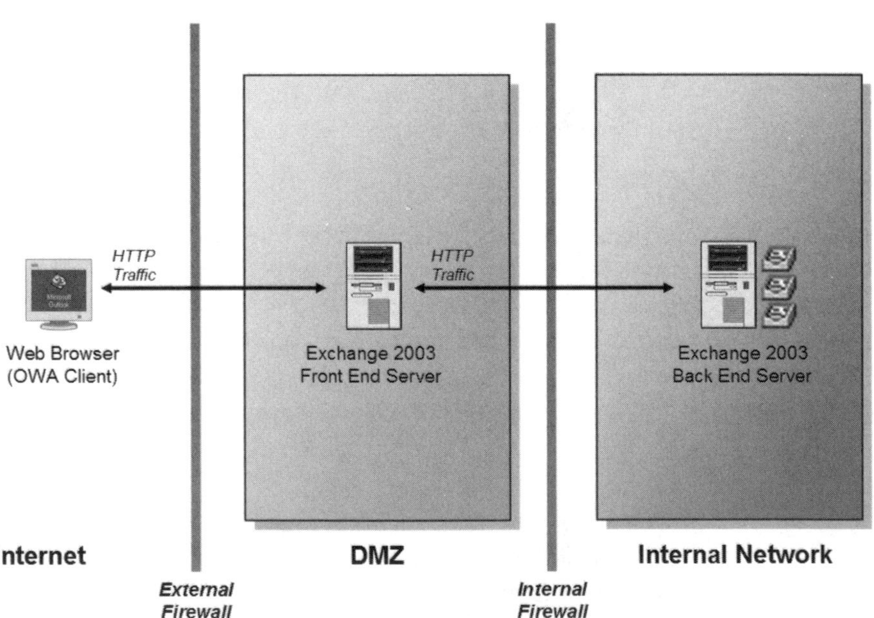

Figure 10-1
OWA Access via Exchange 2003 Front-End Servers in the DMZ

Table 10-1 *Internet to DMZ Port and Protocol Requirements*

Source	Port	Destination	Port/Protocol	Access	Description
*	*	Exchange 2003 Front-End Server	80/TCP (HTTP-basic)	Allow	Connection from Web browser OWA client
*	*	Exchange 2003 Front-End Server	443/TCP (HTTP-SSL)	Allow	Secured connection from Web browser OWA client

nism and is mandatory if you wish to facilitate the changing of passwords from the OWA client.

Table 10-2 defines the open ports that are required for the traffic from the DMZ through the internal-facing firewall to the internal network.

10.3 Exchange, DSAccess, and Firewalls

Versions of Exchange 2000 before Service Pack 2 always used RPCs to facilitate connections from the DSAccess component on the Front-End server to DCs and GC servers in the internal network. However, versions of Exchange since Exchange 2000 Service Pack 2, up to and including Exchange 2003, make significant improvements when it comes to controlling the port access required from DSAccess on Front-End servers in the DMZ to internal DCs and GC servers. Since Exchange 2000 Service Pack 2, LDAP is used for DSAccess to DC/GC server communication, but DSAccess will still attempt to use the NetLogon service to communicate with each DC and GC it discovers. I haven't suggested blocking RPC traffic across the internal-facing firewall to the intranet (for reasons on which I'll expand later), but if you do, then DSAccess will simply determine that the RPC traffic is blocked but that DCs and GC servers are still available. This is not a major problem, but for reasons of performance you should disable the NetLogon checking (described in Chapter 1).

It's also common in DMZ firewall environments to have Internet Control Message Protocol (ICMP) packets blocked by the internal-facing firewall to prevent system discovery and Denial-of-Service (DOS) attacks. However, DSAccess that ships with SP2 uses ICMP pings to validate the availability of DCs and GC servers. Blocking ICMP traffic therefore causes DSAccess to assume that DCs and GC servers are unavailable and to force new topology discoveries using LDAP access to those servers. Similarly, this has a negative performance impact, and again it is advisable to disable DSAccess from performing these ICMP pings to the DCs and GC servers (described in Chapter 1).

Table 10-2 *DMZ to Internal Network Port and Protocol Requirements*

Source	Port	Destination	Port/Protocol	Access	Description
Exchange 2003 Front-End Server	*	Exchange 2003 Back-End Server	80/TCP (HTTP-basic)	Allow	Relayed HTTP traffic. Note that even if the client connection is secured by the means of SSL, the Front-End server communicates with the Back-End server in clear mode (no use of SSL).
Exchange 2003 Front-End Server	*	Windows Active Directory Domain Controller	389/TCP (LDAP)	Allow	Access required for the Front-End server to access the Active Directory Domain Controller (required for Exchange 2003 Configuration information queries).
Exchange 2003 Front-End Server	*	Windows Active Directory Global Catalog Server	3268/TCP (LDAP)	Allow	Access required for the Front-End server to access the Active Directory Global Catalog server (required to determine on which Back-End server a user's mailbox is located).
Exchange 2003 Front-End Server	*	Windows Active Directory Global Catalog Server	88/TCP (Kerberos)	Allow	Access required for the Front-End server for mailbox access authentication.
Exchange 2003 Front-End Server	*	Windows Active Directory Global Catalog Server	88/UDP (Kerberos)	Allow	Access required for the Front-End server for mailbox access authentication.
Exchange 2003 Front-End Server	*	DNS Server	53/TCP (DNS Lookup)	Allow	Access required for the Front-End server to resolve names for Back-End server, Active Directory Domain Controllers, etc.
Exchange 2003 Front-End Server	*	DNS Server	53/UDP (DNS Lookup)	Allow	Access required for the Front-End server to resolve names for Back-End server, Active Directory Domain Controllers, etc.

Table 10-2 (continued)

Source	Port	Destination	Port/Protocol	Access	Description
Exchange 2003 Front-End Server	*	Windows Active Directory Global Catalog Server	135/TCP (RPC Port Mapper)	Allow	RPC endpoint mapper for the Front-End server to query the Active Directory services. This connection will return the RPC service port used by the Active Directory service upon startup of the Domain Controller or Global Catalog server.
Exchange 2003 Front-End Server	*	Windows Active Directory Global Catalog Server	1127/TCP (Windows Active Directory service)	Allow	This is a fixed IP port for the Active Directory to use to advertise its service for replication and logon. The port is normally dynamically assigned in the upper 1024–65365 range. In this case environment, it should be hardcoded using the registry (see below).
Exchange 2003 Front-End Server	*	Windows Active Directory Global Catalog Server	445/TCP (SMB for NetLogon)	Allow	SMB traffic for the NetLogon service, required for communication and authentication of the services
Exchange 2003 Front-End Server	*	Windows Active Directory Global Catalog Server	123/TCP (NTP)	Allow	Network Time Protocol required for synchronizing the time between the various machines. The Active Directory Global Catalog server can be used as the time source, and it is critical that the machines are synchronized to allow proper operation.

10.4 Should You Allow RPCs across Your DMZ?

Table 10-2 described an implementation scenario that allows RPC traffic to travel from servers in the DMZ across the internal-facing firewall through to the intranet. Yet, I've just outlined that DSAccess does not require RPC access to DCs and GC servers on the intranet. So why would you want to see RPC traffic allowed? The short answer is for authentication. When an OWA user connects to a Front-End server, the Front-End server can either authenticate the user immediately or forward the authentication request on anonymously to the Back-End server for authentication there only.

If you wish to prevent all RPC traffic, then you must configure only the Back-End server to perform the authentication. This so-called pass-through authentication is desirable because it requires no trans-firewall RPCs, but it is also undesirable because it complicates the URL addressing that OWA users must specify (i.e., the user must specify the username in the URL so that the Front-End server can look the user up in the AD and forward the request on to the appropriate Back-End server). Also, pass-through authentication is undesirable because all anonymous authentication requests are directed explicitly to Back-End servers within the intranet, and these Back-End servers, which may also be servicing conventional MAPI logons, are susceptible to DOS attacks.

The recommended approach is to use dual authentication, where both Front-End and Back-End servers authenticate OWA user connections with basic authentication. This approach, however, requires the Front-End server to have RPC connectivity to DCs and GC servers within the intranet.

10.5 Generalized Internal-Facing Firewall Requirements

The port definitions shown in Table 10-1 and Table 10-2 are generally indicative of what is required in most situations to facilitate OWA browser access to Front-End servers in the DMZ and Back-End servers in the intranet.

Particular environments may differ. For example, there may be multiple Front-End servers, multiple Back-End servers, multiple DCs and GC servers, load-balancing switches may be used, and so on. Similarly, the source ports and direction of traffic have not been defined, but you should characterize the exact behavior in your own environment because there are almost always differences. It's best to start your testing being as restrictive as you can be, and then gradually open ports and directions as required until normal behavior is observed. Needless to say, this should all be carried out in a strict testing lab environment, carefully documented, and only then transferred over to production.

As pointed out previously, even with the identified required ports and protocols, some configuration still must be performed on DCs and GC servers to specify a fixed port over which AD authentications can be serviced. Table 10-2 indicates that port 1127 should be set on DCs and GC servers for the logon service. You can do this by setting the following registry key:

```
HKEY_LOCAL_MACHINE\System\CurrentControlSet\Services\NTDS\Parameters
Value name: TCP/IP Port
Value type: REG_DWORD
Value data: 1127
```

You might need to consider further port and protocol requirements. In addition to those listed in Table 10-1 and Table 10-2, you may require to open ports for various management and monitoring tools that you could be using in your environment. How are you going to manage the Front-End servers that reside in the DMZ? Even if you are planning to use the basic ESM snap-in, you'll need to open the internal-facing firewall to allow RPC connections to the Front-End servers. (In general, though, outbound connections from the intranet to the DMZ are usually more tolerated because the source of the connections is "trusted.") Alternatives, such as using Terminal Services Remote Desktop Protocol (RDP) over 3389 to access and manage your Front-End servers, are possible. However, even in this case you might want to consider the impact of enabling Terminal Services on vulnerable systems in the DMZ. Perhaps using VPN connections to get to those systems for management is a slightly more robust approach?

Although it is possible to strictly identify the source computer in the DMZ—the Front-End server in this case—and only allow traffic from it to pass through the internal-facing firewall, it is difficult to legislate for those situations when the source computer is compromised and becomes the platform for a malicious attack on internal sections of your network. Upon in-depth analysis of the port and protocol requirements, it is obvious that this approach, although relatively straightforward to implement, certainly does not have the highest degree of associated security. This is most evident when represented graphically, as shown in Figure 10-2.

10.6 Outlook Web Access Security Issues

Placing Front-End servers in the DMZ part of the network results in opening various ports on the internal-facing firewall. Obviously, the more ports that are open on your firewall, the more opportunities there are for unscrupulous individuals (AKA, hackers) to gain unauthorized access to your network. The objective of any security hardening activity is therefore to reduce the number of openings on your firewalls and thus minimize or eliminate such exposure to unauthorized access.

Furthermore, with this model, although the actual communications stream between the OWA Web browser client and the Front-End server may well be secured using an SSL/transport Layer Security (TLS) connection, the communications between Front-End servers and Back-End servers for OWA cannot use such an encryption mechanism. Thus the HTTP-DAV communications stream between the

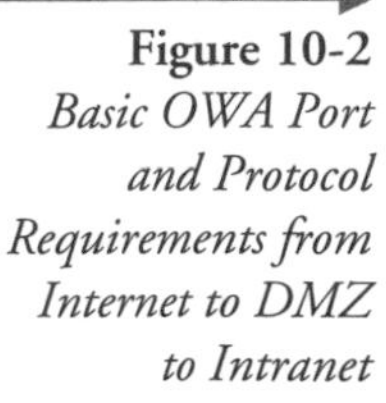

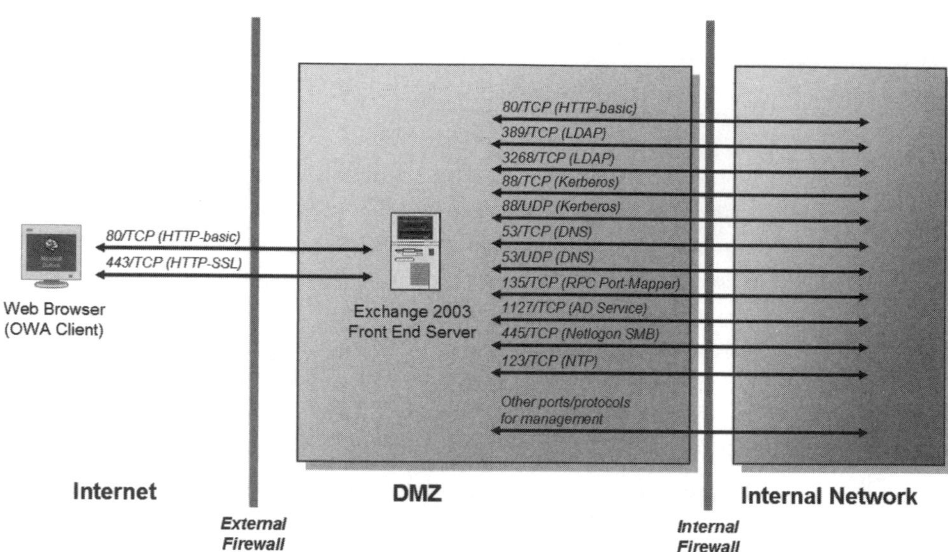

Figure 10-2 *Basic OWA Port and Protocol Requirements from Internet to DMZ to Intranet*

Front-End server and the Back-End server is exposed if your DMZ is compromised. (Although it is possible to have the OWA browser client establish and maintain communication over plain HTTP connections, one would rarely do this in practice because the security exposure would be extreme.)

Both of these problems are shown graphically in Figure 10-3. It is worth noting, however, that you could use an IP Security (IPSec) channel between the Front-End server and the Back-End server to secure the interserver traffic, but if this IPSec connection is itself compromised, then any would-be hackers have an easy path through your internal-facing firewall.

10.7 Secure Architectural Alternative

The most effective approach to securing such an environment uses the concept of a proxy server that resides in the DMZ part of the network. The proxy server effectively receives client requests from the external browser client and forwards those requests on to the Front-End server. For the moment, we'll think of the proxy server as an architectural component, and later look at its implementation: either in software or in hardware.

The proxy-based solution enhances the security of the architecture because it serves two primary purposes: (1) it allows the Front-End server to reside securely on the internal part of the network without all of those openings on the internal firewall; and

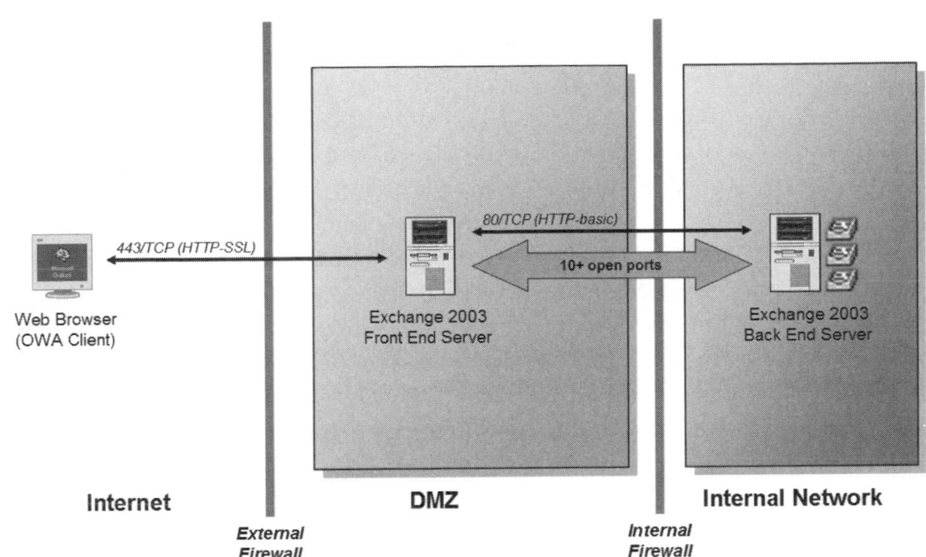

Figure 10-3 *Intrinsic Security Weaknesses with Front-End Server in DMZ*

(2) it facilitates a secure SSL/TLS from the browser client through to the Front-End server. The proxy server allows connections to a Front-End server in one of two fashions: either an SSL/TLS Tunnel or an SSL/TLS Bridge, both of which are shown in Figure 10-4, although typically only one or the other is used.

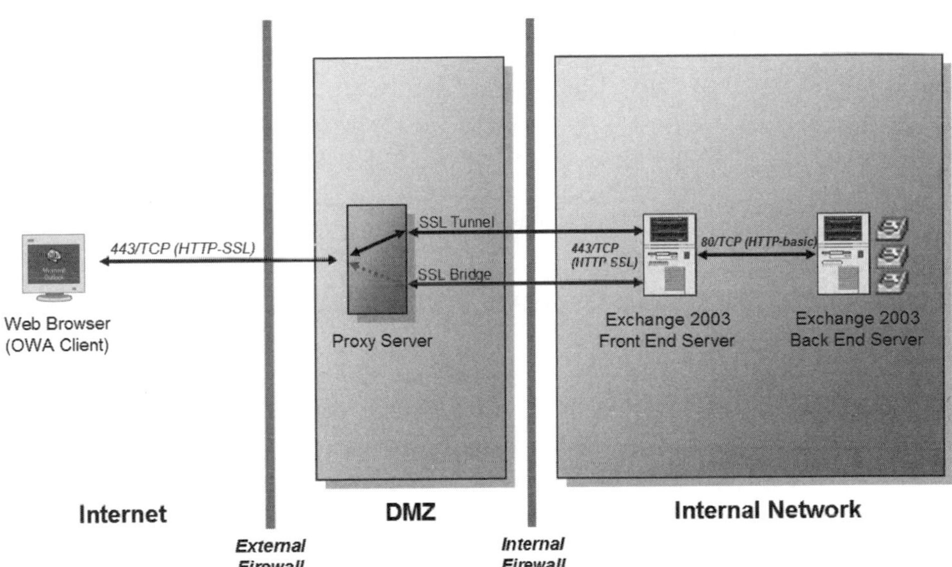

Figure 10-4 *Browser Communications to Front-End Server via Proxy Server*

10.8 Tunneling and Bridging

With the SSL/TLS Tunneling approach, the proxy server effectively receives HTTP packets from the browser client and forwards these packets on to the Front-End server. In this mode of operation, the proxy server is analytically passive and performs no processing of the communications stream between browser client and Front-End server: It simply acts as a conduit to relay packets and allow complete end-to-end security. SSL/TLS Tunneling is a common approach for both hardware and software implementations, but it is particularly relevant for small-scale environments because the SSL/TLS processing load remains with the Front-End server. In general—and of course this is very much related to the nature of the communications stream under study—adding SSL/TLS cryptographic processing workload to a Web server—in this case an OWA Front-End server—results in a CPU processing overhead of at least 15%. So it is not difficult to see why relatively small numbers of OWA users should be supported with this model of proxy server and SSL/TLS Tunneling to a Front-End server (even without crypto-acceleration cards).

However, the proxy server can be used in a different fashion: providing SSL/TLS Bridging functionality as an alternative to Tunneling. In the SSL/TLS Bridging mode of functionality, also shown in Figure 10-4, the proxy server is analytically active and actually terminates the SSL/TLS connection from the browser client in the first instance. The proxy server then establishes a new connection to the Front-End server, typically over an SSL/TLS connection, but potentially over an HTTP-basic connection if so desired. Using an SSL/TLS Bridge is often a desirable approach because it offloads the computationally intensive task of SSL/TLS cryptographic processing from the Front-End server. Thus a large number, typically several thousands, of Web browser clients and OWA users can be supported with this architecture. Furthermore, from a security perspective, it is much better to terminate an SSL/TLS session at a proxy server, inspect the packets, and forward only legitimate sessions on to an application server in the secure part of the network.

10.9 Putting Components into Practice

Using a proxy server to offload the SSL/TLS processing overhead from the Front-End server is obviously a wise tactic, especially with large user populations. However, performing this activity on the proxy server can be taxing. Usually, fewer than 10 or so SSL/TLS connections per second results in server processor saturation. For software-based proxy server implementations, it is common to use dedicated SSL/TLS Peripheral Component Interconnect (PCI) cards, which take on the responsibility of cryptographic processing. A software-based proxy server in Microsoft-centric environments usually consists of a Windows 2000 or Windows 2003 server running software such as Microsoft's Internet Security and Acceleration Server (ISA) coupled with an SSL/TLS accelerator card. These accelerator cards are capable of processing in the region of 500 SSL/TLS connections per second. There are many manufacturers of acceleration cards such as these, and leading examples include the CryptoSwift PCI Accelerator Board from Rainbow Technologies (www.rainbow.com) and the AXL600L SSL Accelerator Card from Atalla (www.atalla.com). Typically these cards retail for about $2,500.

The alternative to a software-based implementation is a dedicated network appliance, which is rather like a network switch but dedicated to cryptographic processing. Hardware-based proxy servers possess even more impressive performance characteristics, typically able to support larger numbers of simultaneous sessions and higher rates of cryptographic processing throughput compared to their software-based counterparts. For example, the Alteon SSL 410 appliance from Nortel Networks (www.nortel.com) can process 2,000 SSL/TLS connections per second and sustain up to 16,000 simultaneous SSL/TLS sessions. Similar SSL/TLS accelerator devices are available from companies such as Cisco (www.cisco.com), Radware (www.radware.com), and F5 Networks (www.f5.com). Few things in life, however, can be obtained for free, and for increased performance one is rewarded with increased price. Prices for hardware-based proxy server appliances range from around $15,000 up to around the $50,000 mark depending on the performance and functionality criteria required. There is no doubt, however, that the largest environments both benefit from and rely on such implementations.

10.10 Using Microsoft ISA Server with OWA

Microsoft ISA Server 2000 (the next version of ISA Server 2004, should ship mid-2004) can be used as a software-based proxy server in either SSL/TLS Tunneling or Bridging mode. (Make sure to be running at least Service Pack 1 of ISA Server 2000—that's build 3.0.1200.166, available from www.microsoft.com/isaserver/downloads/sp1.asp.)

To implement SSL/TLS Tunneling (the least common implementation), you need to use the Server Publishing feature of ISA Server. However, the most common approach is to implement Bridging, and to set this up you need to use Web Publishing. The steps for this are defined in good detail in Technet Article Q290113, but I have reproduced the basic outline here for completeness. All operations are carried out from the ISA Server Management Console.

1. Ensure that the ISA Server is configured to accept incoming Web requests by right-clicking on the server under *Servers and Arrays*, selecting *Properties*, *Incoming Web Requests*, and then *Configure listeners individually per IP address*.

You should be sure to specify that you select an IP address that corresponds to the URL that you publicize for access to OWA. In my environment, I advertise *webmail.cantaz.com* as the DNS name for 62.190.247.149, which is the IP address of the external network interface on my ISA server.

At this point of the configuration, you will specify that you will use a server certificate to authenticate Web browser clients and thus provide SSL/TLS communications.

2. Next you'll need to create a *destination set* (i.e., a grouping of server systems from or to which the ISA server will accept or direct HTTP traffic; in this case it is from the OWA URL). Expand the *Policy Elements* section, right-click *Destination Set*, then *New*, then populate the dialog box in the same way as that shown for my environment in Figure 10-5.

   Be sure to enter path information for */exchange/**, */exchweb/**, and */public/**.

3. Then expand *Publishing*, right-click *Web Publishing Rules*, click *New*, then *Rule,* and proceed to create a new rule using the destination set you have just created and directing HTTP requests to the internal OWA Front-End server (in my case the server is *osbex02.osb.cantaz.net*, as shown in Figure 10-6).
4. You must then stop and restart the Web Proxy and Firewall services before your configuration changes take effect.

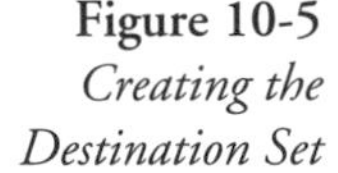

Figure 10-5
Creating the Destination Set

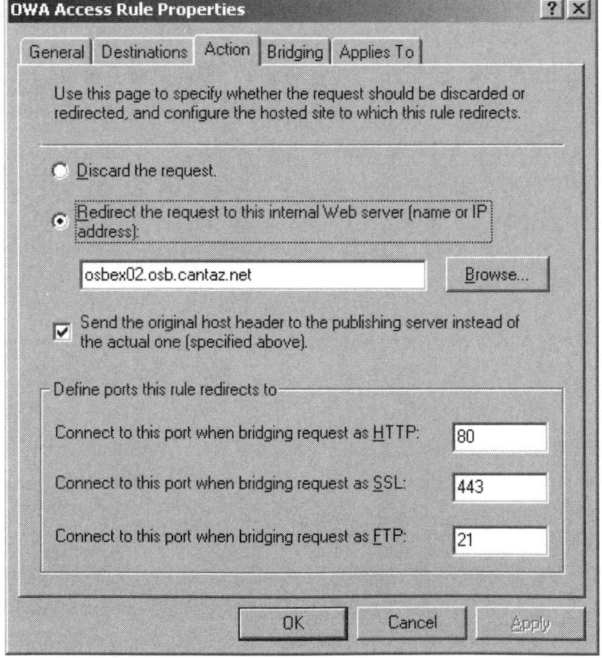

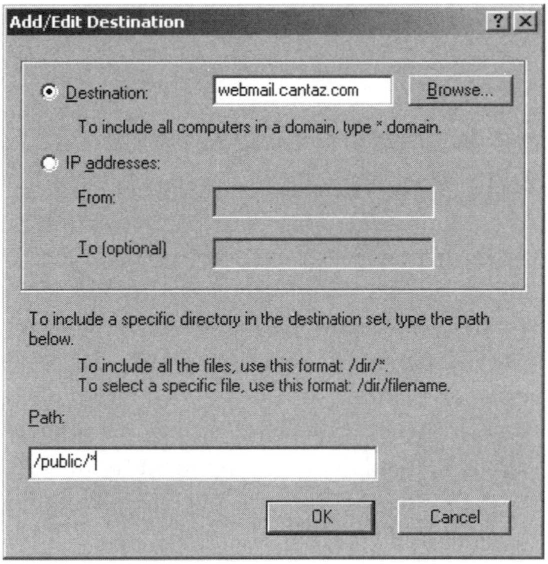

Figure 10-6
Creating the Web Publishing Rule

So the process for configuring ISA Server 2000 to act as a proxy server is relatively straightforward. In fact, it's more straightforward with ISA Server Feature Pack 1, which includes a wizard to help set up the OWA publishing configuration. Basically, the wizard runs through a set of screens asking you for the details of the external URL you wish to publish and to which Exchange server the connections should be directed, as shown in Figure 10-7.

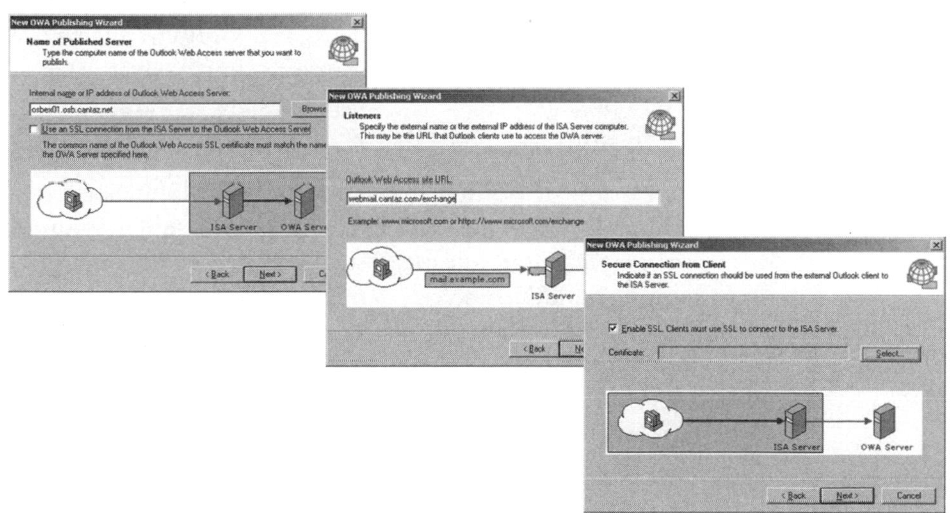

Figure 10-7
OWA Publishing Wizard from ISA Server 2000 Feature Pack 1

Now let's look at possible configurations using hardware-based proxy server implementations.

10.11 Using a Hardware-Based SSL/TLS Proxy Server with OWA

As an alternative to using a Microsoft ISA Server to perform the cryptographic processing of SSL/TLS sessions, it is possible (and often desirable when user loads are high) to employ a dedicated SSL/TLS network appliance. You should not think of such a network appliance as a replacement for an ISA Server (because ISA Server performs important firewall duties, too), but rather as an alternative workhorse for the SSL/TLS processing. In fact, in the architectural options that follow, the hardware-based proxy server is an additional component in an ISA Server secured environment. In many cases the cryptographic processing is performed solely on the network appliance, with a first phase of proxying taking place on an ISA Server and further proxying taking place on the network appliance.

For the purposes of example, I'll describe some topology options that can be implemented using the CertainT 100 SSL Accelerator from Radware, but in general, the same broad topological frameworks can be employed with any hardware-based proxy server device.

In its simplest configuration, the SSL/TLS Accelerator can be employed in an in-line topology, where all traffic is routed through the device, as shown in Figure 10-8.

Figure 10-8 shows inbound connections from browser OWA clients typically to a URL (in my example environment, that's https://webmail.cantaz.com). The ISA server proxies the HTTP requests onto the proxy server, where the SSL/TLS processing takes place before the HTTP packets are forwarded onto the OWA Front-End server (in either plain HTTP or HTTPS).

This is certainly the most straightforward topology to implement using an SSL/TLS accelerator network appliance, but it suffers from a few drawbacks. First, when operating in in-line mode such as this, all traffic, not just HTTPS traffic, must pass through the proxy server, so this is less than ideal from an architectural perspective and less desirable when user loads are high. Only HTTPS traffic is processed, though, with other traffic being effectively bridged from the decryption. Second, in general the proxy server must be on the same subnet as the source and destination of the HTTPS stream, so effectively the proxy server resides on the internal part of the network. Of course, you could implement yet another ISA Server–style proxy device between the proxy server and the OWA Front-End server to provide some form of address transla-

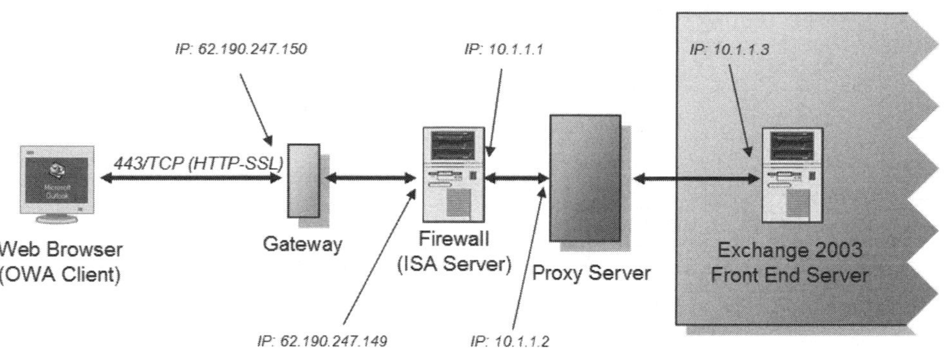

Figure 10-8 *Using a Hardware-based SSL/TLS Accelerator in In-line Mode*

tion, similar to the example shown in Figure 10-9. This really describes a scenario where the SSL/TLS Accelerator proxy server is firmly resident in the DMZ.

Configuring the CertainT 100 SSL Accelerator to operate in this mode is straightforward. You simply connect to the device in the first instance over a serial cable and issue the commands to associate an address with the system and place it into in-line or bridging mode, as shown in Figure 10-10.

Once an address has been associated with the device, you can subsequently connect to it using the HTTP-based management interface. (Some devices from other vendors ship preconfigured with a default address that you can connect to directly using a browser, requiring no serial connection, which can often be useful.)

An alternative architectural approach will use the proxy server in an SSL/TLS Accelerator farm topology, as shown in Figure 10-11.

10.12 Back-End Encryption

Both software-based and hardware-based proxy servers offer the possibility of back-end encryption. That is, while the proxy server takes on the responsibility of the heavy

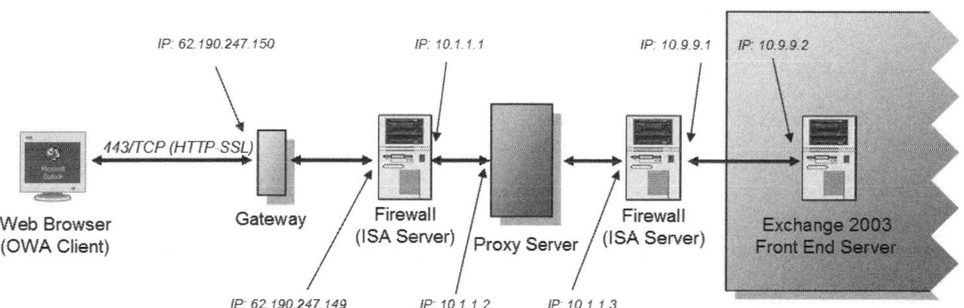

Figure 10-9 *Hardware-based SSL/TLS Acceleration in In-line Mode in the DMZ*

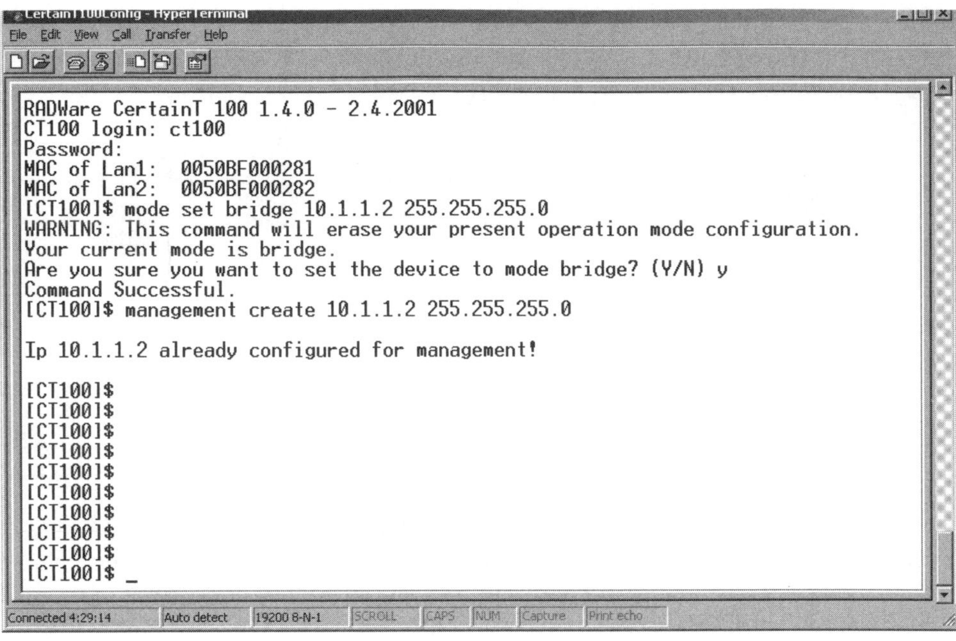

Figure 10-10 *Configuring the CertainT100 SSL/TLS Accelerator for In-line Mode*

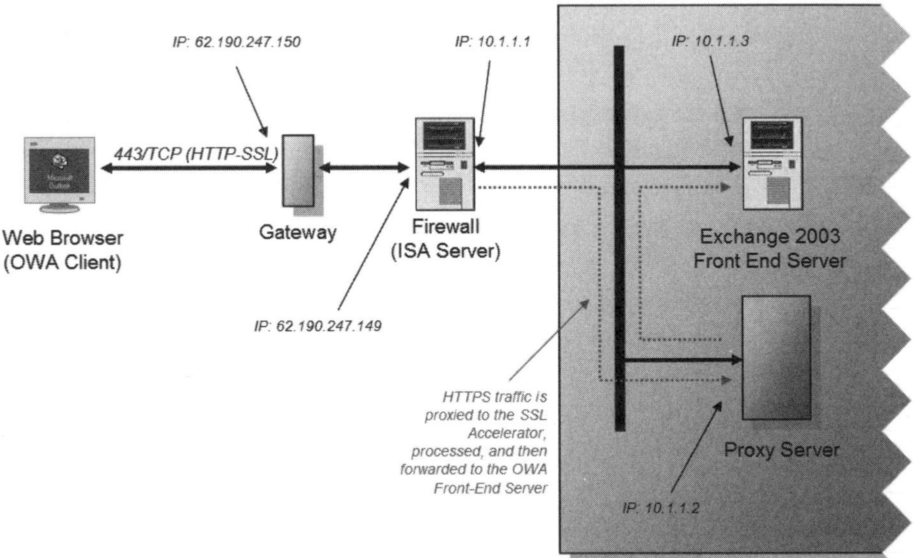

Figure 10-11 *Hardware-based SSL/TLS Acceleration in Server Farm Mode*

cryptographic processing for many hundreds or thousands of simultaneous connection requests, it can still maintain a secure SSL/TLS connection to the Front-End server. So why isn't the cryptographic load on the Front-End server as high as the load on the proxy server? Well, the answer is key-pair management.

The proxy server must deal with the management of many thousands of different key-pairs for each connecting client, basically an N-to-one relationship. This represents the bulk of the cryptographic processing load, but the partnership between the proxy server and the Front-End Server is simply a one-to-one relationship. Thus the management of the key-pairs is considerably simpler, and the encryption strength can often be of a lesser standard, often 56-bit key lengths between proxy server and Front-End Server compared to 128-bit keys used between browser clients and the proxy server.

Of course, there are benefits from not performing back-end encryption at all. As mentioned previously, having the communications stream between the proxy server and the Front-End Server allows for inspection of the packets by, for example, intrusion detection systems, thus providing a more overall secure infrastructure.

10.13 Understanding OWA, Authentication, Front-End Servers, and Redirection

For many organizations, an implementation of Exchange 2003—or even Exchange 2000—OWA has involved Web browser clients either connecting directly to Exchange servers that host the users' mailboxes or to a Front-End server that accepts initial OWA connections from clients and then proxies the connection to the appropriate Back-End server where the user's mailbox is located.

The Front-End model is useful because it allows a normalized or "flat" namespace to be used for the URL specified in the Web browser when multiple Back-End servers are used to host users' mailboxes. For example, users can simply specify the host address of the URL as webmail.acme.com in the Web browser, and so long as this URL resolves to an Exchange Front-End server, the Front-End Server will proxy the connection to the appropriate Back End server. Otherwise, a user would have to know the Back-End server on which the mailbox was located, and thus would have to enter a URL of the form *server1.acme.com*.

If multiple Front-End servers exist, then a mechanism must be used to have the normalized URL direct the browser clients to an arbitrary Front-End server. Typically this is performed by using Windows load-balancing, DNS round-robin, or hardware-based load-balancing switches. It is also important to note that the actual URL specified by a user must consist of more than just the host address part (e.g., *webmail.acme.com*). It is common to specify the URL in the form *webmail.acme.com/exchange*, but you can avoid the need for the */exchange* part of the URL by using an IIS redirection, whereby connections to the root of the Web server (e.g., *webmail.acme.com*) are redirected to the Exchange virtual directory. To do this, you should perform the following tasks:

1. Launch IIS Manager, select the Default Web site, right-click, and then select Properties.
2. Click on the Home Directory tab, then select *A Redirection to a URL.*
3. In the Redirect To field, enter */exchange* and then click on *A directory below this one.*

Although the traditional Front-End/Back-End server model is certainly useful, it has some drawbacks. This section describes the subtleties of authentication and outlines an alternative mechanism for implementing a normalized namespace with OWA and variant of the Front-End server configuration entitled a Pseudo Front-End server.

10.13.1 Traditional Front-End/Back-End server configurations

With the traditional approach to using Front-End and Back-End servers with OWA, all Web browser clients will establish HTTP/DAV connections to a single Front-End server and the Front End server will query an AD GC server to determine the Back-End server on which the user's mailbox resides. The Front-End server will then proxy the HTTP/Distributed Authoring And Versioning (DAV) session to the appropriate Back-End server. All communication between the browser and the Back-End server now takes place via the Front-End server. This is shown in Figure 10-12.

From an architectural perspective, this approach is ideal because the user need only use *webmail.acme.com* as the URL hostname. The complexities of the Back-End server naming structures are never exposed to the user. This represents the central tenet of Front-End/Back-End server architectures in conjunction with OWA.

In this configuration, the Front-End server has some special characteristics that determine it as a Front-End server. First, Front-End servers contain no user mailboxes: All mailboxes in the environment exist on the Back-End servers. In fact, Front-End servers generally do not even have a single Storage Group or Database on them. On the whole there is no need for any databases because they'll never be used, but it is common practice to have a database in place if you are also using the Front-End server to deal with incoming SMTP connections because the SMTP service requires the database in order to generate Non-Delivery Notifications. Second, Front-End servers have the *This is a Front-End server* checkbox enabled to designate them as Front-End servers. If the box is not checked, then the server is for all intents and purposes just another Back-End server. You can set the checkbox from Exchange System Manager/Administrative Groups/<AG-Name>/Servers/<Server-Name>, right-click and select Properties, where AG-Name is the name of the AG in which the server

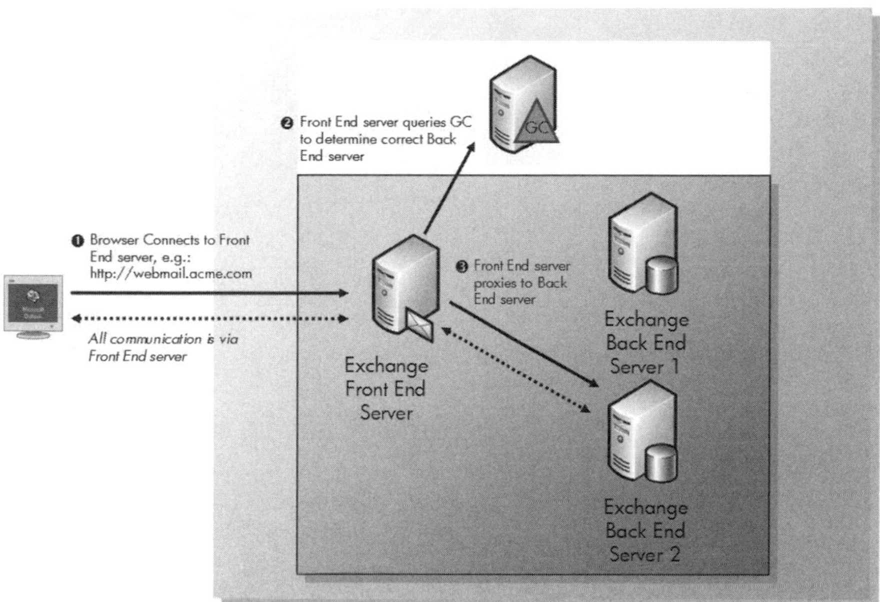
❷ Front End server queries GC to determine correct Back End server
GC
❶ Browser Connects to Front End server, e.g.: http://webmail.acme.com
All communication is via Front End server
❸ Front End server proxies to Back End server
Exchange Front End Server
Exchange Back End Server 1
Exchange Back End Server 2

Figure 10-12 *Traditional Mechanism for OWA Connections*

resides and <Server-Name> is the name of the server. The Properties page is shown in Figure 10-13.

It is worth pointing out that there is no specific configuration option to designate a server as a Back-End server. By default, all servers in an Exchange organization that are not designated as Front-End servers are Back-End servers, if at least one Front-End server has been configured in the environment. In an environment where no Front-End servers exist, it is meaningless to differentiate between server roles using the terms Front-End and Back-End.

10.13.2 Understanding explicit logon and implicit logon

A user may access his or her mailbox through OWA using either explicit logon or implicit logon. When explicit logon is used, information in the URL explicitly specifies the mailbox to which the OWA should be made. An explicit logon URL takes the form:

```
http://<servername>/exchange/<username>/
```

where <servername> represents the name of either the OWA Front-End or Back-End server and <username> specifies the name of the user's Windows account. For example, a typical URL for a user named 'flint' might be:

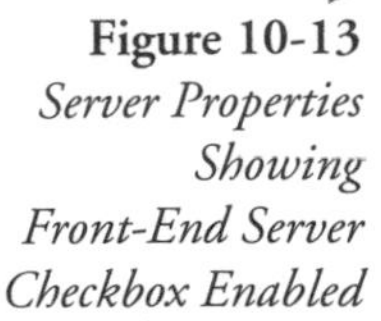

Figure 10-13 *Server Properties Showing Front-End Server Checkbox Enabled*

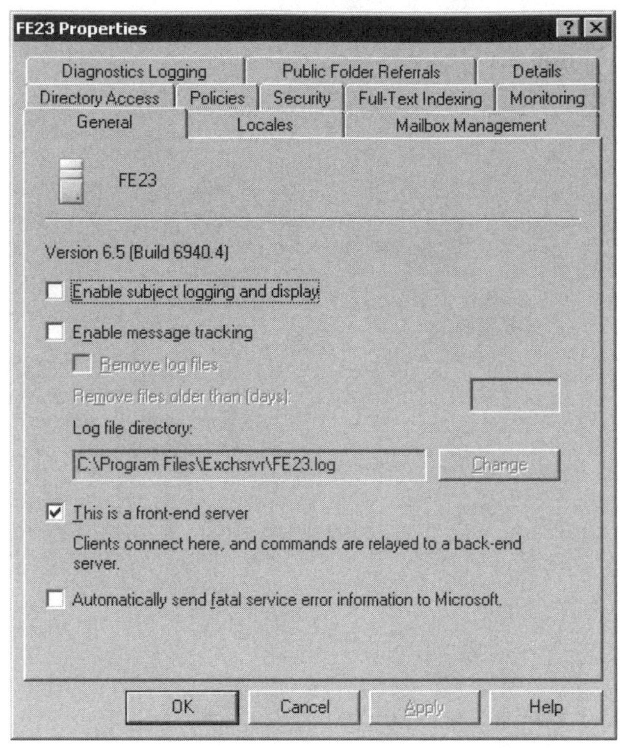


```
http://webmail.acme.com/exchange/flint/
```

When a Front-End server receives an explicit URL from a Web browser client, the specified username part of the URL is extracted and combined with the SMTP domain name associated with the Exchange virtual directory, thus rendering an SMTP address for the user. This SMTP address is used by the Front-End server in a query to a GC, thus allowing the Front-End server to discover on which Back-End server the user's mail is located. With this done, the Front-End server proceeds to forward the request unchanged to the Back-End server, which processes the request as if it came directly from the Web browser. Any response is routed back to the Web browser client via the Front-End server. Explicit logon must be used by the Front-End server if the Web browser session is not authenticated by the Front-End server, but only by the Back-End server.

On the other hand, implicit logon can be used. From a usability and aesthetic perspective, implicit logon is more attractive than explicit logon because the URL specified is much simpler. An implicit logon URL takes the form:

```
http://<servername>/exchange/
```

where <servername> represents the name of either the OWA Front-End or Back-End server. Also note, as described above, that the */exchange/* part can be omitted if the Exchange virtual directory has been appropriately modified. Thus, in its simplest form, an implicit logon URL might be just:

```
http://webmail.acme.com/
```

Few things in life are free, however, and the price to be paid for the ease and simplicity of an implicit logon URL is that the Front-End server must perform authentication on the user connection in the first instance so that it can determine the identity of the user and thus connect to the appropriate Back-End server.

10.13.3 Authentication with traditional Front-End/Back-End server configuration

With the Front-End server/Back-End server model, authentication of a user connection can be handled in one of two ways:

1. *Pass-Thru authentication*, where the Front-End server performs no authentication but merely forwards the request on to the Back-End server, where the authentication takes place
2. *Dual authentication*, where the Front-End server initially authenticates the request and then establishes the connection to the Back-End server, where authentication takes place again

When Pass-Thru authentication is used, explicit logon must be used too because the Front-End server must have some means to determine the identity of the user in order to forward the request to the appropriate Back-End server. Because users often wish to enter the simplest form of URL to access OWA, using Pass-Thru authentication is not desirable. Nor is it a recommended mechanism for OWA access, because Pass-Thru authentication means that anonymous HTTP requests go through to the Back-End server.

Therefore, Dual authentication becomes the desired authentication mechanism because implicit logon can be used, meaning simpler URLs. Because Dual authentication means that both Front-End and Back-End servers perform authentication doesn't mean that users will be prompted twice for credentials. In fact, users get prompted only once when the Front-End server performs authentication and the credentials are then cached within the client browser process. This is the preferred mechanism for the Front-End/Back-End server model and is used almost always except when the Front-End server cannot communicate over RPC with a DC, usually because the Front-End server is separated from the DC by a firewall, resulting in the implementation of Pass-Thru authentication.

Front-End servers support only HTTP Basic authentication. Because HTTP Basic authentication uses a weak encryption of a user's credentials, it is always recommended that connections between OWA clients and Front-End servers always take place over SSL connections. Furthermore, Front-End servers with HTTP Basic authentication cannot support single sign-on, which relies on Windows Integrated Security (essentially either NTLM or Kerberos). This means that even if you are already logged on to your Windows domain, if you connect to a Front-End server, you will always be prompted for your credentials. Both forms of authentication with associated possible logon types are shown in Figure 10-14.

10.13.4 Using a Pseudo Front-End server

So the Front-End/Back-End server model is very useful for normalizing namespaces with multiple Back-End servers, but it does suffer from the lack of single sign-on capa-

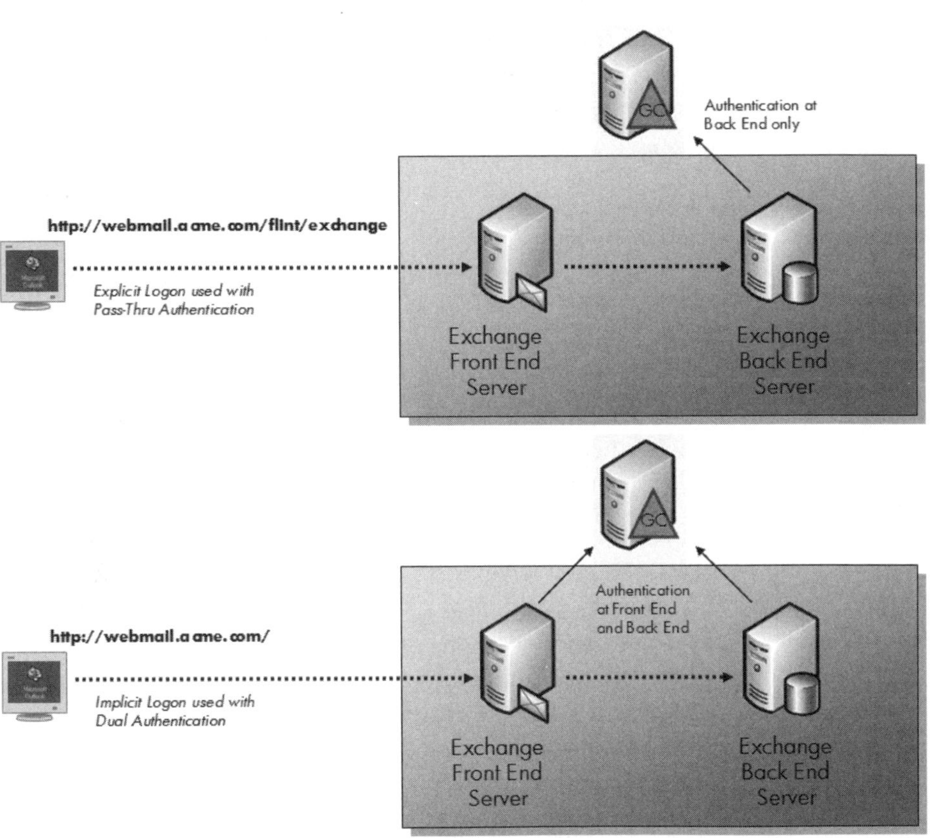

Figure 10-14 *Explicit and Implicit Logon Types with Associated Authentication Models*

bility. However, connecting directly to a Back-End server means that you can use Windows Integrated Security, and thus single sign-on becomes possible.

An ideal situation is to have the combination of both: allowing the user to enter a simple, standard URL and being assured that the browser session will be directed to the appropriate Back-End server; and further, eliminating the need for the user to reauthenticate if he or she has already logged on to the relevant domain.

Fortunately, connecting to any Back-End server—even if it is not the server on which your mailbox is located—will result in a redirection being sent to the client with a new URL that specifies the correct Back-End server to which you should connect. The Web browser client then establishes a direct connection to that Back-End server. The original server that was contacted plays no further role in the communications stream between the client and the Back-End server. This is shown diagrammatically in Figure 10-15.

In Figure 10-15, the Pseudo Front-End server (which is really just another Back-End server) can be referenced by the normalized URL of http://webmail.acme.com/. You can use this Pseudo Front-End server in several ways. You can use it solely to accept initial connections and then redirect the client to the appropriate Back-End

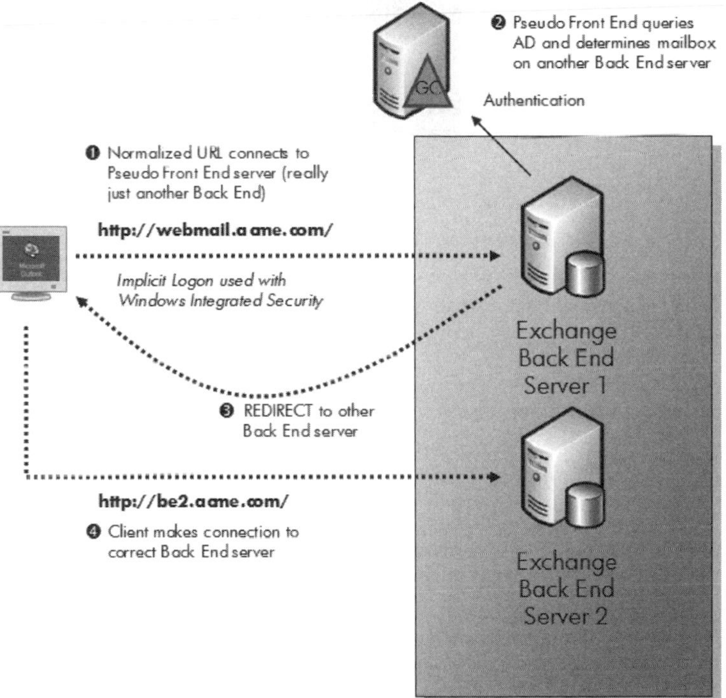

Figure 10-15 *Using a Standard Back-End Server as a Pseudo Front-End Server*

server (i.e., it hosts no user mailboxes). This means that the Pseudo Front-End server does little actual work. Alternately, you can host mailboxes on the Pseudo Front-End server and have it accept the initial connections and perform redirections as additional workload. And as a variation to this, rather than have just one server perform this additional overhead, you could use a load-balancing solution so that all Back-End servers act as Pseudo Front-End servers, sharing the workload.

10.14 Implementing Outlook RPC over HTTP

The combination of Outlook 2003, Windows Server 2003, and Exchange Server 2003 exposes new functionality that allows an Outlook 2003 client to connect to an Exchange Server 2003 system over HTTP. Now the communication is not strictly just using HTTP, but rather HTTP is used as a wrapper around the normal communications between the Outlook client and Exchange server.

This means that in general you can connect a local Outlook 2003 client to a remote Exchange Server 2003 system anywhere that you could normally use a browser to surf the Web. This is a very useful capability given the alternatives of using either OWA, which uses HTTP and has limited functionality compared to the full Outlook client, or via Outlook with a VPN connection, which is often blocked by the network provider. This section describes the mechanism by which this communication takes place and the configuration effort required on both client and server.

10.14.1 Understanding Outlook client and Exchange server interaction

The Outlook client (any version) uses MAPI to interact with an Exchange (any version) mailbox server. To carry out these operations, the Outlook client relies on RPCs over which to execute its MAPI calls. The RPC mechanism is not itself a transport protocol, but it relies on a transport protocol to carry the RPC packets. RPCs have no built-in reliability characteristics of their own, but they typically rely on an underlying transport protocol, such as TCP/IP, for reliability. When implemented on less reliable transports, such as user datagram protocol (UDP), the application must provide timeout and retransmission functionality.

Outlook to Exchange communication need not be restricted to LANs, and in fact the RPC model works well across a WAN. However, the conventional operation of RPC involves an initial handshake between the Outlook client and the Exchange server over a well-known port (UDP port 135; the RPC Endpoint Mapper Port) before establishing a communications channel over a dynamically assigned ephemeral port typically in the 1024 to 1100 range. Although it is possible to control this port assignment to some extent, RPC communications over TCP/IP are generally frowned upon by network security and firewall administrators. Effectively this means that you cannot use Outlook in one company's network to connect to an Exchange server in another company's network.

However, it is very common to find readily available HTTP access from within a company's network that allows external communications. Without it, you couldn't browse the Web from the company's intranet. Typically this communication will be over the standard HTTP port 80 or some variant thereof (e.g., 8080 or 8088) if an HTTP reverse proxy server is being used. In any case, once a client PC's Internet Explorer has been correctly configured with a proxy server, any application can utilize the HTTP protocol for client/server communication. It is also worth noting that HTTP over SSL (or HTTPS) is also typically accessible over port 143.

Rather than have you negotiate with those sometimes less-than-helpful firewall administrators to enable RPC over TCP/IP communications, the clever people in Microsoft's Outlook and Exchange development groups thought it would be simpler if you could just have your Outlook and Exchange RPC communications piggy-back over the HTTP protocol more or less transparently.

10.14.2 RPC over HTTP requirements

For RPC over HTTP communication between an Outlook client and Exchange server, there are strict requirements for the software versions that must be used. You must be running Windows XP SP1 on your client PC and specifically you must be running the Microsoft Q331320 update package (available at http://support.microsoft.com/). You must also be running Outlook 2003.

On the server side, you must be running Windows Server 2003 so that IIS 6.0 and its new Worker Process Isolation Model is available. In fact, you must be running Windows Server 2003 on all systems that will take part in any communications with the Outlook 2003 client. This includes any Exchange servers, GC servers or DC servers, or any other servers (more on this later).

10.14.3 RPC over HTTP architecture

The RPC over HTTP architecture is very similar to the Front-End/Back-End server model used for OWA, IMAP, and POP3 access first introduced with Exchange 2000. The Outlook 2003 client, when suitably configured (described later) connects over HTTP to an RPC Proxy server. This is also referred to as the RPC Proxy Front-End server. The RPC Proxy acts on behalf of the Outlook 2003 client and establishes RPC connections to the appropriate Back-End server, which hosts the requesting client's mailbox. The architecture is shown diagrammatically in Figure 10-16.

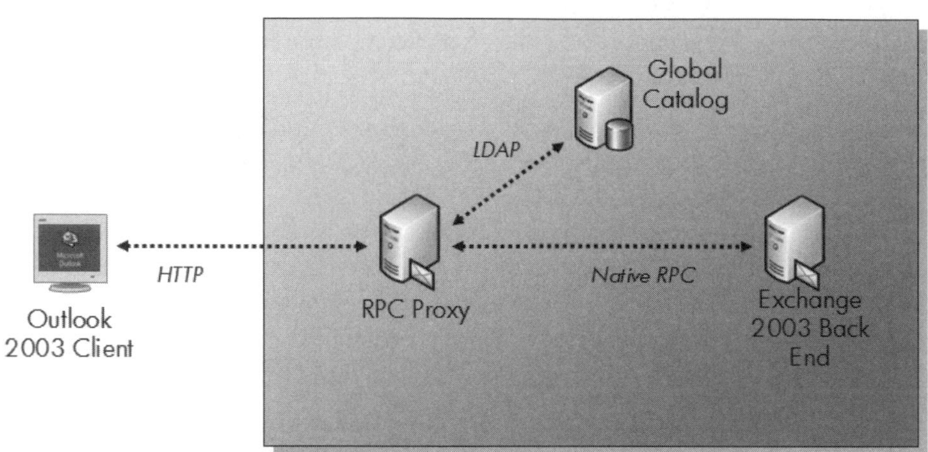

Figure 10-16 *Outlook and Exchange RPC over HTTP Architecture*

There are some important things to note about the implementation of this architecture. First, the RPC Proxy need not be an Exchange Server 2003 system because there are no Exchange components involved in the RPC Proxy functionality. The proxy activity is carried out by an ISAPI filter in IIS 6.0, and therefore the only requirement on the system is that it is running Windows Server 2003. Second, the RPC Proxy server—because it is merely a function of IIS 6.0—can be co-located on the Exchange Server 2003 system, because it also must be running Windows Server 2003. Third, the GC server can be co-located on the Exchange Server 2003 system as well, if required, although this is not recommended. So in essence, all of the server components shown in Figure 10-16 can exist on the same physical server box.

The placement of the various servers also needs to be considered in relation to internal and external firewalls and the resulting DMZ. There are two basic approaches you can take for server placement. In the first instance, you might consider placing the RPC Proxy server in the DMZ, with the Exchange and other AD servers in the internal part of the network, as shown in Figure 10-17.

In general, this approach is not recommended because it causes unnecessary risks as more ports are opened on the internal firewall. This is especially true of the dynamically assigned ports, which must be opened to allow RPC communications between the RPC Proxy and Exchange Server 2003 Back-End, theoretically in the range 1024 to 65535, but the implementation of RPC over HTTP mandates that a narrow range for these dynamically assigned ports be defined (from port 6001 to port 6004), and this is controlled by Registry settings, as described in the next section. Apart from those shown in Figure 10-17, you must also consider the following ports that the RPC Proxy server might require: port 88 (UDP/TCP) for Kerberos services; port 53 (UDP/TCP)

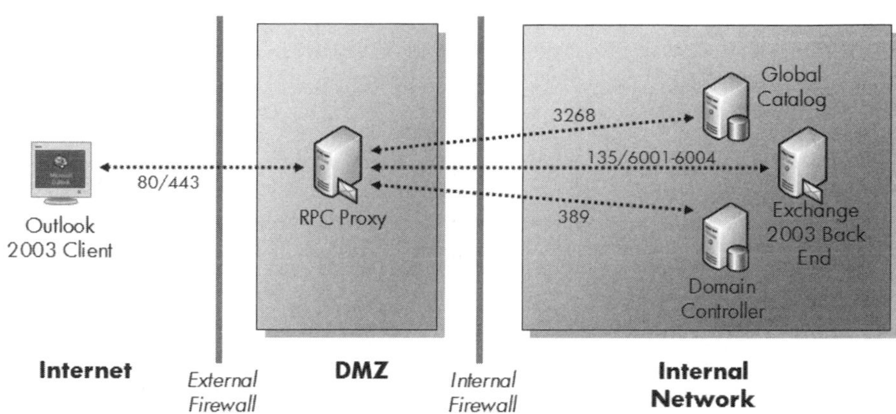

Figure 10-17
RPC Proxy Server Positioned Inside the DMZ

for DNS queries; port 445 for the NetLogon SMB; and any other protocols that might be required for management or monitoring services you will operate.

However, this is not the recommended configuration. Rather, best practice dictates that you should co-locate the RPC Proxy server on the internal part of the network and use a generic HTTP forward proxy in the DMZ, as shown in Figure 10-18.

This is the most secure configuration and benefits from having only one connection from the HTTP forward proxy in the DMZ (in this case an ISA server) to the RPC Proxy server in the internal network. This connection can be either over basic HTTP (port 80) or encrypted with SSL (port 143), or with encrypted RPCs over basic HTTP.

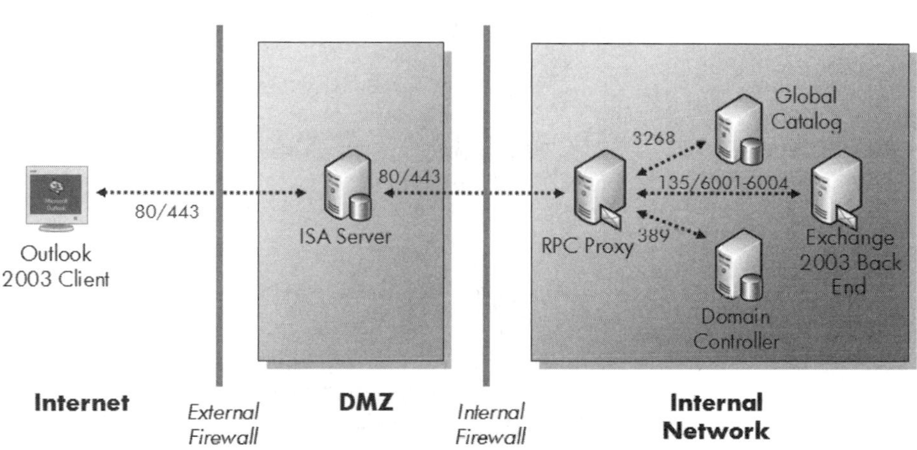

Figure 10-18
RPC Proxy Server Positioned Inside the Internal Network

And there are several means by which you can accommodate this connection. The most conventional approach is to terminate the SSL connection at the HTTP forward proxy and make a basic HTTP connection to the RPC Proxy. This is often done because such HTTP proxy servers are typically equipped with SSL cryptographic accelerator hardware. Alternately, you may either tunnel the inbound SSL connection through the HTTP proxy server untouched and let the RPC Proxy server deal with the SSL encryption, or the HTTP proxy server may terminate the outward-facing SSL session and establish a new SSL session to the RPC Proxy server.

10.14.4 Configuring RPC over HTTP on servers

Several modifications need to be made to servers to implement RPC over HTTP capability. In the first instance, you must ensure that the server you will use as the RPC Proxy server has the *RPC over HTTP Proxy* service installed. You do this from *Control Panel/Add Remove Programs/Add Remove Windows Components,* then select *Windows Components,* and then *Networking Services*. You should ensure that the RPC over HTTP service is selected, as shown in Figure 10-19, and then proceed to install this component.

With the RPC over HTTP Proxy service installed, you should then drill down through the IIS Manager MMC snap-in (*Web Sites/Default Web Site/RPC Virtual Directory*) and select *Properties* of the RPC Virtual Directory. Navigate to the *Directory Security tab* and choose *Authentication and Access Control*, then make sure to disable

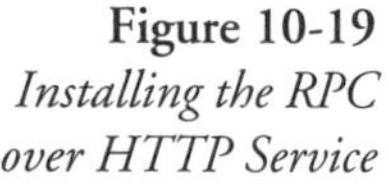

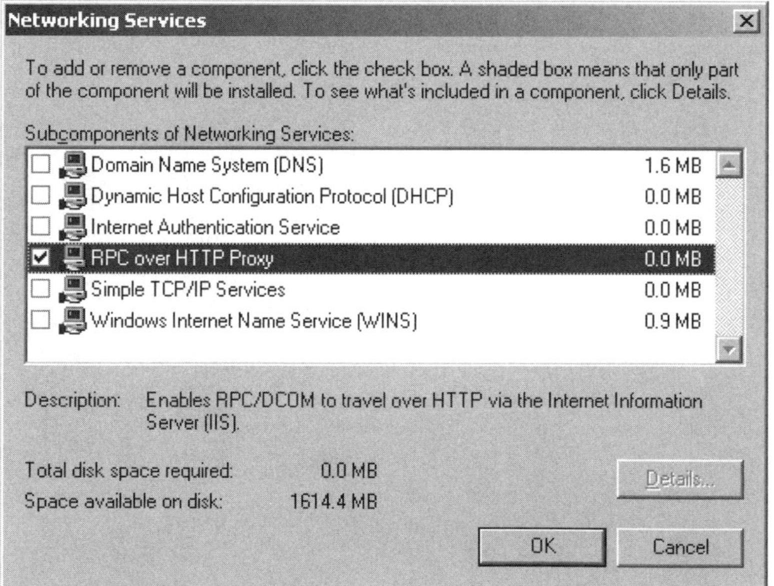

Figure 10-19
Installing the RPC over HTTP Service

Anonymous access and enable either *Integrated Windows Authentication* or *Basic Authentication* if you are using SSL. This is shown in Figure 10-20. Note that if you are implementing the RPC over HTTP functionality over SSL, then you should select Basic Authentication. This means that credentials are sent in clear text, but because the connection will be secure in any event—because of the SSL—this approach is fine.

You must then configure the server to act as the RPC Proxy. You do this by modifying the following registry key on the server:

```
HKEY_LOCAL_MACHINE\Software\Microsoft\Rpc\RpcProxy
Value name: ValidPorts
Value type: REG_SZ
Value data: to servers with which RPC proxy communicates
```

When you set the value for the ValidPorts registry key, you must specify every server with which the RPC Proxy server might communicate. This includes all Exchange 2003 Back-End servers and any DCs or GC servers. Similarly, you must specify the port 593 for each server. This is the well-known port used for the RPC over HTTP Endpoint Mapper service, and it is used for initial connection handshaking and then the port range over which you will allow communication to take place. For example, you may set the value of this string as shown in Figure 10-21. If your GC server is the same server as the one on which you are running Exchange Server 2003, there's no

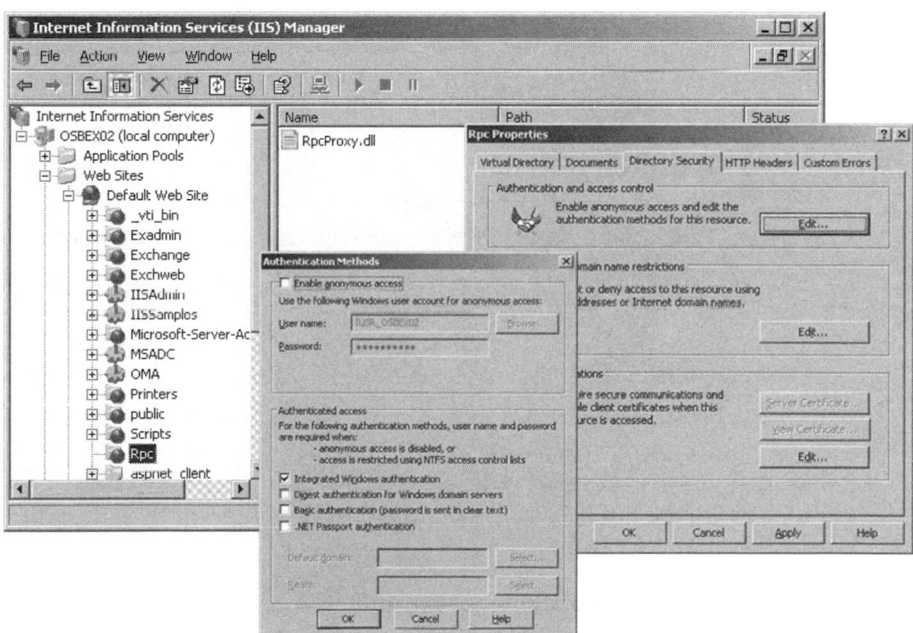

Figure 10-20 *Configuring Authentication on the RPC Virtual Directory*

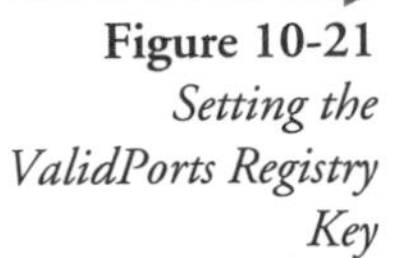

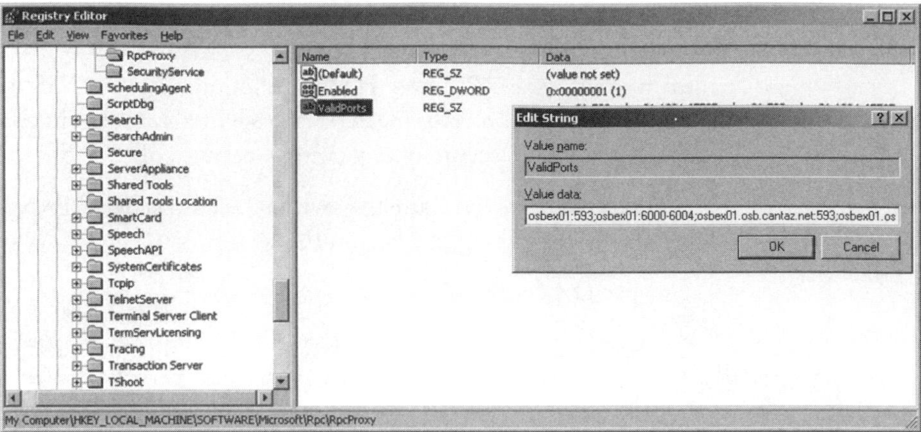

Figure 10-21 *Setting the ValidPorts Registry Key*

need to specify the GC separately from the Exchange system, but you must still have the two entries for the port 593 access and the assigned port range, 6001–6004.

Depending on your environment, your placement of servers, and associated name resolution, you may also wish to specify the Fully Qualified Domain Names (FQDN) of servers in the ValidPorts registry if the short-name formats might not result in correct resolution. Using my configuration as an example, in addition to specifying entries for just osbex01, you should also specify corresponding entries for osbex01.osb.cantaz.net.

If you have tens or even hundreds of Back-End servers and GCs, it might become somewhat tiresome to have to update the ValidPorts registry value with details about every one. Now you can simplify the process of setting the ValidPorts registry key by using a script from Microsoft that automates the task. Microsoft provides the RPCHTTP_setup.VBS (which is available from www.microsoft.com/exchange). This script interrogates the AD and determines the list of servers that are GC servers and Exchange servers and automatically adds the entries to the ValidPorts registry key on the RPC Proxy server. You should run this script every time you make a change to your environment that involves the addition or removal of GC servers or Exchange servers. To run the script you'll need to have Enterprise Admin permissions if the servers exist in multiple domains, or at the very least Domain Admin permissions if the servers exist only within a single domain. You can run the script with an option to pipe the output to a text file, which you can then distribute to local administrators to update their systems directly.

Also as a mechanism to simplify the deployment of the RPC over HTTP environment, Exchange 2003 Service Pack 1 includes a new *Properties* tab for Exchange servers within your organization. The tab, shown in Figure 10-22, allows you to specify those servers that will be involved in Exchange 2003 RPC over HTTP topologies.

10.14.5 Restricting RPC Proxy communications

Setting the port range on the RPC Proxy server defines the range of ports across which RPC over HTTP can function. But you must also explicitly set the ports to be used for the communications on all servers that will be involved in RPC over HTTP communications. (Note that in beta versions of Exchange Server 2003, you could set the ValidPorts registry key to the default range of 1024-65535, and any Back-End servers or GC servers would dynamically choose ports over which to operate; this required no configuration on Back-End or GC servers.)

The Back-End mailbox servers have the most modification, with a total of three registry keys requiring configuration. Fortunately the installation of Exchange 2003 automatically creates and sets these registry keys, so the actual burden of work on the system administrator is reduced. However, it's always worth checking that the values have not been modified if you experience difficulties in your environment. First, you must define the actual port on which the Back-End server will conduct the RPC over HTTP communications with the Exchange Store. To do this you must ensure the setting of the following registry key:

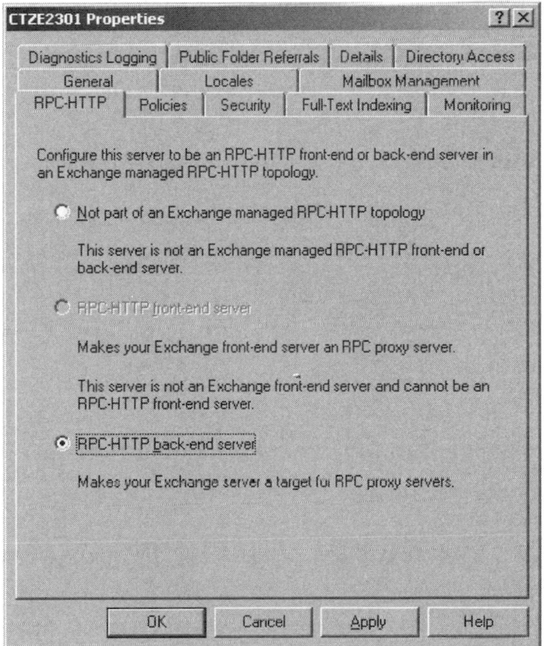

Figure 10-22 *RPC-HTTP Properties Tab in Exchange 2003 Service Pack 1*

```
HKEY_LOCAL_MACHINE\SYSTEM\CurrentControlSet\Services\
  MSExchangeIS\ParametersSystem
Value name: RPC/HTTP Port
Value type: REG_DWORD
Value data: 6001
```

Second, you must configure the Back-End server to provide DS Referral redirection process support. To do this you must ensure the setting of the following registry key:

```
HKEY_LOCAL_MACHINE\SYSTEM\CurrentControlSet\Services\
  MSExchangeSA\Parameters
Value name: HTTP Port
Value type: REG_DWORD
Value data: 6002
```

Third, you must also configure the Back-End server to support DS Proxy access. To do this you must ensure the setting of the following registry key:

```
HKEY_LOCAL_MACHINE\SYSTEM\CurrentControlSet\Services\
  MSExchangeIS\ParametersSystem
Value name: RPC/HTTP NSPI Port
Value type: REG_DWORD
Value data: 6003
```

Remember, you must ensure that these changes are made on all Exchange 2003 Back-End servers that will possibly communicate with the RPC Proxy server.

Any DCs or GC servers that you've specified in the ValidPorts registry key on the RPC Proxy server need to have some configuration to allow them to communicate with the RPC Proxy server over the restricted port range. You must explicitly modify the following registry key on the DC or GC server:

```
HKEY_LOCAL_MACHINE\SYSTEM\CurrentControlSet\Services\
  NTDS\Parameters
Value name: NSPI interface protocol sequences
Value type: REG_SZ
Value data: ncacn_http:6004
```

Note that the modifications to the DCs and GC servers must be done manually: there is no automated mechanism to have these changes made. With all of these registry modifications effected on the various servers in the environment, RPC over HTTP connectivity should be available.

10.14.6 Secure RPC over HTTP communications

Much like using OWA, it is a matter of best practice to conduct RPC over HTTP communications using SSL rather than over an unsecure connection. In the preferred deployment configuration, as shown in Figure 10-18, any SSL-secured client connections should be terminated at the HTTP forward proxy server (e.g., ISA Server) and a non-SSL connection established to the RPC Proxy server. To do this you must have a server certificate installed on the HTTP forward proxy. You can get such certificates from a commercial Certificate Authority (CA) such as Verisign (www.verisign.com) or Thawte (www.thawte.com), or you can create your own certificates using the Windows 2000 or Windows 2003 CA Service.

The default behavior of the RPC Proxy server with respect to non-SSL connections is governed by the AllowAnonymous registry key. If this registry key is nonexistent or its value set to zero, then all non-SSL connections or nonauthenticated connections to the RPC Proxy server will be rejected. When terminating the SSL connection at an HTTP forward proxy, the subsequent connection to the RPC Proxy is normally non-SSL; therefore, the connection would be rejected. You should override this behavior by modifying the registry key with a value of *1*, as shown following:

```
HKEY_LOCAL_MACHINE\Software\Microsoft\Rpc\RpcProxy
Value name: AllowAnonymous
Value type: REG_DWORD
Value data: 1
```

You must restart the IIS service on the RPC Proxy server for this change to take effect.

10.14.7 Client configuration

You must also modify the MAPI profile such that the Outlook 2003 client will connect to the server over HTTP, which may present some challenges.

If the user who wishes to connect to a mailbox using RPC over HTTP already has an existing MAPI profile on his laptop, say, then you need to access the properties of that MAPI profile selecting *Control Panel\Mail* and then choosing the appropriate profile. When selected, choose *Change,* then *More Settings,* then the *Connections* tab. You'll see a checkbox and further options for connection over HTTP at the bottom of the dialog box as shown in Figure 10-23.

Click the *Connect to my Exchange mailbox using HTTP* checkbox, and then click on the *Exchange Proxy Settings...* to complete the rest of the configuration. When the dialog box appears, again as shown in Figure 10-23, you should enter the URL that will direct the client to the RPC Proxy server. This URL can also be the value that is exposed by the HTTP forward proxy server (which will subsequently redirect the packets to the RPC Proxy server. If you choose Basic Authentication, then the URL prefix is automatically changed from *http* to *https* so that only a secure connection can be used.

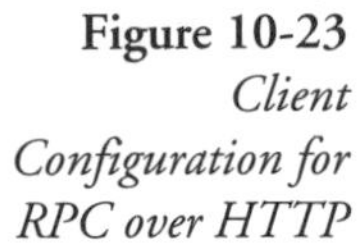

Figure 10-23 *Client Configuration for RPC over HTTP*

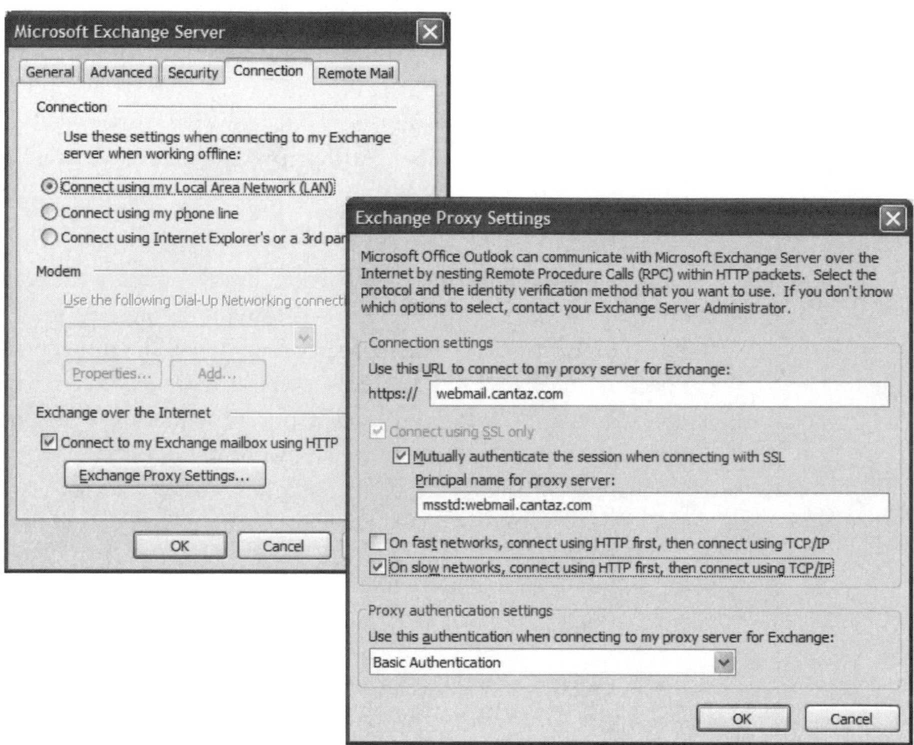

Although not strictly necessary, you may select the *Mutually authenticate the session when connecting with SSL* option. This allows the RPC Proxy server (or HTTP forward proxy) to authenticate the connecting client using the client's certificate as well as the server certificate. If you elect to do so, the client must provide the server (actually the Security Support Provider module on the server) with the expected server Principal name, which using the Microsoft standard syntax uses the prefix *msstd:*, followed by the FQDN of the RPC Proxy server.

Finally, you might check the somewhat confusingly entitled *On slow networks connect using HTTP first...* option if you wish HTTP to be used for the connection when connected remotely. In general, Outlook will try to connect to Exchange over TCP/IP first, but if this fails, it will attempt to use HTTP. Checking this box tells Outlook to bypass the TCP/IP connection attempt in the first instance. The same holds true for the corresponding *On fast networks connect using HTTP first...* option except that HTTP would be tried on a normal LAN connection. (Note that a slow network is considered to be a network connection whereby the Windows network connectoid reports a connection speed of less than 115 kbps.)

Making all of these changes to the MAPI profile assumes that the profile already exists on the client PC. If you have to create the MAPI profile in the first instance, do be aware that the usual process of creating the profile relies on direct RPC access to the Exchange mailbox server over TCP/IP. This happens when you enter the mailbox server name and the username. If you must create MAPI profiles for remote users (i.e., you do not have direct TCP/IP access to the Exchange mailbox server), then you should use the readily available MAPI profile-generation utilities such as ProfGen or the new profile generators that ship with the Office 2003 Resource Kit.

10.15 Summary

The first approach to OWA outlined in this chapter is one that many small environments have implemented to allow OWA access for their users when they are out and on the road. I've known many large corporate environments to implement the same architecture. Although it's a relatively conventional approach, it is far from simple because of the complexity of the configuration, and it is singularly insecure because of the vast number of holes with which internal-facing firewalls must be riddled. There are certainly many different approaches you can take and each approach has its own merits—some are simple to implement, some are highly scalable, some are expensive, but all provide some degree of protection. You may not have the budget to implement the Rolls- Royce solution, but surely some protection is better than none at all.

This chapter has also described how OWA clients interact with Exchange servers, be they Front-End or Back-End servers. The intricacies of different logon formats and the subtleties of authentication may not be too important to many organizations, but there are certainly instances where the default behavior is neither appropriate nor suitable for the user environment. In such circumstances where you require improved ease of use, you might consider the possibility of using a Pseudo Front-End server as described. Its operation is not a radical departure from the norm, but it certainly can be useful.

Using RPC over HTTP as a mechanism to connect Outlook 2003 clients to their mailbox servers has some real advantages. It's a flexible way to provide a user with access to the home mail environment without the constraints of either tunneling or a relatively clumsy Web-based client. However, this functionality does not just work straight out of the box. It requires real planning and configuration on the part of messaging system administrators, and you should certainly think about piloting this kind of service in a production environment so that you can assess its impact on your infrastructure. It is powerful, though, and a real benefit of Exchange 2003!

Lists of Events Generated by the Active Directory Connector

Table A-1 provides a list of the Sources, Event IDs, Symbolic Names, and Severity of events that can be generated by the Active Directory Connector.

Table A-1 *List of Active Directory Connector Event IDs and Symbolic Names*

Event	Symbolic Name	Severity
1	SYNCHRO_CATEGORY	
2	ACCMAN_CATEGORY	
3	AMA_CATEGORY	
4	SERVICE_CATEGORY	
5	LDAP_CATEGORY	
6	ADDRESS_LIST_CATEGORY	
8000	LRALOG_MSG	Informational
8001	MSG_SERVICE_STARTED	Informational
8002	MSG_SERVICE_STOPPED	Informational
8003	MSG_SERVICE_STARTING	Informational
8004	MSG_SERVICE_STOPPING	Informational
8005	MSG_SERVICE_BADREQUEST	Warning
8006	MSG_LDAP_OPENSESSION	Informational
8007	MSG_LDAP_CLOSESESSION	Informational
8008	MSG_LDAP_BIND	Informational

Event	Symbolic Name	Severity
8009	MSG_LDAP_BIND_NULL	Informational
8010	MSG_LDAP_SEARCHWITHFILTER	Informational
8011	MSG_LDAP_SEARCHWITHFILTER_ATTR	Informational
8012	MSG_LDAP_SEARCH_RESULT	Informational
8013	MSG_LDAP_ADD	Informational
8014	MSG_LDAP_ADD_ATTR	Informational
8015	MSG_LDAP_MODIFY	Informational
8016	MSG_LDAP_MODIFY_ATTR	Informational
8017	MSG_LDAP_DELETE	Informational
8018	MSG_LDAP_ABANDON	Informational
8019	MSG_LDAP_NOTIFY_SEARCH	Informational
8020	MSG_LDAP_SEARCHWITHFILTER_ERROR	Warning
8021	MSG_LDAP_ADD_ERROR	Error
8022	MSG_LDAP_MODIFY_ERROR	Error
8023	MSG_LDAP_DELETE_ERROR	Error
8024	MSG_LDAP_INITPAGE_ERROR	Error
8025	MSG_LDAP_GETNEXTPAGE_ERROR	Warning
8026	MSG_LDAP_BIND_ERROR	Error
8027	MSG_LDAP_GC_BIND_ERROR	Error
8028	MSG_LDAP_MODRDN_ERROR	Error
8029	MSG_LDAP_REFERRAL_ERROR	Error
8030	MSG_LDAP_EXTENDED_ERROR	Error
8031	MSG_LDAP_OPENSESSION_ERROR	Warning
8032	MSG_LDAP_SESSION_ERROR	Error
8033	MSG_LDAP_SEARCH_ERROR	Warning
8034	MSG_LDAP_COMPARE_ERROR	Error
8035	MSG_SYNCHRO_MODIFYENTRY	Informational
8036	MSG_SYNCHRO_DELETEDIRSEARCH	Informational
8037	MSG_SYNCHRO_DELETEENTRY	Informational
8038	MSG_SYNCHRO_ADDENTRY	Informational
8039	MSG_SYNCHRO_ENTRY_ATTRVALS	Informational

Event	Symbolic Name	Severity
8040	MSG_SYNCHRO_PROXYRPC_ERROR	Warning
8041	MSG_SYNCHRO_PROXYSOMEFAILED	Warning
8042	MSG_SYNCHRO_UPDATEDIRSEARCH	Informational
8043	MSG_SYNCHRO_DIRSEARCH_ATTRS	Informational
8044	MSG_SYNCHRO_DIRSEARCH_DNLIST	Informational
8045	MSG_SYNCHRO_UPDATETOMBENTRY	Informational
8046	MSG_SYNCHRO_UPDATEEXISTENTRY	Informational
8047	MSG_SYNCHRO_DELETEENTRIES	Informational
8048	MSG_SYNCHRO_NONTOMBSTONEDELETE	Informational
8049	MSG_SYNCHRO_TOMBSTONEDELETE	Informational
8050	MSG_SYNCHRO_ENTRYNOTEXIST	Informational
8051	MSG_SYNCHRO_ENTRYEXISTS	Informational
8052	MSG_SYNCHRO_NODELETEENTRIES	Informational
8053	MSG_SYNCHRO_IMPORTATTRS	Informational
8054	MSG_LDAP_UNBIND_ERROR	Error
8055	MSG_SYNCHRO_NOREPLICATIONAGENTDN	Error
8056	MSG_SYNCHRO_REPLICATESTART	Informational
8057	MSG_SYNCHRO_REPLICATESTOP	Informational
8058	MSG_SYNCHRO_REPLICATEABORTED	Informational
8059	MSG_SYNCHRO_SYNCREMTOLOCAL	Informational
8060	MSG_SYNCHRO_SYNCLOCALTOREM	Informational
8061	MSG_DSCONFIG_READREPLICATIONINFO	Informational
8062	MSG_DSCONFIG_OPENSESSION_FAIL	Error
8063	MSG_DSCONFIG_READ_ROOT_FAIL	Error
8064	MSG_DSCONFIG_READ_OBJECT_FAIL	Error
8065	MSG_DSCONFIG_SEARCH_OBJECT_FAIL	Error
8066	MSG_DSCONFIG_NO_NAMESPACES	Informational
8067	MSG_DSCONFIG_NAMESPACEINFO	Informational
8068	MSG_DSCONFIG_NEW_NAMESPACE	Informational
8069	MSG_DSCONFIG_DELETED_NAMESPACE	Informational
8070	MSG_DSCONFIG_NAMESPACE_ERROR	Warning

Event	Symbolic Name	Severity
8071	MSG_DSCONFIG_SETREMOTELASTUSN	Informational
8072	MSG_DSCONFIG_SETLOCALLASTUSN	Informational
8073	MSG_ACCMAN_INVALIDCOMPUTER	Error
8074	MSG_ACCMAN_ADDUSERLOCALOK	Informational
8075	MSG_ACCMAN_ADDUSERREMOK	Informational
8076	MSG_ACCMAN_LOOKUPSIDERR	Error
8077	MSG_ACCMAN_ADDUSERLOCAL_ERROR	Error
8078	MSG_ACCMAN_ADDUSERREM_ERROR	Error
8079	MSG_ACCMAN_DELACCINVALIDSID	Error
8080	MSG_ACCMAN_DELUSERLOCALOK	Informational
8081	MSG_ACCMAN_DELUSERREMOK	Informational
8082	MSG_ACCMAN_DELUSERLOCAL_ERROR	Error
8083	MSG_ACCMAN_DELUSERREM_ERROR	Error
8084	MSG_AMA_MAPTABLE_ERROR	Error
8085	MSG_AMA_STARTAMAOK	Informational
8086	MSG_AMA_STOPAMA	Informational
8087	MSG_AMA_LOCALTOREMATTRMAX	Informational
8088	MSG_AMA_LOCALTOREMATTR	Informational
8089	MSG_AMA_REMTOLOCALATTRMAX	Informational
8090	MSG_AMA_REMTOLOCALATTR	Informational
8091	MSG_AMA_REMTOLOCALOBJ	Informational
8092	MSG_AMA_LOCALTOREMOBJ	Informational
8093	MSG_AMA_OBJECTNOTFOUND	Informational
8094	MSG_AMA_DESTOBJNOTFOUND	Informational
8095	MSG_AMA_OBJNOATTRS	Informational
8096	MSG_AMA_ATTRFILEEXCEPTION	Error
8097	MSG_AMA_CREATEATTR_ERROR	Error
8098	MSG_AMA_CREATEOBJ_ERROR	Error
8099	MSG_AMA_NOLOCALTREE	Informational
8100	MSG_AMA_NOOBJECTCLASS	Informational
8101	MSG_AMA_NOREMTREE	Informational

Event	Symbolic Name	Severity
8102	MSG_AMA_ATTRNOTFOUND	Informational
8103	MSG_SERVICE_INSTALLED	Informational
8104	MSG_SERVICE_REMOVED	Informational
8105	MSG_SERVICE_NOTREMOVED	Error
8106	MSG_SERVICE_CTRLHANDLERNOTINSTALLED	Error
8107	MSG_SERVICE_CREATESRVCFAIL	Error
8108	MSG_SERVICE_FAILEDINIT	Error
8109	MSG_SYNCHRO_IMPORTFAILURE	Error
8110	MSG_DSCONFIG_SETREMLASTUPDATETIME	Informational
8111	MSG_DSCONFIG_SETLOCLASTUPDATETIME	Informational
8112	MSG_DSCONFIG_UNKNOWN_AUTH_PACKAGE	Error
8113	MSG_DSCONFIG_DYNAMIC_LOAD_DLL_ERROR	Error
8114	MSG_DSCONFIG_DYNAMIC_ENTRY_POINT_ERROR	Error
8115	MSG_DSCONFIG_NT_API_ERROR	Error
8116	MSG_DSCONFIG_SYNCNOW	Informational
8117	MSG_SYNCHRO_BADIMPORTCONTAINER	Error
8118	MSG_SYNCHRO_BADEXPORTCONTAINER	Error
8119	MSG_AMA_INVALIDATTR	Warning
8120	MSG_AMA_INVALIDCONVERSION	Warning
8121	MSG_SYNCHRO_MISSINGMUSTCONTAIN	Warning
8122	MSG_SYNCHRO_INVALIDATTRIBS	Warning
8123	MSG_SYNCHRO_DELETINGMUSTCONTAIN	Warning
8124	MSG_SYNCHRO_BAD_CONFIG	Error
8125	MSG_ALDG_ADDRESS_LIST_NEW	Informational
8126	MSG_ALDG_ADDRESS_LIST_MODIFY	Informational
8127	MSG_ALDG_ADDRESS_LIST_DELETE	Informational
8128	MSG_ALDG_CHANGED_OBJECT	Informational
8129	MSG_ALDG_EVAL_OBJECT	Informational
8130	MSG_ALDG_ADD_TO_OBJECT	Informational
8131	MSG_ALDG_REMOVE_FROM_OBJECT	Informational
8132	MSG_ALDG_CALC_ABORTED	Informational

Event	Symbolic Name	Severity
8133	MSG_ALDG_CALC_COMPLETE	Informational
8134	MSG_ALDG_Q_REQUEST	Informational
8135	MSG_ALDG_NO_RULE	Informational
8136	MSG_ALDG_CRUDE_LOG_FOR_NOW	Informational
8137	MSG_SYNCHRO_BAD_CA_VERSION	Error
8138	MSG_SERVER_UNAVAILABLE	Warning
8139	MSG_SYNCHRO_STALE_TIMESTAMP	Warning
8140	MSG_SYNCHRO_DELAYING_GROUP	Informational
8141	MSG_SYNCHRO_NO_MUTEX	Error
8142	MSG_SERVICE_UNHANDLED_EXCEPTION	Error
8143	MSG_CA_UNHANDLED_EXCEPTION	Error
8144	MSG_SERVICE_MEM_EXCEPTION	Error
8145	MSG_SERVICE_UNHANDLED_EXCEPTION_DETAILS	Error
8146	MSG_SYNCHRO_ERROR_EXCEPTION	Error
8147	MSG_LDAP_MODRDN	Informational
8148	MSG_SYNCHRO_SUMMARY_STATISTICS	Informational
8149	MSG_AD_SERVICE_DISABLED	Informational
8150	MSG_AD_SERVICE_NO_THREADS	Informational
8151	MSG_AD_SERVICE_NO_CONFIG	Warning
8152	MSG_AD_SERVICE_NO_SERVICES	Informational
8153	MSG_AD_THREAD_UNREC_ERROR	Error
8154	MSG_AD_THREAD_RESTART_FAILED	Error
8155	MSG_AD_THREAD_TERMINATED	Informational
8156	MSG_AD_THREAD_STARTING	Informational
8157	MSG_AD_THREAD_WAITING_SCHED	Informational
8158	MSG_AD_THREAD_RUNNING_SERVICE	Informational
8159	MSG_AD_THREAD_CHECK_SCHED	Informational
8160	MSG_ALDG_NO_CHANGE_REQ	Informational
8161	MSG_ALDG_EXCEPTION_WHILE_PROCESSING	Error
8162	MSG_ALDG_THREAD_WAITING_NEXT_TRAN	Informational
8163	MSG_ALDG_THREAD_NEXT_TRAN	Informational

Event	Symbolic Name	Severity
8164	MSG_ALDG_THREAD_IDLE_SHUTDOWN	Informational
8165	MSG_ALDG_EXCEPTION_AL	Error
8166	MSG_ALDG_FAILED_TO_MODIFY	Warning
8167	MSG_ALDG_MODIFIED_USER	Informational
8168	MSG_ALDG_FAILED_TO_MODIFY_USER	Warning
8169	MSG_ALDG_GOT_ALL_UG_CHANGES	Informational
8170	MSG_ALDG_GOT_ALL_AL_CHANGES	Informational
8171	MSG_ALDG_AL_CHANGE_SKIPPED	Informational
8172	MSG_ALDG_CEVT_CYCLE_FAIL	Error
8173	MSG_ALDG_SVC_CHANGES	Error
8174	MSG_ALDG_AL_CHANGE	Informational
8175	MSG_ALDG_UG_CHANGE	Informational
8176	MSG_AD_SERVICE_SHUTDOWN	Informational
8177	MSG_ACCMAN_LOGON_FAILURE	Warning
8178	MSG_SYNCHRO_TARGET_SCHEMA_INVALID	Error
8179	MSG_SYNCHRO_DELETION_FILE_OPENFAILED	Warning
8180	MSG_START_SYNC_WAITING_PERIOD	Informational
8181	MSG_RESUME_SYNC_WAITING_PERIOD	Informational
8182	MSG_SYNCHRO_INVALID_LINK	Warning
8183	MSG_SYNCHRO_IMPORTFAILURE_SECOND	Error
8184	MSG_SYNCHRO_PASSWORD_EXPIRED	Informational
8185	MSG_SYNCHRO_PASSWORD_SHORTAGE	Warning
8186	MSG_SYNCHRO_PASSWORD_SET	Informational
8187	MSG_SYNCHRO_PASSWORD_LSA_READ_ERROR	Error
8188	MSG_SYNCHRO_PASSWORD_LSA_WRITE_ERROR	Error
8189	MSG_Active Directory ConnectorI_START	Informational
8190	MSG_Active Directory ConnectorI_STOP	Informational
8191	MSG_Active Directory ConnectorI_BINDINGS	Informational
8192	MSG_Active Directory ConnectorI_LISTEN_FAIL	Error
8193	MSG_Active Directory ConnectorI_EPREG_FAIL	Error
8194	MSG_Active Directory ConnectorI_USEALL_FAIL	Error

Event	Symbolic Name	Severity
8195	MSG_Active Directory ConnectorI_REGAUTH_FAIL	Error
8196	MSG_Active Directory ConnectorI_REGIF_FAIL	Error
8197	MSG_SYNCHRO_GC_OPEN_FAIL	Informational
8198	MSG_SYNCHRO_GC_OPEN_SUCCESS	Informational
8199	MSG_SYNCHRO_GC_DEMOTED	Warning
8200	MSG_SYNCHRO_GC_UNSUPPORTED_AUTH	Warning
8201	MSG_SYNCHRO_DSBIND_FAILED	Warning
8202	MSG_Active Directory ConnectorI_START_FAIL	Error
8203	MSG_Active Directory ConnectorI_STOP_FAIL	Error
8204	MSG_SYNCHRO_STORE_DELETION_FAILED	Warning
8205	MSG_AMA_IMPORTRULES_ERROR	Error
8206	MSG_SYNCHRO_LSA_NO_PASSWORD	Error
8207	MSG_SYNCHRO_NO_DEL_FILE	Error
8208	MSG_SYNCHRO_FAILED_LOG_DISABLE	Error
8209	MSG_SYNCHRO_DISABLE_OBJECT	Informational
8210	MSG_SYNCHRO_DISABLE_FAIL	Error
8211	MSG_SYNCHRO_DISABLE_EX_OBJECT	Informational
8212	MSG_SYNCHRO_FAILED_LOG_EX_DISABLE	Error
8213	MSG_SYNCHRO_CANNOT_FIND_DC_FOR_DOMAIN	Error
8214	MSG_AD_SERVICE_NO_DOMAIN_SPECIFIED	Error
8215	MSG_AD_SERVICE_RUNNING_DOMAIN_CHECK_FSMO	Informational
8216	MSG_AD_SERVICE_COMPLETE_DOMAIN_CHECK_FSMO	Informational
8217	MSG_AD_SERVICE_ADDING_NEW_DOMAIN_SERVICE	Informational
8218	MSG_AD_SERVICE_SUCCESSFUL_NEW_DOMAIN_SERVICE	Informational
8219	MSG_AD_SERVICE_FAILED_NEW_DOMAIN_SERVICE	Error
8220	MSG_AD_SERVICE_DELETING_SERVICE	Informational
8221	MSG_AD_SERVICE_SUCCESSFUL_DELETE_SERVICE	Informational
8222	MSG_AD_SERVICE_FAILED_DELETE_SERVICE	Error
8223	MSG_SYNCHRO_CONFLICTING_ATTRIBUTE	Warning
8224	MSG_SYNCHRO_CONFLICTING_ATTRIBUTE_REPLICATION_FAILED	Error
8225	MSG_SYNCHRO_BEGIN_UNMERGED_CLEANUP	Informational

Event	Symbolic Name	Severity
8226	MSG_SYNCHRO_FINISH_UNMERGED_CLEANUP	Informational
8227	MSG_Active Directory ConnectorI_ACCESS_DENIED	Warning
8228	MSG_Active Directory ConnectorI_ACCESS_GRANTED	Informational
8229	MSG_ALDG_UNSUPPORTED_POLICY_GROUP	Error
8230	MSG_ALDG_EXTERNAL_PROVIDER_EXCEPTION	Error
8231	MSG_ALDG_EXPROV_PERM_FAILURE	Error
8232	MSG_ALDG_EXPROV_WRONG_VERSION	Error
8233	MSG_ALDG_EXPROV_CALLING_PROVIDER	Informational
8234	MSG_ALDG_EXPROV_ERROR	Error
8235	MSG_ALDG_EXPROV_PROVIDER_CALL_COMPLETE	Informational
8236	MSG_ALDG_EXPROV_MAX_EXCEPTION	Error
8237	MSG_ALDG_EXPROV_LOADED	Informational
8238	MSG_ALDG_EXPROV_UNLOADED	Informational
8239	MSG_ALDG_EXPROV_STARTED	Informational
8240	MSG_ALDG_EXPROV_STOPPED	Informational
8241	MSG_SYNCHRO_DELETEBRANCH	Informational
8242	MSG_SYNCHRO_NOCLEARTEXT	Error
8243	MSG_SYNCHRO_INVALID_LINK1	Warning
8244	MSG_SYNCHRO_INVALID_LINK2	Warning
8245	MSG_SYNCHRO_INVALID_LINK3	Warning
8246	MSG_SYNCHRO_INVALID_LINK4	Warning
8247	MSG_ALDG_EXPROV_RESTART_AFTER_FAIL	Error
8248	MSG_LDAP_NOTIFY_RETURN	Informational
8249	MSG_DUPLICATE_SERVER_TRACKING	Informational
8250	MSG_DSCONFIG_NT_API_ERROR_CODE	Error
8251	MSG_AL_DSCONFIG_READ_OBJECT_FAIL	Error
8252	MSG_AL_DSCONFIG_SEARCH_OBJECT_FAIL	Error
8253	MSG_AL_DSCONFIG_NO_NAMESPACES	Informational
8254	MSG_AL_DSCONFIG_NAMESPACEINFO	Informational
8255	MSG_AL_DSCONFIG_NEW_NAMESPACE	Informational
8256	MSG_AL_DSCONFIG_DELETED_NAMESPACE	Informational

Event	Symbolic Name	Severity
8257	MSG_AL_DSCONFIG_NAMESPACE_ERROR	Warning
8258	MSG_AL_SYNCHRO_REPLICATESTART	Informational
8259	MSG_AL_SYNCHRO_REPLICATEABORTED	Informational
8260	MSG_AL_DSCONFIG_OPENSESSION_FAIL	Error
8261	MSG_AL_DSCONFIG_SYNCNOW	Informational
8262	MSG_AL_SYNCHRO_BAD_CONFIG	Error
8263	MSG_AL_SYNCHRO_NO_MUTEX	Error
8264	MSG_AL_SYNCHRO_ERROR_EXCEPTION	Error
8265	MSG_CONFIG_MISSING_DXA_LOCAL_ADMIN_ATTR	Warning
8266	MSG_CONFIG_MISSING_REMOTE_CLIENT_ATTR	Error
8267	MSG_SYNCHRO_TIMEVETO_DELETION	Informational
8268	MSG_SYNCHRO_USERVETO_DELETION	Informational
8269	MSG_SYNCHRO_DELETE_ENTRY_SPECIAL	Informational
8270	MSG_LDAP_TRANSACTION_FAILED	Error
8271	MSG_SYNCHRO_REPLICATED_OBJECT	Informational
8272	MSG_SYNCHRO_NOT_REPLICATING_OBJECT	Warning
8273	MSG_SYNCHRO_NO_REPL_INTERFOREST	Warning
8274	MSG_SYNCHRO_NO_REPL_DELETED	Warning
8275	MSG_SYNCHRO_NO_REPL_READ_ONLY	Warning
8276	MSG_SYNCHRO_NO_REPL_NOT_BRIDGEHEAD	Warning
8277	MSG_SYNCHRO_NO_REPL_LATENCY	Warning
8278	MSG_SYNCHRO_NO_REPL_CONVERTDN	Warning
8279	MSG_SYNCHRO_NO_REPL_OBJECTCLASS	Warning
8280	MSG_SYNCHRO_NO_REPL_CONFLICT	Warning
8281	MSG_SYNCHRO_NO_MASTERACCOUNTSID	Warning
8282	MSG_SYNCHRO_NO_REPL_NO_REASON	Warning
8283	MSG_CONFIG_CANT_MODIFY_PT_OBJECT_IN_55	Warning
8284	MSG_ALDG_NO_ADDRESS_LIST	Warning
8285	MSG_SYNCHRO_NO_REPL_MB_TO_CONTACT	Warning
8286	MSG_SYNCHRO_NO_REPL_CR_TO_MB	Warning
8287	MSG_SYNCHRO_NO_REPL_INTERORG_NOTBRIDGE	Warning

Event	Symbolic Name	Severity
8288	MSG_SYNCHRO_NO_REPL_INTRAORG_DIFFORG	Warning
8289	MSG_SYNCHRO_NO_REPL_INTRAORG_NOINFO	Warning
8290	MSG_SYNCHRO_NO_REPL_INTRAORG_SAMEORG	Warning
8291	MSG_SYNCHRO_NO_REPL_WRITEABLE_SITE	Warning
8292	MSG_SYNCHRO_GENERIC_MAPPING_FAILURE	Warning
8293	MSG_SYNCHRO_SUCCESSFULLY_IMPORTED_OBJECT	Informational
8294	MSG_SYNCHRO_BAD_ATTR_DELETE	Warning
8295	MSG_LDAP_RENAME_ERROR	Error
8296	MSG_LDAP_RENAME	Informational
8297	MSG_CONFIG_PUT_SERVER_IN_ROUTING_GROUP	Informational
8298	MSG_CONFIG_MASTERED_OUT_OF_55	Warning
8299	MSG_CONFIG_NO_MAPI_PUBLIC_STORE	Warning
8300	MSG_CONFIG_HOME_SERVER_NOT_REPLICATED	Warning
8301	MSG_CONFIG_CANNOT_DETERMINE_CORRECT_RG	Warning
8302	MSG_CONFIG_NEW_FILE_VERSION_ON_TARGET	Warning
8303	MSG_CONFIG_SITE_PROTOCOLS_NOT_REPLICATED	Warning
8304	MSG_CONFIG_PROTOCOL_TYPE_NOT_REPLICATED	Warning
8305	MSG_CONFIG_MISSING_REQUIRED_ATTRIBUTES	Warning
8306	MSG_CONFIG_MISSING_TARGET_ENTRY_IN_AD	Warning
8307	MSG_CONFIG_DELETIONS_NOT_REPLICATED_TO_AD	Warning
8308	MSG_CONFIG_MASTERED_OUT_OF_ACTIVE_DIRECTORY_NO_TARGET_DN	Warning
8309	MSG_CONFIG_MASTERED_OUT_OF_ACTIVE_DIRECTORY	Warning
8310	MSG_CONFIG_PRIVATE_STORE_DELETION_NOT_REPLICATED	Warning
8311	MSG_CONFIG_NON_MAPI_PUBLIC_STORE_NOT_REPLICATED	Warning
8312	MSG_CONFIG_DELETIONS_NOT_REPLICATED_TO_55	Warning
8313	MSG_CONFIG_DONOT_REPLICATE_RGC_IN_SAME_AG	Warning
8314	MSG_CONFIG_DONOT_REPLICATE_GWART_FOR_OSMIUM_RID_SERVER	Warning
8315	MSG_ALDG_ENTRY_DACL_PROTECTED	Warning
8316	MSG_ALDG_CONTAINER_DACL_PROTECTED	Warning
8317	MSG_ALDG_RETRY_DACL_PROTECTED_FAILED	Warning

Table A-2 describes each Active Directory Connector event and provides an explanation and possible recovery action.

Table A-2 *Active Directory Connector Event Description and Explanations*

Event	Description	Explanation	User Action
1	Replication		
2	Account management		
3	Attribute mapping		
4	Service Controller		
5	LDAP Operations		
6	Address List		
8000	%1.		
8001	The service was started.		No user action is required.
8002	The service was stopped.		Usually, no user action is required. If the service was shutdown unexpectedly due to errors, start the service manually. If the service will not start, check the event log with Event Viewer for more details about related errors. If the service continually shuts down due to errors, contact Microsoft Product Support Services.
8003	The service is starting.		No user action is required.
8004	The service is stopping.		No user action is required.
8005	The service received an unsupported request.	The Service Control Manager has returned an invalid request.	If the problem persists, contact Microsoft Product Support Services.
8006	Opening LDAP session to directory %1 on port %2. %3		No user action is required.
8007	Closing LDAP session to directory %1. %2		No user action is required.
8008	Binding to directory %1 as user '%2'. %3		No user action is required.
8009	Binding to directory %1 as service account. %2		No user action is required.

Event	Description	Explanation	User Action
8010	Searching directory %1 at base '%2' using filter '%3'. %4		No user action is required.
8011	Searching directory %1 at base '%2' using filter '%3' and requesting attributes %4. %5		No user action is required.
8012	Search of directory %1 at base '%2' returned %3 objects. %4		No user action is required.
8013	Adding entry '%1' to directory %2. %3		No user action is required.
8014	Adding entry '%1' to directory %2. Attributes are %3. %4		No user action is required.
8015	Modifying entry '%1' on directory %2. %3		No user action is required.
8016	Modifying entry '%1' on directory %2. Modifications are %3. %4	This message is logged whenever Active Directory Connector modifies a directory entry.	No user action is required.
8017	Deleting entry '%1' on directory %2. %3	This message is logged when the Active Directory Connector deletes an object in the directory.	No user action is required.
8018	Abandoning request '%1' on directory %2. %3		No user action is required.
8019	Requesting LDAP notification for base '%1' on directory %2. %3		No user action is required.
8020	LDAP Search of directory %1 at base '%2' using filter '%3' was unsuccessful. Directory returned the LDAP error:[0x%4] %5. %6	If the accompanying Lightweight Directory Access Protocol (LDAP) message refers to LDAP_OTHER, the directory service may be out of disk space.	Check network connectivity. Verify the user name, password, and port address are correct, and try again. If the problem persists, verify that the remote Exchange server is configured to support LDAP.
8021	LDAP Add on directory %1 for entry '%2' was unsuccessful with error:[0x%3] %4. %5	If the accompanying Lightweight Directory Access Protocol (LDAP) message refers to LDAP_OTHER, the directory service may be out of disk space.	Check network connectivity. Verify the user name, password, and port address are correct, and try again. If the problem persists, contact Microsoft Product Support Services.

Event	Description	Explanation	User Action
8022	LDAP Modify on directory %1 for entry '%2' was unsuccessful with error:[0x%3] %4. %5	If the accompanying Lightweight Directory Access Protocol (LDAP) message refers to LDAP_OTHER, the directory service may be out of disk space.	Check network connectivity. Verify the user name, password, and port address are correct, and try again.
8023	LDAP Delete on directory %1 for entry '%2' was unsuccessful with error:[0x%3] %4. %5		Check network connectivity. Verify the user name, password, and port address are correct, and try again. If the problem persists, verify that the remote Exchange server is configured to support Lightweight Directory Access Protocol (LDAP).
8024	LDAP Search Initial Page on directory %1 at base '%2' with filter '%3' was unsuccessful. Directory returned the LDAP error:[0x%4] %5. %6	The Connection Agreement may be requesting too many objects based on the configuration setting of the target directory, or the target server may have failed.	Check network connectivity. Verify the user name, password, and port address are correct, and try again. If the problem persists, verify that the remote Exchange server is configured to support Lightweight Directory Access Protocol (LDAP).
8025	LDAP Get Next Page call on directory %1 for pagesize %2, was unsuccessful with error:[0x%3] %4. %5	The Connection Agreement may be requesting too many objects based on the configuration setting of the target directory, or the target server may have failed.	Check network connectivity. Verify the user name, password, and port address are correct, and try again. If the problem persists, verify that the remote Exchange server is configured to support Lightweight Directory Access Protocol (LDAP).
8026	LDAP Bind was unsuccessful on directory %1 for distinguished name '%2'. Directory returned error:[0x%3] %4. %5	Lightweight Directory Access Protocol (LDAP) allows you to query and manage directory information using a TCP/IP connection.	Check network connectivity. Verify the user name, password, and port address are correct, and try again. If the problem persists, verify that the remote Exchange server is configured to support LDAP.
8027	The LDAP Bind to the global catalog on %1 with credential '%2' was unsuccessful. The Directory returned error:[0x%3] %4. %5		Either promote to a Global Catalog the Active Directory Server that the Connection Agreement points to, or modify the Connection Agreement to point to a Global Catalog.

Event	Description	Explanation	User Action
8028	LDAP ModifyRDN on directory %1 for entry '%2' was unsuccessful with error:[0x%3] %4. %5	If the accompanying Lightweight Directory Access Protocol (LDAP) message refers to LDAP_OTHER, the directory service may be out of disk space.	Check network connectivity. Verify the user name, password, and port address are correct, and try again.
8029	LDAP Referral on directory %1 for entry '%2' was unsuccessful with error:[0x%3] %4. %5		
8030	LDAP Extended result on directory %1 for entry '%2' was unsuccessful with error:[0x%3] %4. %5		No user action is required.
8031	Unable to open LDAP session on directory '%1' using port number %2. Directory returned the LDAP error:[0x%3] %4. %5	Lightweight Directory Access Protocol (LDAP) allows you to query and manage directory information using a TCP/IP connection.	Check network connectivity. Verify the user name, password, and port address are correct, and try again. If the problem persists, verify that the remote Exchange server is configured to support LDAP.
8032	LDAP Session result on directory %1 for entry '%2' was unsuccessful with error:[0x%3] %4. %5		
8033	LDAP search result on directory %1 for entry '%2' was unsuccessful with error:[0x%3] %4. %5	If the accompanying Lightweight Directory Access Protocol (LDAP) message refers to LDAP_OTHER, the directory service may be out of disk space.	Check network connectivity. Verify the user name, password, and port address are correct, and try again.
8034	LDAP compare result on directory %1 for entry '%2' was unsuccessful with error:[0x%3] %4. %5		
8035	Successfully modified entry '%1' on directory %2. %3		No user action is required.
8036	Searching EXPORT directory on directory '%1' for 'deleted' entries. Search base is: %2, filter is: %3. %4		No user action is required.
8037	Successfully deleted entry '%1' on directory '%2'. %3		No user action is required.

Event	Description	Explanation	User Action
8038	Successfully added new entry '%1' on directory '%2'. %3		No user action is required.
8039	Completed the transaction... %1 %2		No user action is required.
8040	Server '%1' could not generate e-mail addresses for entry '%2'. Was unsuccessful with error:[0x%3] %4. %5	Active Directory Connector (Active Directory Connector) could not contact the System Attendant service on the Exchange server.	Make sure that the Exchange server domain has trust with the Windows 2000 computer domain, and that the Exchange server's service account shares the same domain as the Windows 2000 computer.
8041	Server '%1' could not generate some e-mail addresses for entry '%2'. Was unsuccessful for type(s): %3. %4	A unique e-mail address could not be generated based on the entry name. The Exchange 5.5 server service account may be in a different domain than the Windows 2000 server.	In the Add-ins or E-Mail Address Generator container, select the connector or address generator being accessed. On the General tab, verify that the specified DLL file is not corrupted and exists in \Exchsrvr\Add-ins or \Exchsrvr\Address in the proper directory on the server.
8042	Searching EXPORT directory on directory '%1' for new or changed entries. Search base is: %2, filter is: %3. %4		No user action is required.
8043	Directory search requested attributes: %1. %2		No user action is required.
8044	Search of EXPORT directory returned %1 entries: %2. %3		No user action is required.
8045	CImportDir::UpdateEntry, Destination entry marked as deleted, Adding new entry: (Server:%1, Entry distinguished name:%2). %3		No user action is required.
8046	Update existing entry '%2' on directory '%1'. %3		No user action is required.
8047	%1 directory entries were deleted since last replication: %2. %3		No user action is required.
8048	Using 'Non-Tombstone' deletion method, the following entries will be deleted: %1. %2		No user action is required.
8049	Using 'Tombstone' deletion method, the following entries will be deleted: %1. %2		No user action is required.

Event	Description	Explanation	User Action
8050	Entry '%1' does not exist in IMPORT directory. %2		No user action is required.
8051	Entry '%1' already exists in IMPORT directory. %2		No user action is required.
8052	No directory entries were deleted since last replication. %1		No user action is required.
8053	Attribute values for entry '%1' in IMPORT Directory: %2. %3		No user action is required.
8054	LDAP Unbind on directory %1 was unsuccessful. Directory returned error:[0x%2] %3. %4	If the accompanying LDAP message refers to LDAP_OTHER, the directory service may be out of disk space.	Check network connectivity. Verify the user name, password, and port address are correct, and try again. If the problem persists, verify that the remote Exchange server is configured to support LDAP.
8055	Could not read Replication Agent distinguished name from registry. Cannot begin replication. %1		
8056	Starting replication for Connection Agreement '%1'.		No user action is required.
8057	Finished replication for Connection Agreement '%1'.		No user action is required.
8058	Stopped replication for Connection Agreement '%1'.	Synchronization was canceled.	No user action is required.
8059	Replicating from remote directory '%1' to local directory '%2'. %3		No user action is required.
8060	Replicating from local directory '%1' to remote directory '%2'. %3		No user action is required.
8061	Reading configuration information on directory '%1' using entry '%2'. %3		No user action is required.
8062	Could not open LDAP session to directory '%1' using local service credentials. Cannot access Connection Agreement configuration information. Make sure the server '%1' is running. %2	Active Directory Connector could not gain access to Windows 2000 domain controller.	Make sure the Active Directory Connector service account has permissions to read its configuration information from the Active Directory.

Event	Description	Explanation	User Action
8063	Could not read the root entry on directory '%1'. Cannot access configuration information. %2		Verify network connectivity. Attempt to read attributes on the directory. Make sure the Active Directory Connector service account has permissions to read its configuration information from the Active Directory.
8064	Could not read entry '%1' on directory %2. Cannot access Connection Agreement information. Make sure that service was installed properly. %3	Active Directory Connector could not find its service object.	Make sure the Active Directory Connector service account has permissions to read its configuration information from the Active Directory.
8065	Could not search under entry '%1' on directory %2. Cannot access Connection Agreement information. %3	Active Directory Connector could not find the Connection Agreements Container or does not have permissions to read the container.	Make sure the Active Directory Connector service account has permissions to read its configuration information from the Active Directory.
8066	Object '%1' on directory %2 has no Connection Agreements defined.		No user action is required.
8067	Object '%1' on directory %2 has the following Connection Agreements defined: %3		No user action is required.
8068	Found new or changed Connection Agreement '%1' on directory %2.		No user action is required.
8069	Connection Agreement '%1' was deleted or had its owning service changed on directory %2. Shutting down thread for this Connection Agreement.		No user action is required.
8070	The Connection Agreement '%1' on directory %2 could not be loaded due to an error. Make sure that the Connection Agreement is configured properly.	There may be a network problem, or you may not have the appropriate permissions to perform this operation, or the Connection Agreement may be configured incorrectly.	Check network connectivity and the Connection Agreement configuration. If the Active Directory Connector service account does not have the appropriate permissions, ask someone with administrative permissions to modify them. If the problem persists, restart the Active Directory Connector service.

Event	Description	Explanation	User Action
8071	Setting Remote last USN value to: %1. %2	The Unique Synchronization Number (USN) is monotonically increasing value; after every directory update the current USN is stamped on the modified object (by the directory) and then the USN is incremented.	This message requires not action and is informational only.
8072	Setting Local last USN value to: %1. %2		No user action is required.
8073	Could not add Windows 2000 user account, the computer name supplied is invalid. %1	The computer name has been entered in error.	Enter a valid server name and try again.
8074	Added Windows 2000 user %1 on local computer.		No user action is required.
8075	Added Windows 2000 user %1 on computer %2. %3		No user action is required.
8076	Could not retrieve security identifier(SID) for given account. %1	A user may no longer exist. Security identifiers (SIDs) are unique numbers that identify users who are logged on to the Windows 2000 security system. A security ID can identify an individual user or a group of users.	Verify this user exists on this domain. If the problem persists, create the Windows 2000 user account or delete the mailbox from the remote server.
8077	Could not add Windows 2000 user %1 on local computer. %2	Data may have been entered in error.	The account specified must have Change access to the Exchange directory. Verify the connection agreement account being used has the appropriate permissions to perform this task.
8078	Could not add Windows 2000 user %1 on computer %2. %3	Data may have been entered in error.	Verify the connection account has the appropriate permissions to perform this task. The account specified must have Change access to the Exchange directory.
8079	Could not delete Windows 2000 user account, invalid security identifier (SID). %1	The account may have been deleted and re-created. This action creates an account with the same name but a different security identifier (SID), which Windows 2000 views as a different account.	Run the User Manager program to manually delete the account.

Event	Description	Explanation	User Action
8080	Deleted Windows 2000 user %1 on local computer. %2		No user action is required.
8081	Deleted Windows 2000 user %1 on computer %2. %3		No user action is required.
8082	Could not delete Windows 2000 user %1 on local computer. %2		
8083	Could not delete Windows 2000 user %1 on computer %2. %3		Verify the connection account has the appropriate permissions to perform this task and that the Windows 2000 user exists.
8084	Could not load mapping table. %1		Verify that the Active Directory Connector account has permission to read the Connection Agreements and all of their attributes. If so, restart your computer and try again. If you still get this message, create a new Connection Agreement.
8085	Started attribute mapping agent. %1	As part of the replication process, a mapping table is generated.	No user action is required.
8086	Stopped attribute mapping agent. %1		No user action is required.
8087	Mapped local attribute '%1' to remote attribute '%3'. Local attribute value: %2, Remote attribute value: %4. %5		No user action is required.
8088	Mapped local attribute '%1' to remote attribute '%2'. %3		No user action is required.
8089	Mapped remote attribute '%1' to local attribute '%3'. Remote attribute value: %2, Local attribute value: %4. %5		No user action is required.
8090	Mapped remote attribute '%1' to local attribute '%2'. %3		No user action is required.
8091	Mapped remote object '%1' to local object '%2'. %3		No user action is required.
8092	Mapped local object '%1' to remote object '%2'. %3		No user action is required.

Event	Description	Explanation	User Action
8093	Could not find object: %1. %2	The object does not exist.	
8094	Could not find destination object: %1. %2		
8095	Object has no attributes, object is: %1, destination object is: %2. %3	The attribute tree is empty or all attributes in the attribute map are turned off.	Turn on all attributes in the attribute map, if they are turned off.
8096	File Exception %1, occurred handling attribute mapping file: %2. %3		
8097	Could not create new attribute.	The Connection Agreement attribute map is corrupted.	Create a new Connection Agreement. If the problem persists, uninstall and then reinstall MSActive Directory Connector (Microsoft Active Directory Server).
8098	Could not create new object.	The Connection Agreement attribute map is corrupted.	Create a new Connection Agreement. If the problem persists, uninstall and then reinstall MSActive Directory Connector (Microsoft Active Directory Connector).
8099	Cannot find object class, local tree is empty. %1		If the problem persists, create a new Connection Agreement or try to reinstall the Active Directory Connector.
8100	No mapping configured for object: %1		
8101	Cannot find object class, remote tree is empty. %1		If the problem persists, create a new Connection Agreement or try to reinstall the Active Directory Connector.
8102	No mapping configured for attribute: %1	Attributes are a list of mappings between NT and Exchange 5.5 object attributes.	No user action is required. Currently there is no way to configure the attributes to be replicated. In the future you will be able to modify the list of attributes on an object to be synchronized through the Synchronization Agreement Properties page.
8103	The service was installed successfully.		No user action is required.
8104	The service '%1' was removed successfully.		No user action is required.

Event	Description	Explanation	User Action
8105	The service '%1' could not be removed.	This message is logged when an uninstall of the Active Directory Connector fails. The service account may not have the appropriate permissions to perform this task.	Verify that the service account has administrative privilege on the specified computer.
8106	The control handler could not be installed.		Note that the service account has administrative privilege on the specified computer. Check the event log with Event Viewer for more details about related errors.
8107	Could not create Windows 2000 Service object.	Setup has failed. This message is the last in a series of errors which occurred during setup.	Review all related event message and try again. Note that the service account has administrative privilege on the specified computer.
8108	The initialization process failed.		Review the Event Viewer for related entries to determine the cause of this failure.
8109	Could not import the entry '%1' into the directory server '%2' in the first attempt. %3	There may be a network problem or the import failed for another reason. The Active Directory Connector will try once more to import.	Check the event log for additional information. Check network connectivity.
8110	Setting remote last update time value to: %1	As a part of the directory service configuration, the last update time is written to the header.	This message requires no action and is informational only.
8111	Setting local last update time value to: %1	As a part of the directory service configuration, the last update time is written to the header.	This message requires no action and is informational only.
8112	The authentication package value (%1) is not supported on server %2. Check the Connections tab on the Connection Agreement. %3	The type of authentication being used is not supported on the specified server. The credentials cannot be processed.	On the Connection tab of the Synchronization Agreement property page, modify the authentication options for logging onto the Windows 2000 server. Possible options are: Basic, Basic using SSL, NTLM, and NTLM using SSL. Verify the directory service on the remote server is running. Check the port number. Then try again.

Event	Description	Explanation	User Action
8113	The service could not be initialized because the necessary file %1 could not be found. Make sure that the operating system was installed properly.	Active Directory Connector could not find the file, or the DllMain entry point returned an error upon loading the DLL.	Check the file version and verify that its location is in your executable path.
8114	The service could not be initialized because the necessary entry point '%1' could not be found in the file %2. Make sure that the operating system was installed properly.	Active Directory Connector could not find the file or the entry point within the file to initialize this service.	Check the file version and verify that its location is in your executable path.
8115	The Win32 API call '%1' returned an error. The service could not be initialized. Make sure that the operating system was installed properly.	This is an operating system level error.	Perform the user action specified in the message.
8116	The Connection Agreement '%1' has been signaled to start replication immediately.		No user action is required.
8117	Could not locate the import container %1. Make sure that the configured container exists, or that the account in the Connection Agreement has permissions to access the container. Replication stopped for this Connection Agreement. %2		Perform the user action specified in the message.
8118	Could not locate the export container %1. Make sure that the configured container exists, or that the account in the Connection Agreement has permissions to access the container. Replication stopped for this Connection Agreement. %2		Perform the user action specified in the message.

Event	Description	Explanation	User Action
8119	The schema map in the Connection Agreement '%1' contains an invalid attribute: %2	The schema is missing an attribute which the Active Directory Connector expects to find.	No user action is required. If the problem persists, contact Microsoft Product Support Services.
8120	Syntax conversion from syntax type %1 to syntax type %2 is not allowed. %3	The syntax of an attribute cannot be converted.	Contact Microsoft Product Support Services.
8121	The entry with distinguished name '%1' will not be written to the directory because it is missing the following mandatory attributes: '%2'. %3		Add the required attributes, and ensure that the attributes are enabled in the schema map. Verify that Active Directory Connector has permissions to read the attributes from the source directory.
8122	The entry with distinguished name '%1' will not be written to the directory because it has invalid attributes: '%2'. %3	Active Directory Connector could not write the proposed attributes to the directory.	Disable the invalid attributes in the schema map.
8123	The entry with distinguished name '%1' will not be written to the directory because it is trying to delete the mandatory attributes: '%2'. %3	Active Directory Connector cannot remove the attribute specified because the target directory requires that the attribute exist .	No user action is required.
8124	Processing of the Connection Agreement '%1' has been stopped due to an invalid configuration. Check the event log for more information.	This message follows a previous, related message. That message will usually indicate a missing import or export container, or that the Connection Agreement was created or modified by a different version of Active Directory Connector.	Correct the information on the Connection Agreement.
8125	New address list '%1' found with rule '%2'. %3		No user action is required.
8126	Address list '%1' modified with rule '%2'. %3		No user action is required.
8127	Address List '%1' deleted. %2		No user action is required.
8128	Found change to directory object '%1'. Evaluating address list rules. %2		No user action is required.

Event	Description	Explanation	User Action
8129	Evaluating directory object '%1' against address list '%2' rule '%3'. %4		No user action is required.
8130	'%1' added to '%2'. %3		No user action is required.
8131	'%1' removed from '%2'. %3		No user action is required.
8132	Received request to stop calculations on '%1'. %2		No user action is required.
8133	Calculations complete on '%1'. %2		No user action is required.
8134	Queuing request to process '%1'. %2		No user action is required.
8135	No rule set on '%1', skipping. %2		No user action is required.
8136	'%1'. %2		
8137	This version of Active Directory Connector cannot run the Connection Agreement '%1'. Either upgrade Active Directory Connector on this server, or change the Active Directory Connector service on the General tab to a different server.		Make sure that the Connection Agreement was created using the Windows 2000 version of Active Directory Connector. Active Directory Connector cannot run Connection Agreements created by other versions of Active Directory Connector.
8138	The server '%1' is not available. Check for network problems and make sure that the server is running. All directory updates to or from the server can not be replicated unless the server is available. %2		Perform the user action specified in the message.
8139	The target object '%1' was modified after the source object '%2' Consequently, the following set of updates will not be applied to the target object. If this warning persists, make sure that the time is correctly set on both the source and target servers. %3 %4	The service will not replicate changes from the source object to the target object if the target object has been modified more recently than the source object.	Ensure that the clocks on the source and target servers are synchronized.

Event	Description	Explanation	User Action
8140	Delayed processing of group/distribution list: '%1' %2	To replicate objects as quickly as possible, distribution lists and groups are delayed until after users, mailboxes, custom recipients, and contacts have been replicated.	No user action is required.
8141	The operating system has run out of resources. The Connection Agreement will shut down and then restart. If this problem persists, try restarting the service or the server.	Other applications running on the system share resources. This is a Windows-level error that indicates a shortage of resources for all applications.	Perform the user action specified in the message. Reduce the load on resources by restricting any other unnecessary applications from running on the server.
8142	The service threw an unexpected exception.		Restart the service. Verify that there is enough disk space and memory. If the problem persists, contact Microsoft Product Support Services.
8143	The Connection Agreement %1 threw an unexpected exception.		Review related event logs to determine the appropriate action.
8144	The service threw an out of memory exception.		Increase the swap file size, close some other applications, or restart the service. If the problem persists, contact Microsoft Product Support Services.
8145	Exception %1 was raised at address %2.		Restart the service. Check for sufficient disk space and memory. Check that the target directory and source directories are running. If the problem persists, contact Microsoft Product Support Services.
8146	An operation on server '%1' returned [0x%2] %3. The Connection Agreement %4 stopped.		Restart the service. Check for sufficient disk space and memory. Check that the target directory and source directories are running. If the problem persists, contact Microsoft Product Support Services.
8147	Changing the relative distinguished name of entry '%1' to '%2' on directory %3. %4		No user action is required.

Event	Description	Explanation	User Action
8148	Synchronization summary for Connection Agreement '%1' —- %n [Destination Server: %2] %n [Start Time: %3] %n [End Time: %4] %n [Number of entries processed successfully: %5] %n [Number of adds: %6, Number of modifications: %7] %n [Number of entries failed: %8]		No user action is required.
8149	The service has been disabled.		No user action is required.
8150	Cannot start service threads. Retry after 1 minute.		Perform the user action specified in the message.
8151	Cannot read service configuration. Retry after 1 minute.		Perform the user action specified in the message.
8152	No services currently configured for server '%1'.		No user action is required.
8153	Function %1[%2][#%3] had an unrecoverable error.		Contact Microsoft Product Support Services.
8154	Function %1[%2][#%3] had an unrecoverable failure on restart attempt.		Contact Microsoft Product Support Services.
8155	Function %1[%2][#%3] terminated with code: %4.		No user action is required.
8156	Function %1[%2][#%3] starting.		No user action is required.
8157	Thread #%1: waiting for next running schedule. %2		No user action is required.
8158	Thread #%1: running service. %2		No user action is required.
8159	Thread #%1: checking for running schedule. %2		No user action is required.
8160	No change required for %1. %2		No user action is required.
8161	Exception occurred while processing '%1'.		Contact Microsoft Product Support Services.
8162	Thread #%1: waiting for next Address List transaction. %2		No user action is required.

Event	Description	Explanation	User Action
8163	Thread #%1: received next Address List Transaction. %2		No user action is required.
8164	Thread #%1: shutting down automatically since idle. %2		No user action is required.
8165	Exception occurred while processing Address List '%1' against user/group: '%2'.		Contact Microsoft Product Support Services.
8166	Could not modify Address List '%1' for user/group: '%2'. %3		Review the event logs. No user action is required.
8167	Modified user/group: '%1'. %2		No user action is required.
8168	Could not modify user/group: '%1'. %2		Review the event logs to determine the cause of the failure of the modification. No user action is required.
8169	Retrieved all user/group changes under: '%1'. %2		No user action is required.
8170	Retrieved all address list changes under: '%1'. %2		No user action is required.
8171	Address List change calculation of '%1' skipped since we are doing full recalculation of users. %2		No user action is required.
8172	Could not initialize scheduled change event cycle, will retry later. %1		Contact Microsoft Product Support Services.
8173	Could not commit changes to service '%1'.	This message usually indicates a problem accessing Active Directory (AD). Or, the service could be down or busy. It may also indicate that the Address List service is either down or busy.	Verify that Active Directory is functioning properly. The system will automatically retry.
8174	Processing change to Address List '%1'. %2		No user action is required.
8175	Processing change to user/group '%1'. %2		No user action is required.
8176	Received request to shut down service '%1'.		No user action is required.

Event	Description	Explanation	User Action
8177	Could not add Windows 2000 user %1 on the primary domain controller %2, due to a logon failure. %3	The logon could fail if the Connection Agreement had permissions to administrate Exchange, but not the Windows 2000 domain. It could also fail if the domain controller was down.	Verify that the user name and password are correct and that they have the required permissions, and try again.
8178	The directory schema on server '%1' is missing the following attribute types required for Connection Agreement '%2' to work properly: '%3'. Make sure that the directory service on '%4' was restarted after the Connection Agreement was created. If it was, either the Connection Agreement is not configured properly or the directory service on the server was re-installed after the Connection Agreement was setup. Please re-create the Connection Agreement.		Perform the user action specified in the message.
8179	Unable to create or open the transaction file '%1' for writing a deleted entry. If the file exists, make sure that it's writable by the service, else make sure that the parent directory is writable and that the disk is not full. %2		The transaction file is in the same directory that Active Directory Connector (Active Directory Connector) is installed in. User account and passwords are shown on the Connection tab in the Connection Agreement Properties dialog box. Make sure that these credentials allow writing, the file is writable, and the disk is not full.
8180	The Connection Agreement '%1' has paused the replication after %2 seconds. The replication will resume in %3 seconds.		No user action is required.
8181	The Connection Agreement '%1' is resuming its replication.		No user action is required.

Event	Description	Explanation	User Action
8182	The service was unable to add the member '%1' to the group '%2'. This is because the group is a Universal Distribution group and it is not allowed to have Domain Local groups as members. %3	By default, Active Directory Connector creates universal groups. Universal groups can have any object as a member. However, the Windows 2000 administrator can choose to create a global group. Global groups cannot have universal groups or domain local groups as members. Exchange does not have this restriction. So, if the Windows 2000 global group is to replicate to Exchange, and the Exchange administrator adds a unversal group to the global group, then the change cannot replicate back to Windows 2000.	Consider alternative architectures where this grouping is not necessary.
8183	Could not import the entry '%1' into the directory server '%2' in the second attempt. %3	If an imported entry fails, Active Directory Connector will retry once. This message is logged after the second attempt fails.	Inspect the user entry that failed for any values that might prohibit its entry, for instance, an e-mail address that would produce a conflict.
8184	The password for the credential %1 has expired after %2 days without use.		Update the password on the Connection Agreement.
8185	The following credentials had their password removed because of shortage in the LSA Private Store. If you have a Connection Agreement that still using one of this passwords go to the Connection Agreement Property and reset the password. %1		Perform the user action specified in the message.
8186	The password for the credential %1 was set successfully. %2		No user action is required.
8187	The following error has occurred when trying to read a password from the LSA Private Store. Error number: %1. Description: '%2'. %3	Active Directory Connector could not read the credential information. This message resulted from a Windows 2000 error.	Review any related Windows 2000 entries in the event log for further information.

Event	Description	Explanation	User Action
8188	The following error has occurred when trying to write a password to the LSA Private Store. Error number: %1. Description: '%2'. %3	Active Directory Connector could not read the credential information. This message resulted from a Windows 2000 error.	Review any related Windows 2000 entries in the event log for further information.
8189	Active Directory Connector RPC Interface started successfully.	Active Directory Connector successfully established an RPC connection.	No user action is required.
8190	Active Directory Connector RPC Interface stopped successfully.	Active Directory Connector Remote Procedure Call Interface allows server credential information to be stored securely.	No user action is required.
8191	Active Directory Connector RPC Interface is available on the following RPC endpoints: %1	Active Directory Connector Remote Procedure Call Interface allows server credential information to be stored securely.	No user action is required.
8192	Active Directory Connector RPC Interface failed when trying to listen for RPC requests. Services handled by this interface will not be available. Error from RPC subsystem: %1.	Some services will still be available without an RPC connection. Services that are not available without RPC include password and credential modification.	This may be caused by a shortage of Windows resources or by corruption of resources used by Active Directory Connector. Restart Active Directory Connector. If this fails, reboot the computer.
8193	Active Directory Connector RPC Interface failed when trying to register endpoints for RPC requests. Services offered by this interface will not be available. Error from RPC subsystem: %1.	Some services will still be available without an RPC connection while others are not. Services that are not available without RPC include the ability to modify Connection Agreement passwords and credentials. This may be caused by a shortage of Windows resources or by corruption of resources used by Active Directory Connector.	Try restarting Active Directory Connector. If this fails, try restarting the computer.

Event	Description	Explanation	User Action
8194	Active Directory Connector RPC Interface failed when trying to use all network transports to accept RPC requests. RPC interfaces might not be available on all network transports. Error from RPC subsystem: %1.	Some services will still be available without an RPC connection while others are not. Services that are not available without RPC include the ability to modify Connection Agreement passwords and credentials.	Verify network connectivity and restart Active Directory Connector. If this fails, restart the computer.
8195	Active Directory Connector RPC Interface failed when trying to register which authentication methods it will accept. RPC requests may be incorrectly denied even though they are authenticated properly to the server. Error from RPC subsystem: %1.	Some services will still be available without an RPC connection. Services that are not available without RPC include password and credential modification.	This may be caused by a shortage of Windows resources or by corruption of resources used by Active Directory Connector. Restart Active Directory Connector. If this fails, reboot the computer.
8196	Active Directory Connector RPC Interface failed when trying to register itself with the endpoint mapper. This RPC interface will not be available. Error from RPC subsystem: %1.	Some services will still be available without an RPC connection. Services that are not available without RPC include password and credential modification. This may be caused by a shortage of Windows resources or by corruption of resources used by Active Directory Connector.	Restart Active Directory Connector. If this fails, restart the computer.
8197	Could not open Global Catalog port on server '%1'. Attempting to find alternate Global Catalog. %2	This occurs when a Connection Agreement is made with a server that is not a Global Catalog (GC). Each time the Active Directory Connector (Active Directory Connector) encounters a server that is not a GC, it logs this event.	Verify that the Connection Agreement points to a GC server and that there is a GC in the Active Directory site to which this server belongs.
8198	Opened Global Catalog port on server '%1'. %2		No user action is required.

Event	Description	Explanation	User Action
8199	The service could not find an active Global Catalog for the domain that contains server '%1'. It will not be able to find objects outside of the domain. %2	Global Catalogs (GC) have been turned off, or the GC server may be down. Some objects will not be available for synchronization or replication until this is corrected.	Verify that the Global Catalog (GC) server is running and that GC's are turned on.
8200	The service could not search for a Global Catalog Domain Controller on server %1 because the Windows 2000 interface for this information does not support the "Basic (Clear Text)" method. Change the Authentication method for the Windows 2000 server on the Connection Agreement. %2		Perform the user action specified in the message.
8201	The service could not bind to server %1. Please check the credentials supplied. %2	While searching for a Global Catalog, Active Directory Connector found a domain controller to which it could not bind due to credential problems.	Verify that the credentials on the Connection Agreement have sufficient permissions to access replication information on the server.
8202	Active Directory Connector RPC Interface failed to start.	This message may be preceded by other related messages. Some services will still be available without an RPC connection. Services that are not available without RPC include password and credential modification. This may be caused by a shortage of Windows resources or by corruption of resources used by Active Directory Connector	Restart Active Directory Connector. If this fails, restart the computer.
8203	Active Directory Connector RPC Interface failed to stop.		Restart the server. If the problem persists, contact Microsoft Product Support Services.

Event	Description	Explanation	User Action
8204	When deleting the Store Mailbox from '%1' on server '%2' the operation failed with the following error code: %3. %4	An attempt to delete the mailbox store failed.	Verify that the mailbox store service is running. If the service is running, manually delete the mailbox store.
8205	Error loading import rules. %1		
8206	Couldn't find the password for the credential '%1' in the LSA Private Data. If this problem persist after 15 minutes, try to reset the password in the Connection Agreement properties. %2		Perform the user action specified in the message.
8207	Source object '%1' was deleted. No file exists for recording deleted objects, so target object '%2' will not be affected. Make sure there is enough disk space and this Connection Agreement has permission to write to the path where log files are stored. %3	The Active Directory Connector requires more disk space to write the log file.	Perform the user action specified in the message.
8208	Unable to disable target object '%1' because an error occurred while adding the object to disable log file '%2'. Make sure there is enough disk space and this Connection Agreement has permission to write to the log file. %3		Perform the user action specified in the message.
8209	Successfully disabled target object '%1' and added the object to deletion log file '%2' because the source object '%3' was deleted. %4		No user action is required.
8210	Source object '%1' was deleted. Attempt to disable target object '%2' failed. %3		Check the event log for related errors.

Event	Description	Explanation	User Action
8211	Source object '%1' was deleted. This Connection Agreement is configured to not replicate deletions, so target object '%2' will not be deleted. The target object has been successfully added to deletion log file '%3'. %4		Manually delete the target object.
8212	Source object '%1' was deleted. An error occurred while adding target object '%2' to disable log file '%3'. Make sure there is enough disk space and this Connection Agreement has permission to write to the log file. %4		Perform the user action specified in the message.
8213	Couldn't find an accessible writable domain controller for domain '%1'. %2		Use System Manager to verify that the domain name on the Recipient Update Service is correct.
8214	Invalid domain name specified for service '%1', cannot process changes %2		Use System Manager to verify that the domain name on the Recipient Update Service is correct.
8215	Running Domain Change FSMO Check on '%1' %2		No user action is required.
8216	Completed Domain Change FSMO Check on '%1', '%2' new domain services created, '%3' domain services deleted %4		No user action is required.
8217	Adding new domain service for domain: '%1' as '%2' %3		No user action is required.
8218	Successfully added new domain service for domain: '%1' %2		No user action is required.
8219	Failed to add new domain service for domain: '%1' %2		Contact PSS.
8220	Deleting domain service: '%1' %2		No user action is required.
8221	Successfully deleted domain service: '%1' %2		No user action is required.

Event	Description	Explanation	User Action
8222	Failed to delete domain service: '%1' %2		Contact PSS.
8223	The service cannot add the mail address %1 to %2 because this address is already assigned to %3 %4		Assign the object a different address or change the address of the other object using the address.
8224	The service cannot replicate %1 because too many of its attributes conflict with other objects. %2		
8225	Searching for unresolved references in naming context '%1'. This Connection Agreement will resolve all references to existing objects. %2		No user action is required.
8226	Completed search for unresolved references in naming context '%1'. %2		No user action is required.
8227	A client did not have the correct rights to access the Active Directory Connector password interface.		Verify that the use is authorized to access the Active Directory Connector password interface. If so, modify the user's permissions.
8228	A client has successfully connected to the Active Directory Connector password interface.		No user action is required.
8229	Unsupported or unloadable policy group: '%1'. %2		Contact Microsoft Product Support Services.
8230	Exception occurred while calling policy group provider for '%1':'%2'. %3		Contact Microsoft Product Support Services.
8231	Permanent failure reported by policy group provider for '%1':'%2', error=%3. Taking provider offline. %4		Contact Microsoft Product Support Services.
8232	Invalid policy group provider version for '%1':'%2'. Taking provider offline. %3		Contact Microsoft Product Support Services.

Event	Description	Explanation	User Action
8233	Calling policy group provider '%1':'%2':'%3'. %4		No user action is required.
8234	Error reported by policy group provider '%1':'%2', error=%3. %4		Contact Microsoft Product Support Services.
8235	Completed call to policy group provider '%1':'%2':'%3'. %4		No user action is required.
8236	Maximum allowed exceptions occurred while calling policy group provider for '%1':'%2'. Taking provider offline. %3		Contact Microsoft Product Support Services.
8237	Loaded policy group provider for '%1':'%2'. %3		No user action is required.
8238	Unloaded policy group provider for '%1':'%2'. %3		No user action is required.
8239	Started policy group provider for '%1':'%2'. %3		No user action is required.
8240	Stopped policy group provider for '%1':'%2'. %3		No user action is required.
8241	The entry '%1' and all corresponding child entries (if any) have been deleted successfully from the directory server '%2'. %3		No user action is required.
8242	The authentication type Clear Text is not supported by this service. Please use the Active Directory Connector Management tool to change the authentication type for this Connection Agreement. %1	Active Directory Connector does not support LDAP Clear Text authentication method.	Change Connection Agreement to authenticate using another method.
8243	Active Directory Connector was unable to add the member '%1' to the group '%2'. This is because the group is a Domain Local Security group and it is not allowed to have others Domain Local groups as members. %3		Change the group type from a domain local security group to domain global or universal. For more information on security groups, see the Windows 2000 online documentation.

Event	Description	Explanation	User Action
8244	Active Directory Connector was unable to add the member '%1' to the group '%2'. This is because the group is a Global Security group and it is not allowed to have others groups as members. %3		Change the group type from a global security group to a universal security group. For more information on security groups, see the Windows 2000 online documentation.
8245	Active Directory Connector was unable to add the member '%1' to the group '%2'. This is because the group is a Global Distribution group and it is not allowed to have Domain Local groups or Universal groups as members. %3		Change the group type from a global security group to a universal security group. For more information on security groups, see the Windows 2000 online documentation.
8246	Active Directory Connector was unable to add the member '%1' to the group '%2'. This is because the group is a Universal Distribution group and it is not allowed to have Domain Local groups as members. %3		Change the group type from a universal security group to a global security group. For more information on security groups, see the Windows 2000 online documentation.
8247	Address List Service is restarting this instance because policy group provider '%1':'%2' returned a fatal error. %3		Contact Microsoft Product Support Services.
8248	LDAP notification search returned no results. Return code [0x%1] %2. %3	A problem occurred while reading changes to connection agreements.	Check the status of the domain control server.
8249	%1 = %2		
8250	The Win32 API call '%1' returned error code [0x%2] %3. The service could not be initialized. Make sure that the operating system was installed properly.		Perform the user action specified in the message.
8251	Could not read entry '%1' on directory %2. Cannot access Address List information. Make sure that service was installed properly. %3	A permissions problem may have occurred.	Verify that the Address List service has permissions to read the object.

Event	Description	Explanation	User Action
8252	Could not search under entry '%1' on directory %2. Cannot access Address List information. %3	A permissions problem has occurred.	Verify that the Address List has the correct permissions to access the object.
8253	Object '%1' on directory %2 has no Address Lists defined.		No user action is required.
8254	Object '%1' on directory %2 has the following Address Lists defined: %3		No user action is required.
8255	Found new or changed Address List '%1' on directory %2.		No user action is required.
8256	Address List '%1' was deleted or had its owning service changed on directory %2. Shutting down thread for this Address List.		No user action is required.
8257	The Address List '%1' on directory %2 could not be loaded due to an error. Make sure that the Address List is configured properly.		Perform the user action specified in the message.
8258	Starting replication for Address List '%1'.		No user action is required.
8259	Stopped replication for Address List '%1'.		No user action is required.
8260	Could not open LDAP session to directory '%1' using local service credentials. Cannot access Address List configuration information. Make sure the server '%1' is running. %2	The directory may not be available or the name of the domain controller could be incorrect in the service.	Check the status of the directory and verify that the DC name is correct in the Recipient Update Services.
8261	The Address List '%1' has been signaled to start replication immediately.		No user action is required.

Event	Description	Explanation	User Action
8262	Processing of the Address List '%1' has been stopped due to an invalid configuration. Check the event log for more information.		Review the event log for more information. Delete and recreate the Address List service as a possible fix, but be aware that this increases the resources on the domain controller.
8263	The operating system has run out of resources. The Address List will shut down and then restart. If this problem persists, try restarting the service or the server.		Perform the user action specified in the message. If the problem still persists, contact Microsoft Product Support Services.
8264	An operation on server '%1' returned [0x%2] %3. The Address List %4 stopped.		Delete and recreate the Address List that caused the error. Be aware that this action is resource-intensive. It may overload network traffic and CPU utilization on the domain controller.
8265	The target object '%1' will be missing the dXALocalAdmin attribute because the Active Directory Connector was unable to map the original value (%2) from the source object. %3	The Active Directory Connector will log this message while replicating the MSMail DXA objects (DXA-Site-Server, Remote-DXA or DX-Requestor) if it is not able to map the dXALocalAdmin attribute.	Manually change the target object.
8266	Replication of the source object '%1' failed because the Active Directory Connector was unable to map DXA-Remote-Client attribute (original value '%2') to a target object in the Active Directory. %3	The DXA-Remote-Client attribute is a critical attribute on a DX-Requestor or Remote-DXA object and the requestor or remote DXA cannot function properly without this value. When Active Directory Connector is not able to map this attribute from the source object, it does not allow the replication of the object.	Make sure you have a user Connection Agreement that is replicating the recipient specified by the DXA-Remote-Client attribute to Active Directory. Make sure the recipient replicates to Active Directory and then force a full replication on the configuration Connection Agreement.
8267	The entry '%1' was not deleted because it was modified after the source entry. %2	Active Directory Connector will not delete objects in cases where the target is newer than the source.	Manually delete the object or wait for it to replicate back in next cycle.

Event	Description	Explanation	User Action
8268	The entry '%1' was not deleted because it is a user enabled account. %2	Active Directory Connector will not delete enabled user accounts.	Manually delete the user account.
8269	The entry '%1' was deleted because it will be recreated as a different object class. %2	Active Directory Connector deletes and recreates an object when the source object changes from a mailbox enabled to a mail enabled user or vise versa.	No user action is required.
8270	LDAP returned the error [%1] %2 when importing the transaction %3 %4		Check the event log for related messages.
8271	Successfully replicated the object '%1' to object '%2'. %3		No user action is required.
8272	Active Directory Connector is deliberately not replicating %1. %2	Active Directory Connector has been explicitly configured to not replicate this kind of change.	Change the configuration of the Connection Agreement if you want to replicate this kind of change. If not, no user action is required.
8273	This Connection Agreement does not allow back replication. As a result, the Active Directory Connector cannot replicate %1 to %2. %3		
8274	Active Directory Connector could not replicate %1 to %2 because the target object is deleted. %3		No user action is required.
8275	Active Directory Connector could not replicate %1 to %2 because the target object is not writable %3	Active Directory Connector is attempting to replicate to a system object or an object in a different naming context that is not writable.	Replicate to a different object.
8276	Active Directory Connector could not replicate %1 to the target directory because this Connection Agreement is not a primary connection agreement. %2	If the Connection Agreement is not a primary Connection Agreement, then Active Directory Connector will not create new objects.	Change the primary bit on the Connection Agreement, or take no action.

Event	Description	Explanation	User Action
8277	Active Directory Connector could not replicate %1 to the Active Directory because the object came from the configured active directory, yet the Active Directory Connector cannot find it in active directory. This can happen the Active Directory Connector is configured to use multiple DCs, and the DCs are out of sync with each other. The Active Directory Connector will try to re-replicate the object. %2	The security ID (SID) on the object indicates that it came from this domain, but Active Directory Connector cannot find it in the domain.	Try again. If the problem persists, modify the SID on the source object to a valid account.
8278	Active Directory Connector could not replicate %1 to the target directory because it could not convert the DN. %2		Contact Microsoft Product Support Services.
8279	Active Directory Connector could not replicate %1 because it could not convert the object class %2	Active Directory Connector cannot find a mapping for this object class.	Contact Microsoft Product Support Services.
8280	Active Directory Connector could not replicate from %1 to %2 because there are too many similarly named objects in the target directory. %3	Active Directory Connector could not create a unique name for the object.	Manually rename the source object.
8281	Active Directory Connector could not replicate the msExchMasterAccountSid to %1 because this sid is already on the object %2. %3	Exchange requires each object to have a unique security ID (SID).	Assign the SID to the desired object and change SID on the other object.
8282	Active Directory Connector could not replicate from %1 to %2 %3		Review the event log for related messages.

Event	Description	Explanation	User Action
8283	Active Directory Connector will not replicate entry '%1' to the Active Directory because the target object '%2' should be administered using the Exchange Server 2000 administration snap-in only. Active Directory Connector will also force a back-replication of the target entry in order to overwrite any modifications made in the Exchange 5.5 directory. %3		Perform the user action specified in the message.
8284	We couldn't find the Address List Root which is located in the Exchange Service entry under the attribute addressBookRoots. This might have been caused by a permission problem. %1		To check permissions of the server, use ADSIEdit or LDP support tools available on the Windows 2000 compact disk. Check if the server has access to CN=Microsoft Exchange, CN=Services, CN=Configuration, DC=..
8285	Active Directory Connector will not replicate from %1 to %2 because both objects are not mailbox enabled. The source object is a mailbox. The target object is either a Contact or a mail enabled user. If this is a problem, consider making the Connection Agreement an Inter-Organizational Connection Agreement. %3		Perform the user action specified in the message.
8286	Active Directory Connector will not replicate from %1 to %2 because the source object is a Custom Recipient but the target object is a mailbox. If this is a problem, consider making the Connection Agreement an Inter-Organizational Connection Agreement. %3		Follow the instructions in the message.

Event	Description	Explanation	User Action
8287	Active Directory Connector will not replicate %1. Even though this is an Intra-Organizational Connection Agreement, it is not a primary Connection agreement to the target directory, Consequently, over this Connection Agreement, Active Directory Connector is not allowed to create new objects. %2		Change the primary agreement, or take no action.
8288	The Active Directory Connector will not replicate %1. The current connection agreement is not a primary Connection agreement, and %1 came from a different organization. As a result, Active Directory Connector is not allowed to create a new target for this object. %2	If the Connection Agreement is not a primary Connection Agreement, then Active Directory Connector will not create new objects.	Change the primary agreement, or take no action.
8289	The Active Directory Connector will not replicate %1. The current connection agreement is not a primary Connection agreement, and Active Directory Connector cannot determine the name of the source organization. As a result, Active Directory Connector is not allowed to create a new target for this object. %2	If the Connection Agreement is not a primary Connection Agreement, then Active Directory Connector will not create new objects.	Change the primary agreement, or take no action.
8290	The Active Directory Connector cannot replicate %1. The site that the object belongs in is read only on the connected Exchange 5.5 Server. If another connection agreement can replicate this object to a 5.5 server in the correct site, then ignore this message. %2		Perform the user action specified in the message. If you do not have a connection agreement that will work, create a new one to a server that can replicate this object.

Event	Description	Explanation	User Action
8291	The Active Directory Connector cannot replicate %1 because it does not have a legacyExchangeDN for the site it belongs in. %2	Active Directory Connector recognizes that the object belongs in a particular site but cannot determine what it should be named.	Wait for the recipient update service to stamp the object with its distinguished name, and then try again.
8292	The Active Directory Connector cannot replicate %1 because it failed to map the entry. %2		Review the event log for other related messages.
8293	Successfully imported the object '%1'. %2		No user action is required.
8294	The %1 attribute is not present on the import object %2. This can happen when Active Directory Connector does not have permissions to see all links. Please ensure that the Active Directory Connector has Read permissions to the all of the source directory, including the Microsoft Exchange Configuration Container. %3		Perform the user action specified in the message.
8295	LDAP Rename on directory %1 for entry '%2' (to '%3') was unsuccessful with error:[0x%4] %5. %6		Try again or wait for Active Directory Connector to retry. If the problem persists, manually rename the object.
8296	Renaming entry '%1' to '%2' on directory %3. %4		No user action is required.
8297	Active Directory Connector will attempt to add the server '%1' to routing group '%2'. %3		No user action is required.

Event	Description	Explanation	User Action
8298	Active Directory Connector will not replicate entry '%1' to the Active directory because the target object '%2' should be administered using the Exchange Server 2000 administration snap-in only. Any changes applied to the object in the Exchange 5.5 directory will get over-written the next time the Active directory object replicates back to the Exchange 5.5 directory. %3		Perform the user action specified in the message.
8299	Active Directory Connector will not replicate the private information store '%1' because it was not able to find the corresponding MAPI public store object in the Active directory. %2	Every Exchange 5.5 mailbox store points to a public folder server (Home-Public-Server attribute). The corresponding attribute on an Exchange 2000 private store is called msExchHomePublicMDB and points to a public store object (instead of pointing to a server object). When Active Directory Connector replicates a 5.5 mailbox store to the AD(Active Directory), it tries to map the Home-Public-Server setting to the NT5 DN (distinguished name) of a MAPI public store under the server specified. If Active Directory Connector doesn't find a MAPI public store corresponding to the 5.5 setting, it logs this message.	Make sure the public store object for the specified public folder server exists in the Active Directory. If the public folder server is an Exchange 5.5. server, investigate why the public store object did not replicate to the AD. You may also try performing a full-replication on the configuration Connection Agreement and see if it replicates over. If the public folder server is an Exchange 5.5 server, investigate if the MAPI public store for that server was deleted. If you conclude that the Exchange 5.5 mailbox store object is pointing to the wrong public folder server, just re-point the mailbox store to a different public folder server (which has a corresponding MAPI public store object in the AD) and the new value should replicate over to the Active Directory during the next replication cycle of the configuration Connection Agreement.

Event	Description	Explanation	User Action
8300	Active Directory Connector will not replicate the entry '%1' to the Active directory because it was not able to find the home server (corresponding to the %2 attribute on the source object) in the Active directory. %3	Most connectors are homed on a particular server (usually specified by one of Home-MTA, Home-MDB or Responsible-Local-DXA attributes). While replicating a connector object from 5.5 to the AD, if the Active Directory Connector is not able to map the home server setting for the connector to a target DN in the Active Directory, it will not replicate the connector. This is done because the home server setting determines which routing group to put the connector into and if we can't find the home server in the target directory, we can't find the correct routing group to put the connector into. The failed object is put on the retry list and it usually succeeds on retry.	If the failed connector hasn't replicated over yet to the AD, try doing a full replication on the configuration Connection Agreement so that the object specified by the home server setting replicates over to the Active Directory successfully, which in turn will enable the connector to replicate over also.
8301	Active Directory Connector will not replicate the connector '%1' because it was not able to determine the correct target routing group for the connector. %2	While replicating a connector object from the Exchange 5.5 directory to Active Directory, Active Directory Connector was not able to determine the correct target routing group for the connector, and failed to replicate the object. This failure can occur if the home server for the connector is not part of any routing group. It can also occur if the home server on the connector changed, so that the original and the new routing groups are in two different administrative groups.	Investigate the cause of the conditions outlined in the explanation and try to rectify them.

Event	Description	Explanation	User Action
8302	Active Directory Connector will not replicate entry '%1' to '%2' because the target object has a higher file version than the source object. %3	In Exchange 5.5, the Addr-Type objects that describe the proxy-address generation DLLs reside at the site level, while in Exchange 2000 these objects reside at the organization level. When Active Directory Connector replicates these objects, if an object of the same type in the target Active Directory and if it has a file version higher than the source object, the Active Directory Connector will not replicate the source object.	No user action is required.
8303	Active Directory Connector will not replicate entry '%1' because site-level protocol settings are not replicated from the Exchange 5.5 directory to the Active directory. %2	The Active Directory Connector only replicates server-level protocol settings from Exchange 5.5 to the AD(Active Directory) but since site-level protocols settings are also exported out of the 5.5 directory, Active Directory does not replicate these objects.	No user action is required.
8304	Active Directory Connector will not replicate entry '%1' because protocol settings for this protocol type are not replicated from the Exchange 5.5 directory to the Active directory. %2	Active Directory Connector only replicates three protocols types: Internet Message Access Protocol version 4 (IMAP4), Postoffice Protocol version 3 (POP3), and Network News Transfer Protocol (NNTP). For all other server-level protocol type object, for example, Lightweight Directory Access Protocol (LDAP), this message appears.	No user action is required.
8305	Active Directory Connector will not replicate entry '%1' because the following required attribute(s) are missing from the source entry: %2. %3		Determine why the required attributes are missing from the source entry and rectify the condition.

Event	Description	Explanation	User Action
8306	Active Directory Connector will not replicate entry '%1' because it cannot find the target entry '%2' in the Active directory. The target entry needs to be present in the Active directory in order to replicate the source entry. %3		Determine why the target entry is missing from the target directory and rectify the condition.
8307	Active Directory Connector will not replicate entry '%1' because it does not replicate deletions of object class '%2' from the Exchange 5.5 directory to the Active directory. %3		No user action is required.
8308	Active Directory Connector will not replicate entry '%1' to the Exchange 5.5 directory because the target object should be administered using the Exchange 5.5 administration program only. Any changes made to the object in the Active directory will get over-written the next time the Exchange 5.5 object replicates back to the Active directory. %2		No user action is required.
8309	Active Directory Connector will not replicate entry '%1' to the Exchange 5.5 directory because the target object '%2' should be administered using the Exchange 5.5 administration program only. Any changes made to the object in the Active directory will get over-written the next time the Exchange 5.5 object replicates back to the Active directory. %3		No user action is required.

Event	Description	Explanation	User Action
8310	Active Directory Connector will not replicate deletion of private store object '%1' to the Exchange 5.5 directory because there are existing private information stores on the same server in the Active directory that map to the same target object '%2' in the Exchange 5.5 directory. %3		No user action is required.
8311	Active Directory Connector will not replicate entry '%1' to the Exchange 5.5 directory because only MAPI public store objects are replicated to the Exchange 5.5 directory. %2		
8312	Active Directory Connector will not replicate entry '%1' because it does not replicate deletions of object class '%2' from the Active directory to the Exchange 5.5 directory. %3		No user action is required.
8313	Active Directory Connector will not replicate entry '%1' to the Exchange 5.5 directory because it does not replicate routing group connectors between two routing groups in the same administrative group. %2		No user action is required.
8314	Active Directory Connector will not replicate entry '%1' to the Exchange 5.5 directory because the routing calculation server for the administrative group is an Exchange 5.5 server. %2		No user action is required.

Event	Description	Explanation	User Action
8315	The service could not update the entry '%1' because inheritable permissions are not propagated to this object. The inheritable permissions may be disabled because the object belongs to a Windows 2000 administrative group or the inheritable permissions were disable explicitly by an administrator. %2		
8316	The service could not update the entry '%1' because inheritable permissions have been explicitly disabled to all objects within the container '%2'. In order for this object to be mail-enabled properly, you will need to enable inheritable permissions on the security tab for this container so that the permissions can be propagated correctly to the entry that the service is trying to process. %3		
8317	The service could not update the entry '%1' because inheritable permissions may not have propagated completely down to this object yet. The inheritance time may vary depending on the number of Active Directory objects within the domain and also the load of your domain controllers. To correct this problem, verify that the Exchange permissions have been propagated to this object and then force a rebuild for the Recipient Update Service on this domain. %2		

B

Connection Agreement Attributes

Connection Agreements have three categories of attributes:

- General attributes;
- Exchange server-specific attributes that are attributes and values associated with any target Domain Controllers all beginning with the prefix *msExchServer1.*; and,
- Windows server-specific Attributes that are attributes and values associated with any Exchange 5.5 Directory Service servers all beginning with the prefix *msExchServer2.*

msExchHomeSyncService

Attribute syntax: single-valued distinguished name

The distinguished name of the Active Directory Connector service that is responsible for running this Connection Agreement.

msExchCASchemaPolicy

Attribute syntax: single-valued distinguished name

The Distinguished Name of the Active Directory Connector policy that this Connection Agreement uses, which contains the schema maps, object matching rules, and other configuration data. Normally set to CN=Default ADC Policy, CN=Active Directory Connections, CN=Microsoft Exchange, CN=Services,CN=Configuration, Domain Controller=<*domain*>

versionNumber

Attribute syntax: single-valued integer

The version number of the Connection Agreement. This is used, for example, to ensure that an Exchange 2000 Active Directory Connector does not try to run an Exchange 2003 Connection Agreement. The versionNumber of existing Exchange 2000 Connection Agreements will be updated during the Active Directory Connector upgrade from Exchange 2000 to Exchange 2003.

ActivationStyle

Attribute syntax: single-valued integer

Controls the Connection Agreement replication.
0 = never, 1 = selected times, 2 = always

ActivationSchedule

Attribute syntax: single-valued octet string

A bitmap of when the Connection Agreement is scheduled to run. Each bit is one 15-minute increment. Begins at 12.00 am through 11.45 pm.

msExchADCOptions

Attribute syntax: single-valued integer

A set of flags that control Active Directory Connector replication. The flags are:

0x00000004 Replicates secured objects from Active Directory.

0x00000008 Indicates an inter-organizational connection agreement.

0x00000800 Replicates memberships of hidden distribution lists.

0x00001000 Replicates from Windows first on a two-way connection agreement.

msExchDoFullReplication

Attribute syntax: Boolean

If True, all objects will be synchronized on the next replication cycle.

msExchIsBridgeheadSite

Attribute syntax: Boolean

Specifies whether "This is a primary Connection Agreement for the connected Exchange Organization" is selected, and thus whether the Active Directory Connector can create new objects in the Exchange 5.5 directory.

msExchRemotePrivateISList

Attribute syntax: single-valued Unicode string

Contains a list of the Exchange distinguished names of all of the private Information Stores in the site, separated by the § symbol (Hex 0x00A7).

msExchRemoteServerList

Attribute syntax: single-valued Unicode string

Contains a list of the Exchange distinguished names of the message transfer agent (MTA) objects for all servers in the site, separated by the § symbol (Hex 0x00A7).

msExchReplicateNow

Attribute syntax: Boolean

If True, the Active Directory Connector performs a replication cycle immediately for this Connection Agreement. This flag is usually set by the Active Directory Connector Management snap-in. Because it exists within the configuration naming context that is replicated around the forest, you can set this value remotely.

msExchIsConfigCA

Attribute syntax: Boolean

Specifies whether or not a Connection Agreement is a ConfigCA. You should not modify this attribute.

msExchExchangeSite

Attribute syntax: single-valued Unicode string

Contains the Exchange 5.5 Distinguished Name of the site that the Exchange server is in.

For example: ou=<site>,o=<org>

msExchInterOrgAddressType

Attribute syntax: single-valued Unicode string

For inter-organizational Connection Agreements, controls whether or not Custom Recipients/Contacts retain their existing targetAddress when replicated, or if the targetAddress is updated to the primary SMTP address of the object.

msExchSynchronizationDirection

Attribute syntax: single-valued integer

Specifies whether the Connection Agreement is one-way Exchange to Windows, one-way Windows to Exchange, or two-way.

0 = Two-way, 1 = Windows to Exchange, 2 = Exchange to Windows

msExchADCObjectType

Attribute syntax: single-valued integer

Specifies whether a Connection Agreement is a user connection agreement or a ConfigCA.

0 = Recipient CA, 1 = ConfigCA

msExchServer1IsBridgehead

Attribute syntax: Boolean

Specifies whether "This is the primary Connection Agreement for the connected Windows Domain" is selected, and thus whether Active Directory Connector can create new objects in Active Directory.

msExchServer1AlwaysCreateAs

Attribute syntax: single-valued integer

Specifies the type of object Active Directory Connector should create to represent an unmatched mailbox.

0 = Contact, 1 = Disabled User, 2 = Enabled User

msExchServer1AuthenticationCredentials

Attribute syntax: single-valued Unicode string

The credentials for connecting to the Windows server.

For example: Domain\User name

msExchServer1AuthenticationType

Attribute syntax: single-valued integer

Specifies the authentication protocol to be used.

4 = NTLM (Windows Challenge/Response)

msExchServer1DeletionOption

Attribute syntax: single-valued integer

Specifies whether the Active Directory Connector will replicate deletes from Exchange to Windows.

0 = Replicate deletes, 1 = write deletes to an .LDF file

msExchServer1ExportContainers

Attribute syntax: multivalued Unicode string

Specifies which containers to export from Windows, using the distinguished name of the container.

msExchServer1Flags

Attribute syntax: single-valued integer

Special flags that apply when replicating with Windows. Defaults to 0.

0x2 = Do not overwrite RDN with the Exchange 5.5 Alias attribute.

msExchServer1HighestUSN

Attribute syntax: single-valued large (64 bit) integer

The highest USN last found against the Windows 2000 or Windows 2003 Domain Controller that the Connection Agreement is replicating with. The Active Directory Connector uses this value to determine which objects it has already replicated from Active Directory.

msExchServer1HighestUSN

Attribute syntax: multivalued Unicode string

Keeps track of the highest USN of all of the Domain Controllers in the forest. By keeping track of the USN values on all servers that correspond with the highest USN on the local server, if the Connection Agreement is pointed to a different domain controller, the Active Directory Connector will not have to do a full replication from Windows. (If your organization has more than 800 Domain Controllers in the forest, you may need to set a registry key to control how many values are stored in this attribute, see TechNet article Q314950).

msExchServer1ImportContainer

Attribute syntax: single-valued Unicode string

Specifies the distinguished name of the default destination in Active Directory where Active Directory Connector should create new objects.

msExchServer1LastUpdateTime

Attribute syntax: single-valued Generalized-time attribute

Timestamp (UTC) of the last change from the source Active Directory container that the Connection Agreement is aware of. (Deprecated)

msExchServer1NetworkAddress

Attribute syntax: single-valued Unicode string

The host name of the Domain Controller that is the Windows endpoint of the Connection Agreement.

msExchServer1PageSize

Attribute syntax: single-valued integer

Specifies the LDAP page size to use when replicating with Active Directory. The default value is 20.

msExchServer1Port

Attribute syntax: single-valued integer

Specifies the LDAP port to use when connecting to the Active Directory server. The default port is 389.

msExchServer1SearchFilter

Attribute syntax: single-valued Unicode string

Specifies the LDAP search filter that Active Directory Connector uses when searching for objects to export from Active Directory. The value will differ depending on the objects being exported and the type of connection agreement. For example, for a Recipient Connection Agreement that is set to replicate users, groups, and contacts, the value is: (|(objectClass=user)(objectClass=contact)(objectClass=group))

msExchServer1SSLPort

Attribute syntax: single-valued integer

Specifies the LDAP port used for SSL communications with the Active Directory server. The default port is 636.

msExchServer1Type

Attribute syntax: single-valued integer

Specifies the type of server.

0 = Active Directory Domain Controller

msExchServer2AuthenticationCredentials

Attribute syntax: single-valued Unicode string

The credentials for connecting to the Exchange server.

For example: Domain\User name

msExchServer2AuthenticationType

Attribute syntax: single-valued integer

Specifies the authentication protocol that is used.

4 = NTLM (Windows Challenge/Response)

msExchServer2DeletionOption

Attribute syntax: single-valued integer

Specifies whether Active Directory Connector will replicate deletes from Windows to Exchange.

0 = Replicate deletes, 1 = Write deletes to a .CSV file

msExchServer2ExportContainers

Attribute syntax: multivalued Unicode string

Specifies which containers to export from Exchange, using the distinguished name of the container.

msExchServer2Flags

Attribute syntax: single-valued integer

Special flags that apply when replicating with Exchange. The default is 0.

No special flags currently exist.

msExchServer2HighestUSN

Attribute syntax: single-valued large (64 bit) integer

The USN last found against the Exchange server or Site Replication Service the Connection Agreement is replicating with. The Active Directory Connector uses this to determine which objects it has already replicated from the Exchange directory.

msExchServer2ImportContainer

Attribute syntax: single-valued Unicode string

Specifies the distinguished name of the default destination in Exchange where the Active Directory Connector should create new objects.

msExchServer2LastUpdateTime

Attribute syntax: single-valued Generalized-time attribute

Timestamp (UTC) of the last change from the source Exchange container that the Connection Agreement is aware of.

msExchServer2NetworkAddress

Attribute syntax: single-valued Unicode string

The host name of the Exchange server or SRS that is the Exchange endpoint of the Connection Agreement.

msExchServer2PageSize

Attribute syntax: single-valued integer

Specifies the LDAP page size to use when replicating with Exchange. The default value is 20.

msExchServer2Port

Attribute syntax: single-valued integer

Specifies the LDAP port to use when connecting to the Exchange server or SRS. The default port is 389; however, when replicating with an SRS the port is 379. If the Exchange 5.5 server's LDAP port has been changed from 389 to a different value, this attribute must be changed too.

msExchServer2SearchFilter

Attribute syntax: single-valued Unicode string

Specifies the LDAP search filter that the Active Directory Connector uses when searching for objects to export from Exchange. The value will differ depending on the objects being exported and the type of Connection Agreement. For example, for a User connection agreement that is set to replicate mailboxes, distribution lists, and custom recipients, the value is: (|(objectClass=organizationalPerson)(objectClass=remote-address)(objectClass=groupOfNames))

msExchServer2SSLPort

Attribute syntax: single-valued integer

The LDAP port used for SSL communications with the Exchange server. The default port is 636.

msExchServer2Type

Attribute syntax: single-valued integer

Specifies the type of server.

1 = Exchange 5.5 server or SRS.

C

Active Directory Connector Registry Keys

There are a number of registry keys that can be set that have an effect on the operation of the Active Directory Connector. All the registry keys are homed in the following location:

```
HKEY_LOCAL_MACHINE\System\CurrentControlSet\Services\MSADC\Parameters
```

And the individual registry keys that can be manipulated are shown below in Table C-1.

Table C-1 *Active Directory Connector Registry Keys*

Key	Value	Description
Transaction Directory	REG_SZ	The directory to which ADC logs all the deletes and failures. Defaults to MSADC\ in the ADC directory.
Sync Sleep Delay (secs)	REG_DWORD	When ADC is not synchronizing, how long it waits before it should poll or resume work. Defaults to 300 seconds.
Max Continuous Sync (secs)	REG_DWORD	The maximum length of time ADC will replicate. The default is 300 seconds.
Password Expiration	REG_DWORD	The number of days ADC stores unused passwords. The default is 0, and if the default value is used, the actual number of days depends on the number of passwords stored. This can range from 60 to 180 days.
Export Block Size	REG_DWORD	How big a block of USNs ADC exports before ADC commits the connection agreement. The default is 20000. This is the starting value that ADC uses when replicating. After the first block, the block size is variable and is set to 10% of the remaining USNs.

Key	Value	Description
Maximum Export Block Size	REG_DWORD	The maximum allowed export block size. The default is 0xFFFFFFFF.
Deletion Depend On Store	REG_DWORD	If the Exchange store mailbox delete fails, should the directory object delete fail? Used as a Boolean, 0 to disable, and 1 to enable. The default is 0.
ADCI TCP/IP Port	REG_DWORD	Sets the remote procedure call (RPC) port for setting passwords on ADC connection agreements, so that it can be accessed through a firewall. The default is not set, so the RPC port is defined dynamically.
Disabled Windows User Account Description	REG_SZ	Allows you to choose the description that is set when ADC creates a disabled user. The default is "Disabled Windows user account". For more information, see Microsoft Knowledge Base article 288084, "XADM: How to Change the Description Set on Disabled Users by the ADC" (http://support.microsoft.com/?kbid=288084).
UMAC Timeout	REG_DWORD	Period for unmerged attribute cleanup, in seconds. The default is 43,200 seconds (12 hours).
Merge Bad Links	REG_DWORD	Specifies if bad links on a target object (with incorrect syntax or ADC Global Name values that are in the same site and organization as the import container) should be stamped on the source object during back replication. Used as a Boolean value. The default is 1 (TRUE).
Replication-Sensitivity	REG_DWORD	Specifies the default Replication-Sensitivity value set on an object. The default is 20. For more information, see Microsoft Knowledge Base article 291944, "XADM: Mailboxes Do Not Have Trust Level When Created in Active Directory" (http://support.microsoft.com/?kbid=291944).
Max DC State Vector	REG_DWORD	Available with the Exchange 2000 Service Pack (SP) 3 ADC. This value sets an upper limit on the number of domain controllers that ADC keeps track of in the *msExchUSNVector* attribute on the connection agreement. This is useful if you have 800 domain controllers in the environment. For more information, see Microsoft Knowledge Base article 314950, "XADM: The ADC Does Not Work in an Environment That Contains More Than 800 Domain Controllers" (http://support.microsoft.com/?kbid=314950).

Index

B

C

D

E

R

S

T

U

V

W